take the kids
London

JOSEPH FULLMAN

About the series

take the kids guides are written specifically for parents, grandparents and carers. Each guide not only draws on what is of particular interest to kids, but also takes into account the realities of childcare – from tired legs to low boredom thresholds – enabling both grown-ups and their charges to have a great day out or a fabulous holiday.

Cadogan Guides
Highlands House, 165 The Broadway,
London sw19 1NE
info@cadoganguides.co.uk
www.cadoganguides.com

The Globe Pequot Press
PO Box 480, Guilford,
Connecticut 06437–0480

Copyright © Joseph Fullman 2000, 2002, 2004
Maps © Cadogan Guides,
drawn by Kingston Presentation Graphics

Art direction: Sarah Rianhard-Gardner
Series design: Andrew Barker
Original Photography: Travel Pictures
www.travelpictures.co.uk
Cover Photos: © Travel Pictures except for: Hamley's © Nicholas Kane 2000; © Geffyre Museum, London; Regent's Park © Kicca Tommasi

Managing Editor: Antonia Cunningham
Editor: Jacqueline Grosch Lobo
Series Editor: Melanie Dakin

Proofreading: Catherine Bradley
Indexing: Isobel McLean
Production: Navigator Guides Ltd
Printed and bound in Italy by Printer Trento srl.
A catalogue record for this book is available from the British Library
ISBN 1-86011-145-9

Additional Picture Credits: p.131 © Museum of London; p.40, p.44, p.58, p.63, p.71, p.76, p.109, p.133 © Kicca Tommasi; p.42–3 © Zoological Society of London; p.46 © Alex Robinson; p.47 © The Wallace Collection, London; p.51, p.59 © Nicholas Kane 2000; p.52 © The British Museum; p.54 © Nigel Young; pp.56, p.57, p.75, p.81 © Pollock's Toy Museum; p.60 © The British Museum Shop; p.62 © Yo! Sushi; p.65 © London Tourist Board, © National Portrait Gallery; p.68

© National Gallery; pp.78–9 © London's Transport Museum; p.73 © Rainforest Café; p.83 © Peter Durant/arcblue.com; p.100, p.111, p.113 © Imperial War Museum; p.103. p.107 © Dali Universe; p.106 © London Aquarium; p.107 © London IMAX; p.114, p.116 © London Dungeon; p.114, p.122 © Hay's Galleria, © Shakepeare's Globe Theatre; p.132 © Barbican Centre/ J.P. Stankowski; pp.135–6, p.139 © Science Museum; p.138 © The Natural History Museum; p.141 © Victoria & Albert Museum; p.142 © HRP 2001; p.143 © Royal Albert Hall.

The author and publishers have made every effort to ensure the accuracy of the information in this book at the time of going to press. However, they cannot accept any responsibility for any loss, injury or inconvenience resulting from the use of information contained in the guide.

Please help us to keep this guide up to date. We have done our best to ensure that information is correct at the time of printing, but places and facilities are constantly changing, and standards and prices fluctuate. We will be delighted to receive your comments concerning existing entries or omissions. Authors of the best letters or emails will receive a copy of the Cadogan Guide of their choice.

About the authors

Joseph Fullman

Joseph Fullman is a professional travel writer who has lived in London all his life and cherishes happy childhood memories of traipsing around the country with his determinedly enthusiastic mum and dad. He is the author of Cadogan's *take the kids* England, Navigator Guides, *Britain's Top Tourist Attractions* and co-author of *take the kids* Paris & Disneyland® Resort Paris, as well as guides to Britain's steam railways and London's markets. He has also contributed various articles to newspapers, websites and WAP guides.

Series consultant

Helen Truszkowski is series consultant of Cadogan's *take the kids* series, author of *take the kids* Travelling and author of *take the kids* Paris & Disneyland® Resort Paris. Helen is an established travel writer and photographer. Over the past decade her journeys have taken her around the globe, including six months working in South Africa. She contributes to a range of magazines worldwide, and is a former travel editor of *Executive Woman* magazine. Helen's eight year-old son, George, has accompanied her on her travels since he was a few weeks old.

Series editor

Melanie Dakin is series editor of Cadogan's *take the kids* series, having previously acted as consultant editor on the Time Out *London for Children* guide and editor of *Kids Out* magazine. As a mother of two, Eve aged nine and John Hunter aged three, Melanie has spent a great deal of time navigating London with children, pushchairs, toys and luggage. To date, only a couple of baby bottles and a small coolbag have been left behind.

(4) **Contents**

There's more for kids to do in London than you probably think.

You may know that the Science Museum is one of the best interactive museums in the country, but do you also know that it organizes sleep-overs for children wanting to explore and experiment in the dead of night? And were you aware that you can catch a canal boat to London Zoo where you can stroke a snake, watch flying displays by birds of prey and get up close and personal with creepie crawlies? Or that at the Victoria & Albert Museum you can have a go at reconstructing the Crystal Palace built for the Great Exhibition of 1851? Or spend the night pretending to be pirates aboard the *Golden Hinde*, a replica 17th-century sailing ship? And did you realize that not only are most of London's major museums and galleries now free, but they offer a huge range of facilities for families ranging from backpack trails and activity sheets to workshops and storytellings? Or that kids can ride horses in Hyde Park or explore the cosmos and the ocean depths at the IMAX 3D cinema in Waterloo? Well, you do now.

London is one of the most accommodating cities on earth for young visitors. Almost every month some new attraction opens. The amphibious Duck Tours, the Museum in Docklands, the Natural History Museum's Darwin Centre, the Hungerford Foot Bridge and the revamped Trafalgar Square are among the most recent additions to the thriving London scene. In the near future these will be joined by the Spiral Extension at the Victoria & Albert Museum, a revamped Museum of the Moving Image on the South Bank and a new Unicorn Children's Theatre in Southwark.

This guide aims to spring more than a few surprises of its own, bringing to your attention London's lesser-known sights and some tales of life in the capital, as well as giving you the low-down on all the main attractions – the parks, palaces, museums, cinemas, arcades and experiences that make London perfect for discerning families and fun-hungry kids.

Guide to the Guide

Finding your way around this guide is easy. It is divided into four manageable sections as follows:

Travel provides information on every aspect of getting to and around London.

Ideas, Ideas is full of helpful hints and tips to help you get to know the city: what you can do for free, a London calendar, some days out organized along themes and some stress-free tours.

See it, Do it is the main sightseeing section – the heart of the book, divided into 15 child-size areas. In each we've identified the primary sights, and secondary sights nearby; the best local shopping and places to eat; and other worthwhile attractions around and about. For every attraction there is up-to-date information on how to get there, access, opening times and admission prices, as well as workshops and activities specifically organized for kids. Some indication of appropriate age ranges is also given, as well as how long you should allow for each attraction. Throughout, the text is sprinkled with questions and challenges designed to help you and your children get the most from your stay, plus stories to keep them occupied as you travel from A to B. 'Kids in' details the capital's best indoor attractions and entertainment, including everything from theatre shows and cinema clubs to music workshops and backstage tours. 'Kids out' identifies the best outdoor ones from parks to farm trips. There's even a section on the best places to watch and participate in a number of sports and activities. Should you fancy a change of scenery, we've also provided details of day trips – to historic Windsor and the university towns of Cambridge and Oxford, or to Chessington and Thorpe Park for some roller-coaster thrills – all within around an hour's journey of the city.

Need to know makes up the final section of the guide with chapters covering all the practical information you need for living and travelling in London: essential details on medical care, post offices, supermarkets, banks, policemen, nappies and so on, as well as a selection of the best child-friendly hotels, restaurants and shops.

Get ready, the adventure begins here.

TRAVEL

(8) GETTING THERE

London is one of the busiest gateway cities in the world, welcoming thousands of flights every day. Competition between airlines on the major routes is fierce and, wherever you're flying from, you should be able to pick up a cheap deal. Of course, when travelling with children, you may decide to forgo potential savings in return for extra comfort and some in-flight care and entertainment.

> **Flight times to London**
> **New York** 6–7 hours
> **Miami** 4–5 hours
> **Los Angeles** 9–10 hours
> **Hawaii** 18 hours
> **Montreal** 6 hours
> **Toronto** 7 hours

Flights

Many of the larger airlines, including British Airways, Air Canada and Cathay Pacific, provide on-board services for families. These can include such life-savers as designated flight attendants, play packs, seat-back computer games and children's TV channels. Charter flights may be cheap but they can be particularly hellish for children, who will not necessarily tolerate sitting in a cramped seat with nothing to do for eight hours or more. An international air ticket for a child aged 2 or under should cost just 10 per cent of the adult fare. (Remember, only one reduced fare is allowed per adult.) Between the ages of 3 and 11, your child will be charged anything between 50 and 85 per cent of the full adult fare but once over 12 your child is, in the eyes of the airline, officially an adult and no longer entitled to any form of discount.

Pushchairs are usually carried free on airlines and can often be taken right up to the point of boarding. Carrycots, however, are not supposed to be brought on board, although some airlines allow the collapsible kind. It can make more sense to pre-book a sky cot or bassinet.

Transatlantic flights

Transatlantic flights touch down at London's two major airports: Heathrow, **t** 0870 000 0123, **www**.baa.co.uk/heathrow, situated 15 miles west of central London, one of the world's largest airports with four terminals (work on a controversial fifth terminal will start in the near future), and Gatwick, **t** 0870 000 2468, **www**.baa.co.uk/gatwick, some 25 miles to the south, with two terminals.

Of London's other three airports, Stansted, **t** 0870 000 0303, **www**.baa.co.uk/stansted, is the furthest from central London – some 35 miles to the northeast. It's also the largest, the busiest (specialising in budget flights and cut-price deals) and has a pleasant, open-plan terminal designed by architect *du jour* Norman Foster. London City, **t** (020) 7646 0088, **www**.londoncityairport.com, is the closest, 9 miles east – it welcomes just a handful of flights each day from Britain and Europe – while Luton, **t** (01582) 405 100, **www**.london-luton.co.uk, which like Stansted mainly handles budget flights from Europe, is 31 miles to the north.

From North America

The cheapest tickets offered by the major airlines are Apex and Super Apex, which must be booked 21 days before departure and involve a stay of at least seven nights. Also, check out online discounts and consolidators – companies which buy blocks of unsold tickets to sell on at a discount. Because of the restrictions on flight times, high cancellation fees and the potential for delays, charter flights are not recommended when travelling with children.

Major airlines
Air Canada
t US/Canada (888) 247 2262
www.aircanada.com
American Airlines
t US (800) 433 7300
www.americanair.com
British Airways
t US (800) AIRWAYS
www.britishairways.com
Continental Airlines
t US/Canada (800) 231 0856
www.continental.com
Delta Airlines
t US/Canada (800) 241 441
www.delta.com
United Airlines
t US (800) 538 2929
www.ual.com
Virgin Atlantic Airways
t US (800) 862 8621
www.virgin-atlantic.com

Consolidators in North America
Air Brokers Travel
t US (800) 883 3273
www.airbrokers.com
ELT Express
t US (201) 541 3867
www.eltexpress.com
UniTravel
t US (800) 325 2222
www.unitravel.com

Australia and New Zealand
Air New Zealand
t Australia (1 800) 809 298
t New Zealand (0800) 737 000
www.airnz.co.nz
British Airways
t Australia (1 300) 767 177
t New Zealand (0800) 274 847
www.britishairways.com
Cathay Pacific
t Australia (13) 1747
t New Zealand (09) 379 0861
www.cathaypacific.com
Qantas
t Australia (13) 1211
t New Zealand (09) 357 8900
www.qantas.com.au

Arriving by plane

Arriving at an airport after a long-haul flight can be a fraught experience. Thankfully, Heathrow and Gatwick have good facilities to help ease the strain.

Heathrow
Train – the Heathrow Express
t (0845) 600 1515
www.heathrowexpress.co.uk
Every 15mins between 5.10am–12 midnight
Fares Adult single First Class £21, Express Class £13; child single First Class £10, Express Class £6

The Heathrow Express, a direct train link between the airport and Paddington mainline station, is by far the quickest route into town. The journey costs £13 each way but takes just 15 minutes – tickets can be bought at Heathrow, on the train or in advance online which entitles you to a 10 per cent discount (allow at least three days for

Cheap flight websites
www.cheapflights.com
www.cheap-flight-finder.com
www.cheaptickets.com
www.farebase.net
www.lastminute.com
www.moments-notice.com
www.ryanair.com
www.travelocity.com

delivery within the UK, five days for abroad). Paddington is connected to London's underground network with stations on the Bakerloo, Hammersmith and City, Circle and District lines. There is a black cab rank outside.

Underground
5.30am–12 midnight daily
Fares Adult single £3.60, child £1.50

One-Day Travelcards, which allow you unlimited travel on London's buses, trains and underground, are available from 9.30am on weekdays and at any time on weekends. *See* **Getting Around**, p.14.

Heathrow is the first stop on the eastbound Piccadilly Line, which means you should be able to get a seat and find somewhere to put your luggage. On the downside, it can take up to an hour to reach central London and, unless your eventual destination is on the Piccadilly Line (Knightsbirdge, Green Park, Piccadilly Circus, Leicester Square, etc.), you will have to face the prospect of negotiating corridors and escalators whilst laden with luggage and children as you change to another line. Alternatively, you may prefer to get off at ⊖ Earl's Court or South Kensington and take a taxi the rest of the way.

Airbus
t 0870 580 8080
www.nationalexpress.com
Every 20–30mins from 5.30am–6pm, then every hour till 9.35pm
Fares Adult single £10, child £5, under-3s **free**
Equipped for disabled passengers

There are over 40 National Express Airbus departures a day from Heathrow bound for London Victoria by way of Notting Hill, Marble Arch and Russell Square. The journey takes 1hr 40mins.

Taxi
This is the most expensive option. Make sure you take a licensed black cab from the official rank. The

cab fare from Heathrow to central London should be around £30–£35 (£40–£50 if travelling after 8pm when a higher tariff applies).

Gatwick

Train – the Gatwick Express
t 0845 850 1530 for timetable information
www.gatwickexpress.co.uk
The first train is at 5.20am, then every 15mins between 5.50am and 0.50am, then every hour after that at 35mins past the hour
Fares Adult single First Class £18, Express Class £11; under-16s pay 50% of the adult fare, under-5s free

By far the most practical way to get into town. The trains are not quite as speedy as their Heathrow counterparts but make good time – 30mins platform to platform from Gatwick to Victoria – and they run through the night. There is also a stopping service during the day for passengers requiring East Croydon (20mins) or Clapham Junction (35mins), which takes 50mins to reach Victoria. Tickets can be bought at Gatwick, on the train (Express service only) or pre-booked on the phone or online (which entitles you to a discount, although allow at least three days for delivery within the UK, five days for abroad).

Airbus
t 0870 580 8080
www.nationalexpress.com
Hourly from 4.50am–9.15pm
Fares Vary but, depending on the time of day, can be bought for as little as adult £5, child £2.50

The Airbus is cheaper than the train, but is very slow and can take over two hours to reach Victoria, calling at Coulsdon, Wallington, Mitcham, Streatham and Pimlico on the way.

Taxi
Only an option for the seriously wealthy or the seriously tired out. The journey will take over an hour and cost upwards of £70. There is a black cab rank outside the arrivals hall.

London City Airport
t (020) 7646 0088
www.londoncityairport.com
Train – Docklands Light Railway
Trains run Mon-Sat till 12.30am, Sun till 11.30pm
Fares (See Top tips p. 8 for DLR savings.)
DLR runs a service connecting Canning Town (reached from the airport via shuttle bus) with

Tower Gateway or Bank stations on the east side of the city. Adult £2.50, child £1. There is also a shuttle bus to DLR at Canary Wharf. Adult £3, child £1.

Airbus
There is a shuttle bus service to Liverpool Street mainline station.
Every 20mins between 6.50am and 9.10pm
Fares Adult £6, child £2, under-5s free
A taxi from the airport should take around 30mins to the city centre and cost around £15.

Luton
t 01582 405 100
www.london-luton.co.uk
Train – Luton Airport Express
A free shuttle bus connects the airport to Luton Parkway station in about 5mins.
Mon-Fri 7am-10pm, Sat & Sun 9am-8pm. Journey time is 25-35mins
Fare Adult single £10, child £5
Thameslink runs a service to King's Cross. Some trains go via Wimbledon and Sutton in South London.

Airbus
t 0870 580 8080
www.nationalexpress.com
t 0870 608 7261
www.greenline.co.uk
Greenline and National Express run express services to central London and the West End daily, 24hrs a day. Stops include Brent Cross, Finchley Road, Baker Street, Marble Arch and Victoria. Buses depart about every hour, but times vary during the day and run less frequently between 11pm and 3am. The bus takes 1hr 15mins (an extra 15mins during peak times).
Fares Adult single £8/£7, child £5.50/£3.50, under-3s (not occupying a seat) free

Stansted
t 0870 0000 303
www.baa.co.uk/main/airports/stansted/
Train –The Stansted Express
t (0845) 8500 150
www.stanstedexpress.co.uk
The first train is at 5am and runs every 30mins till 8am, then every 15mins till 4pm, every 30mins till 11pm
Fares Adult single £13, child single £6.50

The train links Stansted aiport with Tottenham hale on the Underground's Victoria Line and Liverpool Street Station (east of the city centre). The journey takes 42mins.

Airbus
t 0870 580 8080
www.nationalexpress.com
Approximately every 30mins, 24hrs a day
Fares Adult single, £10 child single £5

Slightly cheaper than the train, the bus takes over an hour longer (journey time 2hrs), stopping en route at Finchley Road and Marble Arch before ending up at Victoria Station. However, this could be an advantage with luggage, as long as you have plenty of time.

Arriving by rail, road or ferry

By rail
Eurostar
t 0870 600 0782
t 0870 167 6767 for a brochure
www.eurostar.com
Twenty times a day from Paris and Brussels
Fares Vary. A Leisure Return, which must be booked 14 days in advance, can be bought for as little as adult £59, child £50, under-4s free. The closer you leave booking to departure, the more expensive the fare
Check-in time 20mins.
No baggage weight limit.
Wheelchair users need to inform Eurostar staff of their requirements when booking

It takes just three hours to reach London from Paris or Brussels aboard a Eurostar train. Time spent under the sea is just 25 minutes. At present the trains arrive at Waterloo, although a new high speed link to St Pancras is currently being built (this will cut journeys by around half an hour, although it won't be operational for several years yet). Waterloo International leads into Waterloo mainline station, which, in turn, is connected to ⊖ Waterloo. Once through Customs, you're just a few minutes away from central London. Trains run from here to other mainline stations such as Victoria and Charing Cross; the Underground

station is on the Northern and Bakerloo Lines. A taxi to the city centre should cost about £7–£12 (more after 8pm when a higher tariff applies). There's a black cab rank outside the station.

By ferry
The completion of the tunnel in the early 1990s transformed the cross-Channel travel industry. The much-hyped advantages of ferry travel – duty free shops, restaurants and bars, fabulously bad cabaret *et al* – have paled in comparison to a seasick-free jaunt under the Channel. And now that duty-free shopping has finally been abolished, ferry companies are really beginning to feel the strain.

Nonetheless, for all its problems, ferry travel is still well worth considering. The main ferry links land you at Dover, Newhaven or Portsmouth, from where you can continue your journey to one of London's eight mainline stations: Charing Cross, Euston, King's Cross, Liverpool Street, Paddington, St Pancras, Victoria or Waterloo. All have connections to the Underground network.

Prices are highly competitive, with companies offering a range of deals in the hope of drawing some custom away from the Channel Tunnel. Under-4s usually travel free , there are discounts for under-14s, and most lines can boast good family facilities – restaurants, baby-changing rooms, children's play areas and video rooms.

Calais–Dover is the quickest and most popular ferry route. P&O Ferrries, **t** 0870 5202 020, (www.posl.com) operate 35 sailings a day in the high season; the journey takes 1 hour 15 minutes. Fares vary hugely and it's best to shop around for the best current deal. A family of four travelling in a medium-sized car should expect to pay anything between £120 and £180 for a flexible return, depending on the time of year.

Driving via the Channel Tunnel
Eurotunnel – Calais to Folkestone
t 0870 535 3535
www.eurotunnel.com
Four departures an hour during peak times
Fares Flexible return tickets start at around £150 if you travel before 7am. The fare is for car space only regardless of the number of passengers
Check-in time At least 25mins but no more than 2hrs before departure.

No baggage weight limit. Wheelchair users need to inform staff of their requirements when booking

Eurotunnel transports cars on purpose-built carriers through the Channel Tunnel between Calais and Folkestone. The French terminal is situated off junction 13 of the A16 motorway, while the British equivalent can be reached via junction 11a of the M20. The journey time is a mere 35 minutes. Most people choose to stay in their car, although you can get out and wander down the corridor to stretch your legs. Toilets and a buffet service are provided. It is advisable to book in advance, although it is possible just to turn up and wait. Space is given on a first-come, first-served basis.

The carless alternative

You may want to consider arriving in Britain without your car and renting one once you get here. Airlines and many travel agents can arrange 'fly-drive' packages for you on request. *See* **Getting around**, p.16, for rental companies in London.

If you're arriving from the Continent, remember to adjust the dip of your headlights for driving on the left. Wearing seatbelts is compulsory in Britain, front seats and back.

By bus
National Express/Eurolines
52 Grosvenor Gardens, London SW1
t 0870 580 8080
www.nationalexpress.com

Coach trips are invariably a balancing act, being both the cheapest and the least pleasant way to travel long distances. National Express do not charge for under-5s, and under-16s travel half-price. They also offer annual family coachcards for £8 (1 adult, 1 child) and £16 (2 adults, 2 children) which allow children to travel free on all services for a year. However, these savings are generally far outweighed by the misery of sitting in a tiny cramped seat for hours on end.

National Express operates coach routes to all the major cities in Britain and Europe. Be aware, however, that its convoluted routes mean that it can often take many hours to reach your destination. London's main coach station is at Victoria, 10 minutes' walk from the train/underground station along Buckingham Palace Road.

Passports and visas
From Europe

Although a member of the European Union – which technically gives all union citizens the right to move freely in and between member states – it is still necessary for EU citizens to present their passports or identity cards upon entering the country, particularly in the current climate.

From elsewhere

Nationals from the US, Canada, Australia, New Zealand, South Africa, Japan, Mexico and Switzerland do not need a visa in order to visit Britain for a holiday of up to three months, but must present their passport upon arrival and should expect to answer a few routine questions relating to the nature of their visit. Other nationals should check out their particular entry requirements with their respective embassies.

Customs

EU nationals over the age of 17 are no longer required to make a declaration to customs upon entry into another EU country, and so can now import a limitless amount of goods for personal use. For non-EU nationals the limits are 200 cigarettes, one litre of spirits, two litres of wine, 60ml of perfume, two cameras, one movie camera and one TV.

Retail Export Scheme

Visitors from non-EU countries can make savings on purchases made in London via the Retail Export Scheme. Pick up a form from participating shops.

Pets' Passports

Until recently, no pet could be brought into the country unless it had first spent six months in quarantine to make sure it wasn't carrying any infectious diseases (particularly rabies). The rules have now relaxed slightly allowing visitors from Western Europe (and certain island states such as Cyprus and Malta) to bring in pets so long as they fulfill the following strict criteria: the pet to be brought in must not have been outside the qualifying area at any time; each pet must be fitted with an identification microchip and have been innoculated against rabies; the owner must carry with them a document (known as the Pet's Passport) proving this. The animal must undergo a further blood test 30 days after entry.

Getting to London from elsewhere in the UK

By air

The ever-increasing demands of business mean that it is now possible to fly to London from most of the UK's main cities, although it's not really a cost- or time-effective option unless you're travelling from the north of England or Scotland (or can pick up a very cheap deal).

British Airways, t 0870 850 9850, **www**.britishairways.com, **British Midland, t** 0870 607 0555, **www**.flybmi.co.uk, and the low-cost airlines **Easyjet, t** 0871 750 0100, **www**.easyjet.com, **Ryanair, t** 0871 246 0000, **www**.ryanair.com and **Bmibaby** (British Midland's budget subsidiary), **t** 0870 264 2229, **www**.bmibaby.com, all offer services and a bewildering array of fares. As a simple rule of thumb, the earlier you book your flight, the cheaper it will be. If travelling Super Apex (which must be booked at least 14 days in advance) or Apex (7 days in advance), you should be able to get a flight from Edinburgh to London on a major carrier for between £70–£90. A flight booked just a few days before departure will rise to £160–£180. Occasionally, you may find a low-cost carrier offering flights for as little as £19.99 (sometimes even cheaper) from Glasgow–London, but, again, these have to be booked well in advance. **Easyjet**, in particular, operates an escalating fare policy. The first people to enquire about a particular flight will get the cheapest deal but, as the service fills up, so the prices will rise until they are more or less compatible with those of the major carriers.

By rail

All train tracks lead to London. You can get to the city from anywhere in the UK and, as with air travel, the earlier you book your journey, the cheaper it will be. Super Apex fares (which must be booked at least 14 days in advance) are the cheapest, Apex (7 days in advance) the next cheapest and you can also buy Super Savers which, though even cheaper, can only be used Sat–Thurs outside peak hours. Perhaps the best option is to pick up a family railcard which, for just £20 a year,

entitles up to 4 adults to a 30% saving and up to 4 children to a 60% saving on most services, **www**.family-railcard.co.uk. Contact National Rail Enquiries, **t** 0845 748 4950, **www**.nationalrail.co.uk, for more information.

The UK is served by four main train companies:
First Great Western t 0845 700 0125, **www**.great-western-trains.co.uk
West of England, including southwest peninsula
GNER t 0845 722 5225, **www**.gner.co.uk
East Midlands, Yorkshire, northeast and Scotland
Scotrail t 0845 755 0033, **www**.scotrail.co.uk
Northwest England and Scotland
Virgin t 0845 722 2333, **www**.virgintrains.co.uk
West coast, West Midlands, northwest and Scotland

By bus

See p.12.

TRAVEL

Making your way around the maze of London's streets can be tricky. They have neither the block-by-block clarity of New York nor the accessibility of Paris. The most convenient option, if you are new to the city, is to take the Underground (the 'Tube'). This in itself can be exciting for children, especially if they have never travelled on an underground system before. When you, and they, are a little more at home in London, you'll find that buses make a welcome change, allowing you to see the sights as you travel around, albeit at a more leisurely pace. Other forms of transport, such as London's famous black cabs, can also be fun, though expensive.

By Underground

Travelcards

If you're travelling after 9.30am on a weekday or at anytime on a weekend, your best bet is to get a One-Day Travelcard, which lets you make unlimited journeys on London's Tubes, buses (except night buses) and trains until 3am the following morning. See **Top tips** p.18.

There are 12 interconnecting lines (colour-coded) which criss-cross London from Heathrow out to the west to Upminster in the east, and from Barnet in the north to Morden in the south. In central London you're never more than five minutes from a Tube station, though the system becomes more sparse the further from the centre you get. Tube trains run from 5.30am to 12midnight (7am on Sundays) every day apart from Christmas. Try to avoid travelling at peak times (Mon–Fri 7.30am–9.30am and 5pm–7.30pm). This is especially important if you are using a pushchair.

The Docklands area in east London is served by the DLR (Docklands Light Railway), an overground monorail which links up with ⊖ Bank and ⊖ Tower Gateway. For information, call the DLR customer services **t** (020) 7363 9700. **www**.dlr.co.uk. Trains run to 12.30am Mon–Sat, 11.30pm Sun.

Follow procedure

You must buy your Underground ticket in advance. Travelcards are available from Tube

Question 1
In Paris it's le métro, in New York it's the subway, so what is it called in London?
answer on p.249

Useful numbers
Transport for London Travel (24hr)
t (020) 7222 1234
www.tfl.gov.uk
National Rail Enquiries
t (08457) 48 49 50

and train station ticket windows and machines, and from many newsagents. Weekly and monthly passes can also be purchased from newsagents.

At most Underground stations you will find an 'Assistance and Tickets' window, where you can pay by card or cash, plus a bank of electronic ticket machines which accept coins and notes (not £20 notes). You can buy a carnet of 10 tickets for £10 or a weekly pass from some machines.

Some stations have ticket inspectors; most, however, have automated barriers. Place your ticket with the black magnetic strip face down and to the right into the slot at the front of the machine. The ticket will reappear from a slot at the top of the machine. Take your ticket and the barrier will open.

Few Tube stops have lifts, which means taking the stairs or (if you're sensible) the escalator. Pushchairs must be folded up and held on the escalator. It is the custom to stand on the right-hand side and walk on the left and people may get very sniffy with you if you get this wrong. On crowded trains, young, fit passengers are supposed to give up their seats for senior citizens, pregnant women and parents with babies or toddlers. Sometimes this even happens.

By bus

Despite the presence of the odd bus lane, London's ongoing traffic congestion problems make the bus an impractical choice for anyone in a hurry. If you're not working to a deadline, however, it can make a very pleasant alternative to sub terranean travel. Looking out of the window from the top deck of a slow-moving double decker is a great way of getting to know the city.

Attempts are being made to speed up the bus service. The introduction of the Congestion Charge (see p.16) has slightly reduced the volume of traffic during the week and most buses in central London now operate a 'pay before you board' policy. To take a ride on a conductor-less bus, you now have to purchase your ticket in advance from one of the new ticket machines located by the bus stop (or from a newsagent) rather than from the driver. You can, however, still buy your ticket from the conductor aboard traditional, open-back 'routemaster' buses. The standard single fare is adult £1, child 40p. You can also buy saver tickets – 6 singles cost adult £3.90, a saving of £2.10, child £2.10, a saving of 30p – and one day bus passes giving you unlimited travel on all the city's routes for adult £2, child £1.

There are two types of bus stop: white, at which buses must stop, and red, which are request stops. To hail a bus at a red stop, stick your arm out. To alight at a request stop, ring the bell.

Night buses

Standard buses stop operating around midnight, at which point N-prefixed night buses take over until 5am the following morning. There are far fewer night bus routes – you can pick up a night route map from any Underground station and most newsagents. One-Day Travelcards are not valid on night buses.

By train

For nipping around central London, stick to the Tube. For longer journeys out into the suburbs, however, you may wish to switch to the train. London's rail network links up with the Tube at various points and, unlike the Tube, there are certain services (particularly the airport routes) that run all night. To find out how trains are running throughout Britain call **t** (08457) 48 49 50, **www**.nationalrail.co.uk, for details of family rail-cards *see* p.13. All train and Tube stations have a map, known as a Journey Planner, showing London's combined Tube and train network. If you buy a Travelcard (*See* p. 18 **Top tips**), you can chop and change your mode of transport throughout the day, using as many trains, Tubes and buses as you like.

Tickets and passes

Fares in London are based on a zonal system. The capital is divided into six concentric rings or 'zones'. Zone 1 is the centre, Zone 6 the outskirts. Your fare is worked out according to the distance of your journey within and between these zones. For instance, a single tube fare within Zone 1 is adult £1.60, child 60p, whereas a single fare between Zone 1 and Zone 2 rises to adult £2, child 80p. Children's fares apply between the ages of 5 and 15. After the age of 12 children need to show an age

identification photocard (available from any Tube or train station) when they purchase their ticket; under-5s go free.

Taxis

London is justifiably proud of its black cabs. Though undeniably expensive, they make up one of the most efficient and reliable taxi services in the world. Cabbies must train for two years and pass a strict test before qualifying for their taxi licences. During this time they must learn every street and major building in the capital, as well as 468 separate routes – a mean feat of learning known simply as 'The Knowledge'.

London cabs are easily recognizable. Most are black although, in this consumer age, some now sport the coloured livery of advertisers. All have orange 'For Hire' signs on their roofs which light up when the cab is available. Carseats are fitted as standard in all TX1 black cabs. The seats are built into the central arm rest in the rear of the cab and can accommodate children between 22 and 36kg. You may hail a cab on the street (by sticking out your arm and shouting 'Taxi!') or, if staying at a hotel, you can ask the doorman to do it for you. There are taxi ranks outside all major railway stations and also some Tube stations. Alternatively, call Dial-A-Cab, **t** (020) 7253 5000. To track down that mislaid umbrella or teddy bear, call Black Cab Lost Property on **t** (020) 7833 0996. Black cabs are licensed to carry four people at a time (sometimes five), with space next to the driver for luggage. Most black cabs can accommodate wheelchairs. Bear in mind that fares increase after 8pm when a higher tariff applies.

Minicabs are cheaper, but less reliable and largely unregulated. A driving licence is pretty much all that's required to qualify as a minicab driver. Hiring a minicab can therefore be rather a risky business. There are some reputable firms, however, including:

Greater London Hire
t (020) 8340 2450
www.glh.com

Lady Cabs
t (020) 7254 3501
A specialist service run by women (all the drivers are female) for women.

By car

Driving in central London is recommended only for the very patient or the very rich. There's also a new factor – the Congestion Charge. Introduced by the Mayor of London, Ken Livingstone, in early 2003, this scheme sought to reduce traffic by detering motorists from making unnecessary journeys and to raise revenue to improve the city's public transport system. All drivers entering central London between 7am and 6.30pm Monday to Friday must pay a flat rate £5 to do so. The scheme has proved to be at least a partial success. Congestion has, it's estimated, been reduced by between 10 and 15 per cent; however, the much-needed improvements to public transport have yet to take effect.

The Congestion Charging Zone currently stretches around central London from King's Cross in the north to Elephant and Castle in the south, and from Hyde Park Corner in the west to Tower Bridge in the east. Entry points are clearly marked by a big red 'C' painted on the road. However, there is talk of extending the zone. The system is enforced by a network of CCTV cameras which monitor number plates. Drivers have until midnight of the day of travel to pay the charge (a £5 surcharge applies to applications made after 10pm), by phone, t (0845) 900 1234, online at www.cclondon.com or at shops bearing the red 'C' symbol. You can pay on a daily, weekly, monthly or annual basis, although there is no discount for doing so. Failure to pay will result in a £40 fine (£80 if you fail to pay within 14 days).

If you do use your car, beware the parking restrictions. Going over the allotted time at a parking meter can have dire consequences. Your car may end up with a wheel clamp or, if you're particularly unlucky, it may be towed away. To find out which pound to go to to reclaim your car call t (020) 7747 4747 – the main ones are at Marble Arch, Earl's Court and Camden. The fine will be a staggering £150. Using the car for trips outside London, however, does make a little more sense. Before setting off, buy a copy of the British Highway Code (available from post offices) in order to familiarize yourself with the British way of motoring. You don't need to carry your papers with you but, if stopped, you will usually be asked to present them at a police station within five days. If you are hiring a car, you need to be at least 21 years old (more usually 25), with a year's driving experience. Most airlines will be able to arrange fly-drive packages on request and most have factored the cost of the Congestion Charge into their prices.

Car rental companies

Alamo
UK t 0870 400 4562
www.alamo.co.uk
US t (1 800) 462 5266
www.alamo.com
Avis
UK t 0870 010 0287
www.avis.co.uk
US t (1 800) 230 4898
www.avis.com
Hertz
UK t 0870 844 8844
www.hertz.co.uk
US t (800) 654 3131
www.hertz.com
Thrifty
UK t (01494) 751 600
www.thrifty.co.uk
US t (800) 847 4389
www.thrifty.com

By bike

London is not terribly cycle-friendly – certainly not when compared with somewhere such as Amsterdam. Extreme congestion, rising pollution and a limited number of cycle lanes are just some of the hazards awaiting you. Cycling as part of a large tour-guided group (see below) is a much safer option. Here are some rental companies that provide bikes and helmets for families. Hire rates are approx adult £2.50 per hour, child £2 per hour.

On Your Bike
52–4 Tooley Street
t (020) 7378 6669
www.onyourbike.net
⊖ London Bridge

Dial-a-Bike
t (020) 7828 4040
Delivers to major hotels in London.

Capital Sport Ltd
t (1296) 631 671
www.capital-sport.co.uk
Offers self-guided tours along the Thames.

IDEAS, IDEAS

17

The best of kids' London

This is our selection of the very best that London has to offer younger visitors: all the best things to see, eat, visit, shop, ride and play with that can be found in England's capital city.

Best animal attraction
London Zoo, *see* p.42.

Best annual jamboree
Totally Covent Garden – The Festival, *see* p.35.

Best café
Food for Thought, for veggie delights in Covent Garden, *see* p.233.

Best Christmas experience
Going skating on the outdoor ice rink at Somerset House, *see* p.233.

Best church
For views and all round 'wow' factor, St Paul's Cathedral, *see* p.129.

Best cinema
The big, big screen: Imax 3D Cinema, *see* p.107.

Best firework display
At the end of the Lord Mayor's Show, *see* p.37.

Best for gruesomeness
The London Dungeon's grisly tableaux, *see* p.116, or the Old Operating Theatre), *see* p.119.

Best interactive fun
The Wellcome Wing at the Science Museum, *see* p.139.

Best market
For budding fashionistas: The Stables in Camden Market, *see* p.49.

Best museum
The Natural History Museum, for its animatronic dinosaurs and sheer number of beasts, *see* p.138.

Best park
Regent's Park, for the boats, playgrounds, wildfowl, open air theatre and sports facilities, *see* p.46.

Best restaurant
Giraffe, where you can sip a fruity shake or tuck into a bowl of noodles while listening to world music, *see* p.225.

Best shop
Semmalina, *see* p.242, or Niketown, *see* p.246.

Best sightseeing tour
Sailing down to Greenwich on a Bateaux London-Catamaran Cruiser, *see* p.29.

Best sports event
The racy to the downright wacky: the Oxford-Cambridge Boat Race, *see* p.33, the London Marathon, *see* p.153, or the superannuated vehicles in the London to Brighton Vintage Car Run, *see* p.37.

Best statue
Nelson on his column, *see* p.66.

Best toy shop
Hamley's, of course, *see* p.247.

Best view
From a capsule in the London Eye, *see* p.108, from Hampstead Heath, *see* p.174, or from the top floor café of the National Portrait Gallery, *see* p.73.

Tips for getting around

▶ London has one of the most extensive public transport systems of any city in the world. Trying to get around the city's traffic-filled streets in your own car is painful (and expensive following the introduction of the Congestion Charge, *see* 'By Car', p.16). Using taxis for more than the odd journey is an expensive option and, again, you'll often be stuck in traffic.

▶ Children aged from 5 to 11 travel for less than half the full fare, and under-5s travel for free, provided they do not take up a seat, on nearly all local transport. *See* 'Travel discounts', p.20.

▶ **Don't** buy tickets every time you use public transport. Travelcards and a *carnet* (a block of ten tickets) can be used for the Tube (Underground/subway), buses, the DLR and train system. This works out cheaper than single tickets and you won't have to queue to pay your fare every time you travel. See 'Getting Around', p.14.

▶ London offers a wide range of **sightseeing tours**. These are some of the best and most enjoyable ways of getting an idea of the city – since they often involve just sitting and looking from a boat or bus. The classic boat trips on the Thames are among London's don't-miss attractions, but don't pass over less well-known rides like the open-top bus tours, canal trips, the madcap fun of the amphibious Frog Tours, or for the energetic, guided walks. For details, *see* p.21.

Getting more for less

London is one of the wealthiest cities in the world and much of what it has to offer does not come cheap. Even so, it is still possible to have a fun day out without breaking the bank.

Churches

Admission to all the churches in London is free – except for St Paul's Cathedral and Westminster Abbey. Carol services take place at several times a year, most notably at Christmas and Easter.

City farms

Coram's Fields and Vauxhall City Farm allow families to pet and stroke their animals and engage in a range of country crafts free of charge. *See* p.176.

Entertainment

Free foyer concerts are often given at the Royal National Theatre, Royal Festival Hall and the Barbican in the early evening. Covent Garden plays host to some of the country's top buskers and street performers on a daily basis (*see* p.79). The Covent Garden Festival of Street Theatre takes place every September.

Events & festivals

Various free events take place in London each year. *See* p.32 for more details of the London year.

Daily events
Changing of the Guard
Outside Buckingham Palace.

Ceremony of the Keys
The Tower of London.

Hyde Park Gun Salutes
By the Royal Horse Artillery; these take place on 6 February (Accession Day), 21 April (Queen's birthday), 2 June (Coronation Day), 10 June (Prince Philip's birthday), and the State Opening of Parliament in November. Note if any of the above dates fall on a Sunday, the salute will be fired on the following Monday.

Museums & galleries

The number of museums and galleries that don't charge for admission is, believe it or not, actually increasing. Some of the capital's most prestigious collections, including the Natural History Museum, Science Museum, Museum of London, National Maritime Museum and the Imperial War Museum, have recently taken the decision to waive their entrance fees.

Apsley House *see* p.92
Bank of England Museum *see* p.131
Bethnal Green Museum of Childhood *see* p.161
British Library *see* p.58
British Museum *see* p.54
Bruce Castle Museum *see* p.161
Clowns International Gallery *see* p.161
Geffrye Museum *see* p.162
Horniman Museum *see* p.162
Houses of Parliament *see* p.99
Imperial War Museum *see* p.111
Kenwood House *see* p.163
London International Gallery of Children's Art *see* p.164
Museum of London *see* p.130
National Gallery *see* p.67
National Army Museum *see* p.164
National Maritime Museum *see* p.150
National Portrait Gallery *see* p.69
Natural History Museum, *see* p.138
Petrie Museum of Egyptian Archaeology *see* p.57
Prince Henry's Room *see* p.133

Museum trails
Several museums and galleries produce free leaflets and trails that children can use to make their visit more enjoyable. Ask at the foyer on entry if there are any audio guides, backpacks or free leaflets for kids to use.

IDEAS, IDEAS

Queen's House *see* p.151
Ragged School Museum *see* p.164
Royal Air force Museum *see* p.164
Royal Observatory *see* p.150
Royal Naval College *see* p.151
Science Museum *see* p.139
Serpentine Gallery *see* p.144
Sir John Soane's Museum *see* p.83
Tate Britain *see* p.100
Tate Modern *see* p.117
Theatre Museum *see* p.79
Victoria & Albert Museum *see* p.141
Wallace Collection *see* p.47
Wandsworth Museum *see* p.165

Museums free for children

Apsley House: The Wellington Museum *see* **p.92**
Cabinet War Rooms *see* p.100
Courtauld Gallery *see* p.84
Dulwich Picture Gallery see p.161
Gilbert Museum see p.85
Guards' Museum *see* p.101
HMS Belfast see p.120
Kew Gardens *see* p.172
London's Transport Museum *see* p.78
Museum in Docklands *see* p.153

Parks & views

From elegantly manicured royal gardens to great swathes of ancient woodland, London's parks are all free. Wherever you're staying in London there will be a park, usually with a children's playground, not too far away. *See* **Kids out p.171** for more information. For stunning views try Hampstead Heath, The Mall, Oxo Tower, Westminster Bridge or the London Eye.

On foot

London comes in two different sizes: Greater London, which is huge – 28 miles north to south, 35 miles east to west; and central London, where the majority of the capital's tourist attractions are located, which isn't very big at all. Touring on foot is the best way to get to know the smaller version; you can explore all the hidden nooks and crannies you would miss if you relied exclusively on public transport. A few words of warning, however.

▶ **Vehicles travel on the left on Britain's roads, so when crossing remember to look right, then left, and not vice versa.**

▶ Never cross the road except at a designated crossing zone such as a set of traffic lights, a pelican crossing (a green man will light up to let you know when it's safe to cross) or a zebra crossing – a black and white striped crossing point with an orange flashing beacon on either side. In theory, traffic should stop as soon as you put your foot on a zebra. Do, however, make sure that it has done so before you start to cross.

Travel discounts

Your cheapest bet is to get a One-Day Travelcard which lets you make unlimited journeys on London's Tubes, buses (except night buses) and also entitles the holder to a 33% discount on most scheduled Thames riverboat services (*See* 'Getting Around', p.14). At the time of writing, a Travelcard covering Zones 1 and 2 costs adult £4.10, child £2; a Travelcard covering all six zones is adult £5.10, child £2. London Transport offers a special family deal on Travelcards which, if purchased together, can be bought for adult £2.70, child 80p for a pass covering Zones 1–2 and adult £3.40, child 80p for a pass covering all 6 zones. You can also buy weekly and monthly Travelcards which provide even greater savings, but these are only really worthwhile if you plan to use public transport all through the week. You will need to provide a passport-sized photograph of yourself for the accompanying photocard.

If you travel beyond the limits of your ticket, you will be liable for an on-the-spot penalty fare. This is £10 on Tubes and trains and £5 on the buses.

There are also a number of tourist buses plying their trade in the capital. The best is probably the Big Bus Company, **t** (020) 7233 9533. Adult £17, child £8 – for 24hours unlimited travel on BBC buses.

London Pass

An all-in-one sightseeing ticket, the London Pass gives you free entry to selected museums, river cruises, historic houses, zoos, cinemas, galleries, guided walks etc., plus special offers at restaurants (including Planet Hollywood), theatres and shops. Prices range from: one day (adult £23, child £15); two days (adult £36, child £25); three days (adult £44, child £29); six days (adult £62, child £41). Tickets including free public transport range from one day (adult £27, child £17) to six days (adult £94, child £52). Holders also receive a free 132-page guide to the capital. Available in person from the British Visitor Centre or by logging on at **www**.londonpass.com

Useful London websites

Contact the relevant local borough council for details of local and seasonal events (firework nights in particular), plus free festivals. Council websites are as follows:

www...nameofborough....**gov.uk**
eg: **www**.barnet.**gov.uk**
www.londontown.com
The official tourist board site with various attractions, hotel details etc.
www.thisislondon.co.uk
The *Evening Standard*'s website. The kids' section is full of jolly ideas and up-to-the-minute events
www.timeout.com/london
Time Out magazine's website. The kids' section is selective and has some interesting features
www.londonnet.co.uk
This site doesn't have a huge kids' section, but its savvy attitude is appealing
www.kidslovelondon.com
The London Tourist Board's dedicated kids' site with links to top attractions, listings of upcoming events, online games and reviews by primary age children (5–11 years).

London Rail and River Tour

Gives an overview of the best the capital has to offer both old and new, from historical sights and attractions to the latest shopping and restaurants around Canary Wharf and Docklands. The Rail and River Rover Ticket is valid for one day and allows unlimited travel on the Docklands Light Railway and City Cruises River Boats, which run between Westminster, Waterloo, Tower Hill and Greenwich

Fares Adult £8.80, child £4.40, family £23 (2 adults and up to 3 children), **www**.citycruises.com, **t** (020) 7740 0400, **www**.tfl.gov.uk/dlr, **t** (020) 7363 9700.

Fun & games

Just in case the kids have time to be bored, which we very much doubt, here are a few ways to keep them occupied.

Pub cricket

Pubs in London have names like the Dog & Duck and The Red Lion. You can play a game called pub cricket in which you score runs according to the number of legs a pub has, i.e The Dog & Duck scores six runs (a dog having four legs and a duck two). Just as in cricket, the object of the game is to score as many runs as possible. If you spot a pub with no legs, such as The Crown, then you lose a wicket. Ten wickets and you're out and it is someone else's turn to score a few runs. The game can get a little more complicated with a pub such as the Horse & Hounds – decide for yourself just how many hounds are to be counted.

What am I?

A London version of the guessing game What Animal Am I?
Q. What London landmark am I?
eg
I am quite tall
I have a pointed roof
I make a noise every hour
I have numbers on my face
A. Big Ben

Quick draw

You will need:
pocket-sized pad of plain paper
a pen that glides easily across the page
This really is the simplest game imaginable, rest the pad on your knee and lightly poise the pen over it. As the vehicle you are in moves around the pen will jump leaving a crazy pattern on the paper. Kids can either take turns making the patterns or trying to figure out what the drawings look like. They could even spend time colouring in the shapes should you experience a long delay to your journey.

IDEAS, IDEAS

Sometimes children can get madly interested in a particular subject, such as football, animals, film or the theatre. When this occurs, everything else becomes dull and uninspiring and just a little bit pointless. With this in mind, here are a number of suggested days out for excitable kids with abiding passions.

Stagestruck kids

Itinerary 1

Morning Take the Tube to Covent Garden for the Theatre Museum, where you can explore the history of the performing arts and kids get to dress up in theatrical costumes. *See* p.79.
Lunch At the Covent Garden Market Café watching the performers on the Piazza.
Afternoon Take the Tube to Waterloo for a tour of the Royal National Theatre. *See* p.109.

Theatre Museum
Russell Street, WC2
t (020) 7836 7891
www.theatremuseum.org
Open Tues–Sat 10–6
Free

Royal National Theatre
South Bank, SE1
t (020) 7452 3400
www.nationaltheatre.org.uk
Tour Mon–Sat 10.15, 12.45 & 5.30
Adm Backstage tours: £5 per person, concs £4.25

Itinerary 2

Morning Take the Tube or train to London Bridge for a tour around the reconstructed Globe Theatre to see how plays were performed in Shakespeare's day. *See* p.170.
Lunch In the Globe Café or the nearby Anchor Inn. *See* p.230.
Afternoon Take a gentle walk along the riverfront past the South Bank (where a free performance may be taking place on Theatre Square outside the Royal National Theatre) to Waterloo. From Waterloo you can take the train to Wimbledon to catch an afternoon performance at the Polka Theatre, the only purpose-built children's theatre in the country. *See* p.169.

Shakespeare's Globe Theatre
Bear Gardens, Bankside, New Globe Wall, Southwark, SE1
t (020) 7902 1400
www.shakespeares-globe.org
Open 10–5 daily, for performance times call in advance
Adm Museum: adult £8, child £5.50 (under-5s **free**), concs £6.50, family ticket (2+3) £24

Anchor Inn
34 Park Street, Bankside, Southwark, SE1
t (020) 7902 1400
Open Mon–Sat 11am–11pm, Sun 12 noon–10.30pm

Globe Café
Bear Gardens, Bankside, New Globe Wall, Southwark, SE1
t (020) 7902 1576
Open May–Sept 10am–11pm, Oct–April 10–5

Polka Theatre
240 The Broadway, SW19
t (020) 8543 4888
www.polkatheatre.com
Open Tues–Fri 9.30–4.30, Sat 11–5.30
Adm Tickets for performances range from £5–£10; a one-day workshop is £25

Toy-mad kids

Itinerary 1

Morning Take the Tube to Goodge Street for a trip to the wonderful Pollock's Toy Museum, a delightful collection of Victorian toys and trinkets. *See* p.57.
Lunch At Pizza Express on the adjacent Charlotte Street or, if you feel up to it, take the Tube to Oxford Circus for the café in the basement of Hamleys on Regent Street where you can tuck into your burgers surrounded by bleeping video machines.
Afternoon Browse through Hamleys' six toy-stuffed floors (*see* p.247).
1 Scala Street, W1 (*entrance on Whitfield Street*)
t (020) 7636 3452
www.pollocksweb.co.uk

Pollock's Toy Museum
Open Mon–Sat 10–5 (last entry 4.30)
Adm Adult £3, child (under 18) £1.50

Pizza Express
7 Charlotte Street, W1
t (020) 7580 1110
www.pizzaexpress.co.uk
Open 12 noon–11.30 daily

Hamleys
188 Regent Street, W1
t (020) 7734 3161
www.hamleys.com
Open Mon–Wed, Fri 10–7, Thurs 10–8, Sat 9.30–7,
Sun 12 noon–6

Life at sea

Morning Take a riverboat cruise from Charing
Cross Pier to Greenwich with Bateaux London-
Catamaran Cruises, to visit the *Cutty Sark* and
National Maritime Museum with its vast collection
of nautical equipment. *See* p.150.
Lunch In the Trafalgar Tavern, Park Row, over-
looking the river.
Afternoon Take the train from Greenwich to
London Bridge for HMS *Belfast*, a Second World
War destroyer moored permanently on the river-
front. *See* p.120.

Bateaux London–Catamaran Cruisers
t (020) 7925 2215
www.bateauxlondon.com
Fares A Circular Cruise (from central London to
Greenwich and back): adult return £7.50, child
return £5.50, family £19.50

The Trafalgar Tavern
Park Row, SE10
t (020) 8858 2437
Open Mon–Sat 11.30–11, Sun 12 noon–10.30

National Maritime Museum
Romney Road, Greenwich, SE10
t (020) 8 858 4422
Infoline **t** (020) 8312 6565
www.nmm.ac.uk
Open 10–5 daily (last entry 4.30)
Free

HMS *Belfast*
Morgan's Lane, off Tooley Street, SE1
t (020) 7940 6300
www.hmsbelfast.org.uk
Open Mar–Oct 10–6 daily, Nov–Feb 10–5 daily
Adm Adult £6, child **free**, concs £4.40

Gory kids

Morning Take a Tube or train to London Bridge for
the London Dungeon, the capital's premier
gorefest. *See* p116.
Lunch At Pizza Hut in the London Dungeon or Café
Rouge in the nearby Hay's Galleria.
Afternoon If you still feel like grossing out, head
either to the Old Operating Theatre, where
surgeons gaily butchered people in the early 19th
century (*see* p.119), or the Clink Museum (*see* p.121),
built on the site of a former prison, which holds a
collection of medieval torture instruments.

London Dungeon
Tooley Street, SE1
t (020) 7403 7221
www.thedungeons.com
Open Mon–Wed 10.30–9, Thurs–Sun 10.30–6.30
(last entry 4.30)
Adm Adult £12.50, child (under 14) £7.50, under-5s
free, concs £9.50

Café Rouge
Hay's Galleria, SE1
t (020) 7378 0097
www.caferouge.co.uk
Open 10am–11pm daily

St Thomas' Old Operating Theatre
9a St Thomas Street, SE1
t (020) 7955 4791
www.thegarret.org.uk
Open 10–4 daily
Adm Adult £4, child £2.50 (under-8s **free**), family
ticket (2+2) £10

Clink Museum
1 Clink Street, SE1
t (020) 7403 6515
www.clink.co.uk
Open 10–6 daily
Adm Adult/child £4, concs £3, family £9

Animal-mad kids

London Zoo (⊖ Camden Town or Baker Street) is still one of the best places for kids to come and learn about animals. *See* p.42.

11.15 Reptile Round-Up – meet some of the zoo's more cold-blooded inhabitants (you can stroke a snake's skin and hold an alligator tooth) at the Reptile House.

12.00 noon Flying display by predatory birds on the Display Lawn.

12.30 Lunch at the zoo's self-service café.

1pm Pelican Picnic – once you've had your fill, watch the pelicans tucking their huge bills into buckets of fish.

1.30 A Gorilla's Story – meet the gentle giants at the Ape and Monkey Enclosure.

2pm Animals in Action in the Amphitheatre – leaping lemurs and flying parrots demonstrate their skills.

2.30 Feeding Time – for the penguins in the Penguin Pool, the fish in the Aquarium and (Fridays) the snakes in the Reptile House.

3pm Happy Families – meet large groups of meerkats, otters and marmosets at the new Happy Families Area.

3.30 B.U.G.S – get up close and personal with creepy crawlies at the Web of Life building.

4.30 Flying display by predatory birds on the Display Lawn.

5pm Watch the giraffes being put to bed at the Giraffe House. (Note: this takes place at 3.15pm in winter when some of the other events may not take place. Times vary on weekdays during term-time).

London Zoo
Regent's Park, NW1
t (020) 7722 3333
www.londonzoo.co.uk
Open Mar–Oct 10–5.30 daily; Nov–April 10–4 daily
Adm Adult £12, child (under 15) £9, under-3s **free**, concs £10.20, family £38

Movie-mad kids

There's absolutely no way you can mention film anymore without reference to the Harry Potter phenomenon. London, of course, features in both the Potter books and on-screen, plus in a number of other movies besides.

Itinerary 1

Morning Take the Tube to Camden Town or Baker Street, then take the 274 bus to London Zoo. Linger around the Reptile House and see if your kids can communicate with the serpents as well as young Harry does. *See* p.42.

Lunch Stroll over to Regent's Park for a picnic and see if you can spot any of Dodie Smith's *One Hundred and One Dalmatians* or head further north to Primrose Hill to re-enact the twilight barking. *See* p.46 and p.48.

Afternoon Hop on the Bakerloo Line down to Waterloo and catch a state-of-the-art film show at the 3D Imax cinema. *See* p.107.

London Zoo
Regent's Park, NW1
t (020) 7722 3333
www.londonzoo.co.uk
Open Mar–Oct 10–5.30 daily; Nov–April 10–4 daily
Adm Adult £12, child (under 15) £9, under-3s **free**, concs £10.20, family £38

IMAX 3D Cinema
1 Charlie Chaplin Walk, SE1
t (020) 7902 1234
www.bfi.org.uk/imax
⊖/ ≋ Waterloo
Bus 12, 53, 76, 77, 109, 211, 507, D1, P11
Open Mon–Thurs 12.30–8, Fri 12.30–9.15, Sat 11.45–9.15, Sun 12 noon–8
Adm Adult £7.50, child (5–16) £4.95 (£6 for evening shows), under-3s **free**, concs £6.20; prices for Hollywood blockbusters start at around £11.50

Itinerary 2

Morning Though not the best spot for hanging around with the kids, St Pancras (exterior) and King's Cross (interior) stations are a must for all Potter-ites, but do try to restrain them from throwing themselves at the barrier in an attempt to locate Platform 9¾. Instead move swiftly along to the Piccadilly Line and head to Leicester Square

– the heart of London's movie-going scene to watch the latest blockbuster or gaze at the hand-prints of famous stars set into the pavement around the square. *See p.72.*

Lunch On a fine day you can grab a picnic and sit in Leicester Square. Alternatively, catch a Northern Line train to Waterloo or Embankment and have a snack in the NFT café underneath Waterloo Bridge. *See p.72 and p.112.*

Afternoon Stay in the NFT for an afternoon screening of an old black and white classic or a special kids' film. On Saturdays kids can also take part in a film-related workshop.

Leicester Square Cinemas

Empire
t 0870 010 2030
www.uci-cinemas.co.uk
Odeon Leicester Square & Odeon West End
t 0870 505 0007
www.odeon.co.uk
Warner Village West End
t 0870 240 6020
www.warnervillage.co.uk

National Film Theatre

t (020) 7928 3232
www.nft.org.uk
Adm 'Movie Magic' film screenings: Child £1, accompanying adult £5

Arty kids

Self-expression is vital to a child's creative development. Thankfully London has plenty of galleries where children can not only go for inspiration, but also have a go at making a masterpiece themselves.

Itinerary 1

Morning Take the Tube or train to London Bridge for the vast Tate Modern, which offers tailor-made kids' audio guides and organizes weekend activities for children, including art trails and creative workshops. *See p.117.*

Lunch The Tate Modern café can get very busy, so opt for an early lunch. The brasserie-style food is a bit pricey but it's worth it just for the spectacular view of the River Thames.

Afternoon Head north on the Northern Line or walk over the new Hungerford footbridge to Charing Cross and the newly revamped Trafalgar Square. If it's fine you can always picnic in the square before stopping off at the National Gallery for a look at the famous paintings. The gallery hosts a variety of family events, including story-telling sessions and drawing days under the tutelage of a professional artist. *See p.67.*

Tate Modern

Bankside, SE1
t (020) 7887 8000
www.tate.org.uk
Open Sun–Thurs 10–6, Fri and Sat 10am–10pm (closed 24–26 Dec; open 1 Jan)
Free

National Gallery

Trafalgar Square, WC2
t (020) 7747 2885
www.nationalgallery.org.uk
Open 10–6 daily, Wed till 9pm
Adm Free, charges apply for some temporary exhibitions

Itinerary 2

Morning Art 4 Fun. Let your children's imaginations run riot painting plates or designing their own pots at these popular, creative workshops. There are five locations in London including Notting Hill and West Hampstead. *See p.167.*

Lunch The ICA (⊖ Charing Cross) has a good café and a shop selling jewellery, gadgets and prints made by local artists. *See p.92.*

Afternoon Take the Tube or train to Vauxhall for Tate Britain. Families could easily spend a whole day wandering around the galleries here, but it's also good for interactive fun. On Sundays – and daily in the school holidays – look out for the art trolley doing its rounds, packed full of arty materials for kids to try. *See p.100.*

Art 4 Fun/Colour Me Mine

Branches in Chiswick, Notting Hill, Muswell Hill and West Hampstead
t (020) 8959 7373
www.art4fun.com
Open 10–6 daily
Adm £3.95 per person, charges apply for the hire of brushes, paints etc

ICA Gallery

The Mall, SW1
t (020) 7930 3647
www.ica.org.uk
⊖ Picadilly Circus, Charing Cross
Bus 2, 8, 9, 14, 16, 19, 22, 36, 38, 52, 73, 82
Open Galleries 12 noon–7.30
Adm Membership Mon–Fri Adult £1.50, concs £1, Sat, Sun Adult £2.50, concs £1.50

Tate Britain

Millbank, SW1
t (020) 7887 8000
www.tate.org.uk
Open 10–5.50 daily
Free, charges for some temporary exhibitions

Mini-monarchists

Of course, there are any number of royal exhibits in London – the following is our pick of the bunch.

Morning Take the Tube to St James's Park for the Buckingham Palace tour (summer only). The tour has been criticised for including just 18 of a possible 600 rooms and giving little sense of what it's like to live there, but young royalists won't be happy without it. *See* p.90.

11.27 If you time things well, you could watch the Changing of the Guard after your 45-minute tour of the palace. Allow yourself time to get the children out and find a place to stand.

Lunch Unless Her Majesty has invited you to lunch, it's not so easy to find a royal-themed eatery. You could, however, encounter the royalty of rock (including The Artist Formerly Known as Prince and, of course, Queen) at the nearby Hard Rock Café. *See* p.94.

Afternoon Princess Diana's palace in Kensington Gardens (⊖ High Street Kensington) has guided tours through the plush historic apartments and an excellent exhibition of royal clothes. Get there by 2.30 as it closes early: it might be easier (and less exhausting) to skip the Changing of the Guards today. After you've seen the Palace, the gardens provide a refreshing break from pomp and ceremony. *See* p.143.

Buckingham Palace

St James's Park, SW1. The ticket office for purchasing tickets on the day is located in Green Park at Canada Gate
t Booking line (020) 7766 7300/1
www.royal.gov.uk
Open Early Aug–Sept 9.30–5.30 daily (last entry 4.15)
Adm Buckingham Palace: adult £12, child (under 17) £6, under-5s **free**; Queen's Gallery: adult £6.50, child £3, under-5s **free**, family £16. There is a £1 booking fee for tickets booked online or over the phone.
The tour lasts 45mins

Changing of the Guard

t (020) 7930 4832
www.royal.gov.uk
Times The ceremony takes place every morning between April and August at 11.27 sharp and on alternate days for the rest of the year
Free
The ceremony lasts over 1hr

Hard Rock Café

150 Old Park Lane, W1
t (020) 7629 0382
⊖ Hyde Park Corner
Open Mon–Thurs 11.30am–12.30pm, Fri–Sat 11.30am–1am

Kensington Palace

The State Apartments, Kensington Gardens, W8
t 0870 751 5170
www.hrp.org.uk
Open Mar–Oct 10–6 daily, Nov–Feb 10–5 daily
Adm Adult £10.20, child £6.60, concs £7.70, family £31

SEE IT, DO IT

So you're ready to hit the town, but what to do first? Do you rush headlong at the nearest attraction and proceed in haphazard fashion? Not if you want to preserve a little sanity to go home with at the end of the day. Here are a few ways of getting a snapshot of the city before taking the plunge. Then you can move on to the sightseeing chapters in earnest.

Walks

It may seem an arduous task with kids in tow, but pushchair-bound kids need to limber and stretch. On a clear day there's really nothing nicer than a leisurely stroll along the river, and on a misty morning where better to take a trip than through London's murky past?

The Original London Walks

PO Box 1708
London NW6 4LW
t (020) 7624 3978
http://london.walks.com

The original and best – there are several companies offering walking tours of London, but this one (London's oldest) is easily the pick of the bunch and certainly the most child-friendly (under 15s go free if accompanied by an adult, adults £5). As well as organizing tours around several specific areas of London, including the City, Greenwich, Westminster and Hyde Park, London Walks offer various themed treks including 'Shakespeare's London', 'Ghosts of the West End', 'Jack the Ripper Haunts' and 'Christopher Wren's London – Bloody, Flaming, Poxy London'. The tours are led by knowledgeable, entertaining guides.

Globe Walkshop

Find out more about the decadent history of Southwark on a Globe Walkshop; a guided tour taking in the prisons, inns and theatres which used to make up the bulk of the area's buildings (10–12 noon every Saturday; **adm** £6, concs £5, student £4; **t** (020) 7902 1433). *See p.119.*

London Silver Jubilee Walkway

A 10-mile walk is not every child's idea of a great day out. This walkway is generally more for strong-thighed adults than children, but it's still worth considering for a family trip. The route is split into

seven sections – which run from Leicester Square through Westminster across the river to the South Bank and then back through The City to Covent Garden – each topped and tailed by a Tube stop, so you can walk as much or as little as you like. The route is marked by discs set in the pavement (there are 400 in total); kids love being the first one to 'find' the marker. The walk was created in 1977 to commemorate the Queen's Silver Jubilee, hence the name. For more information, visit the London Tourist Information Office at Victoria.

Millennium Mile

London's latest walkway, the Thameside path between Westminster Bridge and Tower Bridge, has recently been spruced up and rechristened the Millennium Mile. As a result, what was once one of the city's more tatty districts is now much smarter and one of the best places to come to for a family walk. The route is dotted with some of the capital's best attractions, including the London Aquarium, London Eye, the National Theatre, the Oxo Tower, the Tate Modern, the Globe Theatre, HMS *Belfast* and Tower Bridge. You can find out more by visiting **www.**southbanklondon.com/walk-this-way.

The Thames Path

For a more *ad hoc* walking experience, you might like to try a portion of the Thames Path, a designated nature trail along the banks of the Thames. You might have a job finishing the route, however, as it stretches the entire length of the river, all 180 miles of it. For more information contact the Thames Barrier Visitor Centre, **t** (020) 8305 4188.

Blue Plaque Tours

Have you ever noticed that some London houses have blue plaques adorning their walls? These were erected by English Heritage (**www.**english-heritage.org.uk) to indicate that a famous person used to live there.

It can be quite good fun using these plaques as the basis for a walk around the city. It allows you to explore streets and areas not normally covered on official sightseeing itineraries. *See box opposite.*)

Pub Signs

As you walk around the city, look out for the painted signs hanging up outside pubs, particularly old pubs. The names displayed are often very distinctive, not to say occasionally rather peculiar – Lamb and Flag, Hoop and Grapes, Black Friar, Old

Blue plaque tours

If visiting the British Museum, try finding the following, all within 10 minutes' walk :

7 Fitzroy Square: Home of **George Bernard Shaw**, author of *Pygmalion* (which was subsequently used as the basis for the musical *My Fair Lady*) and the modernist writer Virginia Woolf.

110 Gower Street: Home of **Charles Darwin**, one of the world's greatest scientists and the man who, in his book *The Origin of Species*, published in 1859, first put foward the now widely accepted Theory of Evolution. This states that every living creature on the earth has come about as a result of natural selection over millions of years rather than divine creation.

At **48 Doughty Street**, you'll find the former home of **Charles Dickens**, Victorian Britain's most famous and celebrated novelist. His works, including *Oliver Twist*, *Nicholas Nickleby*, *David Copperfield* and *Great Expectations*, are still widely read today and have been filmed on numerous occasions. His house is open to the public and is filled with period furniture and memorabilia relating to his life. *See* p.56.

If shopping on Oxford Street, look out for the following:

15 Poland Street: Home of the romantic poet **Percy Byshe Shelley**.

28 Dean Street: Home of **Karl Marx**, founder of Marxism (and buried in Highgate Cemetery).

23 Brook Street (it's just off New Bond Street): Home of the legendary rock guitarist **Jimi Hendrix**.

24 Brook Street, (next door to the above): Home of the 18th-century composer **George Handel;** among his most famous works is the choral classic *The Messiah*.

If shopping on the King's Road, try and spot the following:

18 St Leonard's Terrace: Home of **Bram Stoker**, author of the first vampire novel, *Dracula*.

23 Tedworth Squre: Home of **Mark Twain**, the American author of children's favourites *Tom Sawyer* and *Huckleberry Finn*.

56 Oakley Street: Home of **Captain Scott**, the famous Polar explorer who died in the early 20th century on the return journey following his unsuccesful attempt to become the first man to reach the South Pole.

13 Mallord Street: Home of **A.A. Milne**, creator of the Winnie the Pooh stories and one of the most popular children's authors of all time.

Cheshire Cheese, Bleeding Heart Tavern, Red Lion, White Swan, Coach and Horses etc. These were chosen specially because of the ease with which they could be illustrated on the pub sign. Remember, back in the 17th and 18th centuries, a large proportion of London's population couldn't read or write and would have had to rely on such images to make sure they found the right pub.

Look out, in particular, for pubs bearing the name 'The Royal Oak'. If you look closely at the tree depicted in the sign, you should after a while be able to pick out the image of a man hiding in its branches. This is the young Stuart prince Charles (later Charles II) who, after his Royalist army was defeated by the Parliamentarians ('Roundheads') at the the the end of the Civil War in 1652, had to hide in an oak tree for a whole day to avoid capture.

Boat trips

The following companies offer sightseeing boat trips along stretches of the Thames. The frequency depends on the time of year. For more details, visit the London River Services website www.tfl.gov.uk/river, where you can download a comprehensive Thames Boat Service guide and map, or call **t** (020) 7941 4500. Note that Travelcard holders (both adults and children) are entitled to a 33% discount on most scheduled riverboat services.

Bateaux London–Catamaran Cruisers

t (020) 7925 2215

www.bateauxlondon.com

Fares Circular Cruise (from central London to Greenwich and back): adult return £7.50, child return £5.50, family £19.50

Bankside Pass: adult £16.25, child £9.50, family £48.25 (includes entry to St Paul's Cathedral)

Tower Pass: adult £18, child £11 (includes entry to Tower of London)

Hopper Pass: adult £9, child £4.50, family £21 (allows unlimited use of service for one day enabling you to hop on and off at different sites)

River cruises with recorded commentary in purpose-built catamarans sailing between Embankment, Waterloo, Westminster, Greenwich and the Thames Barrier.

City Cruises

t (020) 7740 0400

www.citycruises.com

Fares Westminster–Tower Pier: adult single £5.20, return £6.30; child single £2.60, return £3.15, under-5s **free**

Westminter–Greenwich: adult single £6.60, return £8; child single £3.25, return £4, under-5s **free**

Rail & River Rover: adult £8.80, child £4.40, family £23, under-5s **free**

Runs between Westminster Pier, Waterloo Pier, Tower Pier and Greenwich. The huge boats, which seat up to 500, are easily recognized by their bright red livery. City Cruises also offers a 'Rail and River Rover Ticket' allowing unlimited travel for a day on both their boats and the Docklands Light Railway.

Tate to Tate

t (020) 7477 6892

www.thamesclippers.com

Fares Adult £4.50, child £2.25, family £10; tickets are valid all day with a maximum of three return journeys

Surely 'Tate à Tate' would have been a better name? Never mind, the latest addition to the capital's river traffic provides a welcome direct boat link between two of the capital's great art galleries. Services are run by Thames Clippers (who commissioned Damien Hirst to design the livery of one of their boats) and run every 40 minutes between Bankside Pier (for Tate Modern) and the new Millbank Pier (for Tate Britain) and back again, stopping off at Waterloo Pier (for the South Bank).

Thames River Services

t (020) 7930 4097

Fares Westminster–Thames Barrier: adult single £7.50, return £9; child single £3.25, return £4.50

Take a cruise downriver from Westminster past St Katharine's Pier to the East End, where aspects of the reconstructed Globe theatre of Shakespeare and St Paul's Cathedral merge with converted warehouses, wharves and smoking chimneys. The Thames Barrier itself is a sight to behold, with light gleaming off its magnificent gleaming carapaces. *See* opposite.

Westminster Passenger Service

t (020) 7930 4721

www.wpsa.co.uk

Fares Westminster–Kew (return): adult £15, child £7.50, family £37.50

Westminster–Richmond (return): adult £16.50, child £8.25, family £41.25

Westminster–Hampton Court (return): adult £18, child £9, family £45

Head upriver with some spicy commentary about the occupants of a few well-appointed flats in Chelsea and titbits from the history of London. From Hammersmith onwards the journey becomes more serene and pastoral as you glide towards Kew Gardens, Richmond and Hampton Court.

Canal trips

Several companies make a leisurely journey along Regent's Canal between Little Venice and Camden Town, passing through London Zoo on the way.

Jason's Trip

60 Bloomfield Road, Little Venice, W9

t (020) 7286 3428

www.jasons.co.uk

⊖ Warwick Avenue

Tours Every two hours, 10.30–4.30 in summer and 10.30–2.30pm in winter

Fares Adult single £5.95, return £6.95; child single £4.75, return £5.50; under-4s **free**; family (2+3) £22

Also runs trips to the Canal Museum.

London Waterbus Company

Camden Lock, Camden Town, NW1

t (020) 7482 2550

⊖ Camden Town

Tours April–Oct 10–5 daily; Nov–Mar 10–3 daily; boats run hourly

Fares Adult single £4.80, return £6.20, child single £3.10, return £4, under-4s **free**; combined canal trip and zoo visit: adult £12.90, child £9.40, under-3s **free**

Trips aboard traditional, painted narrow boats, stopping off at London Zoo – you get a reduction on the price of admission.

Sightseeing buses

Various companies offer services, but the Big Bus Company – recognizable by its distinctive maroon and cream livery – is perhaps the best. It operates three colour-coded routes: Green, the West End and Bloomsbury; Blue, Knightsbridge and Mayfair; and Red, from Victoria to the Tower of London. Main departure points are Marble Arch, Green Park, Baker Street and Victoria, although you can board at any stop along the route.

The Big Bus Company
48 Buckingham Palace Road, SW1
t (020) 7233 9533
www.bigbus.co.uk
Fares Adult £17, child £8
Ticket allows 24hrs unlimited travel on BBC buses

Visitor centres

Heathrow Airport
Uxbridge, Middlesex
t (020) 8745 6655
⊖ Hatton Cross
⇌ Feltham
Bus 81, 105, 111, 140, 222, 285, 555, 556, 557
Open 10–5 daily
Free (£3 for 2hrs parking)
Wheelchair accessible, adapted toilets. Suitable for ages 8 and over
Allow at least 1hr

Heathrow Airport isn't every adult's idea of a great day out, but children tend to love the place, as it is busy, noisy and brash, with plenty to do and see. At the Visitor Centre they can find out the history of the world's largest and busiest airport. The Centre is big on interactivity. Kids can look inside a replica cockpit, sit in replica aircraft seats, take a ride in a flight simulator game, walk through a metal detector, take rubbings of special plane brasses, read about undercover operations against smugglers and, of course, watch the planes landing and taking off on the runway outside. Quizzes and I-spys are available from the reception desk and there's an outdoor picnic area.

Thames Barrier
1 Unity Way, Woolwich, London, SE18
t (020) 8305 4188
⊖ New Cross, New Cross Gate
⇌ Charlton
River Cruise Regular service from Westminster Pier, call Thames River Services **t** (020) 7930 4097
Open Mon–Fri 10–5, Sat–Sun 10.30–5.30
Adm Adult £1, child 50p
Suitable for ages 8 and over
Allow at least 1hr

One of the marvels of modern London, the Thames Barrier is an astounding piece of engineering. Spanning the river's 1,700-ft width, these 10 huge steel gates (each the size of a five-storey house) are often all that stands between a dry London and one under 10 feet of water. The gates, which lie on 10,000-tonne concrete sills on the riverbed, can be raised into position in an astonishing 10 minutes flat in the event of a flood.

The barrier's construction was prompted by a flood in 1953 which killed 300 people. You can find out more about London's battle with its ever-rising river at this small 'Information and Learning Centre'. Here you can see a working model of the barrier, watch a video detailing its construction and look at a map showing which unfortunate parts of London would now be regularly submerged if it wasn't in place. Time it right and you might even get to see the mighty metal behemoth in action – the barrier is tested once a month, and the Centre can provide details of the schedule.

Whatever time of the year you visit London, there's always something going on. From festivals and parades to major sporting events and exhibitions, hardly a week goes by without a noteworthy event. London is always busy, always fun, always buzzing, and if you grow tired of the capital you must be, as Dr Johnson famously said, tired of life.

Daily events

Ceremony of the Keys
Tower of London, EC3
t 0870 756 6070
www.hrp.org.uk
⊖ Tower Hill
Bus 15, 25, 42, 78, 100, D1
Adm Free. Every day at 9.53pm
The ceremony lasts about 20mins

The nightly locking of the Tower of London is one of the oldest military ceremonies in the world. For free tickets apply at least two months in advance (remember to include a SAE) to The Ceremony of the Keys, HM Tower of London, London EC3N 4AB.

Changing of the Guard
Buckingham Palace, SW1
t (020) 7930 4832
www.royal.gov.uk
Infoline **t** (020) 7766 7300
⊖ St James's Park, Green Park, Victoria
Bus 7, 11, 139, 211, C1, C10
Free

An hour of pomp and pageantry outside Buckingham Palace beginning at 11.27am sharp everyday April–June and on alternate days for the rest of the year, *see* p.91 for further details.

Annual events

January
London Parade
New Year's Day
Parliament Square to Piccadilly by way of Whitehall and Trafalgar Square
t (020) 8566 8586
www.londonparade.co.uk
⊖ Westminster, Embankment, Green Park, Piccadilly Circus
Adm Free along route

The estimated 10,000 performers and over a million spectators make this one of the the biggest New Year's Day parties in Europe.

Chinese New Year Festival
Late January or early February
Gerrard Street, Lisle Street & Newport Place, WC1
⊖ Leicester Square
Bus 6, 7, 8, 10, 12, 13, 14, 15, 19, 23, 25, 38, 53, 55, 73, 88, 94, 98, 139, 159, 176, X53
Free

Chinatown celebrates its annual rebirth with firecrackers, paper lanterns and papier-mâché dragons that dance down the street

February
Accession Day Gun Salute
Accession Day, 6 February, 12 noon
Hyde Park
⊖ Hyde Park Corner, Knightsbridge, South Kensington, Lancaster Gate, Queensway
Bus 2, 9, 10, 12, 14, 16, 19, 22, 36, 52, 70, 73, 74, 82, 94, 137
Free

This is the first gun salute of London's year. The Royal Horse Artillery gallop furiously into Hyde Park and unleash an extremely noisy 41-gun salute. The practice is repeated several times: on the Queen's birthday (21 April), Coronation Day (2 June), Prince Philip's birthday (10 June) and the State Opening of Parliament in November. Note that if any of the above dates fall on a Sunday, the salute will be fired on the following Monday.

Spitalfields Pancake Race Day
Shrove Tuesday
Spitalfields Market, E1
t (020) 7372 0441
⊖ Liverpool Street
Bus 5, 8, 26, 35, 43, 47, 48, 67, 78, 149, 242, 344
Free

On Shrove Tuesday competing teams of costumed runners race around Spitalfields Market, tossing pancakes as they go. A similar event takes place in Soho, call **t** (020) 7289 0907.

March
Ideal Home Exhibition
Mid- to late-March

National holidays
► New Year's Day (1 Jan)
► Good Friday (9 April 2004, 25 March 2005)
► Easter Monday (12 April 2004, 28 March 2005)
► May Day (3 May 2004, 2 May 2005)
► Summer Bank Holiday (30 Aug 2004, 29 Aug 2005)
► Christmas Day (Dec 25)
► Boxing Day (Dec 26 plus Dec 27 if either Christmas or Boxing Day falls on a weekend)

Earl's Court Exhibition Centre, Warwick Road, SW5
t 0870 606 6080
www.idealhomeshow.co.uk
⊖ Earl's Court
Bus 31, 74, C1, C3
Adm Adult Mon–Fri £11, Sat–Sun £13; child Mon–Fri £7.50, Sat–Sun £8.50; family £43.50; under-5s **free**

At Europe's largest consumer show you'll find masses of designer bathrooms, bedrooms and other house interiors as well as all the latest labour-saving gizmos – juicers that cut as they peel and boil an egg etc.

Easter
Oxford–Cambridge Boat Race
www.theboatrace.org
Saturday before Easter or Easter Saturday
The Thames between Putney Bridge and Mortlake
For start ⊖ Putney Bridge;
for finish ⇌ Mortlake
Bus For start 22, 265; for end 209, 485, R69
Free

The two teams have been battling it out over the 4½-mile Thames course for over a hundred years now. The best viewing points (and the places with the best atmosphere) are Putney Bridge and Chiswick Bridge.

Easter Parade
Easter Sunday
Battersea Park, SW11
⇌ Battersea Park, Queenstown Road
⊖ Sloane Square
Bus 44, 137, 319, 344, 345
Open Dawn till dusk
Free

Easter Sunday carnival with a fairground, parade and special children's village featuring a bouncy castle, playground, clowns and puppet shows. Special events, such as displays by freefall parachute teams, are often laid on.

April
London Marathon
t (020) 7902 0184
www.london-marathon.co.uk
Sunday in late April. Race starts at 9am
26 miles 385 yards between Blackheath and Westminster Bridge by way of the Isle of Dogs, Victoria Embankment and St James's Park.

Over 30,000 people put mind and body to the test each year over the 26-mile course between Blackheath and Westminster Bridge. There's a mini-Marathon for stretching little legs as well.

May
Museums Moonth
www.campaignformuseums.org.uk
In participating museums throughout the capital

This annual celebration of the nation's collections and treasure troves is the largest museums promotion anywhere in the world. Over 850 museums participate, organizing a range of hands-on activities and events, many of which are free and family-friendly. Check out the above website which provides a year-round selection of games, science packs and activities for kids to download free of charge.

May Fayre and Punch & Judy Festival
Nearest Sunday to 9 May
St Paul's Church, Covent Garden
t (020) 7375 0441
⊖ Covent Garden, Leicester Square
Bus 9, 11, 13, 15, 23, 77a, 91, 176
Free

An annual celebration of puppet marital disharmony in the grounds of St Paul's Church.

June
Wildlife Week
First week of June
Various locations around London
t (020) 7261 0447
www.wildlondon.org.uk

During the first week of June, the London Wildlife Trust organizes a range of events throughout the capital (including nature walks, pond dippings, beast hunts etc) designed to get Londoners better acquainted with their native flora and fauna.

Trooping the Colour

Second Saturday in June, starts at 10.45am
Buckingham Palace to Horse Guards Parade
t Booking line (020) 7766 7300/1
www.royal.gov.uk
⊖ Charing Cross, St James's Park
Free along route

Tickets for this top piece of British pageantry are awarded by ballot – you must apply by the end of February. Write to the Brigade Major (Trooping the Colour), Household Division, Horse Guards Parade, SW1, enclosing a stamped addressed envelope. There is a maximum of two tickets per application. The ceremony, which marks the official birthday of the Queen, takes place at Horse Guards Parade and is preceded by a Royal Air Force jet display.

Biggin Hill International Air Fair

Mid-June weekend, starts at 8am
Biggin Hill Airfield, Biggin Hill, Kent
t 01959 572 277
www.airdisplaysint.co.uk
⇌ Bromley South, Croydon East or West, from where a shuttle bus links with the airfield
Bus 246, 320, 4664, R2
Adm Adult £22, child £7, family £49

Every summer, plane enthusiasts from all over the country gather in order to get up close and personal with the truly high-flying machines of the aviation world. Second World War Spitfires and Hurricanes are the biggest draws, but there are lots of other planes to see both on the ground and in the sky. A host of displays, fly-pasts and skydives takes place over the two days, and there's also a funfair and exhibition stands.

Henley Royal Regatta

Wed–Sat late June (sometimes early July)
The Thames at Henley
t (01491) 572 153
www.hrr.co.uk
⇌ Henley
Free

This grand society occasion provides an elegant backdrop for a Thames-side picnic.

Wimbledon

Last two weeks in June
All England Lawn Tennis and Croquet Club, Church Road, Wimbledon, SW19
t (020) 8946 2244
www.wimbledon.org
⊖ Southfields, Wimbledon

≈ Wimbledon
Bus 39, 93 or shuttle bus from any of the above stations
Adm Centre Court tickets start at £28 for the first Monday rising to £72 for the final Sunday. Ground tickets start at £14 for the first Monday (£8 after 5pm), dropping to £10 for the final weekend (£6 after 5pm)

The world's most prestigious tennis tournament. Tickets for Centre and No.1 courts are obtainable only by ballot, which must be entered the previous September. You can queue up during the tournament for a ground pass which gives you access to all the courts apart from Centre and No.1. Obviously, the major stars will play most matches on the show courts, but the atmosphere on the outside courts is sometimes more exciting and you should be able to see a few famous faces. From 2pm onwards, you can queue up to buy resale show court tickets from a kiosk near 'Henman Hill'.

City of London Festival
Late-June–mid-July
t (020) 7377 0540
www.colf.org

Musical kids can hit the high notes at this three-week festival of sound held in the magnificent churches and halls of the City. Free lunchtime recitals featuring everything from classical to jazz take place daily.

July
Coin Street Festival
Mid-July–mid-September
The South Bank at the Oxo Tower Wharf, Gabriel's Wharf and the Bernie Spain Gardens
t (020) 7401 2255
www.coinstreetfestival.org
⊖ Waterloo, Westminster, Blackfriars
Bus 4, 68, 76, 77, 149, 168, 171, 176, 188, 211, P11, 501, 505, 507, 521, D1, P11
Free

There's plenty to please the kids at this three-month free arts festival on London's South Bank organized by the Coin Street Community Builders. Highlights include the splendid Latin-flavoured Gran Gran Fiesta, which features a children's fancy dress parade, and the popular 'Arts Desire' creative workshops.

Greenwich & Docklands Festival
Ten days in mid-July

Various venues in Greenwich
t (020) 8305 1818
www.festival.org
⊖ North Greenwich
DLR Island Gardens
≈ Greenwich
Bus 177, 180, 188, 199, 286, 386
Free

This popular arts festival combines concerts and theatre as well as children's events, and starts with a bang with an opening night firework display.

Kenwood House Lakeside Concerts
July–August
Hampstead Lane, NW3
t 0870 333 1181
www.english-heritage.org
⊖ Archway
Bus 210
Adm Adult £16.50–£30, child £2–£4, under-5s **free**

Families flock to this series of popular classical concerts and firework displays in the grounds of this grand old house. (*see* p.163).

August
Notting Hill Carnival
August Bank Holiday Sunday and Monday
Notting Hill and surrounding streets
t (020) 8964 0544
www.rbkc.gov.uk/nottinghill
⊖ Westbourne Park, Ladbroke Grove (due to crowds avoid Notting Hill Gate)
Free

The largest carnival in the world after Rio. Steel bands, floats, costumed dancers, fancy dress, jugglers, face-painting, exotic food: this is one of the year's most intense experiences. In fact, it can be a little hairy for very young children. Older kids, however, will have a great time. There is a special children's parade on the Sunday.

August Bank Holiday Funfairs
Funfairs set up for business during the summer's premier bank holiday weekend at many of London's parks including Alexandra Palace Park and Hampstead Heath.

September
Totally Covent Garden – The Festival
Early September
Covent Garden, WC2
t (020) 7932 2000

www.coventgardenmarket.co.uk
⊖ Covent Garden, Leicester Square
Bus 9, 11, 13, 15, 23, 77a, 91, 176
Free

The home of impromptu theatrical and musical performance plays host to a week-long festival featuring performances by West End stars and opera singers, a competition to find 'London's Best Busker', a 'Celebrity Shop Assist' (which translates as TV stars helping out in shops for charity), a food market, a fashion show, a car rally and various kids' events organized by the London Transport Museum and the Theatre Museum.

CBBC Proms in the Park

Early September, on Sun after 'Last Night of the Proms'
Hyde Park
t 0870 899 8001
www.bbc.co.uk/proms
⊖ Hyde Park Corner
Adm Adult £12, child £7.50, under-3s **free**

The BBC Philharmonic club together with the latest pop sensations to bring an afternoon of easy on the ear classical tunes, West End musical sing-a-longs and tweeny bop hits.

Covent Garden Festival of Street Theatre

Early September
Covent Garden
t (020) 7836 9136
www.coventgarden.org.uk
⊖ Covent Garden, Leicester Square
Bus 9, 11, 13, 15, 23, 77A, 91, 176
Free

Fire-eaters, escapologists, stilt-walkers, unicyclists and comedians put on a week of performances in Covent Garden's Piazza.

Regent Street Festival

Early September
Regent Street, W1
t (020) 7440 5530
www.regent-street.co.uk
⊖ Oxford Circus, Piccadilly Circus
Bus 3, 12, 15, 23, 139, 159
Free

This annual street fest began in 2000 and is going from strength to strength. For one Sunday only, the section of Regent Street between Oxford and Piccadilly Circus is closed to traffic and families are free to wander round the stalls and enjoy a series

of staged events throughout the day. Many of the shops, such as Hamleys and The Disney Store, stay open for the occasion and some offer discounts, too. There's also a funfair, plus children's activity areas and play tents.

Thames Festival

Mid-September on second weekend of Autumn school term
Various points on the Thames between Waterloo and Blackfriars Bridge
t (020) 7928 8998
www.thamesfestival.org
⊖ Embankment, Charing Cross, Southwark, Waterloo
Bus 1, 4, 26, 45, 63, 68, 76, 77, 149, 168, 171, 171a, 172, 176, 188, 501, 505, 507, D1, P11, X68, RV1
Free

The Thames really comes to life with a range of events along the banks, from firework displays to lantern processions. There's a food village, artworks and installations, river races, stalls, music and funfair rides. During the day there are craft workshops.

October

Costermongers' Pearly Kings and Queens Harvest Festival

First Sunday in October, starts at 3pm
St Martin-in-the-Fields, Trafalgar Square, WC2
t (020) 7766 1100
www.pearlies.co.uk
⊖ Charing Cross, Leicester Square
Bus 9, 24, 109
Free

A Harvest Festival with added sequins – London's community of Pearly Kings and Queens descends on St Martin-in-the-Fields on the first Sunday of the month for an old-fashioned knees-up.

display over the Thames. With over 5,000 participants and 70 floats, this is one of the largest street parades of the year. The Lord Mayor rides at its head in the Lord Mayor's Coach which, for the rest of the year, is on display in the Museum of London.

The Christmas Lights

Mid-November
Oxford Street, Regent Street and Bond Street

The elaborate street illuminations are turned on in mid-November by a celebrity *du jour* – usually a soap star or pop singer.

December

Carol Service

December–early January
Trafalgar Square, WC1
⊖ Charing Cross, Leicester Square
Bus 9, 24, 109
Free

Carol singing takes place around the huge Trafalgar Square Christmas tree every evening from early December to early January. The tree itself is lit from dusk till midnight until the twelfth day of Christmas (6 January).

Pantomime Season

Mid-November to mid-February
All over the capital

Come December, a motley collection of retired sportsmen, soap stars and TV magicians will join forces with a host of actors to produce a very British institution. For details of performances check out the listings section of the *Evening Standard* or *Time Out*.

Royal Institution Christmas Lectures for Young People

Between Christmas and New Year
21 Albemarle Street, W1
t (020) 7409 2992
www.rigb.org/events/christmaslecture
⊖ Green Park
Bus 8, 9, 14, 19, 22, 38

A series of lectures aimed at schoolchildren (aged 11 and over) on a variety of scientific subjects.

New Year's Eve in Trafalgar Square

The traditional venue for London's end of year bash, Trafalgar Square is within easy listening distance of Big Ben's bongs. The celebrations can get a little boisterous and it isn't recommended for young children.

November

London to Brighton Vintage Car Run

First Sunday in November, starts 7.30am
Hyde Park to Brighton
t (01753) 651 736
www.hcvs.co.uk
⊖ Hyde Park Corner, Marble Arch
Bus 2, 8, 9, 10, 14, 16, 19, 22, 36, 73, 82, 137
Free

Entry to the race is free to all so long as you're in possession of a car built before 1905. This parade of clunking, clanking contraptions is one of London's great annual spectacles. It attracts hordes of well-wishers to see them off at the start.

Bonfire Night

5 November
In parks and recreation grounds across London, *see* **www**.londontouristboard.co.uk for more details.

Remember, remember the fifth of November... Parks all over London hold firework displays on this date to celebrate the capture and execution of Guy Fawkes and his failure to blow up James I and the Houses of Parliament. Some of the best displays take place at Blackheath, Wimbledon Park and Alexandra Palace Park.

Lord Mayor's Show

Second Saturday in November, starts at 11am
Mansion House to the Old Bailey
t (020) 7606 3030
www.lordmayorsshow.org
⊖ Mansion House, Blackfriars
Free

The ceremonial parade to mark the beginning of the Lord Mayor of London's year in office starts at Mansion House and wends its way to the Old Bailey. The event ends with a spectacular firework

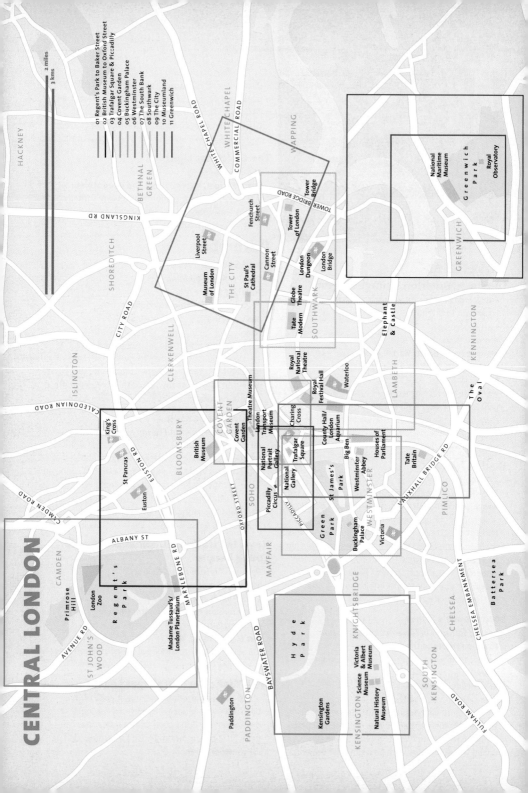

CENTRAL LONDON

01 Regent's Park to Baker Street
02 British Museum to Oxford Street
03 Trafalgar Square & Piccadilly
04 Covent Garden
05 Buckingham Palace
06 Westminster
07 The South Bank
08 Southwark
09 The City
10 to Museumland
11 Greenwich

2 miles
3 kms

HACKNEY

BETHNAL GREEN

WHITE CHAPEL

WAPPING

SHOREDITCH

KINGSLAND RD

WHITE CHAPEL ROAD

COMMERCIAL ROAD

CITY ROAD

CLERKENWELL

ISLINGTON

CALEDONIAN ROAD

CAMDEN ROAD

ST JOHN'S WOOD

CAMDEN

AVENUE RD

Primrose Hill

London Zoo

Regent's Park

Madame Tussaud's/
London Planetarium

ALBANY ST

EUSTON RD

MARYLEBONE RD

King's Cross

St Pancras

Euston

BLOOMSBURY

British Museum

COVENT GARDEN

Theatre Museum

Covent Garden

London Transport Museum

OXFORD STREET

SOHO

National Portrait Gallery

Piccadilly Circus

National Gallery

PICCADILLY

MAYFAIR

Charing Cross

Trafalgar Square

Green Park

St James's Park

Buckingham Palace

Victoria

WESTMINSTER

County Hall/
London Aquarium

Big Ben

Westminster Abbey

Houses of Parliament

Tate Britain

PIMLICO

VAUXHALL BRIDGE RD

LAMBETH

Royal National Theatre

Royal Festival Hall

Waterloo

Elephant & Castle

The Oval

KENNINGTON

SOUTHWARK

Tate Modern

Globe Theatre

London Dungeon

London Bridge

TOWER BRIDGE ROAD

Tower Bridge

Tower of London

Fenchurch Street

Cannon Street

St Paul's Cathedral

THE CITY

Liverpool Street

Museum of London

BATTERSEA Park

CHELSEA

CHELSEA EMBANKMENT

FULHAM ROAD

SOUTH KENSINGTON

KENSINGTON

Natural History Museum

Science Museum

Victoria & Albert Museum

KNIGHTSBRIDGE

Hyde Park

Kensington Gardens

BAYSWATER ROAD

PADDINGTON

Paddington

GREENWICH

Greenwich Park

National Maritime Museum

Royal Observatory

Regent's Park to Baker Street

Some of the capital's best-loved attractions are grouped around Regent's Park. To the north are the birds and beasts of London Zoo, while to the south, on Marylebone Road, is Madame Tussaud's, London's most popular fee-paying attraction (with the great, green-domed Planetarium next door). And you don't need to be a super-sleuth to find the little Sherlock Holmes Museum on Baker Street or the Wallace Collection's imposing frontage in Manchester Square. Then, of course, there's the park itself, where the whole family could easily idle away a whole day boating on the lake, running through the grass, playing ball, making friends in one of the four playgrounds, or watching a summer performance at the Open Air Theatre.

Highlights

The Wallace Collection's wheely cart

Watching a show aboard the Puppet Theatre Barge

Slurping smoothies in Giraffe

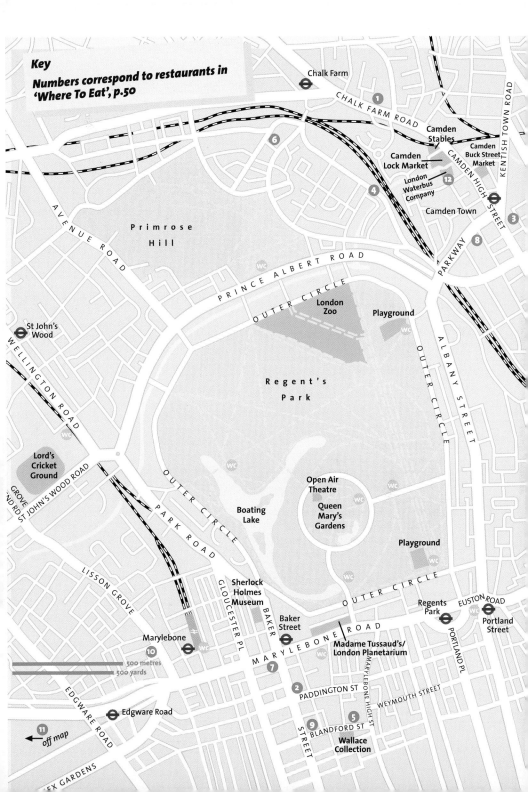

Key

Numbers correspond to restaurants in 'Where To Eat', p.50

Chalk Farm

CHALK FARM ROAD

KENTISH TOWN ROAD

Camden Stables

Camden Buck Street Market

Camden Lock Market

London Waterbus Company

Camden High Street

Camden Town

AVENUE ROAD

Primrose Hill

PRINCE ALBERT ROAD

OUTER CIRCLE

PARKWAY

St John's Wood

London Zoo

Playground

WC

WELLINGTON ROAD

Regent's Park

ALBANY STREET

OUTER CIRCLE

Lord's Cricket Ground

GROVE END RD ST

ST JOHN'S WOOD ROAD

PARK ROAD

OUTER CIRCLE

Boating Lake

Open Air Theatre

Queen Mary's Gardens

WC

WC

Playground

WC

LISSON GROVE

GLOUCESTER PL

Sherlock Holmes Museum

BAKER STREET

Baker Street

OUTER CIRCLE

Regents Park

EUSTON ROAD

Portland Street

PORTLAND PL

Marylebone

Madame Tussaud's/ London Planetarium

MARYLEBONE ROAD

500 metres
500 yards

MARYLEBONE HIGH ST

PADDINGTON ST

WEYMOUTH STREET

EDGWARE ROAD

Edgware Road

STREET

BLANDFORD ST

Wallace Collection

off map

EX GARDENS

1
6
4
12
3
8
2
5
9
7
10
11

London Zoo

Regent's Park, NW1
t (020) 7722 3333
www.londonzoo.co.uk
⊖ Camden Town or Baker Street, then 274 bus
Bus 274
Open Mar–Oct 10–5.30 daily; Nov–April 10–4 daily
Adm Adult £12, child (under 15) £9, under-3s **free**,
concs £10.20, family £38
*Wheelchair accessible for most areas, adapted
toilets, 6 disabled parking bays by the entrance*
First-aid post in the centre of the zoo
Suitable for all ages
Allow a morning or afternoon, or even a whole day

London Zoo is home to thousands and thousands of animals – lions, tigers, gorillas, chimps, giraffes, rhinos, snakes, penguins, camels...the list goes on – and has been a mainstay of school trips and family outings for years. Whatever you may think about the rights and wrongs of big city zoos, there's no doubt that London's famous menagerie does its best to justify its existence in the modern world. These days, its watchwords are conservation and education – simply gawping at animals is no longer the done thing. All the animals are here for a reason, whether, as in the case of the Arabian Oryx, it's because they're now extinct in the wild or, as with the Sumatran tiger, because they soon could be. The zoo runs a very successful captive breeding programme and has played an important part in reintroducing many endangered species back into the wild. This doesn't mean that the zoo has become dry and scientific. It takes its role as an educator very seriously and understands that the best way to get children interested in something is by entertaining and involving them.

Every day the zoo organizes talks and sessions to 'meet the animals'. Turn up at feeding time and you can watch pelicans and penguins gobbling their way through buckets of fish or a snake slowly swallowing a rat – whole.

Spectacular animal shows are held in three special demonstration areas: you can see lemurs and parrots leaping, climbing and flying during the Animals in Action presentations in the Amphitheatre while, on the display lawn, there are regular exhibitions of aerobatic skill by the zoo's birds of prey – keepers will throw pieces of meat into the air for them to swoop down and catch. At the new Happy Families area you can watch animals who live in large groups – meerkats, otters, marmosets etc – scampering around and playing together in a terribly cute way.

It's all very impressive, but your children will no doubt be itching to get involved in a more hands-on way. Take them to the Children's Zoo where, in the Touch Paddock, they can stroke and pet the resident sheep, goats and wallabies and help feed the pigs. To really get into the swing of things, kids

The Original Jumbo

Perhaps London Zoo's most famous inmate was Jumbo the elephant, who in the 19th century became an international star. He was brought to the zoo from Africa in 1865, as a baby. By the 1870s he had transformed into a mighty beast standing some 4m high and weighing over 6 tons – the largest elephant in captivity. You might think that he had quite an appropriate name, but in fact, at that time the word 'Jumbo' didn't mean anything at all. It was simply a misspelled version of the Swahili word 'Jambo', which means 'hello'. Such was Jumbo's fame (and, of course, his size) that soon anything overwhelmingly large came to be known as 'Jumbo-sized'. In 1882 the zoo sold him to the American Circus owner, P.T. Barnum, but Jumbo died a few years later when he refused to get out of the way of a train.

Jumbo still draws the crowds today, however. His huge skeleton is on display at the Museum of Natural History in New York.

can even have their faces painted to look like a lizard, a butterfly or (easily the most popular choice) a tiger. Be sure to visit the tiger enclosure in the main zoo. Stand at the round window when they're on the prowl and you may find yourself just a few inches away from these fearsome beasts.

Even on rainy days, the zoo is still worth visiting. While the animals in the outdoor enclosures take cover, you can do the same at the Aquarium, the Small Mammal Enclosure or the Web of Life Building. Opened a couple of years ago as part of the zoo's Millennium Project, this is the site's undoubted highlight. It's a hugely imaginative exhibition which tries not only to show animals in as natural a setting as possible, but also to demonstrate how various animals and organisms combine to form ecosystems. You can see examples of different habitats from around the world and discover how the resident animals have adapted themselves to their surroundings; how butterflies camouflage themselves against tree bark; how naked mole rats have developed enormous front teeth which allow them to chew their way through the earth; how robber crabs set up home in the shells of other creatures; and how dung beetles use the material other animals reject – watch them carefully rolling their precious balls of dung. Even the tanks housing the exhibits are interesting. Several have magnifying lenses built into the glass to allow you to look at tiny organisms in greater detail, while others are shaped like helmets, enabling you to immerse yourself in the animals' environment. Kids are specially catered for at the Activity Den where they can take part in a

broad range of crafts including brass rubbing and badge making.

The zoo has a central relaxation area with a café, gift shop, fountain and a small children's carousel. There are also several playgrounds dotted about with slides and climbing frames. In the summer there's usually a bouncy castle.

If your kids are really fond of animals, you may want to consider becoming a zoo member. This entitles you to visit the zoo at any time during the year and will also allow your kids to take part in a variety of special 'Children's Activity Days' (such as 'Rumble in the Jungle' or 'Bugtastic') when they can find out more about the zoo's animals and enjoy a range of activities (family – 2 adults, 2 children – £134; family – 2 adults, 1 child – £108; adult £50, child £35). The zoo also plays host to a series of five-day Zoo Camps run under the auspices of AKA Rampage, a professional playscheme registered with Camden Council. On the scheme, children aged 5 and over can, between 10am and 4pm each day, join in games in Regent's Park, arts and crafts activities, animal encounters and zoo tours. The

Can you spot?
Many of the animals in the zoo have managed to adapt themselves to their surroundings. Just as a chameleon will subtly change the colour of its skin, so other creatures have learned to blend in with the environment around them. Can you find any examples at the zoo?

camps must be booked in advance (they fill up very quickly) and cost £1,125 for a full week,
t (020) 7722 5909.

Regent's Canal Trip

Perhaps the most novel way to arrive at London Zoo is aboard a canal boat. The London Waterbus Company runs a service from Little Venice along Regent's Canal to Camden Lock, stopping off at the Zoo on the way. You get a reduction on the price of admission with your ticket.

London Waterbus Company

50 Camden Lock Place
t (020) 7482 2550
⊖ Camden Town, Chalk Farm
Bus 6, 46
April–Oct daily service, boats run hourly from 10–5; Nov–Mar weekends only
Fares Adult single £4.80, return £6.20; child single £3.10, return £4, under-4s **free**; combined canal trip and zoo visit: adult £12.90, child £9, under-4s **free**

The Floating Boater

Waterside, Little Venice, Warwick Crescent, W2
t (020) 7266 1066
www.floatingboater.co.uk
⊖ Warwick Avenue

Jason's Canal Trips

60 Bloomfield Road, Little Venice, W9
t (020) 7286 3428
www.jasons.co.uk
⊖ Warwick Avenue

Madame Tussaud's

Marylebone Road, NW1
t 0870 400 3000
www.madame-tussauds.com
⊖ Baker Street
Bus 13, 18, 27, 30, 74, 82, 113, 159, 274
Open 9–5.30 daily
Adm Prices, which include admission to the London Planetarium, vary according to the time of day ranging from adult £12, child (under-16) £7 for late entry (after 5pm) to adult £19.99, child £16.99 for early entry (9–2). Prices include entry to the 'Chamber Live' show. Prices excluding the show range from adult £10, child £5 for late entry to adult £17.99, child £12.99 for early entry. Under-5s **free**
No pushchairs allowed; baby carriers are provided. Wheelchair accessible
Suitable for all ages, apart from Chamber of Horrors which is only suitable for older children (over 8) Allow at least 1hr

It's strange how this collection of waxen doppelgangers has become one of London's most popular tourist attractions. As famous as it is, with queues that regularly stretch right round the block, it's difficult not to come to the conclusion that it's all a little bit stupid – it's just a load of mannequins, after all, dolled up to look like famous people. It doesn't pay to be too snooty about Madame Tussaud's, however. Whatever its unfathomable attractions may be, your kids understand them and will undoubtedly have a whale of a time, running around pointing at all the famous faces and demanding to have their picture taken with David Beckham (posed scoring his famous World-Cup qualifying free-kick against Greece), Kylie (posed on all fours breathily singing one of her hits) or the Queen (posed, thankfully, standing).

To their credit, the organizers have done their best to invest

Did you know?
Madame Tussaud's always has huge queues. If you buy a joint Planetarium ticket you can, after the Planetary Quest Show, nip into the waxworks via the interior entrance between the two attractions and avoid the wait. You can also get a fast-track combination ticket for Mme Tussaud's and the London Eye at www.ba-londoneye.com

Tell me a story: Max wax

Madame Marie Tussaud was born in France in 1761. When just six years old she was taken by her uncle to Paris, where he instructed her in the art of modelling anatomical figures. By her early twenties, Marie had become so accomplished that she was hired to give art lessons to Louis XVI's children at Versailles; something which, in any other era, would have set her up for life. Unfortunately for her, in 1789 France underwent the Revolution – the monarchy was abolished, the King was executed and Marie, suspected of having Royalist sympathies, was thrown in jail and only released on condition that she attend public executions and sculpt the death masks of the Revolution's more celebrated victims.

In 1802, following a failed marriage, she emigrated to England, taking her two children and 35 of her models with her. To make ends meet, she was forced to tour her waxwork gallery of heroes, rogues, victims and confidence tricksters around the country until, in 1835, a permanent home was found for them in London's Baker Street. By 1850, the year Madame died, 'Tussaud's' was sufficiently well known for the Duke of Wellington to have become a regular visitor. He was especially taken with the Chamber of Horrors and left instructions that he should be informed whenever a new figure was added to its gruesome ranks.

By 1884 the exhibition (now managed by Madame's sons) had grown to over 400 models, forcing it to move to new premises in Marylebone Road, where it has stayed ever since. Madame's last work, a rather eerie self-portrait, is still on display in the Grand Hall.

proceedings with a little excitement. The highlight is probably the Spirit of London Ride where you are carried in a mock-up 'Time Taxi' through representations of London history from Elizabethan times to the present day. There are also sections devoted to sporting figures ('Sporting Heroes') and film stars ('Premiére Night'). Your kids' favourite section, on the other hand, will inevitably be the Chamber of Horrors with its collection of grizzly exhibits (for some reason yet to be explained, all children are fixated with blood, gore and mayhem) where 'live shows' are now put on featuring an array of gruesomely attired actors.

London Planetarium

Marylebone Road, NW1
t 0870 400 3000
www.london-planetarium.com
⊖ Baker Street
Bus 13, 18, 27, 30, 74, 82, 113, 159, 274
Open 9–5.30 daily
Adm Prices, which include admission to Madame Tussaud's, vary according to the time of day ranging from adult £10, child (under-16) £5 for late entry (after 5pm) to adult £17.99, child £12.99 for early entry (9–2). Under-5s **free**
Wheelchair accessible, induction loop for hard of hearing. Suitable for all ages
Allow at least 30mins. Show in auditorium lasts 20mins approx

There really is no better place to find out about the mysteries of the universe than beneath Baker Street's famous green dome (which turns red every two years on Comic Relief or 'Red Nose' Day). The Planetarium is split into two parts, a museum and an auditorium. In the former, known as the 'Planet Zone', you can see waxworks of Neil Armstrong and Buzz Aldrin, the first men on the moon, watch live satellite weather transmissions from space telescopes and step on to a special set of scales which tells you what your weight would be on the moon (where, happily, everyone is much lighter). In the main auditorium, the old 'Planetary Quest' show has been replaced by a new extravaganza called 'Treasure Planet' based on the recent Disney film of the same name and comprising a cartoon romp through the solar system projected on to the ceiling of the dome. Though undeniably more impressive than its predecessor, with black holes and super novas exploding in spectacular fashion, it's also considerably less weighty having dispensed with most of the scientific explanation in favour of whizz-bang effects and a 'yo-ho-ho' narration by Brian Murray (the voice of 'Silver' in the film).

Question 2
Can you name the nine planets that orbit our sun, starting with the nearest?
answer on p.249

Regent's Park

t (020) 7486 7905
www.royalparks.gov.uk/regent.htm
⊖ Baker Street, Great Portland Street, Regent's
Park, Camden Town and then 274 bus
Bus 2, 13, 18, 27, 30, 74, 82, 113, 135, 139, 159, 189,
274, C2
Open 5am to dusk daily
Free
Suitable for all ages

One of London's great parks, Regent's Park has
masses going on. There's the boating lake, home to
a mass of wildfowl including ducks, moorhens and
black swans, where you can hire a rowing boat and
take to the water yourself. There are four playgrounds (open daily from 10.30am), complete with
toilets solely for the use of children (facilities for
parents are separate, usually grouped around a
refreshment kiosk or café), sand pits, swings and
play equipment. Sporty types, meanwhile, can
make use of the tennis courts and several cricket
and football pitches (although many of these will
be dug up and replaced over the next couple of
years as part of a rejuvenation programme). In the
centre are the neatly manicured Queen Mary's
Gardens, best visited in summer when you'll find
bed upon bed of wonderful, colourful roses. The
gardens also house the Open Air Theatre (one of
the most enlivening places to introduce your children to the works of Shakespeare), an ornamental
lake, a sunken garden and a fountain depicting
a man blowing water out of a conch shell. As a
further attraction, the park authorities have
recently started to organize special activities for
families, including nature walks and late night 'Owl
Prowls' (the park is home to a couple of dozen
nesting pairs). For more details **t** 020 7298 2000.

Open Air Theatre

Regent's Park, NW1
t (020) 7486 2431
www.openairtheatre.org
Adm tickets for daytime performances start at
£9.50 (rising to £26); evening tickets cost a flat rate
£6; tickets for family shows are a flat rate £9

This respected theatre company usually puts on
a child-friendly show during the summer holidays
(in 2003, it was 'Granny and the Gorilla') as well as
a selection from Shakespeare and a quality
musical. A few years ago, it premiered a specially
commissioned children's play entitled *The Last
Fattybottypuss in the World*. Although the play
began at the theatre, during each performance the
actors and the audience got up and walked over to
London Zoo where the play's final scene was set.

Sherlock Holmes Museum

221b Baker Street, NW1
t (020) 7935 8866
www.sherlock-holmes.co.uk
⊖ Baker Street
Bus 13, 18, 27, 30, 74, 82, 113, 159, 274
Open 9.30–6 daily
Adm Adult £6, child £4
*No disabled facilities. Suitable for all ages although
older children will get the most out of it
Allow at least 30mins*

It all depends whether your children know who
Sherlock Holmes is. The older ones (10 and over)
may well and if, by chance, they are actually fans of
Conan Doyle's classic detective, they will be
completely bowled over by this little museum. It is
a fictional address, of course, No:221 is actually the
Abbey Building Society, where a secretary is
employed purely to tackle the thousands of letters
sent to the great detective each year.

On entering the museum you are met by a 19th-
century 'Bobby' and shown round the house by a
Victorian maid. The rooms have been faithfully
recreated (or should that be created) according to
the descriptions in the book. Afterwards you can

have a cream tea at Mrs Hudson's Old English Restaurant next door (Mrs Hudson was Holmes' housekeeper in the books). Opposite the museum is a memorabilia shop.

The Wallace Collection

Hertford House, Manchester Square, W1
t (020) 7563 9500
www.wallacecollection.org
⊖ Bond Street, Marble Arch
Bus 2, 13, 30, 74, 82, 113, 139, 159, 189, 274
Open Mon–Sat 10–5, Sun 12 noon–5, Wallace Wheely Cart on Sunday afternoons and school holidays only
Free Wallace Wheely Cart £1
Call ahead **t** (020) 7815 1350 for wheelchair access
Suitable for children over 5, under-8s must be accompanied at all times. Allow at least 1hr

Hertford House, the former home of the Wallace family – 19th-century art collectors *extraordinaire* – is probably not the first place that springs to mind when trying to think of somewhere to take the family. After all, examining one of the country's most important collections of French 18th-century paintings is not every child's idea of a great day out. However, you'd be surprised. The conservators have made a real effort to involve children in the gallery, offering trails and quizzes and running a full programme of holiday activities. So, while parents examine the Sèvres porcelain, priceless furniture and suits of armour, kids may be able to enjoy a puppet show, take an art tour, try on a suit of armour or try their hand at papier-maché mask making, mobile-hanging or collage-making. The gallery also organizes various themed special events where kids can try on historical costumes and handle some of the gallery's extensive collection of weapons (activities usually cost £6 per child, accompanying adult free, and can be booked by emailing hayley.kruger@wallacecollection.org).

The museum recently underwent a millennial refurbishment resulting in four new galleries, a new education centre, a new restaurant, Café Bagatelle and, its most stunning feature, a new glass roof spanning its central courtyard which has been turned into an all-weather sculpture garden and looks a bit like a miniature version of the British Museum's Great Court.

London Canal Museum

12–13 New Wharf Road, N1   t (020) 7713 0836
www.canalmuseum.org.uk
⊖ King's Cross
Bus 10, 17, 30, 45, 46, 63, 73, 91, 205, 214, 259, 390, 476, A2
Free mooring is available outside the museum for canal boats
Open Tues–Sun 10–4.30 (last entry 3.45), open Bank Hol Mons
Adm Adult £2.50, child £1.25 (under-8s **free**)
Wheelchair accessible, with adapted toilets. Suitable for children aged 6 and over. Allow at least 1hr

That rare thing, a museum that makes children appreciate their parents. Back in the 19th century, 'canal kids' were expected to put in 18-hour days leading barge horses along tow paths, opening locks and keeping the boats clean. At the end of the day they would sleep, for just a few hours, on rough wooden benches. This museum tells their story and the story of all the people who tried to make a living ferrying cargo up and down London's industrial canals. It provides a wonderful evocation of a time when childhood was regarded as something less special than it is today. The museum can provide worksheets and organizes occasional activity days for children aged 6–12, usually involving painting or model-making when kids may be able to take a boat trip on the canal.

Lord's Cricket Ground

St John's Wood Road, NW8   t (020) 7266 3825
www.lords.org
⊖ St John's Wood then bus
Bus 13, 46, 82, 113, 139, 189, 274
Tour April–Sept 10am, 12 noon and 2pm daily, Oct–Mar 12 noon and 2pm daily. No tours during Test Matches or Cup Finals
Adm Tickets from £7; tours: adult £7, child £4.50, family £20
Limited wheelchair access, call above number. Suitable for all ages. The tour lasts 1hr 30mins

If your children like cricket, they'll enjoy taking a tour around Lord's (or the Marylebone Cricket Club, to give it its offical title). Lord's is the summer game's official headquarters, and here they can take a walk through the famous longroom, find out about the great W. G. Grace and look at the Ashes Urn, the Holy Grail of cricket. You can also visit the Real Tennis Court.

Question 3
What are the Ashes?
answer on p.249

Puppet Theatre Barge

78 Middleton Road, E8
t (020) 7249 6876
www.puppetbarge.com
⊖ Warwick Avenue
Bus 6, 46
Open Varies, phone ahead
Some wheelchair access by arrangement. Suitable for all ages

A small puppet theatre on an old Thames barge. You can catch a show at Little Venice, to the south of Regent's Park, between October and May. During the summer it sails up and down the Thames putting on performances.

Primrose Hill

If you didn't manage to get your fill of green spaces down in Regent's Park, walk up the hill for some fantastic views over the city. The summit was the setting for the twilight barking in Dodie Smith's *One Hundred and One Dalmatians*, and the area is very popular with families, both canine and human. Regent's Park Road runs adjacent and is good for browsing in book and gift shops.

Camden's markets

⊖ Camden Town, Chalk Farm
Bus 24, 27, 29, 134, 135, 168, 214, 253, 274, C2

Older, more fashion-conscious children will enjoy a visit to Camden's bustling weekend markets which, taken as a whole, are now reckoned to be one of the capital's five most popular attractions. The Camden Stables is the grooviest and grungiest, a casbah-like warren of clothes and fashion stalls; the Lock is craft-based and, as such, a touch more upmarket, while Camden (Buck Street) Market is probably the least interesting – it sells an assorted mixture of clothes, jewellery and general what-nots. In between the markets themselves is an assortment of funky fashion shops, restaurants, pubs and music venues. Come early before the crowds arrive, unless you are willing to let your children mingle with the broadest cross-section of society imaginable spilling out around Camden Town Tube station.

Camden Stables

Off Chalk Farm Road, opposite junction with Hartland Road, NW1
t (020) 7485 5511
www.camdenlock.net/stables

Open Sat, Sun 8–6, though some shops stay open throughout the week

Sells secondhand and designer clothes, jewellery, antiques, books, crafts, furniture, candles, souvenirs, games, memorabilia and old toys. It pays to have a good rummage, for within this extremely popular mish mash of stalls are ones dedicated to musical instruments, street fashions and accessories, plus plenty of places to get yourself tatooed or pierced (over 18s only, of course).

Though there are no plans to close the market, part of the site's southwest corner is soon to be redeveloped into an 'entertainment and commercial complex of bars, shops and media suites' (whatever they are), although developers have promised that this will not change the 'character of the market'. We shall have to wait and see.

Camden Lock

Camden Lock Place, off Chalk Farm Road, NW1
t (020) 7284 2084
www.camdenlock.net
Open Sat, Sun 10–6; some stalls stay open throughout the week

Situated on the river bank, this collection of yards sells craft goods, books, designer clothes, jewellery, food, mirrors, furniture, musical instruments, hand-made soaps, didgeridoos, hand-woven hammocks and sculptures. Thursdays and Fridays see an influx of bric-à-brac, and there's fresh farm produce in abundance on Fridays, too.

Camden (Buck Street) Market

Camden High Street, at junction with Buck Street, NW1
t (020) 7938 4343
Open 9–5.30, daily

The seventies revivalist's dream – the markets stalls are brimming with secondhand clothes, particularly from the days of disco and the perpetually resurfacing gothic phase, plus jewellery, leather belts, handbags and CDs, fruit and veg, as well as a good selection of leather and suede jackets.

WHERE TO EAT

Picnics & snacks

There's no better spot for a picnic than **Regent's Park**. Supplies can be picked up, south of the park, from **Waitrose**, 98–101 Marylebone High Street, W1, **t** (020) 7935 4787 ⊖ Baker Street; **Harts the Grocer**, 112–114 Marylebone High Street, W1, **t** (020) 7846 5610 ⊖ Baker Street; and, north of the park, from the organic store **Fresh and Wild,** at 49 Parkway, NW1, **t** (020) 7428 7575 ⊖ Camden Town.

For a quick bite and a drink, there's the **Primrose Patisserie**, 136 Regent's Park Road, NW1, **t** (020) 7722 7848 ⊖ Camden Town, which serves delicious fruit pastries and hot beverages; **RIBA Café**, 66 Portland Place, W1, **t** (020) 7631 0467 ⊖ Regent's Park, which has a nice roof terrace; **Patisserie Valerie**, 105 Marylebone High Street, W1, **t** (020) 7935 6240 ⊖ Baker Street, a French-style café serving sticky treats. For a swift pint, try **The Queen**, 49 Regent's Park Road, NW1, **t** (020) 7586 0408 ⊖ **Camden Town**, which has a terrace overlooking the park. There's also a very good café in **Regent's Park** itself near the Open Air Theatre. **The Stables** in Camden Market also houses stalls offering takeaway Thai, Chinese and Indian food.

Restaurants

1 Belgo Noord
72 Chalk Farm Road, NW1
t (020) 77267 0718
⊖ Chalk Farm
Open Mon–Fri 12 noon–3 and 6–11, Sat 12 noon–11.30, Sun 12 noon–10.30

2 Caffé uno
100 Baker Street, W1
t (020) 7486 8606
⊖ Baker Street
Open 11am–11pm daily

3 Daphne
83 Bayham Street, NW1
t (020) 7267 7322
⊖ Camden Town
Open Mon–Sat 12 noon–2.30 and 6–11.30

4 The Engineer
65 Gloucester Avenue, NW1
t (020) 7722 0950
⊖ Chalk Farm
Open Mon–Fri 12 noon–3 and 7–11, Sat–Sun 12.30–3.30 and 7–11

5 Giraffe
6–8 Blandford Street, W1
t (020) 7935 2333
⊖ Baker Street
Open 8am–11.30pm daily

6 Manna
4 Erskine Road, NW1
t (020) 7722 8028
www.manna-veg.com
⊖ Chalk Farm
Open Mon–Sat 6pm–11pm, Sun 12.30–3 and 6–11

7/8 Pizza Express
Branches at 133 Baker Street, **t** (020) 7486 0888, ⊖ Baker Street; 85–87 Parkway, **t** (020) 7267 2600, ⊖ Camden Town
Open 12 noon–11.30pm daily

9 Royal China
40 Baker Street, W1
t (020) 7487 4688
⊖ Baker Street
Open Mon–Sat 12 noon–11, Sun 11–10

10 Seashell
49–51 Lisson Grove, NW1
t (020) 7224 9000
⊖ Marylebone
Open Mon–Fri 12 noon–2.30 and 5–10.30, Sat 12 noon–10.30

11 Tiger Lil's
75 Bishop's Bridge Road, W2, **t** (020) 7221 2622 ⊖ Fulham Broadway
15a Clapham Common, SW4, **t** (020) 7720 5433 ⊖ Clapham Common
270 Upper Street, N1, **t** (020) 7226 1118 ⊖ Highbury & Islington
www.tigerlils.com
Branches open Mon–Fri 6pm–11.30pm, Sun 12 noon–11

12 Wagamama
11 Jamestown Road, NW1
t (020) 7487 4688
⊖ Camden Town
Open Mon–Sat 12 noon–11, Sun 12.30–10

See **Eat** p.224 for more details on the above restaurants.
See map on p.41 for the locations of the restaurants numbered above.

British Museum to Oxford Street

There's quite a lot to see here. To the east is the revamped and revitalised British Museum, one of the world's truly great museums, while, to the west lies London's mainstream shopping hub – Oxford Street, Regent Street and Bond Street – one of the best retail districts in Europe. Nonetheless, it's important to time your trip carefully. This whole district is fiercely popular, and on summer weekends or at Christmas the streets can become choked with people. Thankfully, there are a few well-placed small museums to nip into if you need to escape the throng. All in all, there really are few better places to come for an informative day out or a frenzied shopping spree.

Highlights

Walking around the British Museum's Great Court

Handel House Museum's workshops

Watching the new toy demonstrations in Hamleys

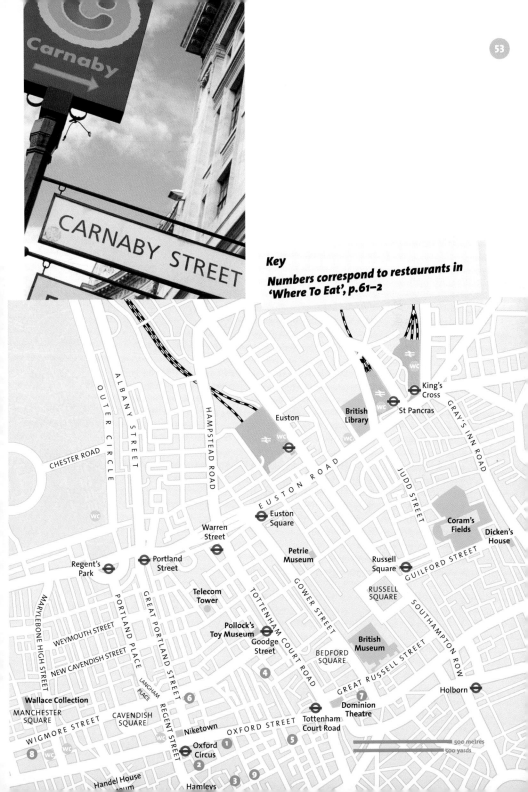

Key

Numbers correspond to restaurants in 'Where To Eat', p.61–2

CARNABY STREET

OUTER CIRCLE

ALBANY STREET

HAMPSTEAD ROAD

CHESTER ROAD

Euston

British Library

St Pancras

King's Cross

GRAY'S INN ROAD

EUSTON ROAD

JUDD STREET

Euston Square

Warren Street

Petrie Museum

Coram's Fields

Dicken's House

Regent's Park

Portland Street

Russell Square

GUILFORD STREET

RUSSELL SQUARE

Telecom Tower

GOWER STREET

SOUTHAMPTON ROW

MARYLEBONE HIGH STREET

PORTLAND PLACE

GREAT PORTLAND STREET

TOTTENHAM COURT ROAD

Pollock's Toy Museum

Goodge Street

BEDFORD SQUARE

British Museum

WEYMOUTH STREET

NEW CAVENDISH STREET

LANGHAM PLACE

4

GREAT RUSSELL STREET

Holborn

Wallace Collection

MANCHESTER SQUARE

CAVENDISH SQUARE

REGENT STREET

6

7

Dominion Theatre

WIGMORE STREET

Niketown

OXFORD STREET

Tottenham Court Road

8

Oxford Circus

1

5

500 metres
500 yards

2

Handel House

Hamleys

3

9

British Museum

Great Russell Street, WC1
t (020) 7636 1555
Infoline **t** (020) 7580 1788
Infoline for disabled visitors **t** (020) 7637 7384
www.british-museum.ac.uk
⊖ Tottenham Court Road, Russell Square, Holborn
Bus 7, 8, 10, 19, 22b, 24, 25, 29, 38, 55, 68, 73, 91, 98,
134, 188, 242
Open Galleries: Sat–Wed 10–5.30, Thurs–Fri
10–8.30; Great Court: Sun–Wed 10–6, Thurs–Sat
9–11. Because of funding problems, some galleries
operate restricted opening times during the week,
check in advance
Free a £2 donation is recommended; charges apply
for some temporary exhibitions
*Wheelchair accessible, with adapted toilets. Suitable
for all ages, but particularly older children, museum
shops (see p.60)*
Allow at least a couple of hours

The British Museum has never looked so good.
Its central courtyard (known as the Great Court,)
which had been closed to the public for nearly 150
years, reopened a couple of years ago following a
spectacular architectural transformation. The
circular Reading Room at its centre, which used to
house the British Library, now holds a public reference library and exhibition galleries. The huge
domed interior looks like a vast cathedral of books,
while the surrounding 2 acres of courtyard have
been landscaped and rebuilt to contain an ethnographic gallery, a new Clore Education Centre, as
well as a lecture theatre, a cinema, seminar rooms
and a young visitor centre offering a huge range of
activities for children. The most stunning development, however, is the new 6,000 square metre
glass roof that arches over the courtyard.

Did you know?
*The British Museum is now over 250 years old. It
was the first museum in the country ever to open
its doors to members of the general public.*

Did you know?
*In the early years of the ancient Egyptian
kingdom, only the rich could afford to be
mummified but, in later times almost everyone
was able to afford it. So many mummies were
dug up in Egypt in the 1800s that people started
using the bodies as fuel and the bandages to
make paper.*

Comprising 3,312 unique triangular panels and
weighing 1,000 tonnes, it makes the courtyard the
largest covered public square in Europe. There's so
much to look at in the museum that you couldn't
hope to do it all in one, or even two, trips. In fact,
once you've had your fill of the awe-inspiring roof,
it's probably best to plan your route around a few
must-see exhibits. From the Great Court, you can
choose from a number of routes into the main
galleries: head west for Egyptian Sculpture, east for
the impossibly huge King's Library and north for
the new Wellcome Wing of Ethnography. Inside the
courtyard, two massive staircases lead up to the
restaurant from where a bridge takes you into the
museum's upper galleries.

Whatever route you chose, however, you won't go
far wrong if you take your children to the ever-
popular Ancient Egyptian Galleries (rooms 62–66)
on the first floor. Here, they'll immediately be capti-
vated by the huge gold sarcophagi, the brightly
coloured frescoes and, of course, the mummies.
These 2,000-year-old dead bodies hold a strange
fascination for kids. The Egyptians, it seems, had a

bit of a thing about mummification. As well as people, you'll find mummified cats, fish and cattle.

Elsewhere, look out for the enormous (11-m high) early 19th-century totem pole that stands by the North Stairs; Lindow Man, the perfectly preserved, leathery remains of a 2,000-year-old Briton (room 35); and the great fat, smiling, ceramic Buddhas in the Oriental gallery (room 33).

The British Museum's other famous exhibits include the controversial Elgin Marbles (room 8), the frieze reliefs from the Parthenon in Athens which, depending on whom you believe, were either rescued or stolen by Lord Elgin, British Ambassador to the Ottoman Empire, in 1802; the Rosetta Stone (room 25), an ancient tablet with the same decree inscribed upon it in three languages, which allowed Egyptian hieroglyphics to be deciphered for the first time; and the Sutton Hoo Treasure (room 41), a jewel-encrusted collection of Saxon swords, helmets, bowls and buckles.

The museum produces a number of themed family tours, known as 'Compass Tours' on subjects such as 'Animal Mummies', 'Anglo-Saxon England', 'Sutton Hoo Treasure' etc., which are available from the information desks in the Great Court and Reading Room (and can also be downloaded from the museum website). The Reading Room also has around 50 computers which you can use to print out the tours for yourself from the website. It's well worth taking a few minutes to explore the museum website as it has a number of resources for children, including puzzles and games, and runs drawing competitions with the best entries displayed on the website.

Do remember, when planning your trip, that the British Museum is a vast place and there's always the danger it can turn into a huge blurry mass for many children, especially the younger ones. So be sure to reserve some time for quiet contemplation in the courtyard.

How to make a mummy

The ancient Egyptians believed that every human being was made up of a *ka* (spirit) and a *ba* (body). When a person died, they would only be able to enter the afterlife if their body was prevented from decaying – hence the fascination with preservation through mummification.

The key to a successful mummification is to dry out the body as quickly and as thoroughly as possible. Remember, the body is 75 per cent water

The Olympics: Then and Now

In 2004 the Olympic Games will return to their birthplace, Greece. In the British Museum's Greek and Roman Antiquities Galleries, several items (including pots, statues and friezes) show images of the ancient games, allowing you to see just how similar they were to their modern counterparts – and just how different.

▶ As with the modern games, the ancient games, were held every four years. Although other cities held their own games, the most renowned were always held in the same location – Olympia.

▶ The modern games have been going for quite a long time. In 2004, it will be 108 years since the first of the modern Olympics. The ancient games, by comparison, went on for a really long time. The first took place in 771 BC, the last in AD 393. In other words, the ancient games were in continuous existence for 1,164 years – that's a lot of races.

▶ The modern games feature many of the same events as the old, including sprinting, long-jump, discus, javelin, wrestling etc, albeit with the odd rule change. For instance, in Ancient Greece long-jumpers took off from a standing start and swung heavy weights in their hands to build up momentum. Modern jumpers are allowed a run-up (but no weights).

▶ Women were not only banned from competing in the ancient games, but could be put to death if caught watching.

▶ The modern Olympics has seen the introduction of gold, silver and bronze medals awarded for 1st, 2nd and 3rd place. Ancient athletes were awarded a simple laurel wreath, although they sometimes also had songs written and performed in their honour.

▶ As important as winning is to the modern athlete, it was much more important in ancient Greece. Winners were exempt from local taxes and often had statues erected in their honour, while losers could be whipped if their performance was particularly bad.

▶ The modern Olympics prides itself on spectacle, but there were certain sights available to ancient eyes that the modern games will never match. For one, all athletes in Ancient Greece competed in the nude. Today, athletes do the next best thing and cover their bodies in the most figure-hugging, aerodynamic material available.

Make friends

The Museum's youth club, 'Young Friends of the British Museum', meets every Sunday. Members are entitled to free entry to all exhibitions and access to a special 'Friends and Family' room, plus preferential admission to a range of special events. These include walking tours through the city and behind the scenes visits to see items not usually seen by the public, as well as the hugely popular 'Egyptian Sleepover' nights when kids (up to four plus one adult) can spend the night in amongst the museum's Egyptian treasures. Kids will also receive the museum's youth magazine 'ReMus' three times a year. Annual membership costs £17.50.

and, in a hot climate such as Egypt's, anything wet or damp rots very quickly. Embalmers used natron, a chemical that occurs naturally in Egypt, to suck the moisture out of the body. The eyes and most of the internal organs, including the brain, kidneys and liver, were taken out. The brain was removed through a nostril, a chisel having first been wiggled around inside the skull cavity to mash it into small pieces. The brain would then be thrown away (for some reason the Egyptians didn't think it would be particularly useful in the afterlife). All the other organs, however, were stored safely inside jars and buried with the body, ready for the post-life

journey. The skull and body cavities were filled with a mixture of natron and plaster, and the eyes replaced with small stones (or, in the case of the unlucky Rameses IV, with two small onions) in order to stop them from becoming sunken. Only the heart was left inside the body; this would have to be weighed in the afterlife against the 'Feather of Truth'. If the feather proved heavier, the heart would be eaten by a monster known as the 'Devourer' and the dead person would be prevented from completing their journey.

Once the body was dry, it was wrapped in bandages. Sometimes over 300 yards of bandages were used, with charms written on pieces of papyrus slipped between the folds. The mummy would then be put into its coffin or sarcophagus and entombed, but not before its mouth had been opened to make sure it could breathe and talk in the afterlife – although, without a brain, conversation was presumably limited.

Dickens' House

48 Doughty Street
t (020) 7405 2127
www.dickensmuseum.com
⊖ Chancery Lane, Russell Square
Bus 17, 19, 38, 45, 55
Open Mon–Sat 10–5, closed Bank Holidays
Adm Adult £4, child (5–15) £2, family £10

Despite Dickens being a bit of a gadabout – much of the south coast lays more or less spurious claim to a pub where he once supped or scribbled, – he did manage to write a fair bit within the walls of this house, now a museum to his literary life. Although only his home for the first two years of his marriage, it was here that Dickens finished *The Pickwick Papers*, and went on to write *Oliver Twist*, *Nicholas Nickleby*, *The Old Curiosity Shop* and *Barnaby Rudge*. As the sole survivor of Dickens' London residences, the museum is chock-full of memorabilia and paintings, and the drawing room has been restored to its mid-1800s state. Special family events are organized throughtout the year. Some are craft-based – kids can learn how to write with a quill pen – while others take the form of storytelling sessions, often featuring tales from one of the author's lesser-known works, 'A Child's History of England'. Tours can be arranged by phoning in advance.

57

Handel House Museum

25 Brook Street, W1
t. (020) 7495 1685)
www.handelhouse.org
⊖ Bond Street, Oxford Circus
Adm Adult £4.50, child £2 (**free** on Saturdays and for family events), concs £3.50
Wheelchair accessible, with disabled toilets.
Audio guide, shop

This was the home of the composer from 1723 until his death in 1759. He used the house as a recital room and a ticket office, besides writing *The Messiah* and many operas on the premises. The house contains artworks relating to the composer's life and times and has been refurbished with items of furniture based on an inventory of his possessions. A handling collection, a children's activity pack (ages 6–12) and costumed actors (some weekends, call for details) are all on hand to bring Handel's world to life and give young visitors a taste of 18th-century living. Musical workshops, storytellings and recitals aimed at a family audience are also put on during the school holidays.

Petrie Museum of Egyptian Archaeology

Malet Place, WC1
t (020) 7679 2884
www.petrie.ucl.ac.uk
⊖ Goodge Street
Bus 10, 73, 29, 134
Open Tues–Fri 1–5, Sat 10–1
Free

Part of University College, London, this hidden gem may well inspire your children to get digging out in the back garden. The assembled artefacts were bequeathed to the University by Sir Flinders Petrie in 1933, following his excavations in Egypt. Among them are assorted pieces of jewellery and the oldest piece of cloth in the world (c.2,800 BC). Mummy enthusiasts will love the 4,500-year-old pot burial and the Egyptian version of a Barbie makeover mannequin – complete with real eyebrows, lashes and a big hairdo. In summer, families can pick up a backpack and follow the trail back in time to the ancient Valley of the Kings.

Pollock's Toy Museum

1 Scala Street, W1
t (020) 7636 3452
www.pollocksweb.co.uk
⊖ Goodge Street
Bus 10, 24, 29, 73, 134
Open Mon–Sat 10–5, (last entry 4.30)
Adm Adult £3, child (under 18) £1.50
No disabled facilities. Suitable for all ages
Allow at least 1hr

This captivating collection of Victorian toys and trinkets is housed in two interlinked 18th-century houses. It's named after Benjamin Pollock, one of Victorian London's leading toy-makers, and is stuffed full of wonderfully crafted playthings: hand-made paper and card miniature stage sets (Pollock's speciality), tin toys, board games, puppets and dolls' houses; as well as folk toys from Russia, Poland and the Balkans. The museum shop is a good source of stocking-fillers – pick up one of the theatre kits based on Pollock's original designs and bring your own version of Cinderella or Aladdin to life. *See* **Covent Garden** p.81 for an additional shop.

AROUND & ABOUT

British Library

96 Euston Road, NW1
t (020) 7412 7000/7332
www.bl.uk
⊖/⤢ King's Cross, Euston
Bus 10, 18, 30, 73
Open Mon, Wed–Fri 9.30–6, Tues 9.30–8,
Sat 9.30–5, Sun 11–5
Free
*Wheelchair accessible, with adapted toilets. Suitable
for older children (over-8s). Allow at least 1hr*

It was completed 10 years behind schedule and
cost a mere £511 million (or £350 million more than
it was meant to), but it's still been hailed as a great
success. The new British Library looks rather ordinary (almost supermarket-like) from the outside,
but inside it's quite magical, with huge, bright
reading rooms. Although many of the public
displays are confined to the (rather dingy) basement, the library it still well worth a visit. It holds
many of the country's most precious manuscripts,
including the Lindisfarne Gospels, the Magna Carta
and Shakespeare's First Folio (look out for Lewis
Carroll's notebook version of *Alice's Adventures in
Wonderland*, complete with hand-drawn illustra-
tions). During the school holidays, the library
organizes craft and creative workshops for children
aged 5 and upwards in which they can try their
hand at calligraphy, block-printing and book-
binding, or perhaps meet a writer or artist.

Camley Street Natural Park

12 Camley Street, NW1
t (020) 7833 2311
⊖/⤢ King's Cross
Bus 10, 30, 73, 91
Open Summer Mon–Thurs 9–5, Sat–Sun 11–5,
closed Fri; winter 10–4, closed Fri
Free

Do not let the sight of King's Cross waste-
transfer station's steely towers put you off. This
hidden two-acre site has been teeming with flora
and fauna since it became a nature reserve at the
hands of the London Wildlife Trust in 1983.
Supervised activities take place all year round, from
pond-dipping and bat walks to mask-making.

Coram's Fields

93 Guilford Street, WC1
t (020) 7837 6138
⊖ Russell Square

Bus 17, 45, 46
Open Summer 9–8 daily, winter 9–dusk
Free

This lovely little park has had a long association
with children. It was here that the eponymous
Thomas Coram established a foundling hospital in
1747 which, following the building's demolition in
1920, was turned into a dedicated children's park.
Today, adults can only visit Coram's Fields in the
company of a child. It's exremely well-equipped.
In addition to lawns, sandpits, a paddling pool, a
basketball court, a helter skelter and a supervised
playground, you'll find the park's undoubted highlight, a small farm home to goats, sheep, pigs,
chickens, geese, rabbits and guinea pigs.

Dominion Theatre

269 Tottenham Court Road, W1
Box office **t** (020) 7413 3546
⊖ Tottenham Court Road
Bus 7, 8, 10, 25, 55, 73, 98, 176
Prices £10–£50

A great place to introduce children to the joys of
the stage in true technicolour musical fashion. Its
productions are nearly always child-friendly and
have in recent years included *The Phantom of the
Opera*, *Notre Dame de Paris* and *We Will Rock You*.

WHERE TO SHOP

Oxford Street, Regent Street and Bond Street together make up one of the busiest shopping districts in the country. You'll find lots of clothes and book shops, all with sections for kids, as well as some well-stocked department stores. There are also a number of shops, like Hamleys and Niketown, which will call to your children like sirens from a rock.

If you're keen on browsing for something to read, Borders on Oxford Street, a massive book, CD and magazine shop, will appeal equally to adults and children, who can both happily spend the best part of an afternoon browsing through its four floors. It's one of the capital's most innovative bookstores, organizing storytellings for children on Saturday mornings – with a roster of costumed characters on hand to enliven proceedings.

Otherwise, head to Charing Cross Road, London's unofficial book centre, and particularly Foyle's, one of the largest bookstores in London. This huge, charming, sprawling shop has a superb collection of children's books. It also has a completely un-fathomable layout, but then looking is half the fun. The nearby branch of Waterstone's at Piccadilly is the largest bookshop in Europe.

If your kids are comic fans try Gosh! on Great Russell Street where you can pick up all your Marvel and DC favourites such as *Superman* and *The Incredible Hulk* (and compilations of news-paper strip cartoons like *Peanuts* and *The Far Side*), or Forbidden Planet on New Oxford Street, full of sci-fi comics, books and models. *See* **Shop** p.238.

Hamleys
188–196 Regent Street, W1
t (020) 7734 3161
www.hamleys.com
⊖ Oxford Circus
Bus 3, 6, 12, 13, 15, 23, 53, 88, 94, 139, 159, X53
Open Mon–Fri 10–8, Thurs 10–8, Sat 9.30–8, Sun 12 noon–6

Toy heaven! Hamleys is one of the largest and certainly the most famous toy shop in the world. You can find absolutely every toy imaginable on its six jam-packed floors. In fact, if Hamleys don't stock it, it probably doesn't exist.

Briefly, this is what you can expect to find. The basement has been turned into an arcade known as the 'Cyberzone', filled with hundreds of video games; there's also a small and rather noisy café. On the ground floor you'll find thousands of soft toys plus all the latest stocking fillers. The first floor is the place for science kits and board games. On the second floor are pre-school toys while the third floor is dedicated to dolls: rag dolls, porcelain dolls and, of course, Barbie. The fourth floor, on the other hand, is packed with more cerebral games: jigsaw puzzles, model kits and computer programmes, as well as an enormous collection of remote-controlled vehicles. The fifth and final floor holds sporting goods, 'Lego World' and a small café.

One of the grand old men of the London shop-ping scene, Hamley's has recently come under foreign ownership for the first time in its 243-year history. It will be interesting to see what changes, if

Did you know?
Watch out! Every time you kick a football, your poor foot has to endure 110kg of pressure!

any, the store's new Icelandic owners will effect on this terribly British toy emporium.

Niketown

236 Oxford Street, W1
t (020) 7612 0800
www.nike.com
⊖ Oxford Circus
Bus 6, 7, 8, 10, 12, 13, 15, 23, 25, 55, 73, 94, 98, 113, 135, 137, 139, 159, 176, 189
Open Mon–Wed 10–7, Thurs–Sat 10–8, Sun 12 noon–6

The biggest sports name in town, the £50 million Niketown is more than just a sports shop. It's a theme store, a mini-museum, an 'experience' – or so the hype would have us believe. It's certainly a fascinating place, and the shop treats sport almost as a religion. Each dedicated section – football, golf, tennis, running etc. – has a distinctly sacred feel, with video images and memorabilia taking the place of rituals and relics. The centre of the store is dominated by an enormous chandelier covered in thousands of sporting pictures. Every now and then the lights will dim for a 'service' when a video of a classic sporting moment will be shown on the store's numerous giant screens to the accompaniment of rousing music – very strange but undeniably affecting.

The Disney Store

360–66 Oxford Street, W1
t (020) 7491 9136
www.disneystore.co.uk
⊖ Oxford Circus
Open Mon–Sat 10–8, Sun 12 noon–6

Videos, play figures, mugs, costumes: the store holds a vast array of merchandise relating to Disney's enormous roster of cartoon characters. The video screen belting out singalong classics never fails to attract a gaggle of painfully warbling children. A selection of toddler's merchandise is in the basement.

British Museum Shops

22 Bloomsbury Street London WC1
t (020) 7637 9449
Open Mon–Sat 9.30–6, Sun 12 noon–6

There are four outlets in total which make up the British Museum shopping experience: a bookshop on the north side of the Great Court; a souvenir shop on the west side which sells inexpensive mementos – mugs, postcards, Rosetta Stone pencil sharpeners etc; the Grenville Shop by the Great Russell Street entrance, which specializes in expensive reproductions of museum exhibits – replica sculptures, jewellery and silk scarves; and, last but not least, a specialist children's shop on the east side of the Great Court, filled with pocket money-priced souvenirs for young visitors.

Question 4
Which London football club has a claret and blue home strip?
answer on p.249

WHERE TO EAT

Picnics & snacks

Green picnic spots are a bit thin on the ground in this most central of locations. You can take food into the Great Court of the **British Museum** which provides a sort of all-weather picnic venue (you can't, however, eat it at the café tables), and there's always **Coram's Fields** on the outskirts of the area. Supplies can be picked up from: **Lina's Stores** Italian delicatessen, 11 Brewer Street, W1, **t** (020) 7437 6482, ✪ Tottenham Court Road; the French delicatessen/bakery/patisserie **Truc Vert**, 42 North Audley Street, W1, **t** (020) 7491 9988, ✪ Bond Street; **Carluccio's** (see p.227), Fenwick, New Bond Street, W1, **t** (020) 7629 0699, ✪ Bond Street; **Fresh and Wild** organic food halls, 69–75 Brewer Street, W1, **t** (020) 7344 3179, ✪ Tottenham Court Road; **Tesco Metro**, 311 Oxford Street, W1 ✪ Bond Street; or, if you really want to splash out, **Selfridges** magnificent food halls, 400 Oxford Street, W1, **t** (020) 7269 1234, ✪ Bond Street.

There are lots of snack bars, sandwich shops, fast-food outlets and chain restaurants where you can grab a quick bite before returning to the dizzying world of retail. Snacks, sandwiches and sticky treats are available from **Patisserie Valerie** (see p.231), 44 Old Compton Street, W1, **t** (020) 7437 3466 ✪ Tottenham Court Road, and **Maison Bertaux**, 28 Greek Street, W1, **t** (020) 7437 6007 ✪ Tottenham Court Road; simple pasta and pizza dishes from **Café Flo**, 13 Thayer Street, W1, **t** (020) 7935 5023 ✪ Bond Street, and **Café Med**, 22–25 Dean Street, W1, **t** (020) 7287 9007 ✪ Tottenham Court Road; and burgers (and, of course, happy meals) from **McDonald's** at 8–10 Oxford Street, W1, 120 Oxford Street, W1, 185 Oxford Street, W1, 291b Oxford Street, W1, 40 New Oxford Street, W1, 310–312 Regent Street, W1, and 134 Tottenham Court Road, W1. If you fancy sampling some slightly more upmarket burgers try **Tootsies** (see p.235), 35 James Street, W1,

Can you spot?

The Telecom Tower? One of London's most distinctive landmarks, the great cylindrical tower (it looks a bit like a huge spark plug) is clearly visible from the north side of Oxford Street. Standing some 580ft high, this was the tallest building in London when it opened in 1964 – it needed to be so tall in order to broadcast clear radio and TV signals over the city's rooftops. The views from the top are said to be fantastic. Sadly, members of the public have been barred from the top of the tower since the closure of the revolving restaurant (yes, a revolving restaurant) in the seventies for security reasons.

t (020) 7486 1611 ✪ Bond Street, a brightly-coloured diner-style bar offering a kids' menu for £4.95.

Restaurants

1 Bodeans Smoke House

17 Poland Street, W1
t (020) 7287 7575
✪ Oxford Circus
Open Mon–Fri 12 noon–11, Sat–Sun 12 noon–10.30

2 Caffé Uno

5 Argyll Street, W1
t (020) 7437 2503
✪ Oxford Circus
Open 12 noon–11.30 daily

3 Masala Zone

9 Marshall Street, W1
t (020) 7287 9966
www.realindianfood.com
✪ Oxford Circus
Open Mon–Sat 12 noon–2.30 and 5.30–11.30,
Sun 12.30–3

4/5 Pizza Express

7 Charlotte Street, W1
t (020) 7580 1110
✪ Goodge Street
10 Dean Street, W
t (020) 7439 8722
✪ Tottenham Court Road
www.pizzaexpress.co.uk
Open 12 noon–11.30 daily

Question 5
How many of the individually-shaped glass panels were used to make up the roof of the British Museum's Great Court?
answer on p.54 or see p.249

6 RK Stanley's

6 Little Portland Street, W1
t (020) 7462 0099
⊖ Oxford Circus
Open Mon–Sat 12 noon–11

7/8 Wagamama

4a Streatham Street, WC1
t (020) 7323 9223
⊖ Tottenham Court Road
101 Wigmore Street, W1
t (020) 7409 0111
⊖ Oxford Circus
www.wagamama.com
Open Mon–Sat 12 noon–11, Sun 12.30–10

9 Yo! Sushi

52 Poland Street, W1
t (020) 7287 0443
www.yosushi.co.uk
Open 12 noon–12 midnight daily
⊖ Oxford Circus, Tottenham Court Road

See **Eat** p.224 for more details on the above restaurants.
See map on p.53 for the locations of the restaurants numbered above.

Trafalgar Square to Piccadilly

The much improved Trafalgar Square, with its newly pedestrianised north side and happy gurgling fountains, provides the centrepiece of this area. Overlooked by a spruced-up Nelson's Column (the square's hundreds of pigeons have had their numbers drastically cut), the square is home to two of the city's great art galleries: the National Gallery and the National Portrait Gallery. Nearby is Leicester Square, London's cinematic heart, and the neon-lit Piccadilly Circus, site of the Trocadero centre where many a teenage adventurer has strayed to sample the arcade rides and games.

Highlights

Trafalgar Square's cooling fountains

The latest arcade thrills at the Trocadero

Eating with chopsticks in Chinatown

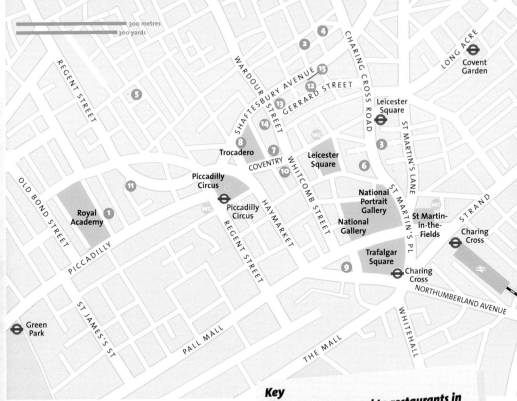

300 metres
300 yards

REGENT STREET

WARDOUR STREET

SHAFTESBURY AVENUE

CHARING CROSS ROAD

LONG ACRE

Covent
Garden

2
4
15
GERRARD STREET
12

Leicester
Square

ST MARTIN'S LANE

5

13

14

8

Trocadero

7
COVENTRY

Leicester
Square

3

WC

10
WHITCOMB STREET

6

11

Piccadilly
Circus

Piccadilly
Circus
WC

HAYMARKET

National
Portrait
Gallery

National
Gallery

ST MARTIN'S PL

St Martin-
in-the-
Fields
WC

STRAND

Charing
Cross

OLD BOND STREET

Royal
Academy
1

PICCADILLY

REGENT STREET

Trafalgar
Square

9

Charing
Cross

Charing
Cross

NORTHUMBERLAND AVENUE

Green
Park

ST JAMES'S ST

PALL MALL

THE MALL

WHITEHALL

Key
Numbers correspond to restaurants in
'Where To Eat' pp.73–4

Trafalgar Square

✪ Charing Cross, Leicester Square, Embankment
Bus 3, 6, 9, 11, 12, 13, 15, 23, 24, 29, 53, 88, 91, 109, 139, 159, 176, 184, 196

Until recently, Trafalgar Square often came as a bit of a let-down to visitors. True, it had many attractions, but the traffic that filled the outskirts of the square, and the huge flocks of pigeons that occupied its centre, made it a noisy, congested and, in truth, rather dirty place. Things, however, have changed. The north side has been pedestrianised and prettified, with traffic now confined solely to the square's southern end, while the pigeons have (for the most part) been sent on their way. The result is a very pleasant public space. It could do with a bit more greenery and some pavement cafés in order to make it compare with Europe's best city squares, but it's certainly moving in the right direction. The grand new staircase at the square's northern end provides a great place to sit and admire the views, which are of course dominated by the 185-ft granite bulk of Nelson's Column. Kids will instinctively roll their heads back in an attempt to catch a glimpse of the one-eyed, one-armed British hero perched on its summit. Lord Horatio Nelson (for it is he) was Britain's greatest naval commander. The square and column were built in the early 19th century to commemorate his victory over the combined Franco-Spanish fleet at the Battle of Trafalgar back in 1805. Unfortunately, Nelson was fatally wounded during the course of the battle and was brought home to Britain for a hero's funeral, his body having been preserved during the journey in a barrel of brandy.

The friendly-looking iron lions at the base were sculpted by Edwin Landseer. They were unveiled in 1870, some 25 years after the construction of the column. Children always fall madly in love with them and will expend remarkable amounts of energy trying to clamber aboard the beasts' great

Did you know?
Just before the 40-ft statue of Nelson was erected in Trafalgar Square, 14 stonemasons had a celebratory dinner perched on top of the column – 145ft in the air. Did you also know that the statue of Charles I (on the south side of the square) is the precise point from which all distances from London are measured?

shiny backs. A photo of your kids sitting between a pair of giant protective forepaws is one of the classic snapshots of London. Alternatively, you could pose them in front of one of the square's great gushing, gurgling fountains which spring into life at 10am. The stairs also provide a fittingly grand approach to the National Gallery, one of the world's finest collections of paintings, which sits next to the National Portrait Gallery, the nation's artistic scrapbook.

Christmas and New Year

Trafalgar Square is particularly popular in winter. Every year the Norwegian government donates a huge Christmas tree to Britain as a thank you for help during the Second World War. The tree is erected in the square next to Nelson's Column. Carol singing takes place around the tree every evening from early December to Christmas Eve. Every 31 December (New Year's Eve) thousands of people cram into Trafalgar Square to celebrate the New Year – waiting for the 12 o'clock chimes of Britain's most famous clock, Big Ben, to ring out.

Can you spot?
Trafalgar Square is home to the world's smallest police station. See if you can find it. Hidden in a lamp post, in the southeast corner of the square, it has room for just one police officer.

National Gallery

Trafalgar Square, WC2
t (020) 7747 2885
www.nationalgallery.org.uk
⊖ Charing Cross, Leicester Square, Embankment
Bus 3, 6, 9, 11, 12, 13, 15, 23, 24, 29, 53, 88, 91, 109, 139, 159, 176, 184, 196
Open 10–6 daily, Wed 10–9
Free Charges apply for some temporary exhibitions
Wheelchair accessible, with adapted toilets, loop system for hard of hearing. Suitable for children aged 8 and over. Allow at least 2hrs

Lots and lots of pictures. Rooms and rooms of paintings. Over 2,300 canvases covering the last eight centuries of European art – and you don't have to pay a penny to see them (although a donation is always appreciated).

All the great artists are here: Cézanne, Constable, Leonardo da Vinci, Picasso, Turner, Van Gogh...think of a famous painter and it can be pretty much guaranteed that you'll find an example of their work here. The sheer size and scope of the gallery can make the prospect of a visit seem daunting for adults, let alone children.

Did you know?
The gallery's collection was begun in 1824 when the government bought 38 pictures from a wealthy merchant, John Julius Angerstein, for £57,000.

To get the best out of the gallery, it's often a good idea to pick perhaps a dozen or so pictures in advance and then plan your tour accordingly. That way you can turn the experience into a sort of treasure hunt. Fortunately, the wonderful resources of the National allow you to plan your trip in exactly this fashion. Your first port of call should be the Micro Gallery in the Sainsbury Wing at the west end of the Gallery. Here you can explore the gallery's entire collection on touch-screen computer terminals and print out your own personalized tour. For very young children, however, it's probably best just to let them wander and point, rather than structuring your trip too rigorously – you'll be surprised at what catches their eye.

The collection is divided into four colour-coded wings: the Sainsbury Wing (blue) shows paintings from 1260 to 1510; the West Wing (green) paintings from 1510 to 1600; the North Wing (yellow) paint-

Tell me a story: Nelson v Napoleon

By 1805 Napoleon, the Emperor of France, had conquered Spain and Italy and was making plans to invade Britain. To this end, he had assembled a fighting fleet of some 33 fearsomely armoured Spanish and French ships which he stationed at Cadiz Harbour under the command of Admiral Pierre de Villeneuve. In September, Villeneuve was ordered to sail the fleet to Italy to prepare for the invasion. The British, however, had different ideas and instructed the Royal Navy's premier commander, Admiral Horatio Nelson, to lead his own fleet of 27 warships in an ambush against Napoleon's ships. Nelson intercepted the enemy at Cape Trafalgar off the Spanish coast, whereupon he gave orders, using a system of flag signals, for his fleet to divide itself into two squadrons, each of which was to attack half the Franco-Spanish fleet. Nelson, meanwhile, would lead the fighting from aboard his flagship, the *Victory*.

At 11.50am, Nelson signalled his now legendary message: 'England expects that every man will do

his duty', and then ordered the fighting to commence. It soon became clear that the British forces would win the day as they quickly smashed through the enemy lines, their heavy cannon causing widespread devastation. A brief counter-attack by the Franco-Spanish forces had little effect and, by 5pm, the battle was over. Twenty enemy ships had been sunk and 7,000 men, including Villeneuve himself, taken prisoner.

It would have have been a time of great rejoicing among the British ranks had it not been for the fact that, at 4.30pm, Nelson, whilst commanding operations from the deck, had been mortally wounded by an enemy sniper. He died, at least, knowing that victory was assured. His final words, spoken to his second in command, Hardy, were supposedly either 'kismet' (which means fate) or 'kiss me' (which means something else entirely).

Nelson's legacy proved to be a lasting one. Not only did his final naval victory thwart Napoleon's plans, but it assured Britain's naval supremacy in Europe for the next hundred years.

ings from 1600 to 1700 and the East Wing (red) paintings from 1700 to 1900.

The Gallery also produces special audio guides for children as well as organising a range of family events including free weekly Gallery talks for 4–11 year-olds, storytellings for under-5s on the Gallery's 'magic carpet' and, on the second weekend of each month, artist-led drawing events. A full programme is available on the Gallery website.

There's a decent self-service café and a more expensive brasserie, but you're probably best off having lunch just around the corner in the Café in the Crypt (see p.225) or bringing your own picnic which can be eaten in the Education Centre's sandwich rooms. The Gallery shop is excellent and well worth a visit. In fact, kids often get as much enjoyment (if not more) from the shop as they do from the Gallery itself. In particular, they love the scale model of Trafalgar Square that sits just outside the shop. Inside there are lots of good introductory art books as well as a variety of art products including pens, drawing pads, CD-ROMs, videos, slides, Renoir umbrellas, Van Gogh back-packs etc. One great new innovation has been the introduction of a print-on-demand poster service. Until recently, only a limited number of the Gallery's artworks could be bought in poster form. Now, thanks to the introduction of a clever new computer imaging system, the whole of the Gallery's collection has become available. So, if a particular picture takes your fancy as you're wandering around, simply head to the shop, request a poster and have it printed out while you wait. Each poster costs a flat £10.

The pictures

There are certain pictures in the National that will especially appeal to children. The colour and vibrancy of many of the Renaissance canvases (to be found in the Sainsbury and West Wings) often touch a nerve with kids, and the subjects – St George killing the Dragon, St Sebastian shot full of arrows, John the Baptist's head on a silver platter – are usually gory enough to impress. Paintings that employ overt forms of visual trickery also often grab children's attention. Here are five paintings they may enjoy.

Hans Holbein

The Ambassadors (above, left; West Wing)

This is a wonderfully bright and colourful picture of two very grand 16th-century courtiers. Everything seems quite normal apart from a strange stretched shape at the bottom of the picture. Get your kids to go as close to the wall on the right hand side of the picture as possible and then look back at the picture. By changing the point of view in this fashion, the stretched shape should now have transformed itself into the picture of a skull.

Can you spot?

Hidden among the fruit and flowers of Jan van Os' picture are the following creatures and objects. How many can you find? There are two butterflies, three flies, a snail, a dormouse, a dragonfly and a bird's nest.

Jan van Eyck

Arnolfini Wedding Portrait (opposite; Sainsbury Wing)

This 15th-century Dutch picture of a couple holding hands seems quite unremarkable on first glance. But if you look closely at the mirror hanging on the wall behind the couple, you should be able to see the reflection of the back of the couple stretching out their hands towards a visitor. The visitor is van Eyck himself, come to paint the couple's portrait. Van Eyck seems to have been very keen for the viewer to know who painted the picture. The words 'Van Eyck fuit hic, 1434' appear on the wall above the mirror. Roughly translated they mean 'Van Eyck made this, 1434'.

Andrea Mantegna

The Introduction of the Cult of Cybele at Rome (Sainsbury Wing)

A 15th-century painting made to look like a sculpture. Mantegna painted this so that, from a distance, it looks carved out of stone.

Samuel van Hoogstraten

Peepshow (North Wing)

Created in the 17th century, this isn't a conventional painting at all, but a wooden box mounted on a plinth. In the side of the box is a peephole. If you look through the hole, you'll see what looks like a miniature house filled with what appears to be 3D furniture. It is, in fact, a 2D painting which cleverly uses perspective to make you think you are seeing things which aren't really there.

Jan van Os

Fruit, Flowers in a Terracotta Vase (East Wing)

This picture, from the late 18th century, is so realistic that it almost looks like a photograph. The trick is in the composition rather than the representation. Although the fruit and flowers in the picture appear quite fresh, in fact they couldn't possibly have all appeared together at the same time as they all ripen at different times of year. The painting was therefore painted over the course of a year, each new fruit and flower being added as it came into season.

National Portrait Gallery

St Martin's Place, WC2
t (020) 7306 0055
www.npg.org.uk
✆ Charing Cross, Leicester Square, Embankment

Can you spot?

Young visitors to the National Portrait Gallery will probably be less concerned with artistic merit than with spotting some famous faces.

See if they can find portraits of the following: Princess Diana, David Beckham, Michael Owen, Barbara Windsor and Ozzy Osbourne.

Bus 3, 6, 9, 11, 12, 13, 15, 23, 24, 29, 53, 88, 91, 109, 139, 159, 176, 184, 196
Open Mon–Wed, Sat–Sun 10–6, Thurs–Fri 10–9
Free Charges apply for some temporary exhibitions
Wheelchair accessible, with adapted toilets. Suitable for older children (8 and over). Allow at least 1hr

If history is, as Sir Thomas Carlyle once claimed, merely the 'biographies of great men', then the National Portrait Gallery is its picture album. Over 2,000 portraits of the greatest figures from the last 700 years of British history are on display here. The collection is arranged more or less chronologically, so it's best to start at the top (there's a lift) with the Tudors (look out for the clever picture of Edward VI by William Scrots which requires you to look at it from an acute angle in order to see the perspective) before making your way slowly down through the centuries via the Balcony Gallery (part of new Ondaatje Wing built for the Millennium) to the 20th-century works on the ground floor – which is also where most of temporary exhibitions are held. On the way children will find themselves putting faces to names they had previously only read about in textbooks or heard in history lessons: kings, queens, soldiers, statesmen, scientists, politicians, artists and sculptors, they're all here. Children might enjoy tracking down the picture of Edwin Landseer, portrayed carving the lions that would eventually go on display just outside in

Trafalgar Square. The Gallery has also introduced a Rucksack Tour of the first floor (children are given a rucksack containing activity sheets and puzzles relating to the displays) and there are 'tour and draw' sessions organized for kids on the last Saturday of each month.

Because the Gallery's pictures have been chosen on the basis of identity rather than ability, the quality and style of the works varies enormously. Note how most of the older paintings have been painted in a very traditional, formal style, while the more modern works have been rendered using a great mish mash of different techniques.

Once you've finished your tour, catch the lift back up to the top floor café which has wonderful views out over Trafalgar Square.

Elsewhere on Trafalgar Square

On the northeast edge of Trafalgar Square stands the church of St Martin-in-the-Fields. Built in 1722, it's the square's oldest building. Today, its church-yard plays host to a rather touristy bric-à-brac market. Inside the church proper, free classical concerts are given every Tuesday lunchtime. Down in the eerie crypt you'll find the London Brass Rubbing Centre – with a selection of over 100 brasses including knights, dragons, griffins and elephants – and an appealingly dungeonesque eaterie, the Café in the Crypt.

London Brass Rubbing Centre

St Martin-in-the-Fields, Trafalgar Square, WC2
t (020) 7930 9306
www.stmartin-in-the-fields.org
⊖ Charing Cross, Leicester Square, Embankment
Bus 3, 6, 9, 11, 12, 13, 15, 23, 24, 29, 53, 88, 91, 109, 139, 159, 176, 184, 196
Open Mon–Sat 10–6, Sun 12 noon–6
Adm Anything from £3 to £15 depending on how many rubbings you do
No disabled facilities

Royal Academy

Burlington House, Piccadilly, W1
t (020) 7300 8000
www.royalacademy.org.uk
⊖ Green Park, Piccadilly Circus
Bus 9, 14, 19, 22, 38
Open 10–6 daily, Fri till 10pm
Adm Depends on the exhibition
Wheelchair accessible for all areas, wheelchair hire available in advance. Suitable for older children (10

Can you spot?

Eros, London's most popular statue, which stands in the middle of Piccadilly Circus, firing 'arrows of love' down the Haymarket. Although everyone calls it Eros, the man who designed it, Sir Alfred Gilbert, insisted that it was in fact meant to be an Angel of Christian Charity and not the God of Love at all. The trouble is, everyone ignored him. Poor old Alfred, he didn't get much pleasure from this statue. When he cast it in 1893, he imagined it sitting on top of a cascading fountain. The people who were paying for it, however, refused to cough up, causing Alfred to fly into a rage and boycott the opening ceremony.

and over). Younger kids may enjoy it but only for short bursts. Allow at least 1hr

The most high-brow entertainment the Piccadilly area has to offer, the Royal Academy specialises in blockbuster temporary art exhibitions, such as its recent Aztec extravaganza and the 'Monet in the 20th Century' show at the end of the last century (which went on to become the most popular temporary art exhibition ever staged in this country). It also holds an annual Summer Exhibition (and has done since 1769, making it the world's longest running art exhibition) made up of works submitted by the public. Anybody, regardless of age, can submit a piece, although obviously only a small fraction goes on display. Even if your piece doesn't make the cut, the Academy is still well worth a visit as it organizes family events throughout the year, including gallery talks, art and music workshops, and provides free guide sheets and art trays for kids.

Question 6
Other than being next to each other, what do Piccadilly Circus, Coventry Street and Leicester Square have in common?
answer on p.249

Piccadilly

Piccadilly's first inhabitant was a wealthy tailor called Robert Baker who built a mansion on fields here in 1612. Baker's friends thought his wealth and fame had gone to his head, and so christened his new house 'Piccadill', meaning 'shirt-cuff', in order to remind him of his humble origins. Today the area is London's neon heart, full of bright lights, traffic and enough video games to last a lifetime.

Trocadero

Piccadilly Circus, WC1
t (0906) 888 1100
www.troc.co.uk
⊖ Piccadilly Circus, Leicester Square
Bus 3, 12, 14, 19, 22, 38

Can you spot?
The Alpine Clock on top of the Swiss Tourist Office. It springs into life at 6pm every day when various clockwork figures come out to parade and dance to the accompaniment of bells and chimes.

Can you spot?

Engraved on a series of brass plaques in Leicester Square's garden (central cobbled area) are the distances in miles from London to all the Commonwealth countries. See who's the quickest to find the distance to the following:

▶ Ottawa in Canada – 3,332 miles

▶ Jamaica – 4,684 miles

▶ Kenya – 4,237 miles

Open Sun–Thurs 10am–12 midnight, Fri–Sat 10am–1am
Free
Some wheelchair access. Suitable for ages 10–15. Allow at least 2hrs

Originally a plush hotel, the Trocadero has been revamped in recent years into a large and very noisy arcade-cum-electronic entertainment centre. It is filled with souvenir shops and fast-food restaurants, not to mention a seven-screen cinema and its biggest draw, Funland – six floors of the latest computer games.

Funland

t (020) 7439 1914
Open Daily 10am–12 midnight, Fri and Sat till 1am
Free
Fast-food restaurants

It may advertise itself as a giant indoor theme park, but Funland is essentially just a giant amusement arcade with six floors of flashing, beeping video games to explore – shoot-'em-ups, fighting games, flight simulators and racing games – interspersed with various 3-D simulator rides as well as a few more traditional attractions such as pool tables, putting, 10-pin bowling, dodgems, etc.

Don't be fooled by the free entry signs. Each video game costs at least £1 and each of the seven 3D rides, £2-£3 (there are small savings to be made by buying a combined ticket to several rides).

Tip *The noise and flashing lights may make it a little overwhelming for very young children. Older children (teenagers in particular), however, will love it.*

Leicester Square

Flanked by four giant cinemas, Leicester Square is *the* place in London to catch a film. This is where all the major film premières are staged and where all the biggest releases get their first runs. Once a fashionable 19th-century meeting place with a Turkish bath, music and dance halls, the square is today (if we're honest) a bit tacky with its souvenir shops, chain restaurants, portrait painters and buskers. Still, the central garden offers some shade on a hot sunny day and you can buy half price tickets for West End shows at the TKTs booth.

Leicester Square Cinemas

Empire
t 0870 010 2030
www.uci-cinemas.co.uk
Odeon Leicester Square and Odeon West End
t 0870 505 0007
www.odeon.co.uk
Warner Village West End
t 0870 240 6020
www.warnervillage.co.uk

WHERE TO EAT

Picnics & snacks

Though the featured area is choc-à-bloc full of fast-food restaurants, cafés and pizza bars, do also remember (particularly if it's a sunny day) that it's also within walking distance of two of the city's best picnic spots – **Green Park** and **St James's Park**. Upmarket supplies, befitting a picnic in a royal park, can be picked up from **Fortnum & Mason's** terribly grand food halls, 181 Piccadilly, W1, t (020) 7734 8040, ⊖ Piccadilly Circus. Less expensive fare is available from **Lina's Stores** Italian delicatessen, 11 Brewer Street, W1, t (020) 7437 6482, ⊖ Tottenham Court Road; the French delicatessen/bakery/patisserie **Truc Vert**, 42 North Audley Street, W1, t (020) 7491 9988, ⊖ Bond Street; **Fresh and Wild** organic food halls, 69–75 Brewer Street, W1, t (020) 7344 3179, ⊖ Tottenham Court Road; and **Tesco Metro**, 311 Oxford Street, W1, ⊖ Bond Street. You can also bring a picnic to eat in the National Gallery's Education Centre's sandwich rooms.

In **Leicester Square**, try **Café Fiori** on the corner of Leicester Square and Charing Cross Road, while if in or around **Trafalgar Square** head either up to the top floor café of the **National Portrait Gallery**, St Martin's Place, WC2, t (020) 7306 0055, ⊖ Leicester Square, which offers wonderful views of the square, or down to the **Café in the Crypt** (see p.225) below St Martin-in-the-Fields church, t (020) 7839 4342, ⊖ Charing Cross. If you fancy a cheap pasta, you could try **Pollo** (see p.225), 20 Old Compton Street, W1, t (020) 7734 5917, ⊖ Leicester Square, slightly further up in Soho. **Piccadilly Circus** can offer little except a very crowded branch of **Burger King**, although if you're in the area, you might want to make your way to the **Fortnum & Mason Fountain Room** (see p.231), 181 Piccadilly, t (020) 7734 8040, ⊖ Piccadilly Circus, a wonderfully elegant tea room set in the basement of the Queen's grocers. It's a haven of old-fashioned style and charm, suitable for older children, or you could splash out on tea at the **Ritz Hotel** (see p.231), 150 Piccadilly, W1, t (020) 7493 8181, ⊖ Green Park. Burgers and happy meals are available at various branches of **McDonald's** at 5 Swiss Court, Leicester Square, ⊖ Leicester Square, 57–60 Haymarket, ⊖ Piccadilly Circus, 69–73 Shaftesbury Avenue ⊖ Leicester Square, and 34–35 The Strand (next to Charing Cross Station). You'll also find branches of the bistro chain **Café Flo** at 103 Wardour Street, t (020) 7734 0581, ⊖ Piccadilly Circus, and 11 Haymarket, t (020) 7734 0581, ⊖ Piccadilly Circus, Charing Cross.

Restaurants

1 Benihana
37–43 Sackville Street, W1
t (020) 7494 2525
www.benihana.co.uk
⊖ Piccadilly Circus, Green Park
Open Wed–Fri 12 noon–3, Mon–Fri 6–11, Sat–Sun 12 noon–11

2 Café Rouge
15 Frith Street
t (020) 7437 4307
www.caferouge.co.uk
⊖ Leicester Square, Tottenham Court Road
Open 10am–11pm daily

3 Caffè Uno
24 Charing Cross Road, WC2
t (020) 7240 2524,
www.caffeuno.co.uk

⊖ Charing Cross, Leicester Square
Open 11am–11pm daily

4/5 Pizza Express

20 Greek Street, W1
t (020) 7734 7430
⊖ Leicester Square
6 Upper James Street, Golden Square, W1
t (020) 7437 4550
⊖ Piccadilly Circus
www.pizzaexpress.co.uk
Open 11.30–12 midnight, daily

6 Pizza Piazza

39 Charing Cross Road, WC2
t (020) 7437 1686
www.pizzapiazza.co.uk
⊖ Leicester Square
Open 11.30am–12 midnight, daily

7 Planet Hollywood

13 Coventry Street, W1
t (020) 7734 6220
www.planet-hollywood.demon.co.uk
⊖ Leicester Square, Piccadilly Circus
Open Mon–Sat 11.30am–1.30am, Sun
11.30am–12.30am

8 Rainforest Café

20 Shaftesbury Avenue, W1
t (020) 7434 3111
www.therainforestcafé.co.uk
⊖ Leicester Square, Piccadilly Circus
Bus 3, 12, 14, 19, 22, 38
Open 12 noon–11 daily, Fri–Sat 12 noon– 12 midnight

9 Texas Embassy Cantina

1 Cockspur Street, SW1
t (020) 7925 0077
www.texasembassy.com
⊖ Charing Cross
Open Mon–Thurs 12 noon–11, Fri–Sat 12 noon–12
midnight, Sun 12 noon–10.30pm

10 TGI Friday's

29 Coventry Street, W1
t (020) 7379 6262
www.tgifridays.co.uk
⊖ Piccadilly Circus
Open Mon–Thurs 12 noon–11.30, Fri 12 noon–12
midnight, Sat 11am–12 midnight, Sun 12 noon–11

11 Veeraswamy

99–101 Regent Street, W1

t (020) 7734 1401
www.veeraswamy.com
⊖ Piccadilly Circus
Open Mon–Fri 12.30–2.30 and 5.30–11.30, Sat
12.30–3 and 5.30–11.30, Sun 12.30–3 and 6–10

Chinatown

The pedestrianized Gerrard Street, just north of
Leicester Square, along with the adjacent Lisle
Street, makes up London's Chinatown district.

It's a fascinating place to go for a meal or just to
explore with its decorative lamps and phone boxes
made up to look like oriental pagodas. Every
Chinese New Year (late January or early February)
paper dragons dance down the street as part of a
week of traditional celebrations.

12 China, China

3 Gerrard Street, W1
t (020) 7439 7502
⊖ Leicester Square

13 Royal Dragon

30 Gerrard Street, W1
t (020) 7734 1388
⊖ Leicester Square

14 Chuen Cheng Ku

17 Wardour Street, W1
t 020 7437 1398
⊖ Leicester Square

15 New World

1 Gerrard Place, W1
t (020) 7734 0396
⊖ Leicester Square

See **Eat** p.249 for more details on the above
restaurants.
See map on p.65 for the locations of the restaurants numbered above.

Covent Garden

Covent Garden is lively and entertaining, but also rather cultured and sophisticated. In other words, children will enjoy themselves and parents won't feel guilty about letting them.

There's lots for kids to do here; they can clamber aboard a vintage bus at the London Transport Museum, dress up at the Theatre Museum or enjoy the ad hoc entertainment provided by the buskers outside in the Piazza. Spend a Saturday morning here and you're bound to encounter at least one impromtu performance from the army of mime artists, fire-eaters, comedians and opera singers that frequent the area. There are also two small markets to rummage around in and various toy and gift shops designed to attract the fancy of children, as well as the wallets of their indulgent parents.

Highlights

Somerset House's fountains/ice rink

The buskers on Covent Garden's Piazza

Messing around on the buses at London's Transport Museum

Key

Numbers correspond to restaurants in 'Where To Eat', p.86

HIGH HOLBORN

CHANCERY LANE

Holborn

Sir John Soane's Museum

LINCOLN'S INN

FIELDS

GT QUEEN STREET

KINGSWAY

Oasis Sports Centre

ENDELL STREET

DRURY LANE

SHAFTESBURY AVENUE

NEAL STREET

NEAL'S YARD

MONMOUTH STREET

SHELTON STREET

❶

LONG ACRE

❼

BOW STREET

RUSSELL STREET

ALDWYCH

❻

Covent Garden

FLORAL STREET

Royal Opera House

WELLINGTON STREET

❹

STRAND

❸

KING STREET

Covent Garden Market

The Piazza

Theatre Museum

GARRICK ST

St Paul's Church

London's Transport Museum

Somerset House

Temple

❽

❷

Leicester Square

ST MARTIN'S LANE

BEDFORD ST

MAIDEN LANE

WC

WC

❺

❿

❾

STRAND

EMBANKMENT

The Savoy

VICTORIA

WATERLOO BRIDGE

WC

Charing Cross

Cleopatra's Needle

National Theatre

NORTHUMBERLAND AVENUE

Embankment

WC

300 metres
300 yards

London's Transport Museum

Covent Garden, WC2
t (020) 7379 6344
www.ltmuseum.co.uk
⊖ Covent Garden/Leicester Square
Bus 6, 9, 11, 13, 15, 23, 77A, 91, 176
Open 10–6 daily, except Fri when it opens at 11am
Adm Adults £5.95, children **free**, concs £4.50
Wheelchair accessible, with adapted toilets
Suitable for all ages
Allow at least 2hrs.

This is a great, child-friendly museum which
neatly combines education (tracing the history of
public transport from 1829 to the present day) with
activity – there are buttons to push, levers to pull
and exhibits to clamber over. Housed in a huge iron
and glass structure (a flower market from the
1870s to 1974), the museum possesses a wonderful,

Did you know?

▶ That in 1900 there were 50,000 horses working
on the London Transport network. Every day, they
helped to transport more than 2,000,000 passengers and left behind over 1,000 tonnes of dung on
London's streets.
▶ That since 1910 over 15 billion passengers have
travelled on London's buses. That's 3 times the
population of the world.
▶ That Victoria is one of Britain's busiest train
stations, with over 86,000,000 passengers a year.
▶ That when London's first Underground line (the
Metropolitan) opened in 1863, the carriages were
pulled by steam trains and the passengers rode in
open-topped wagons. By the end of the journey,
the passengers' faces were usually covered in soot
and smoke.
▶ That in the late 19th century all motorists were
expected to employ someone to walk in front of
their car waving a red flag, so as to prevent anyone
from being run over. The practise was ended in
1896 when the speed limit was raised from 4mph
to 20mph – travelling at that speed, the first
person the car would run over would presumably
be whoever was brave or foolish enough to hold
the flag.

colourful collection of horse-drawn and motorized
trams, buses and trolley cars.

There are 15 hands-on Kids' Zones where children
can find out about the history of transport on
touch screens, take the wheel on a Tube or bus
simulator or hop aboard the Fun Bus (specifically
designed for the under-5s) which sports a see-
through engine and soft play area. A roster of
costumed actors, playing a variety of transport
characters including a First World War bus cleaner,
a Second World War bus conductor and a thirties
tram driver, are on hand to offer information and

Question 7
How many bus stops are there in London?
a) 1,000?
b) 7,000?
c) 17,000?
answer on p.249

advice. The museum has a special learning centre equipped with computers where you can browse the museum website, listen to oral histories and view London Transport films. It also organizes a number of child-orientated special events, such as 2003's 'Adventures Underground', an interactive exhibition designed to teach kids about working on the Tube.

Theatre Museum

Russell Street, WC2
t (020) 7943 4700
www.theatremuseum.org
⊖ Covent Garden/Leicester Square
Bus 6, 9, 11, 13, 15, 23, 77A, 91, 176
Open Tues–Sat 10–6
Free
Wheelchair accessible, with adapted toilets
Suitable for all ages
Allow at least 1hr

The name of the museum is a little misleading. It's dedicated to all aspects of the performing arts, so there are displays on ballet, circus, opera, pop music and magic (you can see the wheelbarrow that the legendary tightrope walker Charles Blondin wheeled across the Niagara Falls in 1859), but there's no doubt that it's theatre and drama which take centre stage. The museum is big on interaction, putting on a daily programme of free workshops and demonstrations where kids can learn how to operate puppets, try on costumes and even walk out on to a stage. Theatrical make-up demonstrations, where you can learn how to make a huge gaping fake scar, are given at 11.30am, 1pm, 2.30pm, 3.30pm and 4.30pm, and there are guided tours (usually given by a wonderfully overwrought professional actor) at 12 noon, 2pm and 5.30pm when, depending on what's showing, you may also be able to take a tour of the nearby Theatre Royal and Drury Lane Theatre. A free theatre workshop club aimed at kids aged 8–12 runs on Saturday mornings (pre-booking is essential as there are only 15 spaces), while their younger siblings can enjoy storytellings (again free) on the first Saturday of every month, as well as on Wednesdays and Fridays in the school holidays.

Question 8
What were decency boards and where would you find them?
answer on p.249

Street performers

Some of the capital's most talented and exuberant street performers strut their stuff at Covent Garden. The approach to the Tube station is usually occupied by a spray-painted mime artist or two, while on the lower levels of the shopping area you will often encounter highly skilled classical and jazz musicians belting out tunes with merry abandon. The proximity to the newly refurbished Royal Opera House means you'll also occasionally find a plain-clothes Carmen or two warbling powerfully. Children who've never heard opera in the raw before will be impressed by the sheer volume of noise produced by these sturdy divas.

The main performing space, however, is the Piazza, in front of St Paul's Church, where some of London's great physical comedians come to ply their trade. You may even spot a star of the future wobbling on his or her unicycle or juggling with fire. This was where comedian Eddie Izzard made his living before he became famous.

On weekends large crowds gather to watch a steady stream of jugglers, mime artists, fire-eaters, unicyclists and escapologists. All the children stream to the front, eager to help out by throwing

Tell me a story: **Covent Garden**

Covent Garden was once part of a great estate owned by the Earls of Beford. Formerly a convent garden (hence the name, the 'n' ceased to be pronounced over time), it came under the ownership of the first Earl during the dissolution of the monasteries in 1552, and was turned into the city's very first square in 1630 by the fourth Earl, who instructed his architect, Inigo Jones, to follow the design of the classical Italian piazza.

Initially inhabited by high society, it became home, for much of its existence, to the capital's great wholesale 'fruit 'n' veg' and flower markets. In 1974, however, the markets relocated to Vauxhall and the square underwent a genteel facelift. The market buildings were transformed into al fresco cafés, chic boutiques and stylish museums, while the square's pedestrianized confines were reborn as a sort of semi-bohemian crafts centre. Today, these gently cobbled streets and shopping arcades are perhaps London's closest approximation of European café culture.

a juggling club, secure some handcuffs or take part in a seemingly death-defying stunt. The masses on the balcony of the Punch and Judy pub overlooking the Piazza offer constant encouragement (and criticism). Remember, these people are not paid to perform and depend on the generosity of the audience. A £1 coin (around $1.50) is usually considered an appropriate donation.

St Paul's Church

Open Mon 9.30–2.30, Tues–Fri 9.30–4.30 and for services on Sunday. The entrance is around the corner through the rose garden

Bordering the Covent Garden Piazza, this is one of the few major buildings in London to survive the Great Fire of London in 1666. Its proximity to the theatres of the West End has gained it the nickname of the 'Actors Church'. If you've seen the film *My Fair Lady*, take a look at the front of St Paul's

Church, the place where the film's two principal characters, Professor Henry Higgins and the Covent Garden flower-seller Eliza Doolittle, are meant to have first met.

Royal Opera House

Bow Street, WC2
t (020) 7304 4000
www.royaloperahouse.org
⊖ Covent Garden/Leicester Square
Bus 6, 9, 11, 13, 15, 23, 77A, 91, 176
Open Tours: Mon–Sat at 10.30am, 12.30pm and 2.30pm
Adm Tours: adult £8, child £7
Wheelchair accessible, with adapted toilets

The magnificently revamped Royal Opera House probably doesn't rank too highly on most families' 'must-visit' list. Most kids, however, enjoy exploring buildings, which is exactly what they can do on a backstage tour given three times a day at 10.30am, 12.30pm and 2.30pm from Monday to Saturday (allow 1hr 30mins). These take in the magnificent concert hall itself, the orchestra pit, the dressing rooms and the costume production department. In fact, these days the Royal Opera House is a good deal more family-friendly than it once was. In an effort to welcome more of the population to opera, public exhibitions and free classical concerts are now staged in its foyer.

Can you spot?

The French-born Claude Duval was one of 17th-century London's most successful and famous highwaymen, holding up hundreds of stage-coaches during his career. He was particularly renowned for the daring nature of his robberies and the gallantry and charm he displayed toward his female victims – many of whom were said to have fallen in love with him. He was hanged in 1670. See if you can find the floor stone in St Paul's on which is written a four-line poem dedicated to this dandy highwayman. It reads:

*Here lies Du Vall: Reader, if male thou art,
Look to thy purse, if female to thy heart...
Old Tyburn's glory, England's
illustrious thief,
Du Vall, the ladies' joy, Du Vall
the ladies' grief...*

There are also six 'School Matineés' a year (tickets only £5 for children and adults), with opera and ballet performances for schools and colleges. Information packs for teachers are available ahead of concerts online at **www**.royaloperahouse.org.

The Jump Zone

Open Summer weekends
Adm £6 for 10mins

The 'Jump Zone' is erected on summer weekends on the eastern side of the piazza next to the Royal Opera House. Essentially, it's a set of four 'bungee trampolines' (you jump on a trampoline attached to a bungy cable) on which your kids can bounce themselves silly over the course of a 10-minute session. There's also a climbing wall and one of those plastic globe things that you sit in while you're spun over and around and up and down (until it stops or you're sick, whichever comes first).

Its museums and street performers aside, Covent Garden is known principally for its shopping. It boasts a number of places that will appeal to families, including a branch of Hamleys, Peter Rabbit & Friends (a shop dedicated to Beatrix Potter's furry creations), a Disney Store, the Candle Shop, 3D Crystal Images and Thornton's chocolate makers. Also look out for the London Dolls House Company, on the lower level of the market building, which contains an amazing and expensive, collection of miniature houses, each a perfect recreation of period style – from Georgian and Victorian to Art Nouveau and Modern. There are stacks of furniture and accessories for the discerning small-house buyer.

Benjamin Pollock's Toy Shop

44 Covent Garden Market, WC2
t (020) 7379 7880
www.pollocks-coventgarden.co.uk
⊖ Covent Garden/Leicester Square
Bus 6, 9, 11, 13, 15, 23, 77a, 91, 176
Open Mon–Sat 10.30–6, Sun 12 noon–6

This lovely little shop (the sibling of Pollock's Toy Museum, *see* p.57), full of olde worlde toys and games, is a great place to take the kids in order to show them that not all toys need batteries and joysticks. Here you'll find hand-painted puppets, carved yo-yos, butterfly kites, dragon mobiles,

intricate paper planes and flying machines powered by ingenious rubber band technology. There are also kaleidoscopes, die-cast soldiers and musical boxes. Pride of place, however, goes to some exquisite replica paper theatre sets, complete with scale scenery and actors. You can buy home assembly kits – suitable for older, more dextrous children.

Apple Market
Open 9–5, daily

This cheerful weekday market occupies part of the old central market building. You'll find a wide variety of craft produce including hand-painted jewellery, knitwear and candles, and on Mondays there's a small antique market.

Jubilee Market
Jubilee Hall
Open 9.30–6, daily

Rebuilt in the 1980s on the site of the old foreign flower market, this deals mainly in tourist fare – Union Jack tea towels and the like. It is, however, a good place to hunt for cheap versions of the latest must-have toys.

3D Crystal Images
26a Covent Garden Market, WC2
t (020) 73799736
www.3dcrystalimages.com
Open Mon–Sat 10.30–7.30, Sun 10.30–6

Come here to pick up a novel souvenir. This new Covent Garden emporium creates what can best be described as three dimensional portraits. A clever computer process scans your 3D image into a block of crystal where it is preserved for posterity. It's undeniably clever, if a bit odd.

Neal Street and Neal's Yard

North of the square past the Tube station and Long Acre lies the real heart of Covent Garden's shopping district. Neal Street, and its surrounding roads, have in recent years become an attraction in their own right, with a flourishing collection of funky fashion boutiques, health food stores and novelty shops. This whole area has a distinctly bohemian vibe attracting a motley collection of punters (not to mention buskers and street performers) on weekends, when it has an atmosphere more akin to a thriving market than a traditional shopping street. Look out, in particular, for The Kite Store, at no. 48, which sells just about every shape and colour kite imaginable, from super-speedy stunt numbers to novelty kites, and, at no. 76, Comic Showcase, one of the capital's best sources of 'graphic novels'. The Tintin Shop, dedicated to the comic adventures of the Belgian boy detective, is a couple of roads away at 34 Floral Street. You might also like to pay a visit to Neal's Yard, just around the corner. This little, alternative-lifestyle Utopia between Long Acre and Floral Street is filled with vegetarian restaurants, health food shops, alternative therapy outlets, herbal treatment stores and world music stockists.

Other notable stores in the area include the Dorling Kindersley shop on King Street – they publish a wide range of high-quality children's books. For clothes, there's a branch of Baby Gap/Kids Gap on Long Acre and, if you fancy splashing out on an item or two of mini-high fashion, Paul Smith for Children on Floral Street. And should you need that little extra adornment there's always the Bead Shop at 21a Tower Street (behind Cambridge Circus), whose shelves are filled with coloured baubles and necklaces.

If you (or perhaps more pertinently your kids) need to take rest from shopping, head to the north end of Neal Street, past Shaftesbury Avenue to Stacey Street where you'll find Phoenix Garden, a lovely little park built on the site of a car park and filled with flowers and wildlife.

The Candle Shop
30 The Market, Covent Garden, WC2
t (020) 7439 4220
www.candlesontheweb.co.uk
Bus 6, 9, 11, 13, 15, 23, 77A, 91, 176
Open Mon–Fri & Sun 10, Sat 10

Hamleys
3 The Market, Covent Garden, WC2
t (020) 7240 4646
www.hamleys.com
Open Mon–Wed, Fri & Sat 10–7, Thurs 10–8, Sun 12 noon–6

Did you know?
The world's first postage stamp, the Penny Black, was introduced in 1840. Previously, the cost of sending a letter was born by the recipient rather than the sender. You can see an example of a Penny Black in the well-stocked Stanley Gibbons stamp emporium (see p.237).

Peter Rabbit & Friends
42 The Market, Covent Garden, WC2
t (020) 7497 1777
www.peterrabbit.com
Open Mon–Sat 10–6

The London Dolls House Company
29 The Market, Covent Garden, WC2
t (020) 7240 8681
www.london-dolls-house.sagenet.co.uk
Open Mon–Sat 10–7, Sun 12 noon–5

The Tintin Shop
34 Floral Street, WC2
t (020) 7836 1131
www.thetintinshop.uk.com
Open Mon–Sat 10–5.30

See **Shop** p.236 for more details on the above shops.

Drury Lane & Bow Street

You could pay a visit to the Drury Lane Gardens, a small enclosed open space for the under-5s with various climbing frames and soft rubbery floors. There are several benches where parents can sit and watch their charges – recommended on sunny days. Built in 1877, this was one of London's first public gardens and was constructed, on the recommendation of the public health reformer Edwin Chadwick, on a former burial ground. Bow Street, one of London's most famous streets, is just east of Covent Garden, while nearby is the architectural oddity of Sir John Soane's Museum, home to a bizarre collection of art and curiosities. After a heavy day's sightseeing, you could cool off with a dip in the Oasis Sports Centre Pool, at 32 Endell Street, just to the north of Covent Garden, WC2, **t** (020) 7831 1804 (*see* p.186).

Sir John Soane's Museum
12–14 Lincoln's Inn Fields, WC2
t (020) 405 2107
www.soane.org
⊖ Holborn
Open Tues–Sat 10–5, til 9pm on first Tues of each month
Free

Situated on Lincoln's Inn Fields, this wonderful museum is made up of three interlinked houses that were once the home of Sir John Soane, the celebrated 18th-century architect (he designed the

original Bank of England building) and collector *extraordinaire*. Inside, it's a real treasure trove. You'll find statues, Egyptian relics, toys, models of buildings, artworks (including a collection of lively Hogarth cartoons – follow the 'Rake's Progress' from wealthy young ne'er-do-well to the madhouse) and jewellery. Everything, in fact, that caught Sir John's eye. Indeed, inveterate horder that he was, his collection grew so big that he was eventually forced to turn his house into a museum.

The museum runs free art workshops for children aged 7–13 during the school holidays. Call **t** 020 7440 4247 for more details.

The Strand & Embankment

⊖ Embankment, Charing Cross
Bus 6, 9, 11, 13, 15, 23, 77a, 91, 176

The Strand, one of London's most famous thoroughfares, runs east from Trafalgar Square just to the south of Covent Garden. Here you'll find the world-famous Savoy Hotel with its elegant tea room, the newly restored Somerset House and the Stanley Gibbons stamp emporium – a must for young stamp collectors everywhere. Determined accumulators should also consider paying a visit to the Charing Cross Collectors' Fair, which is held every Saturday from 8am–4pm in the basement of the PriceWaterhouseCoopers car park on Villiers Street behind Charing Cross Station. Here, as well as stamps and first day covers, you'll find hordes of ancient Roman and British coins for sale.

Until 1860, the great mansions on the Strand's southern side faced on to the Thames. The constant threat of flooding and disease, however (in 1849 over 2,000 people a week were dying of cholera), forced the authorities to construct the Victoria Embankment as a buffer. Today, the Embankment is flanked by a four-lane carriageway and is, in truth, rather gloomy, although its sightseeing potential has been considerably increased by the creation of the new Hungeford Footbridge which links the Charing Cross end of the Embankment with the South Bank Centre and offers great view up and down the river. It stands next to Cleopatra's Needle, a 50ft tall, 1,500-year-old Egyptian monument erected here in 1879 (*see opposite*). There is also an embarkation point for a sightseeing catamaran here that will take you east along the river as far as Greenwich.

Somerset House

The Strand, WC2
t (020) 7845 4600
www.somerset-house.org.uk
⊖ Temple, Charing Cross, Embankment, Covent Garden
Bus 6, 9, 11, 13, 15, 23, 77a, 91, 176
Open 10–6 daily
Adm Entry to Somerset House, the Courtyard and the River Terrace is **free**; Courtauld Gallery: adult £5, child **free**, concs £4; Gilbert Collection: adult £5, child **free**, concs £4, joint ticket adult £9; Hermitage Rooms: adult £6, child £4
Wheelchair accessible, with adapted toilets

Rather overlooked during the Millennium year, what with all the hoopla surrounding the Dome,

the Eye and the Millennium Bridge, the re-opening of Somerset House has, in its way, been more impressive than any of them, particularly for families. Closed to the public for nearly a century, it is now once again possible to explore one of London's great riverside palaces. The building you see today is in fact an 18th-century construction erected on the site of the original Tudor palace built for the Duke of Somerset, and has, over the course of its history, served a variety of functions. It was home to the Navy Board and Inland Revenue and, most famously of all, was for a long time occupied by the Register of Births, Marriages and Deaths. Following a multi-million pound refurbishment, however, its grand wings now provide venues for three outstanding artistic attractions: the Courtauld Gallery, which has a large collection of Impressionist and post-Impressionist paintings (including Van Gogh's *Bandaged Ear*); the Hermitage Rooms, where Russian imperial treasures from the State Hermitage Museum in St Petersburg are displayed; and the Gilbert Collection of jewellery, silverware and other assorted treasures donated by the late American collector and philanthropist, Arthur Gilbert (use the family-friendly 'Royal Trail Guide' to find your way around the dazzling treasures). Interesting though these are, it's the building itself which is the real attraction, with its wonderful river views (particularly from the River Terrace, which is linked by a walkway to Waterloo Bridge) and glorious courtyard, set, in summer with dozens of water jets that have been specially programmed to put on choreographed displays. Dotted with benches, it's a great place to have a picnic. The New York-style ice rink installed here each Christmas is a particularly nice touch.

Refreshment is available at the very grand (and expensive) Admiralty restaurant, the much more relaxed River Terrace Café Bar or the takeaway delicatessen next to the Seaman's Hall. The Courtauld Institute organizes various weekend workshops when kids can take part in a range of activities, such as 'making a silver goblet' and 'animal safaris'. You can also meet strolling players in the courtyard, take part in tours or simply pick up a free family trail guide at the main desk.

Cleopatra's Needle

Cleopatra's Needle, a 50-ft tall, 1,500-year-old Egyptian obelisk, is one of London's odder monuments. When first you see it, plonked somewhat haphazardly in the gloomy surrounds of the Victoria Embankment, your immediate thought is 'why couldn't they have found somewhere nicer to put it?. But, truth be told, it's a wonder they got it here at all. Bequeathed to Britain in 1819, by Mohammad Ali, the Turkish Viceroy of Egypt, it took over 59 years to get to its present site. At first, no one could work out how to move it and then, when an engineer did devise a means of transport using an iron cylindrical pontoon, it very nearly sank. The intended site for the obelisk, near the Houses of Parliament, turned out to be unsuitable because of subsidence, forcing the Board of Works, whose responsibility the needle had become, hurriedly to find a new spot for it on the Victoria Embankment. To top it all, the sphinxes sitting at the needle's base are facing the wrong way.

Buried beneath the Needle are two time capsules. They contain a picture of Queen Victoria, several newspapers, four Bibles, a railway guide and photographs of (allegedly) the 12 prettiest girls in Britain at the time.

Stanley Gibbons

399 The Strand, WC2
t (020) 7836 8444
www.stanleygibbons.com
Open Mon–Fri 9–5.30, Sat 9.30–5.30
The world's oldest stamp dealers is a collector's paradise, selling everything imaginable for the Philatelist.

Boat trips

Bateaux London–Catamaran Cruisers

t (020) 7925 2215
www.bateauxlondon.com
Times April–Oct cruises depart every 30mins between 10.30–4, Nov–Mar cruises depart every 45mins between 10.30 and 3
See p.23 for more details.

Picnics & snacks

If you know where to look, you can find the odd nook and cranny suitable for an alfresco meal in the area. Good spots include **Embankment Gardens** (there's also a small café), Phoenix Gardens, the churchyard of St Paul's Church and Somerset House's courtyard. For supplies, go to **Neal's Yard**, WC2, just north of Covent Garden for **Neal's Yard Bakery**, at no.6, **t** (020) 7836 5199, and **Neal's Yard Dairy** neaby at 17 Shorts Gardens, WC2, **t** (020) 7240 5700, ⊖ **Covent Garden**. There are also branches of **Marks & Spencer** at 107–115 Long Acre, WC2, **t** (020) 7240 9549, ⊖ **Covent Garden**, and a **Tesco Metro** at 22–25 Bedford Street, ⊖ **Covent Garden**.

Watch the world go by in Covent Garden! Try **Fuelbar**, **t** (020) 7836 2187, which can offer ringside seats for the daily entertainment on the Piazza. More wholesome fare can be found at **Food for Thought** (see p.233), 31 Neal Street, WC2, **t** (020) 7836 0239, a cheap and friendly vegetarian café (it can get crowded, so turn up early for lunch) and the **World Food Café**, 14 Neal's Yard, WC2, **t** (020) 7379 0298. For fast food, try **McDonald's** at 68 St Martin's Lane, WC2, ⊖ **Leicester Square**, or the **Rock and Soul Plaice** (see p.226), 47 Endell Street, WC2, **t** (020) 7836 3785, ⊖ **Covent Garden**, the oldest fish and chip shop in the capital, and still one of the best – serving large portions of battered fish and chunky chips. Sticky treats are available from fancy, French patisserie, **Paul**, at 29 Bedford Street, WC2, **t** (020) 7836 3304, ⊖ **Covent Garden**.

Restaurants

1 Belgo Centraal

50 Earlham Street, WC2
t (020) 7813 2233
www.belgo-restaurants.com
⊖ Covent Garden
Open Mon–Thurs 12 noon–11.30, Fri and Sat 12 noon–12 midnight, Sun 12 noon–10.30

2 Brown's

82–84 St Martin's Lane, WC2
t (020) 7497 5050
⊖ Leicester Square, Covent Garden
Open 12 noon–12 midnight daily

3 Calabash

Africa Centre, 8 King Street, WC2

t (020) 7836 1936
⊖ Covent Garden
Open Mon–Fri 12.30–3 & 6–11

4 Café Rouge

34 Wellington Street, WC2
t (020) 7836 0998
www.caferouge.co.uk
⊖ Covent Garden
Open 10am–11pm daily

5 Caffé Uno

37 St Martin's Lane, WC2
t (020) 7836 0998
www.caffeuno.co.uk
⊖ Leicester Square
Open 11am–11pm daily

6 Maxwell's

8/9 James Street, WC2
t (020) 7836 0303
⊖ Covent Garden
Open Mon–Sat 10am–12 midnight, Sun 10am–11.30pm

7/8 Pizza Express

Branches at: 9–12 Bow Street, WC2, **t** (020) 7240 3443, ⊖ Covent Garden; 80–81 St Martins Lane, WC2, **t** (020) 7836 8001, ⊖ Covent Garden, Leicester Square
www.pizzaexpress.co.uk
Open 11.30am–12 midnight, daily

9 Smollensky's

105 The Strand
t (020) 7497 2101
www.smollenskys.co.uk
⊖ Embankment, Charing Cross
Open Mon-Wed 12 noon–12 midnight, Thurs–Sat 12 noon–12.30am, Sun 12 noon–5.30 and 6.30–11

10 TGI Friday's

6 Bedford Street, WC2
t (020) 7379 0585
www.tgifridays.co.uk
⊖ Covent Garden, Leicester Square, Charing Cross
Open Mon–Sat 12 noon–11.30, Sun 12 noon–11

See **Eat** p.224 for more details on the above restaurants.
See map on p.77 for the locations of the restaurants numbered above.

Buckingham Palace

This is picture postcard London at its finest – an elegant, tree-lined boulevard leading down to the magnificent regal architecture of Buckingham Palace where, as every schoolchild knows, the Queen lives, and where you can take a guided tour in summer. Afterwards, why not have a picnic and run around in one of the two great parks flanking the palace, or head to Horse Guards Parade to see the Queen's chocolate-box soldiers parading up and down, before taking a stroll along the nearby King's Road with its fabulous shops and restaurants?

SLOANE SQUARE

Sloan Squar

KINGS ROAD

LWR SLOANE ST

1 2 3 4
5 6 9

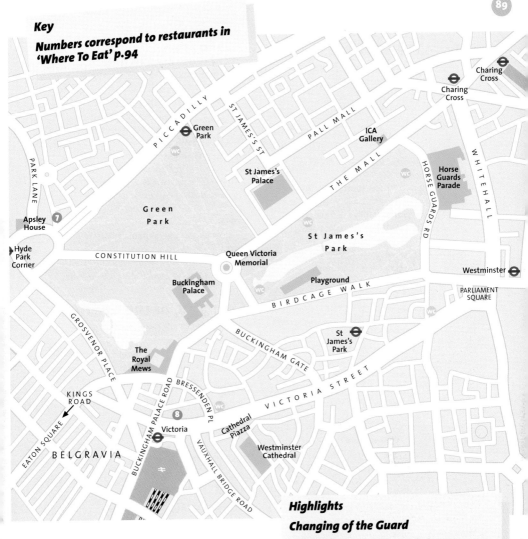

Key

Numbers correspond to restaurants in 'Where To Eat' p.94

Charing Cross

Charing Cross

PICCADILLY

Green Park

ST JAMES'S ST

PALL MALL

ICA Gallery

St James's Palace

THE MALL

Horse Guards Parade

WHITEHALL

PARK LANE

Green Park

HORSE GUARDS RD

Apsley House ⑦

St James's Park

Hyde Park Corner

CONSTITUTION HILL

Queen Victoria Memorial

Playground

Westminster

Buckingham Palace

BIRDCAGE WALK

PARLIAMENT SQUARE

GROSVENOR PLACE

The Royal Mews

BUCKINGHAM GATE

St James's Park

KINGS ROAD

BUCKINGHAM PALACE ROAD

BRESSENDEN PL

VICTORIA STREET

EATON SQUARE

⑧

Victoria

Cathedral Piazza

VAUXHALL BRIDGE ROAD

Westminster Cathedral

BELGRAVIA

Highlights

Changing of the Guard

Following in Wellington's footsteps at Apsley House

Seeing the squirrels in Green Park

Video screens at The Hard Rock Café

Buckingham Palace

St James's Park, SW1. The ticket office for purchasing tickets on the day is located in Green Park at Canada Gate
t Booking line (020) 7766 7300/1
www.royal.gov.uk
St James's Park, Green Park, Victoria
Bus 7, 11, 139, 211, C1, C10
Open Early Aug–Sept 9.30–5.30 daily (last entry 4.15)
Adm Buckingham Palace: adult £12, child (under 17) £6, under-5s **free**; Queen's Gallery: adult £6.50, child £3, under-5s **free**, family £16. There is a £1 booking fee for tickets booked online or over the phone
Wheelchair accessible
Suitable for older children (10 and over)
The tour lasts 45mins

It's all change at the palace. Previously the very private London residence of the Royal Family, the famous 19th-century palace has, since 1993, been opening its doors to the public for two months each summer. Or at least some of its doors; in fact the official guided tour takes in just 18 of a possible 600 rooms (plus a small section of the gardens). These include the Grand Hall, the Throne Room, the State Dining Room, the Music Room, the Royal Picture Gallery and the Silk Tapestry Room. All are quite splendid in a formal, rather haughty sort of way, although the Throne Room is a bit of a disappointment as it doesn't even contain a throne, just two pink and yellow chairs marked EIIR (Elizabeth Regina) and P (Philip). To be honest, the palace will proabably prove a little dull for most children. Many of the more interesting areas are (frustratingly) roped off and the rarefied 'don't touch' atmosphere is a little restrictive, not to say annoying. If it's just a little pomp and circumstance you're after, you would be better off watching the Changing of the Guard from the railings outside.

One new attraction which will be of interest to art fans has been the opening of the new Queen's Gallery on Buckingham Palace Road. Here you can see rotating displays taken from the extensive royal collection (lots of Old Masters), plus occasional touring exhibitions.

Remember, if the Union Flag is raised the Queen is at home; if it's lowered, she's elsewhere.

Tell me a story:
The house that John built

The first house to stand on this site was a modest dwelling built by John Sheffield, Duke of Buckingham in 1702, which was bought by the Royal Family in 1762. George IV thought it might be nice to improve the house, but then he and architect John Nash decided to knock it down and start again. So grand was the scheme that by the time George died in 1830, the new palace wasn't even finished. Parliament, worried about the cost, sacked Nash and gave the job to Edward Blore, who finished the job at the lowest price possible. Nearly the whole of Nash's work was covered with a new façade and his gateway was removed to become Marble Arch. Finally, in 1913, a new façade by the architect Sir Aston Webb replaced Blore's to produce the famous building we see today.

Changing of the Guard

St James's Park, Green Park, Victoria
Bus 1, 16, 24, 52, 73
Times The ceremony takes place every morning between April and August at 11.30 sharp, and on alternate days for the rest of the year
Free
Suitable for all ages
The ceremony lasts about 40mins

This daily costume drama has become a veritable symbol of Britishness attracting hundreds of tourists every day, and yet, it has to be said, it's just a teensy bit dull. To begin with it'll probably capture your interest – the rows of bearskinned, red-coated soldiers, the barked orders, the military band, the complex, regulated marching patterns but, after an hour of the stuff, you could be forgiven for wishing that they'd get to the point (which, in case you're wondering, is to replace the 40 men guarding Buckingham Palace with another contingent from Wellington Barracks). Nonetheless, it's extremely popular, and the views from outside Buckingham Palace can quickly become obscured. Even perched on your shoulders, kids may have trouble seeing. Your best bet for a glimpse of the marching soldiers is to take up one of the alternative vantage points at St James's or Birdcage Walk.

Horse Guards

London's own toy soldiers, the Horse Guards, are perhaps the most photographed military personel in the world. Sitting astride their horses in full dress uniform of red tunic, breastplate and sword, it's an image that has graced a million postcards. The stillness of the soldiers – both horse and man are trained not to move and to look straight ahead – fascinates children, who will try hard to pull the funniest face and break the soliders' concentration. At 11am every summer morning you can see them move as they march to Buckingham Palace for the

> **Can you spot?**
> A famous London monument. It's fairly hard to miss. It's 124-ft tall and supports a statue of George III's son Frederick, the Commander-in-Chief of the British forces during the Napoleonic Wars or, as he's more famously known, the Grand Old Duke of York – yes, that Grand Old Duke of York.

changing of the Guard. They also take part in a great military show in front of the Queen in early June known as The Trooping of the Colour. *See* 'London's Year' p.34.

The Royal Mews

Buckingham Palace Road, SW1
t (020) 7733 2331
www.royal.gov.uk
⊖ St James's Park, Green Park, Victoria
Bus 1, 16, 24, 52, 73
Open Mar–July and Oct 11–4 (last admission 3.15), Aug–Sept 10–5 (last admission 4.15)
Adm Adult £5, child (under 18) £2.50, concs £4
Wheelchair accessible, but call in advance. Suitable for ages 7 and over. Allow at least 1hr

These are the stables where the horses that work for the Royal Family are kept. As you would expect, the stalls themselves are rather magnificent, with tiled walls and gleaming horse brasses. You can touch and pet the horses and admire the beautiful

Question 8
How did Birdcage Walk, which borders St James's Park to the south, get its name?
answer on p.249

gold coach used for coronations – it's so heavy, it takes eight horses to pull it!

The Mall

The capital's most majestic avenue was built in the early 20th century as a memorial to Queen Victoria. It runs from Trafalgar Square to Buckingham Palace. Note the Victoria memorial in front of the Palace gates. The views from Admiralty Arch at the Trafalgar Square end, down the beautiful tree-lined sweep, are particularly impressive.

Double indemnity

In 1842, as Queen Victoria rode through crowds lining the Mall with her husband, Prince Albert, by her side, a man stepped forward out of the crowd and attempted to fire a shot at the Queen. Luckily for Victoria, the gun misfired. The police were unable to catch the culprit, so the incident was dropped. The very next day, however, the same thing happened again, except this time the gun did go off... Luckily for Victoria the bullet was a blank and caused no damage. The gunman, a John Francis, was arrested and sentenced to death, but was then granted a reprieve before execution.

ICA Gallery

The Mall, SW1
t (020) 7930 3647
www.ica.org.uk
⊖ Picadilly Circus, Charing Cross
Bus 2, 8, 9, 14, 16, 19, 22, 36, 38, 52, 73, 82
Open Galleries 12 noon–7.30
Adm Mon–Fri, adult £1.50, concs £1, Sat, Sun, adult £2.50, concs £1.50

The recently refurbished Institute for Contemporary Arts is generally more concerned with presenting arthouse films than entertaining families, but come summer there's plenty for 11–16 year olds to do. The institute runs a number of courses in web design, movie-making and computer game creation for younger visitors, as well as half-term workshops in drawing, sculpture, dance, animation and art history. The shop is good for arty bits and bobs, including original jewellery designs and gifts made by local artists.

Apsley House: The Wellington Museum

Hyde Park Corner, Piccadilly, W1
t (020) 7499 5676
www.apsleyhouse.org.uk
⊖ Hyde Park Corner
Bus 2, 8. 9, 10, 14, 16, 19, 22, 36, 38. 73, 82, 83, 137
Open Tues–Sun 11–5 , closed Mon
Adm Adult £4.50, under-18s **free**
Free entry to all on Waterloo Day (18th June). Sound guides, access via steps to house and lift

London's most singular address (it's officially known as No.1 London) was built by Robert Adam betweeen 1771 and 1778 and was home to the first Duke of Wellington (he of the famous boots and, indeed, famous defeat of Napoleon). It's still the family's London residence.

Ten rooms have been lovingly restored under the auspices of the Victoria and Albert Museum. The collection, assembled by the Duke following his triumphant return from the Battle of Waterloo, includes paintings by Goya, Velaquez, Van Dyck, Landseer and Rubens, as well as medals and memorabilia. Themed sound guides and trails for children (on subjects such as 'servants', 'society parties' and, of course, 'The Battle of Waterloo') are available throughout the year and there are special family-friendly activities organized for Museums and Galleries Month in May, on Waterloo Day in June and at Christmas.

Green Park

Piccadilly W1 & The Mall, SW1
t (020) 7930 1793
www.royalparks.gov.uk/green.htm
⊖ Green Park
Bus 2, 8, 9, 14, 16, 19, 22, 38, 52, 73, 82
Open Dawn till dusk, daily
Free

The most basic of London's Royal parks. The name says it all – this is a green park, with lots of lush grass and trees, but not much else: no pond, no playground, not even any statues. Nonetheless, it's a lovely serene place and very popular with London's children. Every spring, for a few weeks, it becomes a Yellow and Green Park when hordes of daffodils pop up.

St James's Park

The Mall, SW1
t (020) 7930 1793
www.royalparks.gov.uk/james.htm
⊖ St James's Park
Bus 3, 11, 12, 24, 53, 77A, 88, 109, 159, 211, X53
Open Dawn till dusk, daily
Free

A must for all bird-lovers. In the 17th century the park held several aviaries (hence the name of the road that runs alongside the park, Birdcage Walk) and today is home to one of London's finest wild-fowl ponds, a great stretch of water where you can find more than 20 species of bird including ducks, geese and even pelicans (housed in a special enclosure). There's also a playground with a sandpit and a teashop. If your kids have seen the film *One Hundred and One Dalmatians* (the live action version, not the cartoon), they may recognize certain parts of the park – it was the scene of the bicycle chase where poor old Pongo gets thrown into the lake. See if you can spot the black swans that nest on the pond's central island.

King's Road

Buckingham Palace and its adjacent park are just a short walk from the King's Road, one of the very best shopping streets in London. Here you'll find branches of the Early Learning Centre at no.36, the children's clothes shops Brora (no.344), Gap Kids (no.122), Jigsaw Junior (no.124), Joanna's Tent (no.289b), Mothercare (no.85) and Trotters (no.34) as well as the main branch of Daisy and Tom's (no.181), a dedicated kids' department store filled with toys, games, books and clothes. *See* **Shop** p.238 for details of the above stores.

Picnics & snacks

With two of the city's finest parks within easy reach, you really are spoiled for choice. There are few nicer areas to enjoy a picnic than **St James's Park** and **Green Park**. For supplies, head to Elizabeth Street, SW1, ⊖ **Sloane Square**, where there's an excellent collection of quality food shops. Try **Poilâne**, a French bakery at no. 46, **t** (020) 7808 4910, or the **Chatsworth Farm Shop** at no. 54, **t** (020) 7730 3033, which sells great pies, sandwiches, salads and soups, all made with fresh, organic ingredients. Less fancy (not to say less expensive) fare can be picked up at **Tesco Metro** at 18 Warwick Way, SW1, near Victoria Station.

Other than the very good **Cake House Café** in St James's Park, **t** (020) 7930 1973, ⊖ **St James's Park**, and the **Chocolate Society**, a chocolate shop-cum-café, at 36 Elizabeth Street, SW1, **t** (020) 7259 9222, ⊖ **Sloane Square**, there's not much close to Buckingham Palace. For details of cafés in the **Trafalgar Square** area, see p.73–4. Otherwise, your best bet is to head to the **King's Road**. Look out for the **Chelsea Kitchen** (see p.225) at no. 98, SW3, **t** (020) 7589 1330, ⊖ **Sloane Square** an old-fashioned café selling sandwiches, salads and pasta dishes; and **Ed's Easy Diner** (see p.225) at no. 362, SW3, **t** (020) 732 1956, ⊖ **Sloane Square**, a mock 1950s-style 'rock 'n' roll' diner which offers a very reasonably priced kids' menu (£4.45). High chairs available. There are branches of **McDonald's** at 155 Victoria Street, SW1 and in the Victoria Place Shopping Centre in Victoria station.

Restaurants

1 Benihana
77 King's Road, SW3
t (020) 7376 7799
www.benihana.co.uk
⊖ Sloane Square
Open Mon–Thurs 12 noon–2.30 and 6–10 (Fri–Sat till 11pm, Sun till 9.30pm)

2 Big Easy
332–4 King's Road, SW3
t (020) 7352 4071
⊖ Sloane Square
Open Mon–Sat 12 noon–11.30, Sun 12 noon–11

3 Bluebird
350 King's Road, SW3
t (020) 77559 1000

www.conran-restaurants.co.uk
⊖ Sloane Square
Open Mon–Fri 12.30–3 and 6–11.30, Sat 12 noon–4 and 6–11.30, Sun 12 noon–4 and 6–11

4 Blue Elephant
3–6 Fulham Broadway, SW6
t (020) 7385 6595
www.blueelephant.com
⊖ Fulham Broadway
Bus 11, 14. 28, 211, 295, C4
Open Mon–Fri 12 noon–3 and 7–12 midnight, Sat 7–11, Sun 12 noon–3.30

5 Cadogan Arms
298 King's Road, SW3
t (020) 7352 1645
⊖ Sloane Square
Bus 11,19, 22
Open Food from Mon–Sat 11am–11pm, Sun 12 noon–10.30, kids welcome to 8pm

6 Chutney Mary
535 King's Road, SW10
t (020) 7351 3113
www.chutneymary.com
⊖ Fulham Broadway
Open Mon–Sat 12.30–2.30 and 5.30–11.30, Sun 12.30–3 and 7–10.30

7 Hard Rock Café
150 Old Park Lane, W1
t (020) 7629 0382
www.hardrock.com
⊖ Hyde Park Corner
Open Mon–Thurs 11.30am–12 midnight, Fri and Sat 11.30am–1am, Sun 11.30am–11.30pm

8/9 Pizza Express
154 Victoria Street, SW1,
t (020) 7828 1477
⊖ Victoria
152 King's Road, SW3,
t (020) 7351 5031
⊖ Sloane Square
www.pizzaexpress.co.uk
Open 11.30am–12 midnight

See **Eat** p.224 for more details on the above restaurants.
See map on p.89 for the locations of the restaurants numbered above.

Westminster

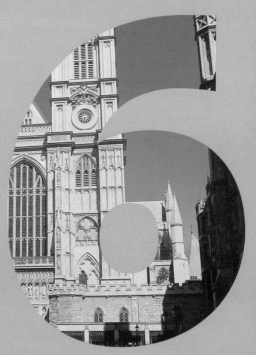

Westminster, the nation's political heartland, is likely to be of most interest to older children, those with some knowledge and under-standing of history, rather than youngsters and toddlers who, once they've finished pointing excitedly at the big clock, will quickly grow bored. Remember, a tour of this area can easily be combined with a trip to Trafalgar Square, or a foray across the Thames to the South Bank.

You could describe Westminster as the very epicentre of Englishness. It's the home of Big Ben, the world's most famous big clock, whose bongs are relaid around the country at midnight every New Year's Eve. Adjoining it are the Houses of Parliament, where the great and good of the country come to thrash out the issues of the day, while across Parliament Square is the 900-year-old Westminster Abbey where the coronation of all British monarchs takes place.

Take a quick walk along Parliament Street and you'll find Downing Street, where the Prime Minister lives, the Cenotaph, the country's most important war memorial, and the Cabinet War Rooms, where Britain's Second World War campaign was formulated. It's all very serious stuff and yet, at the same time, also quite touristy. Should you decide to pay the area a visit, you'll no doubt be accompa-nied on your travels by hordes of camera-wielding tourists, furiously clicking at everything in sight.

Remember, the newly revamped Tate Britain, one of the nation's pre-eminent art galleries and home of the Turner Prize, is just a short walk south along the river.

Highlights

Clock-watching with Big Ben

Getting arty at Tate Britain

Having a dead good time amongst the tombs in Westminster Abbey

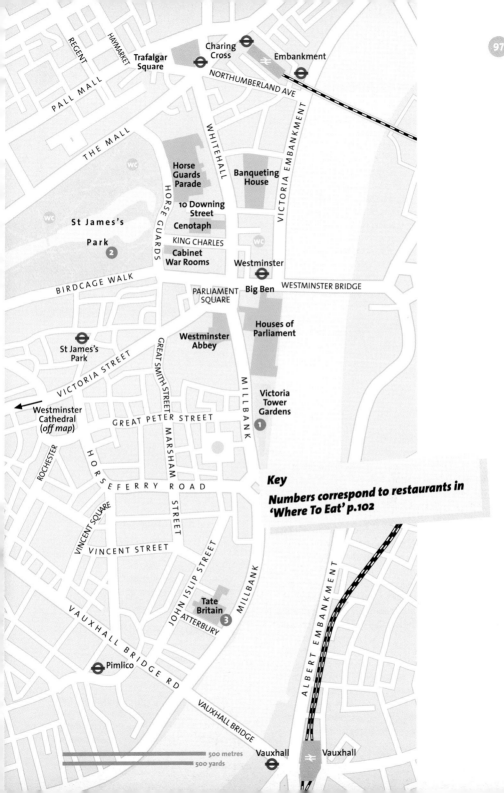

REGENT

HAYMARKET

PALL MALL

Trafalgar Square

Charing Cross

Embankment

NORTHUMBERLAND AVE

THE MALL

WC

St James's Park 2

WC

WHITEHALL

HORSE GUARDS

Horse Guards Parade

Banqueting House

VICTORIA EMBANKMENT

10 Downing Street

Cenotaph

KING CHARLES

Cabinet War Rooms

Westminster

WC

BIRDCAGE WALK

PARLIAMENT SQUARE

Big Ben

WESTMINSTER BRIDGE

St James's Park

VICTORIA STREET

GREAT SMITH STREET

Westminster Abbey

Houses of Parliament

MILLBANK

Westminster Cathedral (off map)

GREAT PETER STREET

MARSHAM

Victoria Tower Gardens 1

ROCHESTER

HORSEFERRY ROAD

Key

Numbers correspond to restaurants in 'Where To Eat' p.102

VINCENT SQUARE

STREET

VINCENT STREET

JOHN ISLIP STREET

ATTERBURY

Tate Britain 3

MILLBANK

ALBERT EMBANKMENT

VAUXHALL BRIDGE RD

Pimlico

VAUXHALL BRIDGE

500 metres
500 yards

Vauxhall

Vauxhall

Westminster Abbey

Broad Sanctuary, SW1
t (020) 7222 5152 or (020) 7654 4900
www.westminster-abbey.org
⊖ Westminster, St James's Park
Bus 3, 11, 12, 24, 53, 88, 109, 159, X53, 211
Open Mon–Fri 9.30–4.45 (last admission 3.45),
Sat 9–2.45 (last admission 1.45)
Adm Adult £6, child £4, under-11s **free**, concs £4
*Wheelchair accessible for most of the abbey; entry
is via a ramp at the north door. Audio guides are
available*
Suitable for ages 6 and over. Allow at least 1hr

Kids are not always interested in churches, even ones as famous and important as this, and you may feel disinclined to subject them to the Abbey, whatever its history or however lovely the stained glass. But, then, it all depends on how you approach it. Left to their own devices your kids will probably have seen enough here in three minutes flat, but point out the fact that the stones they are touching and, often as not, walking over conceal dead bodies, regale them with a few choice stories of how an assortment of the assembled met their ends (*see* below) and they'll find the whole experience much more interesting.

The Abbey could be described, if you were feeling a little disrespectful, as a great indoor graveyard filled with the remains, relics and reminders of the last thousand years of British history. You enter through Statesmen's Aisle, which features memorials to three of the country's most famous past Prime Ministers: Gladstone, Disraeli and Palmerston. Continue on around the Abbey and you'll find the tombs of Elizabeth I and Mary, Queen of Scots whom she beheaded, and what is thought to be the last resting place of the two young princes, Edward V and his brother Richard, who were supposedly murdered by their uncle (later Richard III) in the Tower of London in 1483. Explore further and you'll find the centrepiece of the Abbey – the shrine of St Edward. The Abbey's muddled layout just makes it more interesting for kids who happily wend their way through, under and around the assorted statues, stones, memorials and shrines. See if they can find Poets' Corner where Geoffrey Chaucer was buried in 1400. Ever since, some of the country's most famous poets and writers have ended up here including Dryden, Samuel Johnson, Sheridan, Browning and Tennyson. Others, such as Shakespeare, Shelley and Keats, are memorialized without actually being interred here.

The Abbey is a very beautiful place with great vaulted ceilings and richly coloured stained glass windows, but the best thing about it is that it manages both to engage the macabre interest of children while, at the same time, offering a more serene, reflective air which adults will appreciate.

There's a café and a souvenir shop in the cloisters, the area where the monks who resided in the Abbey until the middle of the 16th century lived

---

Tell me a story: **Emperors' new clothes**
Supertunica and Imperial Mantle may sound like good titles for a couple of glam-rock songs, but actually they are the names given to the Royal Coronation Robes and, when worn together, the outfit weighs in at a hefty 23lbs. The Imperial Mantle was made for the coronation of George IV, whose overall ensemble – including a specially made crown bearing 12,314 diamonds and 204 pearls – was so heavy that he very nearly fainted. Throughout the five-hour ceremony his estranged wife Queen Caroline hammered angrily on the doors of the Abbey in an attempt to gain admittance. She was refused, however, much to the displeasure of the crowd assembled outside, most of whom despised the flashy 'show-off' George.

Can you spot?

The statues in Parliament Square of three of Britain's most famous Prime Ministers: Palmerston, Disraeli and Winston Churchill. How is Churchill's statue different to the others? It is, how shall we put it, cleaner than the other statues. This is because it's heated from the inside to stop pigeon droppings from sticking.

and worked. Audio guides are available for £2 at the front desk.

Houses of Parliament

Parliament Square, SW1. The ticket office is opposite the St Stephen's entrance
t (020) 7219 4272
www.parliament.uk &
www.explore.parliament.uk
↔ Westminster
Bus 3, 11, 12, 24, 53, 77a, 88, 109, 159, 184, 211, X53
Open To watch a debate from the House of Commons Visitors' Gallery, you must queue from 2.30pm onwards Mon–Wed, from 11.30am Thurs and from 9.30am Fri. Seats for Prime Minister's Question Time, which takes place on Wed at 12 noon, are available to UK residents only, who must write to their local MP. Guided tours of the palace when the house is sitting are again available only to UK residents (they take place on Mon, Tues and Wed mornings) and again only via written application to your local MP. In the summer recess (July–Sept) daily guided tours, given by qualified blue badge guides, are available to all visitors (both UK and overseas).
Adm Tours: adult £7, child £5, family £22, under-4s **free**; it is **free** to watch a debate
Wheelchair accessible
Suitable for ages 12 and over

Its official name is the Palace of Westminster, but politicians refer to it simply as 'the House'. Whatever you call it, it is one of the unmistakable

sights of London. Most of the huge building dates from the 1830s, the original medieval structure having burned down in a fire in 1834, although parts of the interior, including Westminster Hall, were built at the end of the 11th century.

This is where the British government goes about its daily business, the ruling party of the day debates policy with the opposition. Here the lords and ladies of the land have, for centuries, come to comment on legislation. Despite its importance, however, it was, until recently, very difficult for members of the public to take a look inside the beautiful, neo-Gothic palace. Happily, guided tours are now available from July to September to all visitors (and to UK residents for the rest of the year via written application to your local MP). The tour includes the House of Commons chamber where the country's most important debates take place. It's surprisingly small, the chamber's plush leather benches having room for just 437 MPs (forcing many of the current 659 MPs to stand during popular debates).

From here it's on to the 'Noes Lobby', where MPs come to vote on legislation. Other places of interest on the tour include the Royal Gallery and Queen's Robing Room, where the Monarch prepares for the State Opening of Parliament; the House of Lords Chamber, and the very Grand Westminster Hall, the oldest part of the whole palace. Though now only used for ceremonial occasions, the hall was once the setting for important state trials. Both Charles I and the Gunpowder plotters were tried (and found guilty) here.

Children wanting to find out more about parliament and its role in British society should visit the special family-friendly website **www**.explore.parliament.uk, which aims to make what is often thought quite a dry and dusty subject interesting for young people.

Big Ben

Big Ben, the great clock tower, completed in 1859, was named after a Mr Benjamin Hill, the portly commissioner of works at the time. Big Ben is actually the name of the bell rather than the tower – its distinctive sound is due to a crack that appeared during its installation. Tours of the clock tower are occasionally available to UK residents (no children under 11) via written application to your local MP.

Cabinet War Rooms

King Charles Street, SW1
t (020) 7766 0120
www.iwm.org.uk/cabinet/index.htm
⊖ Westminster, St James's Park
Bus 3, 11, 12, 24, 53, 77a, 88, 109, 159, 184, 211
Open April–Sept 9.30–6, Oct–Mar 10–6
Adm Adult £7, child **free**, concs £5.50, half-price entry for disabled visitors
Free audio guide available, wheelchair accessible, lift to museum ground floor, adapted toilets
Suitable for ages 6 and over
Allow at least 1hr

This is a great place to take children provided they have some knowledge of the Second World War. These 21 cramped, low-ceilinged rooms 17ft underground were, for the last few years of the conflict, the nerve centre of the British war effort, the headquarters where Winston Churchill and his ministers made decisions that changed history. To visit these rooms today is to take a step back into the past; they have remained untouched since the final days of the war. They are wonderfully evocative, their very smallness (Churchill's office was a converted broom cupboard) giving some sense of the desperate pressure of the times. Each individual detail, so ordinary in itself, becomes, in this context, charged with significance. You can even see Churchill's bedroom from where he made his legendary radio broadcasts. For the full effect, make use of the free, self-paced audio guides, on which you can hear several of Churchill's rousing speeches accompanied by period music. There are also child-orientated audio guides available using children's memories of war, sound effects and recordings of conversations to bring the museum, and its role in the war, alive for younger visitors.

The War Rooms are currently undergoing a fever of reorganization. A new Clore Education Centre has opened, equipped with computers on which you can find out more of the background detail to the conflict, and there are also plans to open a museum dedicated to Winston Churchill (tentatively scheduled for completion in 2005).

Tate Britain

Millbank, SW1
t (020) 7887 8000
www.tate.org.uk
⊖ Pimlico, Vauxhall ⇌ Vauxhall
Bus 2, 3, 36, 77A, 88, 159, 185, 507, C10
Open 10–5.50, daily
Free (charges apply for some temporary exhibitions)
*Lift, wheelchair accessible via the new entrance in Atterbury Street; disabled parking spaces can be booked on **t** (020) 7887 8888*
Suitable for ages 6 and over
Allow at least 1hr 30mins

Although originally intended as a showcase for British art when it opened in 1897, the Tate had ceased to fulfil its role until, in 2000, Tate Modern opened on Bankside (*see* p. 117), allowing the Tate to become Tate Britain, a gallery once again devoted solely to British art.

Can you spot?
The big beige office building with green windows opposite Tate Britain, on the other side of the river. This is the HQ of MI6, Britain's secret service. Until recently, the British government denied that this service existed, which meant that, officially, the building also didn't exist – and neither did the people who worked in it.

Question 10
What did Henry Tate invent that made him rich enough to pay for the Tate Gallery to be established in 1897?
answer on p.249

As with its younger sibling, Tate Britain now organizes its collection according to themes rather than chronology, so you'll find sections named 'Literature and Fantasy', with works by William Blake, Sir John Everett Millais and John William Waterhouse (including his famous *Lady of Shallot*); 'Public and Private', which seeks to explore visions of the city; 'Home and Abroad', with works by war artists such as Paul Nash and John Singer Sargent; and 'Artists and Models', which focuses on self-portraits and nudes, also with an entire room given over to the colourful work of David Hockney.

Families are very well catered for at Tate Britain, whose curators have long understood that children can quickly grow bored. They have thus provided plenty of activities to keep them amused (most of which are, happily, free). In addition to 'Artspace: The Studio', a special art-play area for families equipped with games, jigsaws and clothes for dressing up, the gallery can provide 'Tate Trail' activity sheets and children's audio guides (aimed at 8–12 year-olds) bringing the pictures to life through stories, quizzes, riddles and sound effects.

The ever-popular art trolley is wheeled out on Sundays, Public Holidays and Thursdays during the school holidays between 12 noon and 5pm. Designed for adults and children to work on together, all you have to do is turn up to choose from a range of games and activities related to the many artworks on display.

And, as if that wasn't enough, the gallery also organizes a number of special family events, including 'Activity Days' when children can play with jigsaws, puzzles, handling objects and drawing materials, and 'Tate Tales' storytelling sessions based on the pictures in the collection. Spaces are limited, so be sure to book. Under-8s must be accompanied. Over-8s can be left for the duration of the session while parents explore the gallery. The gallery also organizes holiday art workshops, usually based around whichever temporary exhibition is currently showing (these cost £3 per session and booking is essential).

Tate Britain is linked to Tate Modern by a ferry service (*see* p.30 for more details).

Banqueting House

Whitehall, SW1
t 0870 751 5178
www.hrp.org.uk
✆ Westminster, Charing Cross
Bus 3, 6, 9, 11, 12, 13, 15, 23, 24, 29, 53, 88, 91, 109, 139, 159, 176, 184, 196
Open Mon–Sat 10–5
Adm Adult £4, child £2.60, concs £3
Pushchairs can be used on the ground floor and left in the cloakroom before ascending the stairs to the main hall. Suitable for ages 10 and over
Allow at least 30mins

Next to Horse Guards, this grand old building will be of more interest to parents than children with its magnificent ceiling paintings by Rubens. It does, however, hide one particular secret which may get the young ones pricking up their ears. Charles II was beheaded here, just outside the great dining hall in 1649, following his army's defeat by the forces of Parliament.

Downing Street

You can catch a glimpse of no.10, the house where the Prime Minister lives, through a pair of great black iron railings at the end of the road. Unfortunately, you are no longer allowed to go and have a close-up look. Britain's official centre of power is certainly not as grand as the White House in Washington or the Elysée Palace in Paris. But then, the man who built it, George Downing, never meant it to be anything other than a simple residential house. When Robert Walpole moved here in the mid-18th century (once the preceding tenant, a Mr Chicken, had moved out) he had no idea that all the Prime Ministers would follow in his footsteps, and to this day no one really knows why they have.

Near the junction of Downing Street and Whitehall stands the **Cenotaph**, the nation's chief memorial to the dead of the two World Wars. An official ceremony of remembrance takes place here each year on the Sunday nearest Armistice Day, 11 November, when wreaths of poppies are laid at the memorial.

Guards' Museum

Wellington Barracks, Birdcage Walk, SW1
t (020) 7414 3271
✆ St James's Park
Bus 3, 11, 12, 24, 159
Open 10–4, daily

WHERE TO EAT

Adm Adult £2, under-16s **free**

The museum traces the history of British troops from Cromwell's New Model Army and Charles II's five regiments (who still make up the infantry forces) to the present day, with plenty of battle memorabilia on display. There's also an excellent toy soldier shop. You can compare the mini uniforms here with the real ones at the Changing of the Guard ceremony (*see* p.90).

Westminster Cathedral

Victoria Street, SW1
t (020) 7798 9055
www. westminstercathedral.org.uk
⊖ St James's Park, Victoria
Bus 11, 24, 148, 211, 507
Open Mon–Fri 7am–8pm, Sat 8am-7pm.
Free to the cathedral; *Campanile*: adult £2, child £1, family £5
Wheelchair/pushchair accessible, café, audio guide (£2.50, £1.50 concs) worksheets, tours by arrangement
Suitable for ages 8 and up
Allow at least 30mins

Principally worth visiting for the fantastic views from the platform at the top of St Edward's Tower, some 280ft up – you can see right into the gardens of Buckingham Palace. Built in 1903, Westminster is London's main Roman Catholic Cathedral and has the widest nave in Britain. Its green pillars were hewn from the same stone as the 6th century Basilica of St Sophia in Istanbul. It took over two years to transport them all the way to London. Worksheets for children are available from the cathedral shop.

Picnics & snacks

The closest spot for a picnic is Victoria Tower Gardens (1), a relatively quiet and unvisited stretch of park next to Parliament and overlooking the river. You're also within easy reach of St James's Park (2), just to the west, and if it's raining you can use the picnic area by the Tate Britain café (3) (half portions and baby changing facilities available).

Otherwise, you're not exactly spoiled for choice in the immediate vicinity. Your best bet is to head either up Victoria Street towards the station or to Trafalgar Square and the West End, where you'll find a vast number of eateries. For more details, *see* pp.73–4.

See map on p.97 for the locations of the picnic spots numbered above.

The South Bank

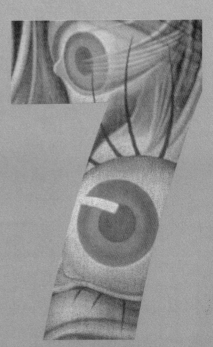

There's a tremendous concentration of attractions in this area. In truth, there should be even more, but the South Bank Centre's much heralded revamp is currently on hold which means that the re-opening of one of the area's very best children's attractions, MOMI (the Museum of the Moving Image) has once again been delayed. No matter, there's still plenty to draw the crowds. Just west of the centre is County Hall, home to the London Aquarium with its thousands of sea creatures, and standing proudly on the riverfront is the London Eye, the biggest big wheel in the world, which takes passengers on a fantastic tour, high up above the London skyline. Back down on the ground there are river walks to enjoy, plus live music events and riverside festivals. Budding movie buffs are spoilt for choice with the National Film Theatre and the IMAX 3D cinema right on the doorstep.

Highlights
Driving into the Thames on a Duck Tour
Watching the London Aquarium sharks
Elevated gazing from the London Eye

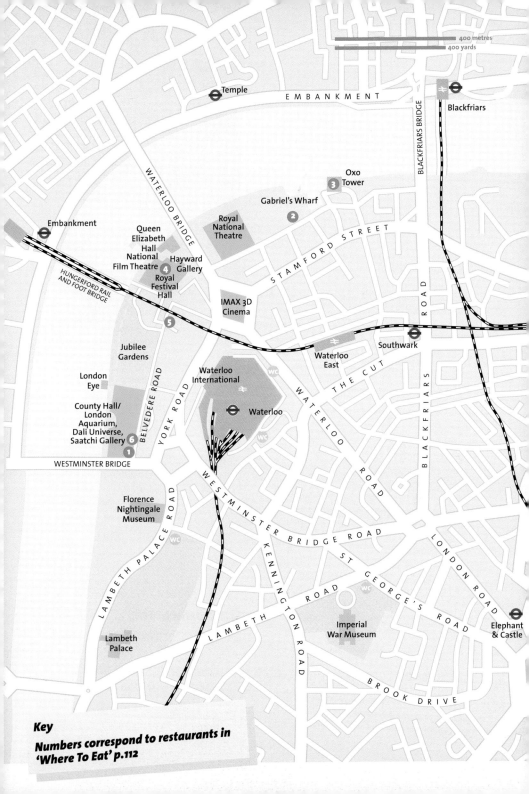

Temple

EMBANKMENT

BLACKFRIARS BRIDGE

Blackfriars

3 Oxo Tower

Gabriel's Wharf

2

Royal National Theatre

STAMFORD STREET

ROAD

Embankment

Queen Elizabeth Hall National Film Theatre

Hayward Gallery

4 Royal Festival Hall

HUNGERFORD RAIL AND FOOT BRIDGE

WATERLOO BRIDGE

IMAX 3D Cinema

5

Waterloo East

Southwark

WC

THE CUT

Jubilee Gardens

London Eye

Waterloo International

Waterloo

WATERLOO ROAD

BLACKFRIARS

BELVEDERE ROAD

YORK ROAD

County Hall/ London Aquarium, Dali Universe, Saatchi Gallery

6

1

WESTMINSTER BRIDGE

Florence Nightingale Museum

WC

WESTMINSTER BRIDGE ROAD

KENNINGTON ROAD

LAMBETH PALACE ROAD

Lambeth Palace

LAMBETH ROAD

ST GEORGE'S ROAD

LONDON ROAD

Elephant & Castle

WC

Imperial War Museum

BROOK DRIVE

400 metres
400 yards

Key
Numbers correspond to restaurants in 'Where To Eat' p.112

SEE IT, DO IT : The South Bank

County Hall

◉ Waterloo, Westminster ⇌ Waterloo
Bus 11, 12, 24, 53, 76, 77, 159, 211, 341, 381, X53

For much of its existence County Hall, the beautiful Edwardian building that sits on the South Bank opposite the Houses of Parliament, was home to London's premier administrative body, the Greater London Council (GLC). Following the council's abolition in 1986, however, the building sat empty for many years, with no one quite sure what to do with it – there was even talk of knocking it down. Thankfully, it has once again found a purpose. The political animals may have long gone, but there are still many weird and wonderful creatures to be found swimming around the vast tanks of the London Aquarium, which now occupies the building's basement. Here, too, can be found Namco Station, a sort of giant video game arcade, The Saatchi Gallery, displaying 'Brit Art', and Dali Universe, a museum dedicated to the great, Spanish surrealist artist, as well as numerous restaurants and hotels.

London Aquarium

County Hall, Riverside Building, Westminster Bridge Road, SE1
t (020) 7967 8000
www.londonaquarium.co.uk
Open 10–6 daily
Adm Adult £8.75, child £5.25 (under-3s **free**), family £25, concs £6.50, registed disabled **free** , carers £3
Wheelchair accessible, with adapted toilets. Suitable for all ages
Allow at least 1hr

In the five years since it opened, the London Aquarium has become firmly established as one of the capital's premier animal attractions. Its vast tanks are home to thousands of sea creatures, from water-spitting archer fish and gruesome-looking eels to multi-coloured corals and translucent

Did you know?
The world's biggest fish is the whale shark which can grow to over 70ft in length. Unlike some other sharks, it is perfectly harmless, feeding only on plankton.

floating jellyfish. It's arranged according to habitat and region, with displays on freshwater rivers, coral reefs, mangrove swamps and rainforests, as well as the Indian, Pacific and Atlantic Oceans. The prime attractions, of course, are the sharks, which swim in lazy circles around the Pacific tank.

More serene pleasures can be found at the touch pool where visitors can stroke the resident rays. Children, who usually need little encouragement to get their hands wet and touch things, love this. Do make sure, however, that they treat the rays gently.

Dotted in among the tanks are a number of interactive terminals where more can be learnt about the aquarium's inhabitants. There are touch-screen quizzes and short-play videos in which cartoon sea creatures explain themselves and their environment to children. More information can be gleaned at the free daily talks given by the aquarium's keepers at the Coral Reef and Pacific Tank (where the sharks live).

Dali Universe

County Hall, Riverside Building, Belvedere Road, SE1
t (020) 7620 2720
www.daliuniverse.com
Open Daily 10–5.30
Adm Adults £8.50, child (10–16) £4.95, under-9s £1, under-3s **free**
Shop, wheelchair accessible

This museum is filled with bizarre sculptures and paintings of the Spanish surrealist. In particular, look out for the sofa designed to resemble an enor-

Question 11
What do lobsters and the Royal Family have in common?
answer on p.249

mous pair of red lips (it was modelled on the Hollywood actress Mae West) and the lobster telephone. Activity sheets for children are available from the front desk.

The Saatchi Gallery

County Hall, Riverside Building, Belvedere Road, SE1
t (020) 7823 2363
www.saatchi-gallery.co.uk
Open Mon–Thurs and Sun 10–6, Fri and Sat 10–10
Adm Adults £8.50, child £6.50, family £25
Wheelchair accessible. Suitable for ages 12 and over

Modern art at its weirdest and most controversial. The advertising mogul, Charles Saatchi, more or less instigated the whole 'Brit Art' movement of the early 1990s when he began buying up works by young artists (many of whom had only just qualified from art school) for huge sums of money. His acquisitions soon became major talking points with countless 'is it art?' debates appearing in the press. Indeed, such was the furore that a few select pieces, including Damien Hirst's shark pickled in formaldehyde and Tracey Emin's unmade bed, took on the status of national icons. Though not to everyone's taste, the gallery's constantly rotating display does provide a good introduction to British conceptual art, although do be aware that many of the pieces explore sexual themes and therefore may not be suitable for young children.

Namco Station

County Hall, Riverside Building, Westminster Bridge Road, SE1
t (020) 7967 1067
www.namcostation.co.uk
Open 10am–12 midnight, daily
Free, although each game costs £1–2

Love it or hate it, this noisy, arcade-ridden labyrinth is packed with hundreds of video games and simulators as well as a full-size car racing game, bowling, dodgems and pool tables. The downstairs section is for over-18s only.

IMAX 3D Cinema

1 Charlie Chaplin Walk, SE1
t (020) 7902 1234
www.bfi.org.uk/imax
⊖/ ≷ Waterloo
Bus 1, 4, 26, 59, 68, 76, 77, 168, 171, 176, 188, 211, 243, 341, 381, 501, 505, 507, 521, RV1
Open Mon–Thurs 12.30–8, Fri 12.30–9.15, Sat 11.45–9.15, Sun 12 noon–8.
Adm Adult £7.50, child (5–16) £4.95 (£6 for evening shows), under-3s **free**, concs £6.20; prices for Hollywood blockbusters start at around £11.50
Wheelchair accessible, lifts, adapted cinema seats and toilets

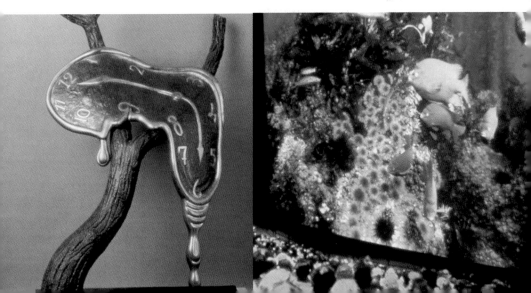

Suitable for all ages
Shows last approximately 1hr each

Britain's largest cinema screen is housed in a seven-storey glass cylinder in the middle of the Waterloo bullring. The screen itself is the height of five double-decker buses, the sound system transmits 11,000 watts and the films are recorded and projected using the most up-to-date 3D format available – it's a pretty all-encompassing experience. The programme changes regularly, but you can be confident of seeing some kind of scifi/wildlife spectacular plus the odd Matrix-style effects-laden Hollywood Blockbuster. *See p.xxx for the IMAX cinema in the Science Museum.*

British Airways London Eye

Next to County Hall, South Bank, SE1
General information and advance booking **t** 0870 500 0600
www.ba-londoneye.com
Open Sept–May Mon–Thurs 9.30–8, Fri–Sun 9.30–9; June Mon–Thurs 9.30–9, Fri–Sun 9.30am–10pm; July–Aug 9.30am–10pm daily
Adm Adult £11, child (5–16) £5.50 (under-5s **free**), concs £10. Tickets must be purchased in advance, online discounts available
Wheelchair accessible

One of the few Millennium projects to have stood the test of time, this 453-ft rotating observation wheel perched on the south bank of the Thames has provided both tourists and London residents alike with a whole new way of looking at the capital. Night rides are particularly spectacular, especially when the Christmas lights go on, although the best sightseeing opportunities are afforded during the day.

Officially the fourth-highest structure in the capital, each of the Eye's 32 enclosed glass-sided capsules (they hold up to 25 people each) takes around 40 minutes to complete its circuit. Don't worry though, it moves so slowly and smoothly there's little chance of travel sickness and there's a central seating area for passengers to sit down.

London Duck Tours

County Hall, Belvedere Road, SE1
t (020) 7928 3132
www.londonducktours.com
Open Daily 10–dusk
Adm Adults £16.50, children £11, family £49, concs £13

A novel approach to sightseeing – London Duck Tours (formerly 'Frog Tours') have adapted a number of former Second World War amphibious vehicles into bright yellow sightseeing 'ducks' capable of tackling London by both road and river. Each duck begins its 80-minute tour on land at County Hall, before crossing Westminster Bridge and making its way to Lacks Dock in Vauxhall, taking in key sights on the way, before 'splashdown' into the Thames. You are then taken on a half-hour sightseeing cruise down the river to the starting-point opposite Dali Universe. It's a different and fun way of navigating through London and the plunge into the river is truly exciting. It may be advisable to wear waterproofs.

South Bank Arts Centre

The South Bank, SE1
General Information **t** (020) 7960 4242
www.sbc.org.uk
⊖ Waterloo, Embankment
≋ Waterloo
Bus 1, 4, 26, 68, 76, 77, 168, 171, 172, 176, 188, 211, 341, 381, 501, 507, 521, RV1, X68
Wheelchair accessible, hearing/blind facilities

One of the world's great art complexes, the South Bank comprises, at present, the Royal Festival Hall, the Queen Elizabeth Hall, the National Film Theatre, the Hayward Gallery and the Royal National Theatre. Together, they put on a range of events suitable for families throughout the year including dance classes, concerts by youth orchestras, ballet performances, theatre shows and poetry sessions.

Royal Festival Hall

t (020) 7960 4242
www.rfh.org.uk
Open 10am–10.30pm daily
   Along with the adjacent Purcell Room and the Queen Elizabeth Hall, this is one of the top venues for classical music in the country. Look out, in particular, for the National Festival of Music for Youth, which takes place every summer, and the drumming festival 'Rhythm Sticks', which features open days and workshops aimed at younger visitors. Free concerts and exhibitions are often put on in the Festival Hall foyer.

National Film Theatre

t (020) 7928 3232
www.nft.org.uk
Adm 'Movie Magic' film screenings: child £1, accompanying adult £5
   The NFT shows a range of classic family films as part of its 'Movie Magic' programme, and organizes movie workshops for children aged 6–12 on the first Saturday of each month. At these, kids can

Can you spot?
The country's one and only floating police station, just to the side of Waterloo Bridge?

learn more about the techniques of film-craft. Supervised by experts, they can try their hand at creating a piece of animation, making movie props and costumes or writing their own short film script. The NFT also stages two-day 'Movie Magic Schools' which take a more in-depth look at the techniques of movie-making (they cost £5.50 per child, accompanying adult £4, and must be booked in advance). The NFT is also the main venue for the London Film Festival, held every November.

Hayward Gallery

t (020) 7690 4242
www.hayward.org.uk
Open 10–6 daily, until 8pm on Wed and Thurs
Adm Varies, depending on the exhibition
   The Hayward has no permanent exhibition, but puts on a series of temporary shows throughout the year, with children's art trails and activities attached wherever possible. It often organizes art and photographic workshops for children in the holidays as well (usually for over-12s). The Hayward shop can be accessed via the foyer and stocks a large and impressive range of art and activity books for children, from board books and bath books to project-based art boxes.

Royal National Theatre

t (020) 7452 3400
www.nationaltheatre.org.uk
Open 10am–11pm daily
Adm Backstage tours: £5, concs £4.25
Wheelchair accessible
   Three theatres in one: in descending size, these are the Olivier, the Lyttleton and the Cottesloe. All offer a year-round programme of drama. For a taster, pop along to Theatre Square, just outside, where free performances are staged throughout the year. Backstage tours of all three stages are available, on which you can see how the costumes are created, how the scenery is shifted around and how even the stages themselves can be moved during a performance. For more details, call **t** (020) 7452 3400. There's also an excellent bookshop.

Coin Street Community Builders

The Coin Street Community Builders (CSCB) is the name given to the non-profit organization that manages Gabriel's Wharf, the Bernie Spain Gardens, the Oxo Tower Wharf and organizes the three-month free Coin Street Arts Festival every summer. From near dereliction in the early 1980s, the CSCB has transformed the area into a thriving arts centre. Contact **t** (020) 7401 2255 or check out the website **www**.coinstreet.org

Gabriel's Wharf

Just down from the South Bank is Gabriel's Wharf, a bohemian collection of shops, restaurants and snack places. Look out for the London Bicycle Tour Company, who will rent you bikes to ride around the capital or arrange a guided bike tour. The endlessly delayed plans to build a floating lido on the Thames in front of the wharf are, as you might expect, once again on hold (**www**.gabrielswharf.co.uk).

London Bicycle Tour Company

1A Gabriel's Wharf, SE1
t (020) 7928 6838
www.londonbicycle.com
Bike hire Adult £2.50 per hour, child £2 per hour

Oxo Tower

Bargehouse Street, SE1
t (020) 7401 2255
www.oxotower.co.uk
⊖ Blackfriars, Waterloo
Bus 455, 63, 149, 172, D1, P11
Open Studios Tues–Sun 11–6; bars and restaurants every day until late

Topped by its famous Art Deco tower (one of the capital's great landmarks), the Oxo Tower Wharf is now an artsy shopping arcade housing designer boutiques, art studios and fashionable eating places, most notably its celebrated rooftop restaurant, which offers fantastic views out across the city – there's also a free viewing gallery next door. On the ground floor is an exhibition detailing the history of the building. In the 1930s, when the Oxo Tower was first commissioned by the famous stock

---

Tell me a story: **Evacuation**

When Britain declared war on Germany on 3 September 1939, Londoners began preparing for the worst. It would surely only be a matter of time, they reasoned, before the German air force began bombing raids on the city (it actually took over a year) and it was therefore crucial that the capital's children (up to aged 15) were quickly evacuated to safer parts of the country. Of course, finding places for all the children to stay (not to mention people with disabilities, teachers and helpers) proved to be no easy task. The sheer numbers involved meant that there was no way of guaranteeing which child went where, with the result that many middle-class kids found themselves in labourers cottages while slum children were billeted in stately homes. In this way, the evacuation process helped to foster a level of social integration that would have been impossible outside wartime. For some it proved to be a frightening and unhappy experience, although others, with fresh food to eat and space to run around in, saw it more as a holiday.

---

cube company, it was their intention to have the company's name spelled out in lights on the top.

Unfortunately, the strict advertising laws of the time forbade this, forcing the company to come up with an ingenious alternative. They instructed the architect to incorporate the Oxo logo into the design of the tower's windows, thus enabling them to claim that it was an architectural feature rather than an advert.

The Coin Street Festival

t (020) 7401 2555
www.coinstreetfestival.org
Three months each summer, usually June–Aug

For three months every summer, the Oxo Tower Wharf, Gabriel's Wharf and the Bernie Spain Gardens play host to a range of art, music and dance events from across the globe.

Although the programme changes each year, the festival usually features a whole host of children's events including creative workshops and a special children's fancy dress parade.

AROUND & ABOUT

Florence Nightingale Museum

2 Lambeth Palace Road, SE1
t (020) 7620 0374
www.florence-nightingale.co.uk
⊖/ ≈ Waterloo
Bus 12, 53, 76, 77, 148, 159, 211, 431, 381, 507
Open Mon–Fri 10–5, Sat, Sun 11.30–4.30, last admission one hour before closing
Adm Adult £4.80, child and concs £3.80, family £12
Wheelchair accessible
Suitable for ages 6 and over
Allow at least 1hr

A wonderful place to take any aspiring doctors or nurses. The museum tells the story of the founder of modern nursing via a mixture of videos, reconstructions and articles from the life of Florence Nightingale, including several of her letters. You walk through a recreated ward scene from the Crimean War where you can see 'the lady with the lamp' tending to the wounded soldiers. The museum is very much geared towards the interest of kids, so there are lots of interactive consoles and audio-visual displays including a 20-minute film on Florence's achievements in health care. The museum is due to undergo a major revamp in 2004 to mark the 150th anniversary of Florence Nightingale's posting to the Crimea.

Imperial War Museum

Lambeth Road, SE1
t (020) 7416 5320
Infoline t (0900) 1600 140
www.iwm.org.uk
⊖ Lambeth North, Elephant & Castle
Bus 1, 3, 12, 45, 53, 55, 63, 68, 100, 159, 168, 171, 172, 176, 188, 344, C10
Open 10–6, daily
Free
Wheelchair accessible
Suitable for ages 6 and over
Allow at least 1hr

Upon catching sight of the enormous 15-inch naval guns by the museum's entrance, you could be forgiven for thinking that this is a place that glorifies war and treats it as some great gung-ho 'Boys Own' adventure. In fact, the museum is largely dedicated to exploring and demonstrating the human experience of war; the lives of the ordinary men and women charged with settling the arguments of nations on the battlefield. It's true, there are some fantastic machines to look at in the large central hall, including tanks, planes, one-man submarines and even a 30-ft Polaris missile, but the museum never loses sight of the very real cost of conflict. For every piece of dazzling equipment, there's a more sobering exhibit – the Trench Experience, for instance, is an affecting recreation of the life of a foot-soldier on the Western Front during the First World War, while the Blitz Experience gives you the chance to see what conditions were like for Londoners during the Second World War, huddled in shelters under the streets as Hitler's bombs rained down overhead.

The museum's latest display, a two-floor exhibition on the Holocaust, is the most moving of all, but is not recommended for children under 14. It charts the rise of Hitler and the Nazi party through to the horror of the Final Solution.

Alongside two galleries devoted to paintings from the First and Second World Wars, you'll find a recreation of a 1940s' house as well as an exhibition on spying called 'Secret War', filled with outlandish surveillance gadgets.

There's a good proportion of interactive exhibits – you can clamber around the cockpits of some of the fighter planes, take the controls of a fighter plane simulator or watch some archive footage on one of the touch-screen TV terminals that dot the museum floor. Children's trails are available at reception and the museum organizes activity workshops in the school holidays, including their very popular 'Do touch the exhibits' days when kids (under supervision) are invited to handle artefacts from the First and Second World Wars.

After a visit, it may come as something of a relief to take a walk to the Tibetan Peace Garden just outside. This small, sculptured, enclosure was opened by His Holiness The Dalai Lama in 1999.

Picnic & snacks

There's not much greenery on the South Bank. The main 'park', **Jubilee Gardens**, is in fact little more than a scrubby lawn set next to County Hall. There are plenty of benches lining the Millennium Walkway next to the riverfront, but these aren't particularly picnic-friendly as you'll find your meal interrupted by a constant flow of pedestrians (not to mention joggers, cyclists, roller bladers and the area's ubiquitous skateboarders).

It may be slightly lacking when it comes to picnic sites, but, as one of the busiest places on the London arts scene, the **South Bank** has more than its fair shaire of fast food outlets and cafés. There's the **51 Café and Coffee Bar** in the Royal Festival Hall, **t** (020) 7921 0946, ⊖/≈ **Waterloo,** which serves pastas, salads, sandwiches and drinks throughout the day; the **Eat Café** on the ground floor of the Oxo Tower, **t** (020) 7401 2255, ⊖/≈ **Waterloo, Blackfriars**, where you can pick up home-made breads, tortilla wraps and smoothies; and, perhaps the pick of the bunch, the **NFT Café**, ⊖/≈ **Waterloo, t** (020) 7928 3232, situated under Waterloo Bridge, next to the Riverside Book Market. While children tuck into pizzas and jacket potatoes, their parents can rummage through the stalls or listen to the musicians who often busk along this vibrant stretch of the river. Slightly further afield, the **Imperial War Museum Café**, Lambeth Road, SE1, **t** (020) 7416 5320, ⊖/≈ **Lambeth North, Elephant & Castle,** provides a 'Hungry Monkeys' menu for kids. A lunchbox with sandwiches, cake, a piece of fruit and a fruit drink can be picked up for £2.45. Gabriel's Wharf also has several snack places including **House of Crêpes** and **Sarnis**, ⊖/≈ **Waterloo,** which specializes in continental sandwiches made from panini, ciabatta, focaccia and baguettes. There's also a branch of **McDonald's** in County Hall, ⊖/≈ **Waterloo.**

Restaurants

1 Fish!
County Hall, 3b Belvedere Road, SE1
t (020) 7234 3333
www.fishdiner.co.uk
⊖/≈ Waterloo
Open Mon–Sat 11.30–3 and 5–11, daily

2 Gourmet Pizza Company
Gabriel's Wharf, 56 Upper Ground, SE1
t (020) 7928 3188
www.gourmetpizzacompany.com
⊖/≈ Waterloo
Open 12 noon–10.30

3 Oxo Tower Restaurant
Oxo Tower, Barge House Street, South Bank, SE1
t (020) 7803 3888
www.oxotower.co.uk
⊖/≈ Waterloo, Blackfriars
Open Mon–Sat 12 noon–3 and 6–11.30, Sun 12 noon–3.30 and 6.30–10.30

4 The People's Palace
Royal Festival Hall, South Bank Centre, SE1
t (020) 7928 9999
www.peoplespalace.co.uk
⊖/≈ Waterloo
Open Mon–Sat 12 noon–3 and 5.30–8

5 Pizza Express
The White House, 9c Belvedere Road
t (020) 7928 4091
www.pizzaexpress.co.uk
⊖/≈ Waterloo
Open 11.30–12 midnight daily

6 Yo! Sushi
County Hall, Belvedere Road, SE1
t (020) 7928 8871
www.yosushi.co.uk
⊖/≈ Waterloo
Open 12 noon–12 midnight, daily

See **Eat** p.224 for more details on the above restaurants.
See map on p.105 for the locations of the restaurants numbered above.

Southwark

There really isn't much that you can't do here. From London Bridge Station it's a short walk to some of London's oldest and best loved attractions, such as the nautical treasures of HMS *Belfast* and The *Golden Hinde*, plus Tower Bridge, Southwalk Cathedral and the ghoulish London Dungeon. There's also a few hidden gems to discover like the Old Operating Theatre, The Design Museum and, if you fancy a spot of retail therapy, Hay's Galleria and the bijou shops around Butler's Wharf. Alternatively, if you really must be up-to-the-minute, head for the very latest blockbusters: Shakespeare's Globe, the Millennium Bridge and Tate Modern, formerly Bankside Power Station.

Highlights

Quoting Shakespeare at The Globe

Gazing at the Crown Jewels

Views from atop the Tower Bridge Exhibition

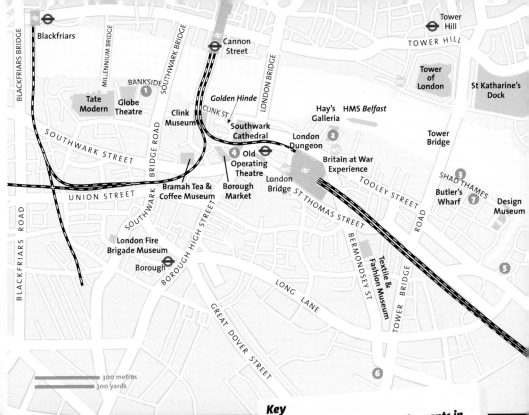

Blackfriars

BLACKFRIARS BRIDGE

MILLENNIUM BRIDGE

SOUTHWARK BRIDGE

Cannon Street

LONDON BRIDGE

Tower Hill

TOWER HILL

WC

Tower of London

St Katharine's Dock

BANKSIDE **1**

Tate Modern

Globe Theatre

Golden Hinde

CLINK ST

Clink Museum

Southwark Cathedral

London Dungeon

Hay's Galleria

HMS *Belfast*

2

Tower Bridge

SOUTHWARK STREET

BRIDGE ROAD

4 Old Operating Theatre

WC

London Bridge

Britain at War Experience

SHAD THAMES **3**

Butler's Wharf **7**

Design Museum

UNION STREET

Bramah Tea & Coffee Museum

Borough Market

ST THOMAS STREET

TOOLEY STREET

TOWER BRIDGE ROAD

5

SOUTHWARK

BLACKFRIARS ROAD

London Fire Brigade Museum

BOROUGH HIGH STREET

BERMONDSEY ST

Textile & Fashion Museum

Borough

LONG LANE

GREAT DOVER STREET

6

300 metres
300 yards

Key
Numbers correspond to restaurants in 'Where To Eat' p.124

Tower Bridge Exhibition

London Bridge, Fenchruch Street
t (020) 7403 3761
www.towerbridge.org.uk
⊖ Tower Hill, London Bridge
Bus 15, 25 (Sat/Sun), 42, 78, 100, RV1
Open 9.30–6, daily (last entry 5)
Adm Adult £4.50, child and concs £3, under-5s **free**, family ticket (2+2) £9.50
Wheelchair accessible for all public areas
Suitable for ages 6 and over
Allow at least 1hr

With its fairytale turrets and huge decks, which raise to let tall ships pass through, this is easily London's most recognizable and popular bridge. At Tower Bridge Exhibition you can see the steam-powered machinery which was used to raise the decks in Victorian times (these days the bridge relies on hydraulics and electricity), play with some interactive models and climb the 200 or so steps (or if you're sensible take the lift) to the covered walkway that runs along the top of the bridge some 150ft above the Thames. From here you can enjoy spectacular views up and down the river and out across London. Look out, in particular, for the new Greater London Authority building next to the bridge, which looks a bit like an enormous glass paperweight. The bridge is still raised at least once a day; you can find out exactly when by calling **t** (020) 7940 3984. Family activities, including 'Meet the Workers' days and storytelling sessions, are put on throughout the year.

London Dungeon

Tooley Street, SE1
t (020) 7403 7221
www.thedungeons.com
⊖/ ≷ London Bridge
Bus 10, 44, 48, 70, 133
Open Oct–Mar 10.30–6, April–July, Sept, Oct, 10–5.30, Nov–Mar 10–5. Mid-July–early Sept 10–8, daily
Adm Adult £12.50, child (under 14) £7.50, under-5s **free**, concs £9.50
Wheelchair accessible
Suitable for ages 8 and over
No unaccompanied children allowed
Allow at least 1hr

The concept behind the London Dungeon is rather odd but it's one that seems perfectly attuned to the interests of children, who often harbour a strange desire to be scared in a 'safe' way. In the dark, candlelit 'dungeon' (actually a series of railway arches next to London Bridge Station), you'll find a series of gruesome waxwork tableaux depicting some of the more grisly episodes from British history: a human sacrifice by druids at Stonehenge; Boadicea stabbing a Roman soldier to death; Anne Boleyn being beheaded, as well as the blotchy, bloated victims of the great plague and the manacled maniacs of Newgate Prison. The highlight, however, is a recreation of the life and times of London's most notorious serial killer, Jack the Ripper. You can walk the streets where his crimes took place and hear the muffled cries of his victims. You'll have to judge for yourselves whether you consider this sort of fare suitable for children. It's probably not a good idea to take very young children to the London Dungeon (those under 8) or anyone (young or old) susceptible to nightmares.

Did you know?

▶ That each bridge deck weighs an astonishing 1,000 tonnes. That's as much as 200 elephants.
▶ That the 'proper' name for one of the bridge's decks is a 'bascule'.
▶ That in 1952 a double decker bus had to jump a three foot gap between the opening bridge decks when the traffic lights didn't turn red?

Tate Modern

Bankside, SE1
t (020) 7887 8000
www.tate.org.uk
⊖/ ≷ London Bridge, Blackfriars
Bus Bus 11, 15, 17, 23, 26, 45, 63, 76, 100, 344, 381, RV1
Open Sun–Thurs 10–6, Fri and Sat 10–10 (closed 24–26 Dec; open 1 Jan)
Free
Wheelchair accessible, hearing facilities, free touch tours
Suitable for ages 8 and over
Allow at least a couple of hours

Tate Modern was one of the unqualified success stories of the Millennium year and has been packing them in ever since the day it opened. Housed in the former Bankside power station, the collection is arranged around a vast turbine hall which serves as both entrance and exhibition space and has to be seen to be believed. Make sure you come in by the main entrance for the full 'wow!' effect.

Inside, the museum has a mighty 100,000 square feet of display space dedicated to modern international works from the 19th century to the present day. That's a lot of art, but don't be put off. There are actually only four (large) galleries to explore and there are lightweight collapsible stools available for you to take round for when your legs start

to get tired (plus plenty of comfy sofas, strategically placed around the galleries). The galleries are arranged thematically rather than chronologically, with umbrella topics used to trace links and resonances between artists who might otherwise seem to have little in common. Much of the work on show, such as Marcel Duchamp's *Fountain* (actually a toilet) and Carl Andre's *Equivalent VIII* (a pile of bricks), are the kind of works of art that the British public love to hate, although there are also many famous works by more 'traditional' artists such as Bacon, Dali, Freud, Hockney, Matisse, Picasso, Pollock, Rothko, Spencer and Warhol.

As with Tate Britain, its sister gallery, Tate Modern provides plenty of resources to help families understand and involve themselves in the collection. After all, modern art, perhaps more than any art form, often needs to be explained (to both adults and children) in order to be properly appreciated and enjoyed. Free activity sheets, which encourage kids to draw their own impressions of the collection, and Explorer Trails, which offer themed routes around the gallery for ages 3 and over, are available from the members' desk. You can also hire a special children's audio tour (aimed at 8–12 year-olds), narrated by the celebrated children's author, Michael Rosen, from the audiotour desk on level 1 (£1 each). The gallery also organizes a programme of art-related activities for children including 'Start', a drop-in event on Sundays between 11–5 (and on certain weekdays during the school holidays) aimed at providing a basic introduction to art for under-5s, and Tate Tales, which offers storytelling and word games for ages 5 and over. Teenagers may be interested in the gallery's 'Raw Canvas' summer school courses for budding young artists aged 15–23.

Before leaving, head up to the top floor where the café offers wonderful views of the river, the Millennium Bridge and St Paul's. And save time for the shop on the ground floor, where you can pick up T-shirts, mugs, umbrellas and a stationery box in the shape of the Bankside building which includes a magnetic 'lightbeam' lid.

Tip Tate Modern is one of the capital's newest and most popular attractions and by mid-afternoon is usually heaving with visitors. To avoid the crush, visit early in the morning or later on in the day.

Tell me a story: The Blitz
The deliberate and systematic bombing of London by the German airforce, or 'Luftwaffe', began on the afternoon of Sunday 7 September 1940. Squadron after squadron hit the East End where the warehouses at Surrey Docks, filled with rubber, paint and rum, were soon ablaze. That night the Luftwaffe struck again and by the dawn of 8 September, 448 Londoners had lost their lives. The 'Blitz', as it came to be known, had begun and continued unabated for the next 76 days, during which time vast swathes of the capital were flattened and thousands of lives lost. There were, however, some miraculous escapes along the way. Buckingham Palace was hit but escaped relatively undamaged, while St Paul's Cathedral, despite the destruction around it, survived the bombing virtually intact and became a symbol of London's defiance. Night after night, Londoners took cover in steel shelters or on the platforms of the Underground stations as the German planes attempted to crush their morale in preparation for a land invasion. Much to the Nazis' chagrin, however, the bombing, if anything, served to stiffen British resolve to resist the enemy at all costs. Even so, London paid a heavy price for its brave resistance. Over the next four years 20,000 people were killed in the air raids and a further 25,000 wounded.

Britain at War Experience

Tooley Street, SE1
t (020) 7403 3171
www.britainatwar.co.uk
⊖/ ⇌ London Bridge
Bus 21, 35, 40, 43, 47, 48, 133, 381
Open April–Sept 10–5.30 daily,
Oct–Mar 10–4.30 daily
Adm Adult £7.50, child (under 15) £4 (under-5s **free**),
concs £5
Wheelchair accessible
Suitable for ages 6 and over
Allow at least 1hr

On Tooley Street, under the same set of arches as the London Dungeon, is perhaps the best place for kids to come and find out what life was like in this country during the Second World War. You start by taking a lift down to a replica underground shelter of the type hidden in by Londoners during the Blitz, when bombs rained down night after night on the city. In order to get a real sense of the times, children can dress up in period costume complete with gas masks, tin helmets and ARP (air-raid patrol)

uniforms. A mixture of sounds, smells and visual effects are used along with archive footage, radio broadcasts and music to conjure up a period atmosphere. The overall effect is fun and exciting, but also informative, successfully conveying a little of the reality of the time: the desperate fear that must have been felt by the people sheltering here, as well as the community spirit that helped them to get through. You finish the tour by walking through a replica bombed street as sirens wail and spotlights criss-cross overhead. It's a great interactive museum where kids can get their hands dirty finding out about what war was like in the past.

Question 12
What is a groundling?
answer on p.249

Globe Theatre

Bear Gardens, Bankside, New Globe Wall, Southwark, SE1
t (020) 7902 1400
www.shakespeares-globe.org
⊖/ ≷ London Bridge
Bus 11, 15, 17, 23, 26, 45, 63, 76, 100, 344, 381, RV1
Open 10–5 daily, for performance times call in advance
Adm Museum: adult £8, child £5.50 (under-5s **free**), concs £6.50, family ticket (2+3) £24
Saturday 'Child's Play' Workshops **adm** £10
Limited wheelchair access, call disabled access information on (020) 7902 1409
Suitable for ages 8 and over
Allow at least 1hr to see the museum
Performances can last a few hours

The Globe is a perfect modern recreation of the Elizabethan theatre where Shakespeare premiered many of his most famous plays, including *Othello*, *Macbeth* and *Romeo and Juliet*. The original theatre burnt down in 1613 during a performance of *Henry VIII*, when an ember from a stage cannon set fire to the thatched roof.

You can take a guided tour of the new Globe (which, begun in the early 1980s, was finally completed in the mid-1990s), visit the multimedia museum which explains the history of the Globe (old and new), or watch a performance of a Shakespeare play almost as his contemporaries would have done: seated on wooden benches or standing in the open in front of the stage. This can add to the atmosphere at performances, but can also serve to obscure children's views.

On certain Saturdays, children aged between 8 and 11 can take part in Saturday afternoon 'Child's Play' sessions at the Globe's Education Centre. While parents watch a matinée performance, kids are treated to storytelling sessions and art and drama workshops before joining the groundlings (*see* question opposite), in front of the stage for the final act (£10 per child, booking essential).

Shakespearian theatre

Welcome to the bad side of town... In the 16th century, when the first Globe theatre was built, this was the area of town frequented by the city's reprobates and ne'er do wells – where people came to indulge in bawdy, rowdy entertainments such as drinking and gambling, bear and bull baiting, cock and dog fighting (any sort of mayhem with

Did you know?
The Globe's roof is the first thatched roof to top a London building since the Great Fire of 1666. In order to prevent another disaster, the thatch sits on an insulating layer of fibreglass and is dotted with sprinklers.

animals seems to have been particularly popular) and, of course, going to the theatre. While, today, we often regard theatre-going as something rather refined and elegant, in Shakespeare's day it was a much more rough and ready form of entertainment. During the summer months, children can find out more about the decadent history of Southwark on a Globe Walkshop; a guided tour taking in the sites of the prisons, inns, brothels and theatres which used to make up the bulk of the area's buildings (10–12 noon Saturday; **adm** £7, concs £5, student £4; call **t** (020) 7902 1433).

Old Operating Theatre

9a St Thomas Street, SE1
t (020) 7955 4791
www.thegarret.org.uk
⊖/ ≷ London Bridge
Bus 17, 21, 22a, 35, 40, 43, 47, 48, 133, 343, 344, RV1
Open 10–4 daily
Adm Adult £4, child £2.50 (under-8s **free**), family ticket (2+2) £10
No wheelchair or pushchair access. Museum is reached via narrow staircase, young children must be carried
Suitable for ages 8 and over
Allow at least 1hr

Just think what it would be like to have your tonsils taken out here, in the country's only surviving example of an early 19th-century operating theatre. These days we tend to think of surgery as a skilled job involving the delicate repair of internal organs by trained professionals. That

Did you know?
In the early 19th century, surgeons were regarded by the medical establishment as being little better than butchers. Even today, when they are among the most highly skilled of all medical practitioners, they do not take the title 'Dr' but remain a simple 'Mr'.

Did you know?
HMS *Belfast*'s huge, deck-mounted guns had a range of 14 miles which means that, from their present position, they could blow up Hampton Court.

wasn't the case in the early 1800s when a surgeon's main task was amputations – the removal of damaged or diseased limbs with a fine-toothed saw. The patient wouldn't even have an anaesthetic (this wasn't cruelty, it hadn't been invented yet). Surgeons relied instead on speed and the bravery of the patient (and six or seven able-bodied men to hold him or her down). Patients could actually watch while someone sawed off their leg – imagine what that must have felt (and looked) like. There was also no antiseptic and standards of hygiene were poor (surgeons often didn't bother to clean their instruments between operations). In fact, a third of all amputees died from an infection caught during surgery – the museum cheerily explains that surgeons often performed operations 'stinking with pus and blood'.

It's a fantastic place, thick with atmosphere and a very real sense of horror. You can see the gruesome medical equipment (almost indistinguishable from the tools of torture at the nearby Clink Museum), the operating table (actually a wooden board that held patients upright) and various pickled bits of unlucky patients in jars.

The theatre itself has had a fascinating history. It was housed in a medieval tower that formed part of the old St Thomas' hospital. When the hospital relocated to Lambeth in 1860, the old building was demolished and only the tower was left standing. The operating theatre within, however, was forgotten about for nearly a century until re-discovered and turned into a museum in 1956.

HMS Belfast

Morgan's Lane, off Tooley Street, SE1
t (020) 7940 6300
www.hmsbelfast.org.uk
⊖/ ⇌ London Bridge
Bus 21, 35, 40, 43, 47, 48, 133, 381
Open Mar–Oct 10–6 daily, Nov–Feb 10–5 daily
Adm Adult £6, child **free**, concs £4.40
Wheelchair accessible for main deck, but not many below-deck areas. Suitable for ages 6 and over Allow at least 1hr

This huge, heavily armed, heavily armoured cruiser was used during the D-Day landings, the

1944 invasion of Normandy that finally turned the Second World War in the Allies' favour. These days it is a kind of floating nautical museum, moored permanently between London Bridge and Tower Bridge. Children love running around the ship's clunking metal decks, looking down the barrels of the huge naval guns, manoeuvring the lighter anti-aircraft guns and exploring the seven floors of narrow winding corridors.

The *Golden Hinde*

St Mary Overie Dock, Cathedral Street, SE1
t 0870 011 8700
www.goldenhinde.co.uk
⊖/ ⇌ London Bridge
Bus 17, 95, 149, 184
Open Call in advance (the ship is only open to casual sightseeing when there are no pre-booked groups visiting)
Adm Adult £2.75, child £2, , family £8, concs £2.35
Guided tours: adult £3.50, child £2.50, concs £3.
Pirate Birthday Parties: £175 for 15 children and food (£10 for each additional child).
Overnight Living History Experiences: £33 per person plus £11 per person deposit.
Daytime Experience £22.50 (ages 6–12 *only*)
No wheelchair access
Suitable for ages 6 and over

Billed as a living museum, this full-size replica of the 16th-century ship on which Sir Francis Drake became the first Englishman to circumnavigate the globe sits in dry dock, just back from the river front. There are five levels to explore including Drake's cabin and a 14-cannon gun deck. As the children roam the ship, the crew, dressed in Tudor costume, will entertain them with tales of adventure and treachery on the high seas. Although a replica, this is a fully functioning vessel and has sailed the Atlantic several times since it was built in 1973. It's available for children's parties and school groups or families are invited to attend the ship's Overnight or Daytime Living History Experiences, which run from 5pm until 10am the next day and 10am until 5pm respectively. During this time the whole family is expected to assume the roles of a crew of Tudor sailors: performing shipboard tasks, eating Tudor food and sleeping in the cabins on the lower decks.

Clink Museum

1 Clink Street, SE1
t (020) 7403 6515
www.clink.co.uk
⊖/ ≷ London Bridge
Bus 17, 95, 149, 184
Open 10–6 daily
Adm Adult & child £4, concs £3, family £9
No wheelchair access
Suitable for ages 8 and over
Allow at least 30mins

If your kids aren't quite up to the big frights of the London Dungeon, try them on the smaller fun-size frights offered here. The museum has attempted to recreate many of the scenes and settings of the medieval Clink Museum which stood on this spot in the Middle Ages. Although the prison building was demolished in 1780, the name 'the Clink' has survived to this day as a nickname for all prisons. It clearly hasn't got the budget of other big-name horror attractions such as the London Dungeon or the Chamber of Horrors and many of its supposedly gory effects are actually a bit ordinary. Even so, it boasts a historical authenticity which the other two attractions can't match and, despite its limitations, still manages to convey something of the eerie gruesomeness of these primitive and brutal forms of punishment.

> **Did you know?**
> Medieval prisoners were expected to pay for the privilege of being manacled and tortured. They had to contribute towards their food, their cells and the wages of the men who kept them locked up. They even had to pay for their own ball and chain!

It's divided into a number of cells, each inhabited by some rather unhappy-looking mannequins undergoing some of the various forms of torture popular during the Middle Ages. There's the Stocks, which is basically two wooden planks used to hold a prisoner's head and hands fast; the Fure, a hole in the ground where trussed up prisoners were left to rot; and the Cage, a wire contraption fitted to the head of 'scolds and gossips' – in other words women who, in the eyes of their husbands, talked too much. In one particular cell you'll find a torture chair to which a victim would be strapped before being forced to confess by use of pincers (for tooth extractions), knives and foot crushers. The section detailing the history of the Stews (medieval brothels) is for over-18s only.

The prison closed soon after the Great Fire of London in 1666 when the local area began to go upmarket. City merchants and investors started moving in, putting the brothels, drinking houses and gambling dens that had provided the majority of the prison's clientele out of business. For a while the building continued to be used as warehouse before finally being knocked down in 1780.

The Millennium Bridge

Designed by Norman Foster, Anthony Caro and the engineering firm Arup, this elegant walkway linking Tate Modern with St Paul's on the other side of the river was definitely not one of the Millennium year's success stories, not to begin with anyway. As people walked across the bridge on its first day of opening, it started shaking from side to side in such an alarming (and potentially dangerous) manner that the authorities were forced to close it. Thankfully, the problems have since been rectified and the now stable bridge provides great views up and down the Thames, not to mention easy access between the City and Southwark.

Bramah Tea & Coffee Museum

40 Southwark Street, SE1
t (020) 7403 5650
www.bramahmuseum.co.uk
⊖/ ≷ London Bridge
Bus 15, 25, 42, 78, 100, 381, RV1
Open 10–6 daily
Adm Adult £4, child and concs £3.50, family ticket (2+4) £10
Suitable for ages 8 and over
Allow at least 30mins

Recently relocated from Butler's Wharf, this charming little museum details the history of the country's two favourite (non-alcoholic) beverages. You can find out how the drinks were introduced to Britain in the 17th century, how public tastes have changed since then and how the ritual of drinking coffee, and particularly tea, has become such a part of British life. Children will like the collection of teapots and coffee-makers. There are over 1,000 in all shapes and sizes: dragons, monsters, lions, pillar-boxes and even policemen. Perhaps the most interesting section is devoted to the way the drinks have been advertised during this century. If all this talk of tea and coffee gets you thirsty, you can always head for the café and sample one of the museum's own blends.

Design Museum

28 Shad Thames, Butler's Wharf, SE1
t (020) 7940 8790
www.designmuseum.org
⊖ London Bridge, Tower Hill
Bus 15, 42, 47, 78, 100, 188, P11
Open 11.30–6, daily
Adm Adult £6, child and concs £4, under-5s **free**, family £16
Suitable for ages 10 and over
Allow at least an hour

This probably won't interest youngsters very much, but older children may well get something out of it. The museum's purpose is to explain why various ordinary, everyday objects – such as telephones, vacuum cleaners, toothbrushes and cars –

look the way they do, examining them from both a functional and an aesthetic perspective. You can sit in some of the outlandish chairs of yesteryear and there's a very good shop selling books and gadgets as well as an attractive (but expensive) Conran-run café, the Blueprint (more of a restaurant really).

Fashion & Textile Museum

83 Bermondsey Street, SE1
t (020) 7403 0222
www.ftmlondon.org
⊖/ ≈ London Bridge
Bus 42, 47, 78, 149, 188, 381, RV1
Open Tues–Sun 11–5.45
Adm Adult £6, child £4, under-5s **free**, family £16
Wheelchair accessible, with adapted toilets; shop.
Suitable for ages 10 and over

Opened in the summer of 2003, the country's first dedicated fashion museum is the brain-child of the leading British fashion designer, Zandra Rhodes. Inside the striking orange, purple and blue building (a fashion statement in its own right), you'll find a constantly rotating exhibition showing the development of fashion and textile production during the latter half of the 20th century. Fashion workshops for kids are run in the summer holidays.

Hay's Galleria

London Bridge, Tooley Street, SE1
t (020) 7940 7770
www.haysgalleria.co.uk
⊖/ ≈ London Bridge
Bus 10, 44, 48, 70, 133
Open 10–6 daily

A rather posh shopping arcade. Its main entrance is on Tooley Street, almost directly opposite the London Dungeon, and it can be used as a quick short-cut to the Thames riverside path. Should you decide to linger you'll find lots of well-to-do shops and restaurants (look out for a branch of the child-friendly chain, Sweeney Todd's), while the kids' attention will no doubt be caught by the great statue-cum-fountain, *The Navigators*, which stands at the arcade's riverside end.

London Fire Brigade Museum

94a Southwark Bridge Road
t (020) 7587 2894
www.london-fire.gov.uk
⊖ London Bridge, Borough
Bus 344

Open Mon–Fri, pre-booked tours only at 10.30am, 2pm
Adm Adult £3, child £2, under-7s **free**
Suitable for ages 7 and over

Once upon a time, every small boy who didn't want to be a train driver wanted to be a fireman. Times have changed, of course, but today's would-be astronauts, pop stars and internet gurus may like to pay a visit (by appointment only) to this museum of fire-fighting to see what they're missing out on. You'll see some 20 historic fire engines ranging from 18th-century hand-pumped affairs to the latest super hi-tech models, find out how the fire service has developed in the 300 odd years since the Great Fire of London and, best of all, kids can try on some of the uniforms. Space travel pales in comparison.

Southwark Cathedral

Montague Close, SE1
t (020) 7407 3708
www.dswark.org
⊖/ ≈ London Bridge
Bus 17, 21, 35, 40, 43, 48, 133, 149, 501, D1
Open Cathedral: 8–6 daily; exhibition: Mon–Sat 10–6, Sun 11–5
Free to the cathedral; exhibition: adult £3, child £1.50, under-5s **free**, family £12.50
Wheelchair accessible, call in advance; restaurant, shop, lifts

The Cathedral's newly landscaped grounds are practically crying out for a picnic. There's also a new interactive museum, 'The Long View of London' with touch-screen computers, a camera obscura mounted on the Cathedral tower showing panoramic views of the city, plus a variety of medieval, Roman and Victorian artefacts.

Picnic & snacks

As with the South Bank, its adjacent area, Southwark, doesn't really go in for inviting expanses of greenery. Its one small park, the **William Curtis Park** by the new GLA building, offers great views of Tower Bridge and is a pleasant enough spot for a picnic, although you can feel a bit hemmed in. The newly landscaped gardens of **Southwark Cathedral** are much more welcoming and you're also welcome to picnic in the Tate Modern's Clore Education Centre.

Supplies can be picked up from **Borough Market**, (just south of Southwark Cathedral, off Borough High Street) which sells a huge array of farmer's market produce: fruit and veg, cheeses, meat etc. and also has a number of delicatessen counters.

There's plenty of choice. The **Hays Galleria**, SE1, ⊖ **London Bridge,** has numerous eateries including **Absolutely Starving**, a delicatessen-cum-sandwich shop, **t** (020) 7407 7417; the **Bagel Factory**, **t** (020) 7407 7616, which serves American-style bagels, cookies and brownies; and **Schulers**, **t** (020) 7378 6968, which serves made-to-order sandwiches and salads. Several of the area's attractions also have good cafés including **Southwark Cathedral**, **t** (020) 7407 3708, where there's outside seating; **Tate Modern**, **t** (020) 7887 8000, which has two cafés, one on the second floor and one on the top (the latter offers great views of the river), and the **Globe Theatre Café**, **t** (020) 7902 1576, which, overlooking the theatre piazza, serves snacks and light lunches throughout the day. Lastly, if you think your stomach can stand it, there's also a branch of **Pizza Hut** in the London Dungeon.

Restaurants

1 Anchor Inn
34 Park Street, Bankside, Southwark, SE1
t (020) 7902 1400
⊖/≷ London Bridge
Open Mon–Sat 11am–11pm, Sun 12 noon–10.30

2 Café Rouge
Hay's Galleria, SE1
t (020) 7378 0097
www.caferouge.co.uk
⊖ London Bridge
Open 10am–11pm, daily

3 Cantina del Ponte
Butler's Wharf Building, Shad Thames, SE1
t (020) 7403 3403
www.conran.co.uk
⊖ London Bridge, Tower Hill
Open Mon–Sat 12 noon–3 and 6–11, Sun 12 noon–3 and 6–10

4 Fish!
Cathedral Street, SE1
t (020) 7836 3236
www.fishdiner.co.uk
⊖ London Bridge, Borough
Open 11.30am–11pm, daily

5 La Lanterna
6–8 Mill Street, SE1
t (020) 7252 2420
⊖ Tower Hill
Open 12 noon–11pm

6 Manze's
87 Tower Bridge Road, SE1
t (020) 2407 2985
www.manze.co.uk
⊖ London Bridge, Tower Hill
Open Mon 11–2, Tues–Thurs 10.30–2, Fri 10–2.15, Sat 10–2.45

7 Pizza Express
Cardomom Building, Shad Thames, SE1
t (020) 7403 8484
www.pizzaexpress.co.uk
⊖ London Bridge, Tower Hill
Open 11,30am–12 midnight, daily

See **Eat** p.224 for more details on the above restaurants.
See map on p.115 for the locations of the restaurants numbered above.

The City

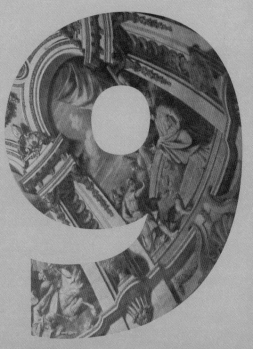

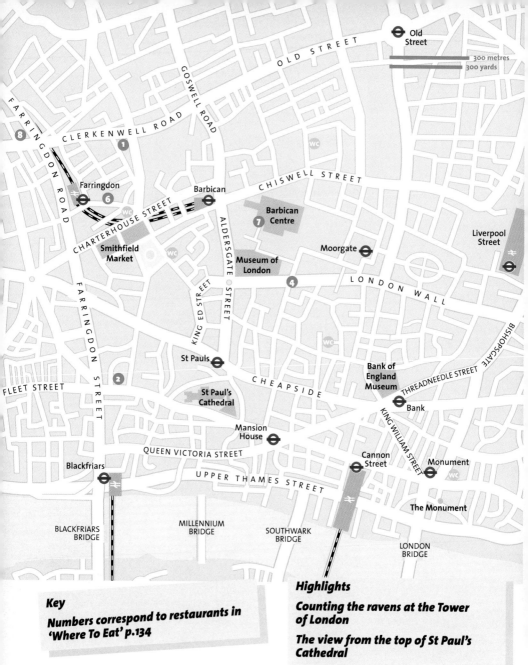

OLD STREET

⊖ Old
Street

300 metres
300 yards

GOSWELL ROAD

CLERKENWELL ROAD

⑧

①

FARRINGDON ROAD

CHISWELL STREET

≋ Farringdon

⑥

CHARTERHOUSE STREET

Barbican
⊖

Barbican
Centre
⑦

Liverpool
Street
≋
⊖

wc

ALDERSGATE STREET

Smithfield
Market

wc

Museum of
London

Moorgate ⊖

LONDON WALL

④

FARRINGDON STREET

KING ED STREET

wc

BISHOPSGATE

St Pauls ⊖

CHEAPSIDE

Bank of
England
Museum

THREADNEEDLE STREET

FLEET STREET

②

St Paul's
Cathedral

Bank ⊖

KING WILLIAM STREET

Mansion
House ⊖

QUEEN VICTORIA STREET

Cannon
Street ⊖

Monument
⊖
wc

Blackfriars
≋

UPPER THAMES STREET

The Monument

BLACKFRIARS
BRIDGE

MILLENNIUM
BRIDGE

SOUTHWARK
BRIDGE

LONDON
BRIDGE

Key

*Numbers correspond to restaurants in
'Where To Eat' p.134*

Highlights

*Counting the ravens at the Tower
of London*

*The view from the top of St Paul's
Cathedral*

*Staring at the gold bars in the Bank of
England Museum*

London's monied heart, the City, is home to the Bank of England, the Stock Exchange and the Royal Mint as well as dozens of other seriously rich institutions. Millions and millions of pounds change hands here every day at the blink of an eye.

It's the most commercial area of London and the least residential. In the Middle Ages, when the City *was* London, people would come here from miles around to sell their goods and livestock at market, as the surviving street names Bread Street, Wood Street and Poultry can testify.

It's an area both filled with history and in a permanent state of reinvention. Dotted with cranes all year round, the City skyline is constantly being reshaped. So, alongside such grand old landmarks as St Paul's Cathedral and the 900-year-old Tower of London, you'll find some of London's newest creations – places like the Swiss Re building, a stunning giant glass cylinder nicknamed the 'Erotic Gherkin' by the press.

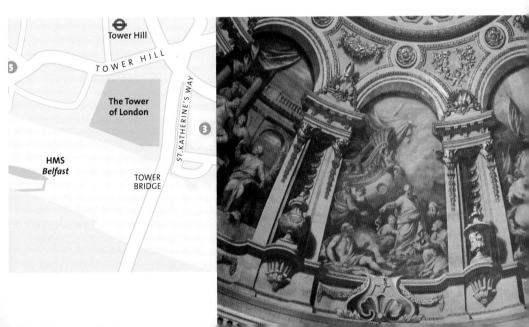

Tower of London

Tower Hill, EC3 (the entrance, while the Tower Hill area is being redeveloped, is via Tower Moat – follow the signs from Tower Hill Underground)
t 0870 756 6060
www.hrp.org.uk
⊖ Tower Hill
Bus 15, 25, 42, 78, 100, D1
Open Mar–Oct Mon–Sat 9–6, Sun 10–6; Nov–Feb Tues–Sat 9–5, Sun–Mon 10–5
Adm Adult £12, child £7.80, concs £9, family (2+2) £36
*Very limited wheelchair access, call **t** (020) 7403 1115 for access guide. The entrance for pushchairs and wheelchair users is via the Tower's West Gate on Lower Thames Street. Tours, family trail guides*
Suitable for ages 7 and over
Allow at least 3hrs

Murders, executions, assassinations, conspiracies and betrayals – the Tower of London has seen them all. So that kids get the most out of their visit here, it's important that they know a little of the history. An old building is not particularly interesting in itself, but if children are told that this is the building in which two princes were murdered and bricked up behind a wall, perhaps by their wicked uncle so that he would become king instead of them, it suddenly becomes much more exciting. The famous Yeoman Warders or 'Beefeaters' come in very handy in this regard, as they are generally more than willing to regale children with tales of intrigue and murder.

At around 900 years old, the Tower is one of London's oldest major landmarks, and also one of the best-preserved medieval castles in the world. The White Tower, at its heart, was built by William the Conqueror soon after his invasion of England in 1066 in order to shore up his position and provide a stronghold against future rebellions. It was to prove a great success; its massive 15-ft walls have never been breached. The Tower has not always served a purely defensive role, however. In the 16th and 17th centuries it proved just as good at keeping people in as it had been at keeping them out. You can visit the spot on Tower Green where the teenage Lady Jane Grey, Walter Raleigh and Anne Boleyn all met their grisly ends – and grisly, in this instance, really means grisly. The sword blow that killed Anne Boleyn, Henry VIII's second wife, was delivered with such speed that her lips supposedly continued to recite a prayer after her head had been removed.

The Tower's fantastic security record led to it being entrusted with the safekeeping of the nation's most precious treasure – the Crown Jewels. You can see them in all their glory at the Jewel House, where you are carried past the

Tell me a story: A Bloody coup

Today the crown jewels are protected by an array of sophisticated security devices, but did you know that in 1671 the fantastically named Irish adventurer and Civil War veteran Colonel Thomas Blood almost succeeded in stealing them from the Tower? On the day in question Blood disguised himself as a clergyman and, accompanied by his wife and nephew, went to the tower where his wife pretended to faint. When the Keeper of the Jewels came to help, Blood hit him on the head with a mallet, knocking him out. Blood then grabbed the crown, which he bent to fit under his cloak, while his nephew put the orb in his pocket. The nephew then tried to file the royal sceptre in half to hide it under his coat. He took so long, however, that the keeper's son was able to raise the alarm and the two men were captured and thrown into a dungeon in the Tower. Charles II was apparently so impressed by the daring shown that he not only granted Blood a pardon, but also gave him a pension of £500 a year (a fortune in those days). Sometimes, it seems, crime really does pay.

priceless crowns, sceptres and orbs on a moving walkway. Be sure to look out for the Cullinans I and II, the largest top-quality cut diamonds in the world. Elsewhere in the Tower you'll find Edward I's medieval palace, where guides dressed in period costume will demonstrate crafts such as calligraphy and quill-making; the Armouries, where there's a display of miniature suits of armour made for royal children (presumably the medieval equivalent of a modern millionaire giving their child a miniature Ferrari), and the White Tower where there's a display of grisly torture instruments. It was here that Guy Fawkes confessed to having tried to blow up James I (only after his legs and arms were almost pulled off on the rack). Do also look out for the Tower's most famous residents, the shiny black ravens which live in the Tower Gardens (although be sure to keep your distance as they can get a bit grumpy). According to legend, if the ravens ever leave the Tower, the country will topple.

Question 13
What was the name of the king who supposedly had his nephews killed in the Tower?
answer on p.249

The Tower is one of the most popular sites in London which means that, if you're visiting in summer, you're going to have to queue. It can also be quite hard on the legs, especially for young children, but it does provide a memorable day out. Family trail booklets are available at the main gate and, during the school holidays, the Tower organizes a whole range of free family activities.

St Paul's Cathedral

St Paul's Churchyard, EC4
t (020) 7236 4128
www.stpauls.co.uk
⊖ St Paul's, Mansion House
Bus 4, 8, 11, 15, 17, 23, 25, 26, 56, 76, 172, 242, 501, 521
Opening times Mon–Sat 8.30–4
Adm Cathedral only: adult £6, child £3, family (2+2) £17, concs £5
Wheelchair accessible for all areas except galleries
Suitable for ages 5 and over
Allow at least 1hr

St Paul's Cathedral is undoubtedly one of London's most recognizable landmarks. Its great plump dome, which seems to dominate the City's skyline, will be familiar to many children from the film of *Mary Poppins*. Unfortunately, over the next two years, much of the building will be obscured behind scaffolding as a huge renovation programme is completed. This is a pity as the creation of the Millennium Bridge to the south and the Paternoster Square retail development to the northwest had opened up views of the cathedral unseen for centuries. We'll just have to wait.

The cathedral will remain open throughout the renovation and is still well worth a visit. It's a great place for kids to come and burn off some excess energy. The 521-step climb, though hard on the thighs, is well worth it. The panoramic views from the top of the dome, 365ft up are stupendous. You can see more or less the whole of London stretched out before you like a great 3D tapestry.

Designed by Sir Christopher Wren, and built in the late 17th century after the original, wooden cathedral burnt down in the Great Fire in 1666, St Paul's is arguably London's most beautiful church. The fantastically decorated interior is almost as impressive as the view from the top of the cathedral, particularly the massive domed ceiling. About halfway up the inside of the dome is the Whispering Gallery. You can test it by doing the following: stand on one side of the Gallery while a friend goes over to the other. Now, providing it's quiet enough, you should be able to whisper something to the wall on your side and have your friend hear it quite clearly on the other, 107ft away.

In the crypt (the largest in Europe) you'll find the tombs of many of Britain's greatest military leaders – Admiral Nelson (his coffin is made out of the main mast of the defeated French flagship at Trafalgar) and the Duke of Wellington (the conqueror of Napoleon at Waterloo) among them – as well as a model of the cathedral, featuring a considerably thinner dome. There's also a shop, restaurant, and a great, child-friendly café.

Museum of London

London Wall, EC2
t 0870 444 3851
www.museumoflondon.org.uk
⊖ Barbican, Bank, St Paul's
Bus 8, 22b, 56
Open Tues–Sat 10–6, Sun 12 noon–6
Free
Wheelchair accessible. Suitable for all ages
Allow at least 2hrs

This fascinating museum tells the story of life in London from prehistoric camps to concrete tower blocks. It may not have the range of one of the great Kensington collections, but this is still a lovely museum with a charm and style all its own.

Can you spot?

The following landmarks, visible from the top of St Paul's. The Thames is due south.

▶ To the west: the British Telecom Tower (formerly the Post Office Tower), a tall, thin, round building that looks like an enormous spark plug. Its sides are covered in transmitters and satellite dishes.

▶ To the northwest: The Old Bailey (the colloquial name for the Central Criminal Courts), which looks a bit like St Paul's but with a much smaller dome. Perched on top is a golden statue of a woman holding a sword in one hand and a pair of scales (representing the balance of justice) in the other.

▶ To the south, across the river: Tate Modern – formerly a power station, this is a huge square brick building with a tall central square tower.

▶ To the east: Canary Wharf, London's (and indeed Britain's) tallest building (812ft), which has a triangular top with a light that winks 40 times a minute to prevent low-flying aircraft from hitting it.

▶ Tower Bridge, with its two great turrets and raising decks.

The museum has created some wonderful scale models, which vividly illustrate the various stages of London's history: there's a prehistoric mammoth hunt, a Viking ship, Shakespeare's Rose Theatre and London during the Great Fire, each rendered in perfect miniature. There are also a number of restored and reconstructed interiors: a Roman kitchen, a Stuart dining room, a cell from the infamous Newgate Prison and a 1920s shop interior. These more traditional displays are augmented by more modern technologies, including computer terminals where you can see films depicting life in the Victorian age, wartime and 1960s London. Also on show, for 364 days of the year, is the ornate Lord Mayor's state coach.

As vast as the museum's collection is, it's constantly expanding thanks to the number of new building projects taking place in the city. By law, no new development can be undertaken within the 'Square Mile' until there's been a thorough architectural excavation of the site. Recent digs at Spitalfields and Gresham Street have uncovered hordes of Roman antiquities (including tombstones, jewellery, kitchenware and even the remains of a water-wheel), many of which have gone on display in the museum just a few weeks after being discovered.

The museum tries hard to make history come alive for its younger visitors. The curators allow families to attend artefact handling sessions on weekends. During the school holidays the museum

Question 14
The Lord Mayor's gold coach resides in the museum for 364 days of the year. Where is it on the remaining day?
answer on p.249

also organizes a number of workshops, demonstrations and performances for children on a range of subjects from metalwork to preparing Roman food.

Bank of England Museum

Threadneedle Street, EC2. The entrance is on Bartholomew Lane
t (020) 7601 5545
www.bankofengland.co.uk
⊖ Bank, Cannon Street
Bus 9, 11, 22
Open Mon–Fri 10–5
Free
Wheelchair accessible
Suitable for children aged 10 and over
Allow at least 1hr

Take a trek through the monetary world to see how financial transactions have developed from paper IOUs to whizzing numbers on a computer screen. The curators have obviously thought long and hard about how to make what is, after all, a

Did you know?
▶ That the first St Paul's Cathedral was built by the Saxons way back in AD 604
▶ That the present cathedral took 35 years to build at a cost of £721,552 (over £50 million in today's money) and was paid for by a tax put on coal coming into the city.
▶ That the cathedral clocktower 'Great Tom' houses Britain's heaviest bell (17 tonnes) and that the dome itself weighs a staggering 65,000 tonnes.
▶ That when the medieval cathedral caught fire in 1666, it generated such a tremendous amount of heat that the 250-year-old corpse of the former Mayor of London, Robert Braybrooke, was blasted out of his grave and thrown clear of the churchyard.

rather dry subject interesting for children. So you'll find a recreation of an 18th-century bank office inhabited by waxwork bankers; lots of interactive video screens where you can find out the history of the bank and, the highlight, a large perspex pyramid filled with gold bars – the kids glued permanently to its side are not part of the exhibit.

The museum also has displays on more modern currency matters – the Stock Exchange, financial trading etc. – which include a (very difficult) inter-active currency trading game. Activity worksheets for kids (there are versions for 5–8 year-olds, 9–12 year-olds and 13–16 year-olds) available from the front desk.

The Monument

Monument Street, EC3
t (020) 7626 2717
⊖ Monument
Bus 15, 22a, 35, 40, 48
Open 9.30–5, daily
Adm Adult £2, child £1, under-5s **free**
No wheelchair access
Suitable for ages 4 and over
Allow at least 30mins

If the Monument were to fall over, its top (provided it fell in the right direction) would land on the very spot in Pudding Lane where the Fire of London began more than 300 years ago. It was designed by Sir Christopher Wren as a memorial

Question 15
The Bank of England Museum has a collection of British coins. However, the bank only issues notes. Who issues British coins?
answer on p.249

for the victims of the Fire. At 202-ft high it was, on completion in 1677, the tallest free-standing column in the world. Of course, by modern stan-dards, 202ft isn't very tall at all, and today the monument is rather obscured by the medium-sized buildings surrounding it. You can climb the 311 steps to the top where you get a close-up look at the great bronze urn that sits on the monu-ment's summit spouting shiny metallic flames. The views are good, albeit not as good as those from the top of St Paul's, but kids will enjoy sending themselves dizzy running down the spiral staircase.

Barbican Centre

Silk Street, EC2
t 0845 120 7598
www.barbican.org.uk
⊖ Barbican, Bank, St Paul's, Moorgate
Bus 4, 11, 21, 76, 100, 141, 153, 214, 271
Wheelchair accessible

Nobody could describe the Barbican as beautiful, but it is one of the capital's major arts centres and, as such, always has a lot going on. These great concrete tower blocks and labyrinthine corridors are home to several of the country's most presti-gious artistic bodies including the London Symphony Orchestra and the English Chamber Orchestra as well as three cinemas, an art gallery and a semi-tropical garden. Special children's events and performances are put on in the school holidays as part of the centre's 'Barbican Family'programme. These include the annual LSO Discovery Concert (*see* p.165), and Discovery Creative Music Workshops, which offer informal instrument tuition for 7–12 year-olds. There's also a Family Film Club for 5–11 year olds which meets every Saturday morning at 10.30 (*see* p.158)

AROUND & ABOUT

Smithfield, the capital's largest meat market, was a popular site for jousting in the Middle Ages and also witnessed the bloody conclusion of the Peasants' Revolt (*see* below). Opposite the market, on the wall of St Bartholomew's Hospital, is a blue plaque marking the spot where another revolt came to an end when William Wallace (as featured in the film *Braveheart*), the leader of the Scots, was hung, drawn and quartered by the English in the 13th century.

Further afield, on Fleet Street, is Prince Henry's Room, one of the few domestic houses to survive the Great Fire of London, while just off King Edward Street is one of the City's few pieces of greenery, Postman's Park. It has a memorial wall dedicated to ordinary people who have sacrificed their lives for others.

Tell me a story: Filthy lucre

Have you heard the one about the man who got into the Bank of England's gold vaults by way of the sewers? It's no joke.

In 1836 the directors of the Bank are said to have received an anonymous letter stating that the writer had discovered an underground passage to the bullion. He offered to meet them there to prove his claim at any hour they chose. Although initially sceptical, the directors were finally persuaded to assemble one night in the vault. At the agreed time they heard a noise under the floor and the mysterious correspondent appeared from below merely by displacing a few floorboards. Apparently he was a sewerman who, during repair work to the tunnels, had discovered an old drain which ran immediately under the bullion vault. He might have carried away enormous sums but he resisted the urge and for his honesty the Bank is said to have rewarded him with a gift of £800. Following the incident, the directors decided to take precautions against further unwanted intrusions. Several letters were sent to George Bailey, the Curator of the Soane Museum*, asking that the architect's plans of the drains beneath the Bank premises be returned to the Bank, just in case of other passages.
* Sir John Soane was the Bank of England's architect from 1788 to 1833. *See* p.83 for more on his extraordinary house, now a museum.

The peasants are revolting

In 1381 a band of commoners marched on London demanding the repeal of the newly imposed Poll Tax (which charged everyone the same amount, regardless of their ability to pay). Once in the City, they stormed the Debtors' Prison and slaughtered as many lawyers and tax collectors as they could find. The 14-year-old king, Richard II, met them at Smithfield to discuss their grievances. At first it seemed that the rebels would get their way, with the king agreeing to a number of concessions including the repeal of the tax and the abolition of serfdom. However, the Mayor of London became so incensed at the protesters' presumption that he stepped forward and stabbed the rebel leader Wat Tyler, fatally wounding him. Rather than continue their protest, the rebels decided to accept the word of the king and disband. Bad move – once they had turned for home, Richard's troops captured and killed as many of the protesters as they could find. A picture of the dagger used to stab Tyler was subsequently incorporated into the City of London's coat of arms.

Prince Henry's Room

17 Fleet Street, EC4
t (020) 7936 2710
⊖ Temple, Blackfriars
Open Mon–Sat 11–2
Free

WHERE TO EAT

Picnic & snacks

With demand for building space so high, there are precious few green spaces to be found within the City limits. A few small courtyards aside, the best strech of greenery is **Postman's Park** on King Edward Street, which makes a nice spot for a picnic (although finding a spot during a sunny summer lunchtime may take a while). Picnics and packed lunches can also be eaten in the school rooms of the **Museum of London** and, if the weather's fine, the museum's **Barber Surgeon's Gardens,** which are bordered by the remains of a Roman fort.

Supplies can be picked up from **Leadenhall Market** on Gracechurch Street, EC3, which has a fine array of grocers and delicatessens; the **Deli Bar** at 117 Charterhouse Street, EC2, **t** (020) 7253 2070, ⊖ Farringdon, and **Tesco Metro** at 80b Cheapside, EC1, ⊖ Bank are two useful examples.

The primary function of the City's food outlets is to assuage the lunchtime appetites of its thousands of day workers. Consequently you'll find plenty of fast food, sandwich bars and cafés (although be aware that many of these are closed on weekends). There are numerous eateries lining **Ludgate Hill** by the west front of St Paul's including a **Starbuck's, M&S Food Halls** and **Fresh Italy** at no.38, **t** (020) 7329 5279, ⊖ St Paul's, a sort of fast-food Italian café where you can pick up simple pasta dishes, salads and foccacia sandwiches. **St Katharine's Dock**, situated next to Tower Bridge, is also a good source of cafés and restaurants. Otherwise look out for **The Place Below,** an excellent vegetarian café situated beneath the 'Cockney' church of St Mary le Bow, Cheapside, EC2, **t** (020) 7329 0789, ⊖ St Paul's, Bank; **Smiths of Smithfield** at 67–77 Charterhouse Street, EC1, **t** (020) 7251 7950, ⊖ Farringdon, which does a very good all-day breakfast; and the **Crypt Café** of St Paul's Cathedral, St Paul's Courtyard, EC4, ⊖ St Paul's. Selling an array of hot and cold drinks, sandwiches, pastries and cakes, this is a cool welcoming spot (particularly on a sunny day) and is open to everyone, regardless of whether they're visiting the cathedral or not. There are also branches of **McDonald's** at 143 Cannon Street, ⊖ Cannon Street, 41–42 London Wall, ⊖ Moorgate, 12 Tower Hill Terrace, ⊖ Tower Hill and 50 Liverpool Street, ⊖ Liverpool Street.

Restaurants

1 Ask Pizza
103 St John Street, EC1
t (020) 7253 0323
www.askcentral.co.uk
⊖ Farringdon
Open 11.30am–11.30pm

2 Café Rouge
Hillgate House, Limeburner Lane, EC4
t (020) 7588 3008
www.caferouge.co.uk
⊖ Blackfriars
Open Mon–Fri 12 noon–2.30 and 6–10.30, Sat–Sun 12 noon–3 and 5–6.30

3 Dickens Inn
St Katherine's Way, E1
t (020 7488 2208)
www.dickensinn.co.uk
⊖ Tower Hill, Tower Gateway
DLR London Bridge

4/5/6 Pizza Express
Branches at: 125 Alban Gate, London Wall, EC2, **t** (020) 7600 8880, ⊖ Barbican, St Paul's **Open** Mon–Fri 11.30–11, Sat 12 noon–10, Sun 12 noon– 8 1 Byward Street, EC3, **t** (020) 7625 5025, ⊖ Tower Hill; 26 Cowcross Street, EC1, **t** (020) 7490 8025, ⊖ Farringdon **Open** 11.30–11, daily
www.pizzaexpress.com

7 Searcy's
Level I, Barbican Centre, EC2
t (020) 7588 3008
⊖ Barbican
Open Mon–Fri 12 noon–2.30 and 6–10.30, Sat–Sun 12 noon–3 and 5–6.30

8 Yo! Sushi
95 Farringdon Road, Clerkenwell, EC1
t (020) 7841 0785
www.yosushi.co.uk
⊖ Farringdon
Open 12 noon–12 midnight daily

See **Eat** p.224 for more details on the above restaurants.
See map on p.126 for the locations of the restaurants numbered above.

Museumland

There are few better places than this to come for an exciting day out. In the morning, start with a quick tour around one of the capital's great museums. You can choose from the Natural History Museum, the Science Museum or the Victoria and Albert Museum. All are within spitting distance of each other, all offer guaranteed entertainment with a huge range of family-friendly exhibits and facilities and, as an added bonus, all are free. From here it's a five minute walk to Hyde Park for a picnic and a quick jaunt in a rowing boat on the Serpentine, before finishing the day with some souvenir and gift shopping in the unforgettable halls of Harrods.

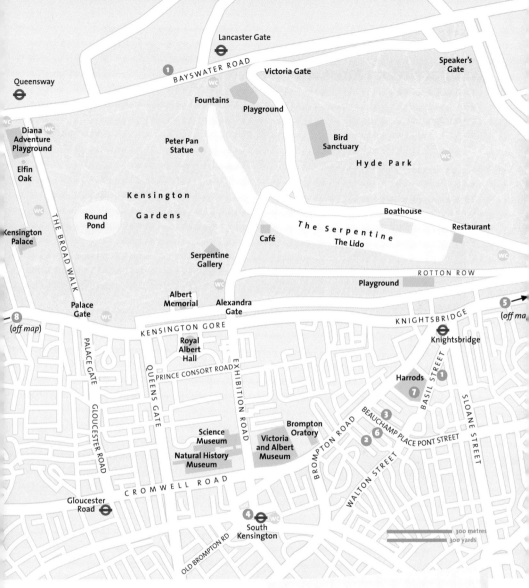

Lancaster Gate

Speaker's Gate

1 BAYSWATER ROAD

Victoria Gate

Queensway

Fountains

Playground

WC

Diana Adventure Playground

WC

Peter Pan Statue

Bird Sanctuary

Hyde Park

WC

Elfin Oak

Kensington Gardens

The Serpentine

Boathouse

Restaurant

WC

Round Pond

Café

The Lido

Kensington Palace

THE BROAD WALK

WC

Serpentine Gallery

ROTTON ROW

Playground

Albert Memorial

WC

Alexandra Gate

KNIGHTSBRIDGE

5

(off ma

Palace Gate

WC

KENSINGTON GORE

8

(off map)

Royal Albert Hall

Knightsbridge

PALACE GATE

QUEEN'S GATE

PRINCE CONSORT ROAD

EXHIBITION ROAD

Harrods

7

BASIL STREET

GLOUCESTER ROAD

Science Museum

Brompton Oratory

3

BROMPTON ROAD

BEAUCHAMP PLACE

PONT STREET

SLOANE STREET

Natural History Museum

Victoria and Albert Museum

6

WALTON STREET

CROMWELL ROAD

Gloucester Road

OLD BROMPTON RD

4

WC

South Kensington

300 metres

300 yards

Key
Numbers correspond to restaurants in 'Where To Eat' p.146

Highlights

The new British Galleries at the Victoria and Albert Museum

Boating in Hyde Park

Encountering the dinosaurs at the Natural History Museum

Natural History Museum

Cromwell Road, SW7
t (020) 7942 5000
www.nhm.ac.uk
◉ South Kensington
Bus 9, 10, 14, 49, 52, 70, 74, 345, 360, 414, C1
Open Mon–Sat 10–5.50, Sun 11–5.50
Free
Wheelchair accessible for most galleries, with adapted toilets. The entrance for wheelchair users is via the Earth Galleries in Exhibition Road
Suitable for all ages
Allow a morning or afternoon

One of the must-see sights in London for both children and adults, the Natural History Museum is, quite simply, a fabulous place. Huge monsters, replica volcanoes, earthquake simulators, creepy crawlies, precious stones, big things, small things, shiny things – there's so much to look at. This is the sort of museum where kids tend to rush off pointing at everything.

It's been revamped in recent years. All the old favourites are still here – the great fossil monsters, the impossibly huge blue whale suspended from the museum ceiling – but these have been augmented with new exhibits and more up-to-date technologies.

Whatever entrance you choose, there's an almost immediate 'Wow!' awaiting you. Walk through the main door and you'll be confronted by the great swooping head of a fossil *diplodocus* looming down above you. Nip around the side and you'll find yourself walking through a guard of honour made up of bizarre futuristic statues before riding up an escalator into a huge clunking, clanking metal globe. The two entrances mark the beginnings of the museum's two themed areas, the Life and Earth Galleries.

Pride of place in the Life Galleries goes to those perennial children's favourites, dinosaurs. There is an illuminated walkway to take you

past the various superstar fossils (T-Rex and the horned-faced Triceratops among them). Videos and interactive displays provide background information and there's an intriguing section looking at how these long-extinct beasts have become staples of popular culture – from *The Flintstones* to *Jurassic Park*. The *pièce de resistance*, however, is the new two-thirds size animatronic *Tyrannosaurus Rex* – it growls, it slavers, it snaps its jaws, it really is rather excellent. It even smells, although not authentically. The stench of rotting meat which presumably would have pervaded from the dinosaur's mouth was considered a touch over-powering. Instead the dinosaur gives off a weaker, 'swampy' odour.

The Earth Galleries play to their strengths. Detailed, in-depth geology has been ditched in favour of spectacular volcano and earthquake exhibitions: videos of exploding craters, models of lava flows, plastercasts of the Pompeii victims frozen in mute agony and, best of all, an earthquake simulator – every five minutes you can stand inside a mock-up Japanese supermarket as it undergoes a minor tremor.

The latest addition to this great cathedral of nature is the Darwin Centre. Built at a cost of £30 million and covering some 10,000 square metres, it provides a showcase for the museum's vast collection of preserved animal species (of which there are around 22 million, although the centre only has space for a mere 450,000). The centre's walls are lined with shelves on which sit hundreds and hundreds of preserving jars, each containing a different animal. There are monkeys, birds, sharks, tortoises, lizards, plus countless others. Several seem to have been put (or rather stuffed) into jars a little too small for them, their distorted features

Did you know?
The Natural History Museum is every collector's idea of paradise. It contains a staggering 68 million plants, animals, fossils, rocks and minerals from all regions of the world.

Question 16

The word 'dinosaur' itself means 'terrible lizard' in Latin. What do the following dinosaur names mean?

a) Triceratops
b) Deinocheirus
c) Baronyx

answer on p.249

creating grotesque visages against the sides of the glass. Amazingly, some of the creatures were actually collected by the great naturalist Charles Darwin himself during his mid 19th-century travels to the Galapagos islands, and provided the evidence for his world-changing theories of evolution via natural selection.

Free behind-the-scenes tours to see the thousands of specimens not on public display, as well as the laboratory facilities used to examine them, are given daily (available to ages 10 and over only).

Interesting though the centre is, it offers little in the way of interaction and kids itching to get involved in a more hands-on way should head to the new Clore Education Centre. Here 7–14 year-olds are invited to take an item (such as a fossil, a plant or a preserved bird or insect) from the 'Specimen Wall' and examine it at one of several workstations, which come equipped with computer terminals, microscopes, magnifiers and measures. The centre also has a display of living creatures – insects, carniverous plants etc. – and a small courtyard garden.

Even if the Education Centre is closed or busy, there's still plenty on offer for families in the museum. Discovery Guides, aimed at all ages from 3–18, are available at the main entrances of the Earth and Life Galleries (samples can be downloaded from the internet). The museum organizes family workshops for both under-7s (storytelling, puppet shows etc) and 7–12 year-olds (hands-on activities, beast hunts in the new museum courtyard etc) on Saturdays and Sundays and some school holiday weekdays. The workshops are free, but can only be booked on the day at the information desk in Gallery 10. The museum also organizes special events and family talks year round.

If it gets the funding, the museum hopes to open yet another extension in 2007 in which it will display some of its collection of 6 million preserved plants and 22 million preserved insects.

Science Museum

Exhibition Road, London SW7
t 0870 870 4868 f (020) 7942 4302
www.sciencemuseum.org.uk
⊖ South Kensington
Bus 9, 10, 14, 49, 52, 70, 74, 345, 360, 414, C1
Open 10–6, daily
Free to all museum galleries. 'Explorer pass' for IMAX and simulator rides: adult £11.50, child £7.50, family (2+2) £34.95, family (2+1) 25.50
Wheelchair accessible, with adapted toilets. An 'Access and Facilities Guide' is available from the information desk
Suitable for all ages
Allow a morning or afternoon

The Science Museum, perhaps more than any other museum, understands children. It understands that children like to be involved with the exhibits; they like to touch, to feel, to press and push as well as merely see. Nowhere is this better demonstrated than in the Wellcome Wing, the museum's £48 million extension which opened in Millennium year. Bathed in futuristic blue light, the new four-storey wing offers state-of-the-art exhibits and lots of hands-on fun. There are three permanent exhibitions: 'Who am I?', which looks at how science has helped us to understand what it means to be human (you can morph your features on a computer to make yourself look older or younger, or even switch gender); 'Digitopolis', which explores today's digital landscape (you can digitally manipulate your voice to sound like Darth Vader or Mickey Mouse), and 'In Future', which predicts how technology will develop over the next 20 years – play the 'In Future' interactive game and decide for yourself which technologies you think will be most relevant in the decades to come. There

Short of time?

There's far too much in the museum to be covered in a single day and you may prefer to plan your tour around a few headline exhibits. Here are some suggestions:

▶ A 1903 Burnley mill engine. This is the showpiece of the Power Gallery on the ground floor, dedicated to the great machinery of the Industrial Revolution.

▶ The Black Arrow. Britain's first and only satellite launch rocket. The enormous craft is attached to the ceiling of the Space Gallery.

▶ The Apollo 10 Command Module. In 1969 it flew three astronauts into space as a rehearsal for the moon landing mission later in the year. Note the scorch marks on the craft, which were caused when it re-entered the earth's atmosphere at great speed.

▶ Foucault's Pendulum. A giant pendulum suspended from the ceiling of the ground floor, designed to demonstrate the rotation of the Earth.

▶ One of the last working mechanical telephone exchanges in Britain. It can be found in the Telecommunications Gallery on the first floor.

▶ Charles Babbage's Difference Machine. This collection of cogs, gears and levers was the world's first ever computer. It is in Computing Then and Now on the second floor.

▶ On Air. Here, on the third floor, kids can learn how a radio station works.

▶ A model of a 16th-century medical teaching theatre and a life-size recreation of a modern operating theatre, in which waxwork doctors perform open-heart surgery. Both are in Glimpses of Medical History on the fourth floor.

is also an IMAX film theatre showing science-related films on huge, four-storey-high screens (adm £7.10) and a simulator ride, 'Virtual Voyages', which takes you on a ride across the solar system to intercept a comet hurtling towards Earth (adm £3.50).

Impressive though this wing is, you'll want to save some time for some of the museum's other exhibits, several of which are specifically designed for children. These include the Launch Pad in the basement where there are various games and pieces of equipment through which kids can learn a few basic scientific principles – they can create a

giant bubble, touch a plasma ball and see electricity following their fingers, build a rubber bridge or perhaps try and tiptoe past the vibration detector. Staff are on hand to guide the youngsters through the apparatus. In the basement there are two further child-centric galleries – the Garden, aimed at 3–6 year-olds, which gives children the chance to experiment with water using pumps, dams and buckets, and Things, aimed at slightly older children (7–11 year-olds), which has a wide range of interactive video displays. Also try not to miss the Secret Life of the Home. This takes a humorous look at domestic gizmos and gadgets from vacuum cleaners and washing machines to WCs, fridges and heaters.

Of course, there are plenty of other galleries which, while not specifically designed for children, will nonetheless appeal. The Flight Gallery, for instance, will bring out the latent pilot in both parents and children. Here, in the 'Flight Lab' hands-on section, you can pedal a propeller to see how helicopters work, sit in the cockpit of a single-seater aircraft, watch as a water-powered rocket is fired across the galler, or take a ride (for a small fee) in a state-of-the-art flight simulator (adults £2.50, children £1.50, height restriction 1.20m) which replicates the experience of sitting in the cockpit of a Harrier jump jet.

Before leaving, make sure you check out the museum shop which is filled with 'science' toys and games – junior astronomy kits, rainbow Slinkies, holograms, binoculars, models, kaleidoscopes and the like. 'Play', the museum's family guide, is available both here and at reception for £2.95.

Science Nights

Kids will like the museum so much that they'll probably wish they could spend the night. Well, guess what? The museum has started running Science Nights when children aged between 8 and 11 (plus an accompanying parent) can come and camp overnight. They are treated to midnight tours of the museum, workshops and bedtime stories.

Victoria & Albert Museum

Cromwell Road, SW7
t (020) 7942 2000
www.vam.ac.uk
⊖ South Kensington
Bus 9, 10, 14, 49, 52, 70, 74, 345, 360, 414, C1
Open Mon–Tues 10–5.45, Wed 10am–10pm,
Thurs–Sun 10–5.45, last Fri of month till 10pm
Free
*Wheelchair accessible. Wheelchair users should use
Exhibition Road entrance where there are also
4 designated disabled parking bays*
Suitable for ages 10 and over
Allow at least 2hrs

Dedicated to the decorative arts, the Victoria and Albert Museum (or the V & A as it is known) has, over its long history, gathered together a huge collection of treasures from all over the world: silverware from European royal palaces, ceramics from eastern temples, sculptures by African tribes and vast hoards of jewellery, furniture, textiles, tapestries and paintings – it's like an enormous magpie's nest, full of the world's most gaudy, glittery things. The Dress Gallery usually appeals to clothes-conscious teens. It traces the evolution of fashion from the 17th century to the present day, from ruffs and crinolins to mini skirts and trainers.

For something to gasp at, head to the Cast Court where you'll find plastercasts of some of the

Tell me a story: Tudor tales

The V&A is home to a number of rare and precious objects, among them Charles Dickens' pen case and manuscript for *Oliver Twist*, as well as Joseph Paxton's first sketch for the Crystal Palace, built for the Great Exhibition of 1851. Here are a selection of Tudor curios, each with its own story. Try and find them on your way round this eclectic museum.

▶ The Great Bed of Ware – over 11-ft long and 10-ft wide, the bed is mentioned in Shakespeare's *Twelfth Night* and in a poem by Lord Byron. Charles Dickens is said to have tried to buy it. It was, in fact, a Tudor marketing ploy, to attract visitors to The White Hart Inn at Ware in Hertfordshire. The bed is also supposed to be haunted.

▶ A rare 16th-century Standing Salt, or ceremonial salt cellar. In the Tudor period salt was a luxury commodity and was kept in a precious container called simply a 'salt'. Distinguished guests sat 'above the salt' at the table and had the choice of the best dishes.

▶ The beautiful hanging panels from Oxburgh Hall were embroidered by, amongst others, Mary Queen of Scots when imprisoned (1569–85).

▶ A fine 16th-century Silver Tankard. These were introduced during the reign of Henry VIII and soon became fashionable gifts at court. They could be engraved with the individual's heraldic insignia, and were used to drink warm beer or ass's milk.

world's greatest (and biggest) statues and monuments – Michelangelo's *David* and Trajan's Column (in two huge pieces) are among them.

The British Galleries 1500–1900 are a welcome addition, with play areas where kids can try on Victorian clothes or attempt to rebuild the Crystal Palace using perspex blocks, as well as touch-screen information points, reconstructed room sets and banks of computer workstations.

There's not much to push or pull in the other galleries, though the museum organizes plenty of

Question 17
How many years did it take to build the V&A Museum's current home and in what year was it finished?
answer on p.249

kids' activities. These are usually themed according to the gallery – origami in the Japanese Gallery, paper clothes-making in the Dress Gallery and jewellery-making in the Silver Gallery. Free themed family trails are available from the information desk daily, and activity backpacks full of jigsaws, stories, puzzles and construction games can be picked up from the Grand Entrance on Saturday afternoons (1–4.30). Designed for ages 5–12, there are six themed packs to choose from (themes include 'Murder Mystery', 'Antique Detective' and 'Magic Glasses'). On Sundays and in the school holidays a roving activity cart tours the museum's seven miles of corridors, while on the first Sunday of each month the museum organizes drop-in events for 5–12 year-olds, based around the current temporary exhibitions and usually involving some artistic activity such as drawing or photography. Note that during the next few years some exhibitions may close temporarily, due to building of the museum's controversial 'Spiral' extension (completion has been tentatively set for 2007).

Hyde Park

t (020) 7298 2100
www.royalparks.gov.uk/hyde.htm
⊖ Hyde Park Corner, Knightsbridge, South Kensington, Lancaster Gate, Queensway, Marble Arch
Bus 2, 8, 9, 10, 12, 14, 16, 19, 22, 36, 39, 73, 74, 82, 94
Free
Suitable for all ages, although only children aged 5 and over can go boating on the Serpentine

A wonderful expanse of greenery, Hyde Park provides a welcome oasis of calm in the hectic, bustling city. In fact, only the eastern side is officially called Hyde Park; the western side is known as Kensington Gardens; but there is no official border and it's really just one big park. In the middle is the Serpentine – a great, snake-shaped lake as the name suggests – populated by swans, ducks, geese and other wildfowl. You can hire rowing boats – a great way to spend a lazy summer afternoon (adults 30mins £3, one hour £4; children 30mins £1, one hour £2; rowing lessons £5). Alternatively, if the kids would rather play on the grass, help yourself to one of the many green and white striped deckchairs that dot the park – an attendant will eventually find you and charge you the required £1. You can also swim in the Serpentine Lido, paddle in the children's pool (between May and September) and clamber aboard the giant model pirate ship in the Princess Diana Adventure Playground. This is located near the famous Elfin Oak (a tree decorated with dozens of tiny elf sculptures) and

Did you know?
Rotten Row, the name of the bridal path running along the southern edge of the park, is a corruption of the French 'route de roi' (king's way). It became the first road in London to have street lighting when William III hung 300 lanterns from the trees along its route in order to deter highwaymen.

features a large adventure galleon (not a pirate ship, it was felt that such violent imagery might be inappropriate). The park's famous Peter Pan statue is also near here. Author J. M. Barrie lived at 100 Bayswater Road, not 500 yards from the park, and erected the statue secretly in the middle of the night.

Because of its location, Hyde Park is extremely popular, but it is also, owing to its sheer size, serene and quiet. Furthermore, it's clean and largely free of dogs. The only real problem is the footpaths, which seem to be the favoured thoroughfares of London's roller-skating and jogging community, and if the weather's fine you may be better off walking on the grass. For more information on the park's flora and fauna, head to the former police observation point in the centre of the park, which has been turned into an education post. The staff

The Albert Memorial

This huge gold statue set in an elaborate 175-ft stone frame was built in the 1860s on the orders of Queen Victoria as a memorial to her late husband, Prince Albert. Around its carved stone sides are tributes to all the important men of letters, arts and sciences of the Victorian era. Women are somewhat few and far between. The statue itself was considered so bright that the gilding was removed during the war to stop it attracting the attention of enemy planes. It has recently been renovated to stunning effect. There are guided tours every Thurs, Fri, Sat–Sun at 2pm and 3pm, adult £3, concs £2.50, **t** (020) 7495 0916.

Can you spot?
Can you find the Pet Cemetery by the Victoria Gates in Hyde Park's northwest corner?

organize occasional beast hunts, pond dippings and nature walks, call **t** (020) 7706 3990. Do also remember that Hyde Park is one of the very few places in central London where you can go horse-riding (although you'll have to pay quite handsomely for the privilege). Hyde Park Stables, on the north side of the park, offer lessons for all abilities, *see* p.183 for more details.

Speaker's Corner

Some of London's more passionate (some would say barmy) citizens have, since 1872, been allowed to let off steam every Sunday at Speaker's Corner, which is located at the northeastern end of the park. People can say whatever they want (about whoever they want) here and, standing on a makeshift platform (traditionally a soapbox), attempt to rally passing pedestrians to their cause (be it Buddhism, Marxism or the uses and abuses of potting compost) – providing they can make themselves heard above the traffic on Park Lane.

Kensington Palace

The State Apartments, Kensington Gardens, W8
t 0870 751 5170
www.hrp.org.uk
⊖ High Street Kensington, Notting Hill Gate, Queensway
Bus 9, 10, 12, 52, 73, 94

Open Mar–Oct 10–6, daily, Nov–Feb 10–5, daily
Adm Adult £10.20, child £6.60, concs £7.70, family £31
Suitable for ages 8 and over, audio-tour guides
Allow at least 1hr

On the western edge of Kensington Gardens, this rather reserved-looking palace is where Princess Diana, the 'People's Princess', lived following her divorce from Prince Charles. The gardens outside were covered in 1.5 million bunches of flowers in the week following her untimely death in 1997. There are guided tours between 10am and 3.30pm, when you can walk through the plush historic apartments and see the Royal Ceremonial Dress Collection. This features a rotating display of items taken from the royal wardrobe – everything from flouncy 18th-century creations and early 20th-century debutante dresses to (always prompting the most interest) some of Princess Diana's glamourous outfits. The palace's very fancy Orangery restaurant offers a children's menu.

Serpentine Gallery

Kensington Gardens, W2
t (020) 7402 6075 **f** (020) 7402 4103
www.serpentinegallery.org
⊖ South Kensington, Knightsbridge, Lancaster Gate
Bus 9, 10, 12, 52, 73, 94
Open 10–6, daily
Free
Wheelchair accessible. Suitable for ages 8 and over

Near the Albert Memorial, the recently revamped Serpentine Gallery specializes in staging temporary exhibitions of modern art. It's at its most family-friendly on Saturday mornings from 10–12 noon, when kids can take tours of the gallery as part of its 'Children's Art Club'.

Royal Albert Hall

Kensington Gore, SW7
t (020) 7838 3110
www.royalalberthall.com
⊖ High Street Kensington, Knightsbridge
Bus 9, 10, 52, 360

A great red barrel of a building, it sits opposite the Albert Memorial on Kensington Gore. Despite its indifferent acoustics and legendary echo, this 19th-century construction is one of London's most popular concert venues, playing host in summer to 'the Proms' – a series of innovative classical concerts that have become a national institution. A special 'Children's Proms in the Park' concert takes place every year in Hyde Park. Call **t** (020) 7859 3203 or log on to **www**.royalalberthall.com for details of concert programmes.

There's Knightsbridge, of course, home to two of the world's most famous department stores – the ultra-chic Harvey Nichols and legendary Harrods, with its enormous toy department and magnificent food halls – as well as the nursery equipment and children's clothes shops of Walton Street. If you've got the shopping bug, however, remember that you're just a Tube stop or two away from two of London's best shopping areas: the King's Road (*see* p.93) and High Street Kensington – look out for the Children's Book Centre at no.237, the department stores – Marks & Spencer (no.113) and Barkers (no.63), and the children's clothes stores Jigsaw Junior (no.65), Hennes (no.123) and Trotters (no.127). See **Shop** p.240 for details of the above stores.

Harrods

87–135 Brompton Road
Knightsbridge, SW1
t (020) 7730 1234 **f** (020) 7581 0470
www.harrods.com
⊖ Knightsbridge
Bus 10, 19, 52, 74, 137
Open Mon–Fri 10–7, Sat 10–6

Harrods, which celebrated its 150th anniversary in 1999, is famous for its luxurious interiors. The food halls, in particular, are fabulously opulent – children may well take a passing interest in the exotic fruit displays, fresh fish sculptures and straw-boatered shop assistants as they drag you towards the toys on the fourth floor. Here you can find everything, from limited edition Steiff teddies and one-third size Ferraris with full leather interior to the latest video games. There's also a children's book department and (parents, at least, might like to know) a children's-wear section. Down a couple of floors is the pet store, full of talking parrots and cute kittens and dogs (plus rather sad-looking birds in cages). There are places to eat on each of the four floors including a tapas bar, an oyster bar, a crêperie, a sea grill, a pizzeria, a diner and a sushi bar. Your kids will probably insist on dining at Planet Harrods, however, next to the toy department, where cartoons play constantly on big screens. Harrods toy department organizes various events and activities for children, including Teddy Bear days and Easter Egg hunts.

Harvey Nichols

109–125 Knightsbridge, SW1
t (020) 7235 5000
www.harveynichols.com
⊖ Knightsbridge
Bus 10, 19, 52, 74, 137
Open Mon–Fri 10–8, Sat 10–7, Sun 12 noon–6

Though less child-friendly than Harrods, this can still provide a singular shopping experience. It's renowned as London's most fashionable department store and always stocks the latest high fashions for men, women and children. Its food halls on the fifth floor are, in their own way, just as impressive as those to be found at Harrods, and offer some great views of the Knightsbridge skyline, especially in the evening.

Picnic & snacks

There's plenty of choice. **Hyde Park**, of course, offers a grand swathe of picnic-friendly greenery, but you should also be aware that the area's three great museums each have designated picnic areas. You can lunch alfresco in front of the **Natural History Museum**, in the **Pirelli Gardens** of the V&A or, if the weather has taken a turn for the worse, in the **Science Museum's 'Megabyte'** picnic area on the first floor. Supplies can be picked up from the grand food halls at **Harrods** and **Harvey Nichols,** or from **Baker & Spice** (a sort of hybrid bakery/delicatessen/patisserie) at 46 Walton Street, SW3, t (020) 7589 4734, or from the Italian delicatessan, **La Picena**, at 5 Walton Street, t (020) 7584 6573, SW3, both ⊖ Knightsbridge

All three Kensington museums have good cafés. The pick of the bunch is probably the **Science Museum's Deep Blue Café,** which can be found on the ground floor of the Wellcome Gallery. Otherwise try **Café Crêperie**, just around the corner at 2 Exhibition Road, SW7, t (020) 7589 8947, ⊖ South Kensington. If shopping in Knightsbridge, be aware that the **Brompton Road**, SW3, is lined with pavement cafés, patesseries and fast food restaurants – look out for branches of **Patisserie Valerie** (*see* p.231) at no.215, t (020) 7823 3997, **Gloriette Patisserie** (*see* p.231) at no.128, t (020) 7589 4750, and **McDonald's** at no.177, ⊖ South Kensington. Though there isn't much in the immediate vicinity of Hyde Park, you can get excellent toasted sandwiches at the **Kensington Gardens Café** on the Broad Walk,⊖ South Kensington, and the **Kensington Kiosk** near the Princess Diana Memorial Playground, ⊖ Queensway.

Restaurants

1 Café Rouge
27–31 Basil Street, SW3
t (020) 7584 2345
⊖ Knightsbridge
Open 10am–11pm daily

See **Eat** p.224 for more details on the above restaurants.
See map on p.137 for the locations of the restaurants numbered above.

2 Monza
6 Yeoman's Row, SW3
t (020) 7591 0210
⊖ South Kensington, Knightsbridge
Open Tues–Sun 12 noon–2.30 and 7–11.30, Mon 7pm–11.30pm

3 Pizza Express
6–7 Beauchamp Place, SW3
t (020) 7589 2355
⊖ Knightsbridge
Open Mon–Sat 11.30am–12 midnight, Sun 11.30am–11.30pm

4 Pizza Organic
20 Old Brompton Road, SW7
t (020) 7589 9613,
www.pizzapiazza.co.uk
⊖ South Kensington
Open 11.30am–12 midnight daily

5 Pizza on the Park
11 Knightsbridge, SW3
t (020) 7255 5273
www.pizzaonthepark.com
⊖ Hyde Park Corner, Knightsbridge
Open Mon–Fri 8.15am–12 midnight, Sat–Sun 9.30am–12 midnight

6 Pizza Pomodoro
51 Beauchamp Place, SW3
t (020) 7589 1278
www.pomodoro.co.uk
⊖ Knightsbridge
Open 12 noon–1am daily

7 Planet Harrods
Fourth Floor, Harrods, 87–135 Brompton Road, SW1
t (020) 7730 1234
⊖ Knightsbridge
Open Mon–Sat 10–7, Sun 12 noon–6

8 Sticky Fingers
1a Phillimore Gardens, W8
t (020) 7938 5338.
www.stickyfingers.co.uk
⊖ High Street Kensington, Holland Park
Bus 9, 10, 27, 28, 31, 49, 94
Open 12 noon–12 midnight daily

Greenwich

Greenwich is just a hop and a jump on the DLR extension from central London, but it has an entirely different ambience. It's as relaxed, cultured and stately as the city is brash, racy and commercial.

Of course, elegance and beauty don't always cut it with children. They want action, not elegantly crafted buildings and parks. Thankfully, Greenwich can also offer plenty of fun.

Despite its proximity to central London, Greenwich is one of the best places to come and learn about life on the ocean waves. There's the National Maritime Museum, stuffed full of ships and nautical equipment for kids to clamber over, the *Cutty Sark*, the fastest tea clipper of the 19th century, and the *Gypsy Moth*, in which Sir Francis Chichester sailed solo around the world in the mid-1960s.

Greenwich is also the home of time (Greenwich Mean Time has been used to set the watches and clocks of the world since 1884). It marks the point of the Prime Meridian, which led to it being chosen as the venue for the nation's Millennium celebrations at the now empty Dome.

At the Royal Observatory you can stand above a line marked on the ground with one foot planted in the world's western hemisphere and one in the east.

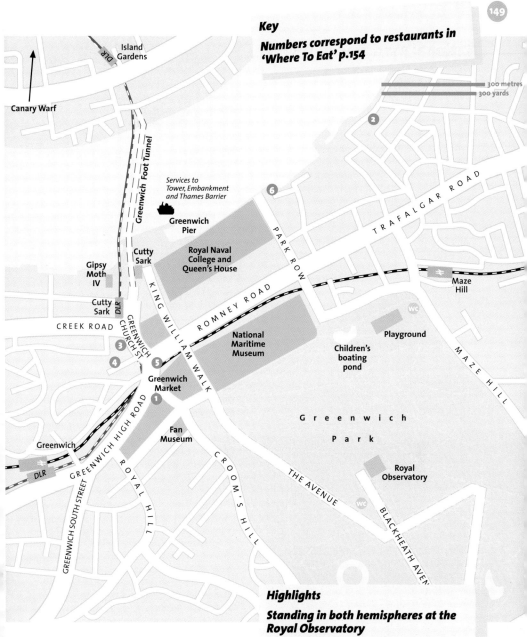

Key

Numbers correspond to restaurants in 'Where To Eat' p.154

Island Gardens

Canary Warf

300 metres
300 yards

DLR

Greenwich Foot Tunnel

Services to Tower, Embankment and Thames Barrier

Greenwich Pier

Cutty Sark

Gipsy Moth IV

Cutty Sark

CREEK ROAD

GREENWICH CHURCH ST

KING WILLIAM WALK

Royal Naval College and Queen's House

PARK ROW

TRAFALGAR ROAD

Maze Hill

ROMNEY ROAD

National Maritime Museum

Children's boating pond

Playground

WC

MAZE HILL

Greenwich Market

Greenwich

DLR

GREENWICH SOUTH STREET

GREENWICH HIGH ROAD

ROYAL HILL

Fan Museum

CROOM'S HILL

G r e e n w i c h

P a r k

THE AVENUE

WC

Royal Observatory

BLACKHEATH AVEN

Highlights

Standing in both hemispheres at the Royal Observatory

Exploring the 12 interactive zones at the Museum in Docklands

Standing under the river in the Thames Tunnel

THE SIGHTS

National Maritime Museum

Romney Road, Greenwich, SE10
t (020) 8 858 4422
Infoline **t** (020) 8312 6565
www.nmm.ac.uk
⇌ Greenwich, **DLR** Greenwich, Cutty Sark
Bus 53, 54, 177, 180, 188, 199, 207, 286, 380, 386,
Open 10–5, daily (last entry 4.30)
Free
Bosun's Café with outdoor seating, souvenir shop
Wheelchair accessible for all floors – ramps and lifts
Suitable for all ages
Allow 1hr

The National Maritime Museum, one of the nation's favourite family museums, has always been good at sparking off controversy. After years of criticism that exhibitions were too 'triumphalist', the curators are now being accused of portraying the British Empire in an unremittingly hostile light. Certainly the exhibition tries to show the spread of Empire, and not just from the victors' point of view.

Besides the 'Trade and Empire Gallery', there are galleries dedicated to 'Explorers', 'Passengers' and 'Hidden Treasures', all filled with great nautical exhibits to explore and study, including reconstructed engine rooms, boat decks and cabin interiors. There's also a special hands-on children's area on the third floor, where kids can experience 'pulling flags', 'firing cannons', sending morse code messages and learning how to steer a Viking longboat. For a little touch of gore, pop into the Nelson Gallery where you can see the bloodstained uniform worn by the famous Admiral during his final battle at Trafalgar. *See p.67 for more on this* famous nautical encounter. Every Saturday the museum runs its 'Shipmates' sessions, in which children aged 7 and over can learn more about the lives and skills of sailors through a series of interactive workshops. Their younger siblings, meanwhile, can enjoy 'Crowsnest' storytelling sessions. Trails and themed backpack tours are available from the front desk, and you can also download lots of quizzes and games from the museum website.

Royal Observatory

Greenwich Park, SE10
t (020) 8858 4422
Infoline **t** (020) 8312 6565
www.rog.nmn.ac.uk
⇌ Greenwich, **DLR** Greenwich, Cutty Sark
Bus 53, 54, 177, 180, 188, 199, 202, 286, 380, 386,
Open 10–5 daily, last admission 4.30pm
Free to observatory. Planetarium shows: adult £4, child £1.50
Limited wheelchair access owing to the age of the building. Guided tours by prior arrangement
Baby changing room
Suitable for all ages
Allow 1hr 30mins

Just behind the Royal Naval College, the Royal Observatory stands on the Greenwich Meridian, the official dividing line between east and west, declared to be 0° degrees longitude. The line is marked out so you can stand with one foot in the western hemisphere and the other in the east. In 1884 the observatory was given the task of setting the time for the whole world, and Greenwich Mean Time (GMT) is still the standard against which all other times are measured. Every day at exactly 1pm, a red timeball on the Observatory roof drops to allow passing ships to set their clocks accurately.

The observatory, built in the late 17th century by Sir Christopher Wren, today houses the country's largest refracting telescope. It has become a compelling attraction for anyone interested in the

Tell me a story: Mean time

Since the late 19th century, the Prime Meridian at Greenwich has been used to calculate Greenwich Mean Time. Before this, almost every town in the world kept its own local time. However, with the vast expansion of the railway and communications networks in the mid-19th century, it became necessary to come up with an international time standard.

In 1884, the International Meridian Treaty established in law that 'every new day begins at mean midnight at the cross-hairs of the Airy Transit Circle telescope at the Royal Observatory'. Forty-one delegates from 25 nations met in Washington DC for the International Meridian Conference and decided 22 to one that Greenwich had won the prize of Longitude 0°. The decision, essentially, was based on the argument that by naming Greenwich as Longitude 0°, it would inconvenience the least number of people.

cosmos. You can visit the apartments of the Astronomers Royal and find out how astronomy has developed, attend a 'space show' in the dome or try some astronomical experiments at the children's 'science station'. The observatory organizes free 'drop-in' summer workshops for children where they can learn more about the techniques of astronomy and even have a go at making their own basic astronomical equipment.

The search for longitude

Until the late 18th century nobody knew how to measure longitude – the distance east or west around the earth. People could work out latitude (the distance north or south) using the position of the pole star, but no such system existed for longitude. In 1754, the government put up a reward of £20,000 for anyone who could come up with a solution. The reward was finally claimed, in 1772, by a clockmaker called John Harrison. He constructed a clock which could measure time accurately at sea, and so permit navigators to calculate a ship's east-west position to within 30 miles.

Royal Naval College

King William Walk, SE10
t (020) 8269 4747
www.greenwichfoundation.org.uk
≈ Greenwich, **DLR** Greenwich, Cutty Sark
Bus 53, 54, 177, 180, 188, 199, 286, 380, 386,
Open 10–5, daily
Free
Coffee shop, souvenir shop
Limited wheelchair facilities. Call in advance
Suitable for ages 10 and over

With its grand classical façades overlooking the river, the Royal Naval College (now home to the University of Greenwich) provides a wonderfully elegant first sight of Greenwich to anyone arriving from the riverside.

The building is the work of three of Britain's most famous architects: Sir Christopher Wren, Nicholas Hamilton and Sir John Vanbrugh, and was originally used as a hospital for disabled sailors before being turned into a college in 1873. It's now home to a visitors' centre, the Greenwich Gateway, with exhibitions on the history of the borough, and, provides information on local attractions. It's located in the Pepys Building. Of the rest of the site, only the chapel and Painted Hall are open to the public. Their fabulously painted interiors were designed by James Thornhill, who also decorated the dome of St Paul's.

Queen's House

Romney Road, SE10
t (020) 8312 6565
≈ Greenwich, **DLR** Greenwich, Cutty Sark
Bus 53, 54, 177, 180, 188, 199, 286, 380, 386,
Open 10–5, daily (last entry 4.30)
Free
Wheelchair accessible

In between the Royal Naval College's façades stands the Queen's House, an earlier Italianate palace designed by Inigo Jones. The interiors are just as sumptuous as the college, adorned with frescoes and paintings, but it's a touch more child-friendly and organizes regular holiday activities and workshops for children.

Cutty Sark

King William Walk, SE10
t (020) 8858 3445
www.cuttysark.org.uk
≈ Greenwich, **DLR** Greenwich, Cutty Sark
Bus 53, 54, 177, 180, 188, 199, 286, 380, 386,
Open 10–5, daily (last entry 4.30)
Adm Adult/child £3.95, concs £2.95, family £9.80, under-5s **free**
Souvenir shop

Can you spot?
The self-portrait of James Thornhill on the wall of the Painted Hall in the Royal Naval College? Despite being paid £1 per foot for decorating the walls and £3 per foot for the ceilings – which, in the early 18th century, was quite a lot of money – Thornhill still decided to paint himself with his hand outstretched as if asking for more cash.

Wheelchair accessible for first floor only
Suitable for all ages

In her time, the *Cutty Sark* was the speediest sailing boat in the world, able to complete the round-Africa journey from Shanghai to London in a record 107 days. Unfortunately, the advent of steam-powered boats in the late 19th century, coupled with the opening of the Suez Canal, put an end to her usefulness. Such was her fame, however, that she was never dismantled, and today is the only surviving example of a tea clipper in the world. You can explore her decks and cabins and learn all about the vessel's illustrious history through a display of pictures and models.

Gypsy Moth IV

King William Walk, SE10
t (020) 8858 2698
Open Easter–Oct Mon–Sat 10–6, Sun 12 noon–6 (last entry 5.30)
Adm Adult 50p, child 30p
Suitable for all ages

Near the very grand *Cutty Sark* stands the tiny 54-ft yacht in which Sir Francis Chichester sailed single-handedly around the world in 1966–7. In honour of his achievement, Chichester was knighted with the very same sword with which Elizabeth I had knighted Sir Francis Drake (the first Englishman to circumnavigate the globe) some 300 years earlier. Children love to explore the tiny cramped cabins and to imagine how they would have coped alone on the high seas for 274 days.

Greenwich markets

Greenwich is home to three excellent weekend markets: a small **antique market** off Greenwich High Road, between junctions with Stockwell Street and Royal Hill (**open** weekends 9–5), where you can often pick up good old toys; **the central market** on Stockwell Street, opposite the Hotel Ibis, **t** (020) 8766 6844 (**open** weekends 9–5; organic food market Sat only; village market **open** Fri, Sat 10–5, Sun 10–6); and the South London Book

Centre, with its enormous collection of comics; and a covered **craft market** on College Approach, with entrances on Turpin Lane (off Greenwich Church Street) and Durnford Street, **t** (020) 7240 7405, www.greenwich-market.co.uk (**open** Fri–Sun 9–5).

Fan Museum

12 Croom's Hill, Greenwich, SE10
t (020) 8305 1441
www.fan-museum.org
➤ Greenwich, **DLR** Greenwich, Cutty Sark
Open Tues–Sat 11–5, Sun 12 noon–5
Adm Adult £3.50, child £2.50, under-7s **free**
Shop, baby changing room
Wheelchair accessible, with adapted toilet
Suitable for all ages

Housed in a beautiful 18th-century townhouse, this is a delightful collection of over 2,000 fans from the 17th century to the present day. It holds regular demonstrations of fan-making.

Thames Tunnel

Open 24hrs daily. Lift open 5–9
Wheelchair and pushchair accessible when lift open

It's a simple pleasure, standing in a tunnel beneath the River Thames, but one which never fails to enthrall children who marvel at the sheer impossibility of being under so much water. The glass-domed entrances to the tunnel are easy to spot on the south side of the river by the *Cutty Sark* and on the north in Island Gardens.

Greenwich Park

Charlton Way, SE3
t (020) 8858 2608
www.royalparks.gov.uk/greenwich.htm
Open Dawn till dusk daily
Free

Everything in Greenwich Park has been touched by the brush of elegance, from the flower gardens and stately avenues to the ornate Ranger's House and landscaped heights offering stunning views over the Thames. The park was created as a hunting ground by Henry VI in 1433 – it still contains a small deer enclosure on its southern side – and was landscaped in the 17th century by the great French gardener André Le Nôtre.

The park will also greatly appeal to children, with a boating lake, well-equipped playground and picnic tables.

Blackheath

Blackheath, SE3
t 020 8854 8888
⇌ Blackheath
Bus 53, 177, 180, 286
Open 24hrs a day
Free

A great windswept piece of common next door to the neatly manicured Greenwich Park, Blackheath is popular with kite flyers. Each year, it holds one of London's best Guy Fawke's night firework displays. It's also where 40,000 runners begin the London Marathon's 26 miles of annual hell.

Museum in Docklands

No.1 The Warehouse, West India Quay,
Hertsmere Road, E14
t 0870 444 3856
www.museumindocklands.org.uk
⊖ Canary Wharf
DLR West India Quay
Bus 115, 277, D3, D6, D7, D8
Open 10–6, daily
Adm Adult £5, concs £3, under-16s **free**; all tickets are valid for a year
Wheelchair accessible, with adapted toilets; shop, café
Suitable for all ages

Question 18
How long did it take Sir Francis Chichester to sail around the world?
answer on p.249

Much delayed and, apparently, a good deal over budget, the Museum of London's sister museum finally opened in the summer of 2003. It's been worth the wait. Housed in a Georgian warehouse on the West India Quay where tea clippers once used to dock, the museum traces the story of 2,000 years of trade on the River Thames – from early Celtic riverside trading settlements to the dock's subsequent post-war decline and recent rejuvenation (of which this museum is part). Five floors and 12 galleries provide a wealth of detail about dockyard life – you can walk through a reconstruction of a Victorian sailors' settlement, *see* depictions of how the Thames has changed over the years (highlights include a scale model of the old London Bridge and the Rheinbeck Panorama, a rare painting showing a bird's eye view of London *c.*1810) and find out about some of the punishments meted out to smugglers and pirates in days past. Best of all for families is the interactive children's gallery made up of 12 zones, each offering a range of hands-on experiments to perform. You can winch and weigh cargoes, make a scale model of Canary Wharf and discover archaeological finds in the 'Foreshore Discovery Box'. The museum makes full use of modern technologies with projectors displaying images on the walls and CD Roms offering close-up details of the exhibits.

Did you know?
The name Cutty Sark is a corruption of the French phrase 'courte chemise' meaning 'short shirt', the garment worn by the ship's figurehead.

Picnic & snacks

Greenwich Park is the obvious choice with its rolling vistas and wide open spaces, but there are also plenty of nice spots by the river overlooking the now defunct Millennium Dome and the far from defunct **Canary Wharf**. Supplies can be picked up from **Sauce for the Goose** delicatessen at 66 Royal Hill, SE10, t (020) 8692 3010, **DLR** Greenwich, and, for a great selection of cheeses, the nearby **Cheeseboard**, 26 Royal Hill, SE10, t (020) 8305 0401, **DLR** Greenwich.

Although there are less places to eat than Central London, Greenwich has plenty of village-style cafés and riverside inns. There's a very good park café near the main entrance to Greenwich park and, situated at 14 King William Walk, SE10, (the road which leads from Greenwich park to the *Cutty Sark*), a very nice tea house. Named, appropriately enough, **The Tea House**, it serves lovely cream teas and makes a welcome afternoon pit stop, t (020) 8858 0803 **DLR** Greenwich. Just around the corner at 39 Greenwich Church Street, SE10, is **Tai Won Mein**, a great, fast-moving noodle house where you eat at Wagamama-style long tables, t (020) 8858 2688, **DLR** Greenwich.

Restaurants

1 Café Rouge
Ibis Hotel, Stockwell Street
t (020) 8293 6660
www.caferouge.co.uk
≈ Greenwich, **DLR** Greenwich, Cutty Sark
Open 10am–11pm daily

2 Cutty Sark
Ballast Quay, off Lassell Street, SE10
t (020) 8858 3146
≈ Greenwich, **DLR** Greenwich, Cutty Sark
Open Mon–Sat 11am–11pm, Sun 12 noon–10.30

3 Goddard's Pie House
45 Greenwich Church Street, SE10
t (020) 8293 9313
www.pieshop.co.uk
≈ Greenwich, **DLR** Greenwich, Cutty Sark
Open Mon–Fri 10–6.30, Sat–Sun 10–7.30

4 The High Chaparral
35 Greenwich Church Street, SE10
t (020) 8293 9143
≈ Greenwich, **DLR** Greenwich, Cutty Sark
Open Mon–Sat 12 noon–11, Sun 12 noon–10

5 Pizza Express
4 Church Street, SE10
t (020) 8853 2770
www.pizzaexpress.co.uk
≈ Greenwich, **DLR** Greenwich, Cutty Sark
Open 11.30am–12 midnight daily

6 The Trafalgar Tavern
Park Row, SE10
t (020) 8858 2437
≈ Greenwich, **DLR** Greenwich, Cutty Sark
Open Mon–Sat 11.30am–11pm, Sun 12 noon–10.30

See **Eat** p.224 for more details on the above restaurants.
See map on p.149 for the locations of the restaurants numbered above.

Kids in

12

Rain, rain, go away, come again another day! London is famous for many things, one of which is the unpredictable weather. It rains here – a lot. Thankfully, there is so such much to do when the rain comes that it hardly matters.

Adventure playgrounds

Indoor play areas are a very good option if you want to give the kids a chance to let off steam. Parents are usually expected to stay on the premises while their children play. Below is a selection of venues in the London area. Alternatively, you could try your nearest shopping centre or leisure complex.

Bramley's Big Adventure

136 Bramley Road, W10
t (020) 8960 1515
www.bramleysbig.co.uk
⊖ Ladbroke Grove, Latimer Road
Bus 7, 23, 52, 74, C1
Open 10–6.30, daily
Adm per hour: under-2s £2, under-5s £2.50, over-5s £3.20 term-time weekdays; £2.40, £2.90, £3.60 weekends, school and bank holidays
Ages up to 11

There are slides, inflatables, monkey ropes and ball pools galore for ages 5–11. There's also a separate area for under-5s and a café for flagging parents. A popular venue for parties with play session, meal, goody bags and balloons thrown in.

Discovery Planet

Surrey Quays Shopping Centre, Redriff Road, SE16
t (020) 7237 2388
www.discovery-planet.co.uk
⊖ Surrey Quays
Bus 1, 47, 149, 188, 225, 381, P13
Open Mon–Sat 10–6, Sun 11–5
Adm Mon–Fri under-10s £2.99, under-2s £2.49; Sat–Sun under-10s £3.99, under-2s £3.49; accompanying adult free
Ages Maximum age 10, under 9-months free

The main area has two slides, two ball pits, lots of soft play equipment, ropes, ladders and swings. There's also a separate baby section, toilets and a Burger King counter on the premises. Birthday parties are available from Monday to Friday at 4 and 5 daily, and any time during opening hours at weekends.

The Discovery Zone

First Floor, The Junction Shopping Centre, SW1
t (020) 7223 1717
⇌ Clapham Junction
Bus 37, 39, 77, 77A, 219, 319, G1
Open Mon–Fri 10–6, Sat–Sun and school hols 10–7, parent and toddler groups daily from 10–1 and 1–3
Adm Mon–Fri £3.99, Sat–Sun £4.99. There's also a 4 o'clock club in term-time when kids can play and eat for £1.99 (Mon–Wed) and £2.99 (Thurs–Fri)
Ages 2–12

Basically, this is just a big room full of coloured soft things for kids to jump about on with enough space for over 500 leaping, bouncing tots. There is also a branch of Burger King and, best of all, a TV room for parents.

Monkey Business

222 Green Lanes, N13
t (020) 8886 7520
⊖ Manor House
⇌ Palmers Green
Bus 121, 329, W6
Open 10–7 daily
Adm Child £2.75, accompanying adult free
Ages 2–14
Height restriction is 4ft11in

Monkey-themed adventure playground aimed at very young children and toddlers. There's a tree house, a ball pond, lots of tube slides, biff-bash bags and a maze.

The Playhouse

The Old Gymnasium, Highbury Grove School, corner Highbury Grove/Highbury New Park
t (020) 7704 9424
⊖ Highbury & Islington
Bus 4, 30, 19, 236
Open Mon–Thurs 10–6, Fri–Sun 10–7
Adm Over-2s £3, under-2s £2.50, babies that are crawling £1.50
Ages Maximum age 10

Superior play area with a three-level climbing frame, 30-ft slide, rope swings, ladders and ball pools. There's a separate section for babies and a café, plus toilets with changing facilities.

Sobell Safari

Sobell Leisure Centre, Hornsey Road, N7

t (020) 7609 2166
Finsbury Park, Holloway Road
Bus 43, 271
Open Mon–Fri 9–5.15, Sat–Sun 9–4
Adm Over 1m tall £3.20, under 1m £2.40

This is a great place for kids to come and play at being pirates with three levels of ropes, slides and punch bags for them to clamber over. There's also a separate soft play area for under-5s.

Rascals

Waterfront Leisure Centre, High Street, Woolwich, SE18
t (020) 8317 5000
Woolwich Arsenal, Woolwich Dockyard
Bus 51, 53, 96, 122, 177, 272, 161
Open Mon–Fri 9.30–5, Sat–Sun 9.30–2
Adm Non-member £3.30, member £2.30, each additioinal child £1.10, happy hour is from 4–5 Mon–Fri when charge is £1 per child
Ages up to 9

Indoor fun for under-9s (climbing frames, biff-bash bags, etc.) with a special soft play area for under-4s. Parents can use the centre's special 'drop and shop' sessions in the school holidays.

Snakes & Ladders

Syon Park, Brentford, Middlesex
t (020) 8847 0946
www.snakes-and-ladders.co.uk
Gunnersbury
Kew Bridge
Bus 116, 117, 237, 267
Open 10–6, daily (last entry 5.15)
Adm Weekdays/term-time, before 4.30: over-5s £4.35, under-5s £3.15; after 4.30: over-5s £3.55, under-5s £2.55; weekends/holidays: over-5s £5, under-5s £3.90
Ages 2–12
Maximum height 4ft8in
Socks must be worn

In the grounds of Syon Park, this is the place to come after a hard day's butterfly hunting or go-

Can you spot?
The pavement surrounding Leicester Square's garden is adorned with the handprints of famous actors and directors. See who can be the first to spot them all.

karting. It's the usual fare – giant slides, ropes, ball ponds, climbing frames – but still very good.

Spike's Madhouse

Crystal Palace National Sports Centre, SE19
t (020) 8778 9876
www.crystalpalace.co.uk/clubs/spike.htm
Crystal Palace
Bus 157, 358, 361
Open Sat–Sun 10–5
Adm Members £2, non-members £2.50
Ages 2–13

Four floors filled with slides, climbing frames and soft play equipment.

Cinemas

London is a great place to go and see a film. It may not have as many screens as it used to – the days when every high street had its own Odeon are now, sadly, long gone – but the cinemas that remain are bigger and better equipped than ever. The biggest and best of all can be found in Leicester Square, London's cinematic heart, where star-studded premières take place and where all the major blockbusters have their first runs. For a full and up-to-date list of what's on where and when, check the weekly listings magazine *Time Out* or the *Evening Standard*'s *Hot Tickets* – a free magazine which accompanies its Thursday edition.

Leicester Square

Empire
t 0870 010 2030
www.uci-cinemas.co.uk
Odeon Leicester Square & Odeon West End
t 0870 505 0007
www.odeon.co.uk
Warner Village West End
t 0870 240 6020
www.warnervillage.co.uk

Both The Odeon and Warner Village Cinemas run special offers for kids at any of their branches apart from Leicester Square, call for details.

Cinema clubs

If you consider Leicester Square's cinematic big boys a bit brash and commercial, and find yourself longing for the halcyon days of Saturday matinées, you could be in for a very pleasant surprise. There are several smaller picture houses in London running Saturday morning film clubs for kids. The films are usually a mix of Disney cartoons and family favourites. To add to the fun, additional entertainments, such as workshops, competitions and seasonal events, are often laid on.

Barbican Centre

Silk Street, EC2
t (020) 7382 7000
www.barbican.org.uk
⊖ Barbican, Moorgate
Bus 8, 22B, 56
Times Club meeting time varies, call ahead
Adm Annual membership £5, films £3 non-members, £2.50 members.
Ages 5–11

The Barbican's Family Film Club for 5–11 year-olds meets at 10.30am each Saturday. Here kids can enjoy a family classic and take part in some film-related activities from the 'Movie Cart' in the foyer. Workshops on movie related skills – screen make-up, set design, animation etc. – are also held on the first Saturday of each month.

Clapham Picture House

76 Venn Street, SW4
t (020) 7498 3323
www.picturehouse-cinemas.co.uk
⊖ Clapham Common
Bus 88, 137, 155, 345, 355
Times Club meets Sat 11.15am, film starts at 11.45am
Adm Members £2, non-members £3, accompanying adult £4; annual membership £3, £5 for 2 siblings, under-5s must be accompanied by an adult
Ages up to 12

At the weekly pre-screening craft workshops, kids can get in the mood for the upcoming celluloid adventures by designing their own space ship, making a cartoon picture book or moulding plasticine. Six times a year the cinema screens doggie-themed movies and invites the residents of nearby Battersea Dogs' Home over for a mutual appreciation session.

Electric Cinema

191 Portobello Road, W11
t (020) 7908 9696
www.electriccinema.co.uk
⊖ Notting Hill Gate
Times Sat, films at 11.30am and 1pm

Adm £3.50 members, £4.50 non-members, accompanying adults
Ages 4–12

Games and activities inspired by the screenings, plus birthday party specials.

Movie Magic at the NFT

National Film Theatre 2, BFI, South Bank, SE1
t (020) 7928 3232
www.bfi.org.uk/moviemagic
⊖ /≈ Waterloo
Bus 1, 4, 26, 68, 76, 168, 171, 176, 188, 341, 501, 505, 521, X68
Times Sat afternoon, workshop time varies, call ahead
Adm Child £1, accompanying adult £5
Ages 6–12

The NFT shows a range of classic family films as part of its 'Movie Magic' programme, and organizes movie workshops for children aged 6–12 on the first Saturday of each month, in which kids can learn more about the techniques of film-craft. Supervised by experts, they can try creating a piece of animation, making movie props and costumes or writing their own short film script. The NFT also stages two-day 'Movie Magic Schools' which take a more in-depth look at the techniques of movie-making (they cost: child £5.50, accompanying adult £4 and must be booked in advance).

Phoenix Cinema

52 High Road, East Finchley, N2
t (020) 8444 6789
⊖ East Finchley
Bus 102, 143, 263
Times Club meets bi-weekly Sat 11am, film starts at 12 noon
Adm Under 12s £4; 'Bringing up Baby' screenings for parents with babies under 1-year old £4; teenage screenings and workshops £7
Ages 6–12

Combining screenings with hands-on activies such as painting and model-making, 'Freddie's Film Club' aims to introduce children to the wonders of World Cinema. The Phoenix also organizes special screenings and workshops in movie-related skills (such as animation and documentary film-making) for 13–19 year-olds.

Ritzy Cinema

Brixton Oval, Coldharbour Lane, SW2
t (020) 7733 2229

www.ritzycinema.co.uk
⊖ Brixton
Bus 35, 37, 118, 196, 250, P4, P5
Times Sat, films start at 10.30am
Adm Child £1, accompanying adult £2
Ages to 12

Shows two separate programmes: one for 7s and under and the other for 8s and over. In truth, this is done more for reasons of social bonding than anything else, and either age group may attend either programme. There are special kids' club events organized and free tea, coffee and news-papers provided for parents.

IMAX 3D Cinema
1 Charlie Chaplin Walk, SE1
t (020) 7902 1234
www.bfi.org.uk/imax
⊖ Waterloo, Westminster
Bus 11, 12, 53, 76, 77, 109, 211, 507, D1, P11
Open Call ahead
Adm Adult £7.50, child (5–16) £4.95 (£6 for evening shows), under-3s **free**, concs £6.20; prices for Hollywood blockbusters start at around £11.50
Wheelchair accessible,with lifts, adapted cinema seats and toilets
Suitable for all ages
Shows last approximately 1hr each

Britain's largest cinema screen is housed in a seven-storey glass cylinder in the middle of the Waterloo bullring (a fancy name for what is essen-tially a roundabout). The screen itself is the height of five double-decker buses, the sound system transmits 11,000 watts and the films are recorded and projected using the most up-to-date 3D format available – it's a pretty all-encompassing experience. The programme changes regularly, but you can usually be confident of seeing some kind of outer space/wildlife-type spectacular, plus the occasional Matrix-style, effects-laden Hollywood Blockbuster. *See* p.140 for the IMAX cinema in the Science Museum.

Internet cafés

If your kids are clamouring to email their mates back home or you fancy sending a cyber postcard, there are plenty of web cafés in London, albeit not quite the variety of outlets there once was now that Easy Internet has begun to dominate the market. You'll also find internet points in most public libraries, main branch post offices and, increasingly, in some fast food outlets.

Easy Internet Café
12–14 Wilton Road, SW1, **t** (020) 7233 8456
Branches at 1160 Kensington High Street; 358 Oxford Street, W1, 9–16 Tottenham Court Road, W1
www.easyEverything.com
⊖/ ⇌ Victoria
Open 10–12 midnight
Cost The minimum payment is 50p, but the exact price depends on the time of day and how busy the café is (the busier, the more expensive)

Internet Exchange
37 The Piazza, Covent Garden, WC2
t (020) 7836 8636
www.internet-exchange.co.uk
⊖ Piccadilly Circus
Open Mon–Fri 10am–10pm, Sat–Sun 10–8
Cost From £1

Museums & galleries

Central London
Please *see* the main sightseeing chapters for details of these establishments.

Bank of England Museum
Threadneedle Street, EC2
t (020) 7601 5545 (*see* p.131)

Bramah Tea & Coffee Museum
40 Southwark Street, SE1
t (020) 7403 5650 (*see* p.122)

Britain at War Experience
Tooley Street, SE1
t (020) 7403 3171 (*see* p.118)

British Museum
Great Russell Street, WC1
t (020) 7636 1555 *(see* p.54)

Cabinet War Rooms
King Charles Street, SW1
t (020) 7766 0120 *(see* p.100)

Clink Museum
1 Clink Street, SE1
t (020) 7403 6515 *(see* p.121)

Fashion and Textile Museum
83 Bermondsey Street, SE1
t (020) 7403 0222 *(see* p.123)

HMS *Belfast*
Morgan's Lane, off Tooley Street, SE1
t (020) 7940 6300 *(see* p.120)

Imperial War Museum
Lambeth Road, SE1
t (020) 7416 5320 *(see* p.111)

London Canal Museum
12–13 New Wharf Road, N1
t (020) 7713 0836 *(see* p.48)

London Dungeon
Tooley Street, SE1
t (020) 7403 7221 *(see* p.116)

London Fire Brigade Museum
94a Southwark Bridge Road
t (020) 7587 2894 *(see* p.123)

London Planetarium
Marylebone Road, NW1
t 0870 400 3000 *(see* p.45)

London's Transport Museum
Covent Garden, WC2
t (020) 7565 7299 *(see* p.78)

Madame Tussaud's
Marylebone Road, NW1
t (020) 7935 6861 *(see* p.44)

Museum of London
London Wall, EC2
t 0870 444 3851 *(see* p.130)

National Gallery
Trafalgar Square, WC2
t (020) 7747 2885 *(see* p.67)

National Portrait Gallery
St Martin's Place, WC2
t (020) 7306 0055 *(see* p.69)

Natural History Museum
Cromwell Road, SW7
t (020) 7942 5000 *(see* p.138)

Old Operating Theatre
9a St Thomas Street, SE1
t (020) 7955 4791 *(see* p.119)

Pollock's Toy Museum
1 Scala Street, W1
t (020) 7636 3452 *(see* p.57)

Royal Academy
Burlington House, Piccadilly, W1
t (020) 7439 7438 *(see* p.70)

Science Museum
Exhibition Road, London SW7
t 0870 870 4868 *(see* p.139)

Globe Theatre
Bear Gardens, Bankside, New Globe Wall,
Southwark, SE1
t (020) 7902 1400 *(see* p.119)

Saatchi Gallery
County Hall, Riverside Building, Belvedere Road, SE1
t (020) 7823 2363 *(see* p.107)

Serpentine Gallery
Kensington Gardens, W2
t (020) 7402 6075 *(see* p.144)

Sherlock Holmes Museum
221b Baker Street, NW1
t (020) 7935 8866 *(see* p.46)

Tate Britain
Millbank, SW1
t (020) 7887 8000 *(see* p.100)

Tate Modern
Bankside, SE1
t (020) 7887 8000 *(see* p.117)

Tower of London
Tower Hill, EC3
t 0870 756 6060 *(see* p.128)

Wallace Collection
Hertford House, Manchester Square, W1
t (020) 7563 9500 *(see* p.47)

Victoria & Albert Museum
Cromwell Road, SW7
t (020) 7942 2000 *(see* p.141)

Outer London

London is a huge, sprawling city, and can prove quite daunting for visitors. You might think you've got more than enough to cope with visiting the attractions in the centre of town, never mind the outskirts. However, it's well worth giving the suburbs some consideration. Not only can they offer smaller crowds, less congestion and better air quality, they are also home to some great local museums. There follows a selection of places that are, in general, a lot less touristy than their central London counterparts, and able to provide you with a much calmer day out. Most are extremely family-orientated and, best of all, free.

Bethnal Green Museum of Childhood

Cambridge Heath Road, E2
t (020) 8983 5200
Infoline **t** (020) 8980 2415
www.museumofchildhood.org.uk
⊖ Bethnal Green
Bus 8, 106, 253, 309, D6
Open Mon–Thurs, Sat–Sun 10–6
Free (donations welcome); under-5s' soft play area costs £1.80 for 40mins
Suitable for all ages, under-8s must be accompanied
Allow at least 1hr

This East London branch of the Victoria and Albert Museum contains a wonderful collection of historic childhood artefacts, including clothes, toys (lots and lots of toys), nursery furniture and baby equipment. Pride of place, however, goes to the two Dolls' House Streets (three centuries' worth of miniature homes) and a chronological display of dolls – from 17th-century porcelain beauties to pink, plastic, modern Barbies. There's plenty of interaction on offer for children, particularly in the redeveloped upper floor; here in the 'What Will I be?' display, kids can dress up in the clothes of their ideal future job – fireman, doctor etc. Other family-friendly facilities include a soft play area for under-5s and free 'Family Fun Bags', which are available at reception and contain activities relating to the displays. The museum organizes lots of events year-round for children, including quiz trails, storytelling sessions and art workshops where children may be able to have a go at decorating their own T-shirts, constructing finger puppets or designing jewellery. In summer, the museum also stages its own theatrical productions.

Bruce Castle Museum

Church Lane, off Lordship Lane, N17
t (020) 8808 8772
www.brucecastlemuseum.org
⊖ Wood Green
Bus 123, 243
Open Wed–Sun and bank hols 1pm–5pm
Free
Wheelchair accessible, with adapted toilets

This lively local history museum is housed in a listed Tudor building. In addition to its art, history and postal history exhibitions, it has a special 'Inventor Centre' filled with interactive experiments for kids to play with and is surrounded by 20 acres of parkland. Free activities for children are laid on on Sundays in term-time and on Wednesdays, Thursdays and Fridays in the school holidays between 2pm and 4pm.

Clowns International Gallery

All Saints Centre, Haggerston Road, E8
t (023) 8087 3700
www.clownsinternational.co.uk
⇌ Dalston Kingsland, London Fields
Bus 38, 236, 243
Open 12 noon–5 first Fri of month
Free
Wheelchair accessible. Suitable for all ages

It's a serious business – wearing large shoes and red noses, driving a collapsible car and having custard pies stuffed down the front of your over-sized trousers – which is why this gallery, dedicated to exploring and explaining the noble art of clowning (the only such gallery in the world) reopened in 2003. Run by volunteer clowns (in plain clothes while on museum duty), the museum traces the history of making people laugh by falling over a lot, from its origins in the 16th century to the present day. Exhibits include clown costumes, clown props (including, of course, a collapsible car) and a collection of painted eggs, each showing a different clown's make-up – as with finger prints, no two clowns' make-up is the same. It's fun, in an oddly reverential way.

Dulwich Picture Gallery

Gallery Road, Dulwich Village, SE21
t (020) 8693 5254
www.dulwichpicturegallery.org.uk
⇌ North Dulwich
Bus P4, P15

Open Tues–Fri 10–5, Sat , Sun and Bank Hol Mon 11–5
Adm Adult £4, child **free**, senior citizens £3, **free** to all on Fridays
Wheelchair accessible. Suitable for ages 10 and over
Allow at least 1hr

Newly reopened following an extensive period of refurbishment and rebuilding – which saw a whole new wing added – this is one of the finest galleries to be found anywhere in the country outside central London. Formerly owned by Dulwich College, a private boys' school now owned by an independent charitable trust, the collection includes Rembrandt's *Girl at a Window* and Gainsborough's *Linley Sisters,* as well as works by Rubens, Poussin, Canaletto and Raphael. Art workshops are held on Sunday afternoons during the summer holidays, when children can take part in a range of activities, such as collage design, T-shirt decoration and badge-making. There's also a Saturday morning art school for 12–15 year-olds and an after-school art club for 10–13 year-olds. The gallery's park makes a pleasant picnic spot.

Firepower Museum

Royal Arsenal, SE18
t (020) 8855 7755
www.firepower.org.uk
⚊ Woolwich Arsenal
Bus 96, 161, 180, 472
Open 10–5, daily
Adm Adult £6.50, child (5–16) £4.50, family £18.
Suitable for all ages, some images may distress
Allow at least half a day

Housed in a former arsenal, the Firepower Museum is like a more whizz-bang version of the Imperial War Museum. It's got a similarly impressive range of military hardware, but perhaps places less emphasis in its displays on the human cost of war than its more famous rival. It's certainly a very noisy affair, with battlefield re-enactments, ping-pong target practice and hands-on computerized simulators used to trace the development of military firepower from the sling-shot to computer guided missiles. Would-be cadets can stock up on their combat gear, toys and ammo in the shop.

Geffrye Museum

Kingsland Road, E2
t (020) 7739 9893
www.geffrye-museum.org.uk

> **Did you know?**
> The museum's founder, Frederick Horniman, was the first man to think of selling tea in small cup-sized packets. These are today known simply as teabags.

⊖ Old Street (south exit 8)
⚊ Dalston Kingsland
Bus 67, 149, 242, 243
Open Tues–Sat 10–5, Sun 12 noon–5
Free
Suitable for all ages, under-8s must be accompanied by an adult
Allow at least 1hr

This charming little museum, housed in a row of 18th-century almshouses, is dedicated to the evolution of Britain's living rooms. It contains dozens of reconstructed interiors from Tudor times to the present day, allowing kids to see what bizarre lives their forebears lived in rooms devoid of TVs, hi-fis, playstations or anything that makes life livable. Though you can't actually go into the rooms, it's still fun to nose around the strange archaic furniture and find out interesting nuggets of domestic history. There is also a collection of period garden rooms and an aromatic herb garden (open April–Oct). The museum holds imaginative workshops on such diverse topics as wig-making, landscape gardening, living room design, enamelling, cookery, block printing and mask-making, and also organizes occasional storytelling sessions for young children. Live jazz is sometimes staged on the museum lawn in summer.

Horniman Museum

100 London Road, SE23
t (020) 8699 1872
www.horniman.ac.uk
⚊ Forest Hill
Bus 63, 122, 176, 185, 312, P4, P13
Open Mon–Sat 10.30–5.30, Sun 2–5.30
Free (charges apply for temporary exhibitions)
Suitable for all ages
Allow at least a couple of hours

A day spent here is easily as rewarding as a day spent in one of the great Kensington collections. It was founded in the early 19th century by the tea magnate Frederick Horniman, and defies classification. It's not really an anthropology museum, although it does contain a vast ethnographic collection including South American tribal masks, African head dresses and Egyptian mummies. Equally, it's not really a natural history museum, but still boasts a fantastic array of animal exhibits including a collection of stuffed creatures – look out for the Goliath beetle, the largest insect in the world – as well as a huge aquarium filled with frogs and fish. Neither is it a museum of music, but it nonetheless holds one of the country's most important collections of musical instruments. It also has a wonderful interactive music display where, using touch-screen computers and head-phones, kids can find out about (and listen to) some of the world's more obscure instruments. In fact, considering its many wonders, it's perhaps best to describe the museum simply as South London's premier treasure trove.

Thoroughly revamped in recent years with a whole new layer of interactivity (not to mention a new education centre) added, the museum is now better than ever. As useful as all the new computer terminals and push-button technologies are, however, it's still the sheer clutter and variety of the museum that enthralls. The trails and activity sheets available at the front desk will help put the collection is some sort of order, while at the new 'Hands-on Base' kids have a chance to touch and examine over 4,000 miscellaneous items.

The museum gardens, which have also been completely overhauled, are equally wonderful, offering great views out over South London and containing nature trails, an exhibition on caring for the environment, a small animal enclosure (home to goats, rabbits and turkeys) and a family picnic area.

The Horniman stages a whole host of family events throughout the year including storytellings, arts and crafts sessions (learn how to make an Ancient Egyptian mummy case, an African mask or an Indonesian shadow puppet) and handling activities with puppets, toys and even animals.

Kenwood House

Hampstead Lane, NW3
t 0870 333 1181
www.english-heritage.org
⊖ Archway
Bus 210
Open Summer 10–5.30, daily, winter 10–4, daily
Free

Wheelchair accessible

Houses a wonderful collection of art including works by Rembrandt, Gainsborough and Vermeer, and has a rather nice tearoom. In summer, the grounds play host to a series of spectacular classical music concerts which usually climax with a firework display.

Kew Bridge Steam Museum

Green Dragon Lane, Brentford, Middlesex, TW8
t (020) 8568 4757
www.kbsm.org
⇌ Kew Bridge Station
⊖ Gunnersbury, Kew Gardens
Bus 237, 267, 391 (Sun only)
Open 11–5, daily
Adm Mon–Fri adult £3.60, child £1.50, concs £2.70, family ticket (2+3) £8; Sat–Sun adult £4.60, child £2.50, concs £3.70, family £11.95; **free** admission to all after 4pm
Wheelchair accessible for most of the museum – no access to viewing platform above beam engines
Suitable for all ages

Just across the river from the gardens (*see* p.172), Kew Bridge Steam Museum offers a nice, down-to-earth contrast to all those flower beds and neatly sculpted lawns. It focuses on the development of London's water supply and sewage system from Roman times to the present day, and houses a wonderful collection of Victorian water-pumping machinery, including the two largest beam engines in the world. In their prime, these noisy behemoths would have pumped six and a half million gallons of water every day into London's reservoirs. You can get some idea of the power involved when the great beasts are switched on for a short time in the afternoon at weekends. Providing water is one thing, but it's the means of taking the waste away that brings the best out of the museum. Kids love the replica London sewage system; spying through peep holes at sewer rats and mice, and finding out about 'flushers' and 'toshers' – 19th-century sewer workers who made their living in quite the most smelly way imaginable. The museum's Water of Life exhibition has plenty of levers and buttons to push and pull to keep children amused, and there's a full programme of family events put on in summer.

London International Gallery of Children's Art

O² Centre, 255 Finchley Road, NW3
t (020) 7435 0903
www.ligca.org
⊖ Finchley Road
Bus 13, 46, 82, 113
Open Tues–Thurs 4–6, Fri–Sun 12 noon–6
Free
Suitable for all ages
Allow at least 30mins

London's only gallery devoted to works of art by children. The collection contains paintings from round the world and organizes free art workshops for children aged 5–12 (involving such activities as mask-making, wire sculpting and musical drawing), as well as special 'Little Artists' sessions for under-5s.

National Army Museum and Royal Hospital

Royal Hospital Road, Chelsea, SW3
t (020) 7730 0717
www.national-army-museum.ac.uk
⊖ Sloane Square
Bus 11, 19, 22, 137, 239
Open 10–5.30, daily
Free
Suitable for ages 10 and over
Allow at least 1hr

Telling the story of British army life from the 16th century to the present day, the museum is well laid out and thoughtful, although perhaps a little dry for younger children. It sits next to the Christopher Wren-designed Royal Hospital, founded by Charles II in the 17th century as a home for army veterans and still home to 400 red-coated Chelsea pensioners today. In May each year the grounds play host to the Chelsea Flower Show, the country's premier gardening event.

Ragged School Museum

46–50 Copperfield Road, E3
t (020) 8980 6405
www.raggedschoolmuseum.org.uk
⊖ Mile End
Bus 25, 277, 309, D6, D7
Open Wed–Thurs 10–5, first Sun of every month 2–5
Free
Suitable for all ages
Allow at least a couple of hours

In the late 19th century, thousands and thousands of children in London were living in abject poverty. There was no free education system or health care as there is today, and many children had to work for a living, often in dangerous conditions. It was an appalling state of affairs and one that Dr Barnardo, a young missionary, decided to do something about. During his life he founded over 90 homes for London's destitute children. He also ran this 'Ragged School', which provided free education for the poorest children of London's East End. Today it is a museum. Kids can walk through the classrooms, sit at the old desks and write on the slates. The museum also organizes a range of period activities, including parlour games and sweet-making sessions.

Royal Air Force Museum

Grahame Park Way, NW9
t (020) 8205 2266
www.rafmuseum.org.uk
⊖ Colindale
⇌ Mill Hill Broadway
Bus 204, 303
Open 10–6, daily
Free
Suitable for ages 5 and over, under-16s must be accompanied by an adult
Allow at least a couple of hours

On the site of the former Hendon Aerodrome, the museum is made up of two huge hangars stuffed full of aeronautical hardware. In Bomber Command Hall you'll find fighter planes from right through the 20th century – from bi-planes and Battle of Britain Spitfires to the awesome vertical take-off Harrier jump jet. Once you've finished marvelling at these fearsome machines, try some of the interactive exhibits in the Aeronauts Gallery, guaranteed to get your and your kids' combative juices flowing. You can clamber inside the cockpit of a Lockheed Tristar, take the controls in a Jet Provost and find out whether you've got the reactions needed to be the 'best of the best' at the Pilot Skills test. You can even line up the sights to send a bouncing bomb crashing through a dam at a special display on the life of the inventor of the bouncing bomb, Barnes-Wallis. The highlight, however, is undoubtedly the flight simulator in which you get to take the controls of a Tornado – be warned, it's pretty intense and certainly isn't recommended if you've had a heavy lunch.

The museum organizes a number of family events throughout the year when kids may be able to try on RAF uniforms, experience life in a mock-up wartime classroom or listen to actors retelling the story of the Battle of Britain, the nation's 'finest hour'. Owing to an extensive redevelopment programme (which should see the creation of a new 'Milestones of Flight' exhibition and an expanded interactive centre) due to begin in the next couple of years, some of the exhibitions may be forced to close temporarily, so be sure to check before visiting.

Wandsworth Museum

11 Garratt Lane, SW18
t (020) 8871 7075
www.wandsworth.gov.uk
⊖ East Putney
⇌ Wandsworth Town
Bus 28, 37, 39, 44, 77a, 156, 170 220, 270, 337
Open Tues–Sat 10–5, Sun 2–5, closed bank hols
Free
Wheelchair accessible, with adapted toilets.
Suitable for all ages
Allow at least 1hr

Organizes regular hands-on sessions for kids inspired by its permanent displays of local history.

Music

Listening to music

Pop is obviously a week-by-week phenomenon with no fixed calender of events. For details of forthcoming pop concerts, consult the listing sections of the *Evening Standard*, London's principal daily newspaper, or the weekly entertainment magazine, *Time Out*. The **London Arena, t** (020) 7538 1212, **www**.londonarena.co.uk, is a key venue for popular shows like *The Tweenies* and *Toy Story on Ice*, as well as pop concerts, as is **Wembley Arena t** (020) 8902 0902. **www**.ticketmaster.co.uk Classical music, on the other hand, does adhere to a calendar (admittedly a rather fluid one) and you might like to keep an eye out for the following.

Kenwood House Lakeside Concerts

Hampstead Lane, NW3
t 0870 333 1181
www.english-heritage.org

⊖ Archway, Golders Green then bus 210
Bus 210
When *July–August*
Adm Adult £16.50–30, child £2–4, under-5s **free**

Kids can play in the grassy grounds during the concert and then rejoin their parents for the fireworks at the end. There are deckchairs and grass seating. Many families take a picnic.

London Coliseum

St Martin's Lane, WC2
t (020) 7632 8300
www.eno.org
⊖ Leicester Square, Charing Cross
Bus 14, 19, 24, 29, 38, 176

Operatic workshops and short performances for ages 7 and over. Children and accompanying adults can take part in plot summaries and improvisation sessions, and listen to a sung excerpt from the opera in question.

London Symphony Orchestra Family Discovery Concerts

Barbican, Silk Street, EC2
t (020) 7638 8891
www.barbican.org.uk
⊖ Barbican
Bus 4, 56
Adm Adult £5, child (under 16) £3
One or two a season, call in advance

A popular annual event designed to get children aged 7–12 interested in classical music. The programmes mainly comprise short pieces and there is lots of audience participation. Orchestra musicians mingle with the crowds during the interval and will give any child who brings along an instrument an impromptu music lesson.

Royal Opera House

Bow Street, WC2
t (020) 7304 4000
www.royaloperahouse.org
⊖ Covent Garden/Leicester Square
Bus 6, 9, 11, 13, 15, 23, 77A, 91, 176
Open Tours: Mon–Sat at 10.30am, 12.30pm and 2.30pm
Adm Tours: adult £8, child £7
Wheelchair accessible, with adapted toilets

As well as the free classical concerts now staged in its foyer, there is an education programme comprising six 'School Matineés' a year (tickets only £5 for children and adults), with opera and ballet performances for schools and colleges. Information packs for teachers are available ahead of concerts online at **www.royaloperahouse.org**.

Stilgoe Family Concerts
Royal Festival Hall, South Bank, SE1
t (020) 7336 0777
www.stilgoeconcerts.co.uk
⊖/ ≋ Waterloo
Bus 1, 4, 26, 68, 76, 168, 171, 176, 188, 341, 501, 505, 521, X68
Adm £4.50–12
Four concerts between Oct and April, Sat at 3.30
Wordsmith and composer Richard Stilgoe leads these family and school concerts, accompanied by the National Children's Orchestra and youth orchestras from around the country. Children can learn a song in advance that Richard Stilgoe has written especially for the performance.

Wigmore Hall
36 Wigmore Street
t (020) 7935 2141
www.wigmore-hall.org.uk
⊖ Bond Street
Adm £5
Bus 6, 7, 10, 12, 13, 15, 23, 73, 94, 98, 113, 135, 137, 139, 159, 189
Organizes Chamber Tots sound workshops for under-5s, hands-on music-making sessions for over-5s (which culminate in a concert) and school holiday music groups for over-11s.

Making Music
Whether it's pop, classical or 'world' music, your kids will always have much more fun making a racket than listening to one.

Guildhall School of Music
Silk Street, Barbican, EC2
t (020) 7638 1770
www.gsmd.ac.uk
⊖ Barbican
Bus 4, 56
This prestigious school runs weekly music courses for all abilities during term time. Children can learn an instrument or have vocal coaching and, if they reach a sufficient standard, join one of two youth orchestras.

Horniman Music Room Workshops
100 London Road, SE23
t (020) 8699 1872
www.horniman.ac.uk
≋ Forest Hill
Bus 63, 122, 176, 185, 312, P4, P13
No fixed calender, call in advance
Free
The Horniman Museum houses one of Britain's largest and most important collections of musical instruments. Children can explore their various sounds at one of the museum's regular workshops. *See* (Museums & galleries), above.

National Festival of Music for Youth
Royal Festival Hall, South Bank, SE1
t (020) 8878 9624
www.mfy.org.uk
⊖/ ≋ Waterloo
Bus 1, 4, 26, 68, 76, 168, 171, 176, 188, 341, 501, 505, 521, X68
In July, a vast collection of school orchestras and youth bands comprising some 12,000 musicians gather at the Royal Festival Hall for a huge musical jamboree (the biggest of its kind in the world), during which music workshops and classes for both adults and children are held. In November, the festival's best musicians also play three concerts at the Royal Albert Hall.

The Music House for Children
Bush Hall, 310 Uxbridge Road, London, W12
t (020 8932 2652)
www.musichouseforchildren.com
⊖ Shepherd's Bush
Bus 207, 260, 283, 607
The Music House for Children, run from Bush Hall, has an extensive music and arts education programme. It provides group tuition throughout the week involving music, dance and drama.

Pottery cafés
Unleash the budding Wedgwood in your family with a spot of ceramic painting. Many cafés prove great venues for parties, and as well as throwing or painting pots, you can sculpt, tie-dye or style your own jewellery. Go create!

Art 4 Fun/Colour Me Mine
196 Kensington Park Road, W11, **t** (020) 7792 4567
www.art4fun.com

⊖ Ladbroke Grove
Adm £3.95; items from £2.50
172 West End Lane, Nw6, **t** (020) 7794 0800
www.art4fun.com
⊖ West Hampstead
Adm £3.95; items from £2.50
44 Chiswick High Road, W4, **t** (020) 8994 4100
www.chiswick.colourmemine.com
⊖ Chiswick Park,
Adm £3.95; items from £2.50
212 Fortis Green Road, N10, **t** (020) 8444 4333,
www.muswellhillcolourmemine.com
⊖ East Finchley **Bus** 102, 234
Adm Adult £4, child £5
Open daily
Suitable for all ages

A magical place where children and parents can paint their own cups, plates (dishwasher safe), T-shirts or picture frames. Also great for original parties: ceramics, clay T-shirt printing and painting, tie-dye and face painting. Take away a souvenir ceramic hand or footprint of your little angel!

Ceramics Café
Branches at Hammersmith, Kew Greeen and West Ealing
t (020) 8741 4140
www.ceramicscafe.com
⊖ Ravenscourt Park
Bus 9, 10, 27, 94
Open Tues–Sat 10–6, Sun 11–6
Adm £2 studio fee, £3–£12 for materials
Suitable for all ages

Personalize plates, mugs and other tableware. Party packages available.

Theatre

On any given night, there will be well over 60 plays, shows and revues showing in the West End. Obviously not everything that gets put on is suitable for children, but there are many theatres specializing in the type of big, glossy, all-singing, all-dancing shows that appeal to a family audience. For further details check the daily newspapers and weekly listings magazines such as *Time Out* .

Performances are typically at 7.30pm Monday to Saturday with a couple of additional matinée performances on Tuesday or Wednesday, and Saturday.

Chitty Chitty Bang Bang
London Palladium, Argyll Street, W1
Box office **t** 0870 890 1108
www.chittythemusical.co.uk
⊖ Oxford Circus
Bus 3, 6, 7, 8, 10, 12, 13, 15, 23, 25, 53, 55, 73, 88, 94, 98, 113, 137, 139, 159, 176, 189, C2
Prices £11–£40

The much loved film – complete with toe-tapping songs, the beautiful Truly Scrumptious, the ever-so-scary Child Catcher and, of course, the famous flying car – brought to the West End stage. Enjoyable knockabout fun. Interestingly, the story on which it's based was written by Ian Fleming, the creator of the rather different-in-tone adventures of 007 James Bond.

The Complete Works of William Shakespeare (abridged)
Reduced Theatre Company, Criterion Theatre, Piccadilly Circus, WC2
Box office **t** (020) 74313 1437
www.reducedshakespeare.com
⊖ Piccadilly Circus
Bus 3, 12, 14, 19, 22, 38
Prices £14.50–£32.50

Don't panic, this isn't a performance of an actual Shakespeare play (which some children might not be too thrilled at the prospect of watching), but rather a hilarious, two-hour romp through the bard's work, with each play's plot, themes and memorable quotes reduced down to bite-sized, easily digestible portions. The reduced theatre company also puts on other 'best bits' shows including a 'Complete History of America (abridged)' on Tuesdays and 'The Bible, the Complete Works of God (abridged)' on Thursdays.

Joseph and the Amazing Technicolour Dreamcoat
New London Theatre, Drury Lane, WC2
Box office **t** (020) 7404 4079
www.reallyuseful.com
⊖ Covent Garden
Bus 1, 68, 91, 168, 171, 188, 501, 505, 521, X68
Prices £10–£40

Another Lloyd Webber production, which means a simple plot, simple catchy songs and lots of jolly choreography.

Les Misérables

Palace Theatre, Shaftesbury Avenue, W1
Box office **t** (020) 7434 0909
www.lesmis.com
⊖ Leicester Square
Bus 14, 19, 38
Prices £10–£42.50

This tale of the Parisian underworld is officially the world's most popular musical. It's been running in London since 1985, so they must be doing something right.

The Lion King

Lyceum Theatre, Wellington Street, WC2
⊖ Covent Garden, Charing Cross
Box office **t** 0870 243 9000
www.disney.co.uk/musicaltheatre/thelionking
Bus 1, 6, 9, 11, 13, 15, 23, 68, 77A, 91, 168, 171, 176, 188, 501, 505, 521, X68
Prices £17.50–£42.50

An all-singing, all-dancing extravaganza set in the heart of Africa, with a plot and songs that most of the audience will already know by heart. Book well in advance.

Mamma Mia!

Prince Edward Theatre, Old Compton Street, W1
Box office **t** (020) 7447 5400
www.mamma-mia.com
⊖ Leicester Square
Bus 3, 6, 9, 11, 12, 13, 15, 23, 24, 29, 53, 88, 91, 109, 139, 159, 176, 184, 196
Performances Mon–Sat 7.30, matinées Wed, Sat 2.30. Duration 2hrs 40mins
Prices £22.50–£45

Theatrical karaoke – all your favourite Abba songs shoe-horned into a rather convoluted story.

The Mousetrap

St Martin's Theatre, West Street, WC2
Box office **t** (020) 7836 1443
⊖ Leicester Square
Bus 14, 19, 24, 29, 38, 176
Performances Mon–Sat 8, matinées Tues 2.45, Sat 5. Duration 2hrs 51mins
Prices £13.50–£31.50

The big daddy of them all – it's the longest-running show in the world, having played continuously for the last 49 years. This gentle Agatha Christie mystery is a good way to introduce kids to the joys of the stage.

We Will Rock You

Dominion Theatre, Tottenham Court Road, W1
Box office **t** (020) 7413 3546
http://queenonline.com/wewillrockyou
⊖ Leicester Square
Bus 3, 6, 9, 11, 12, 13, 15, 23, 24, 29, 53, 88, 91, 109, 139, 159, 176, 184, 196
Prices £10–£50

An absurd Ben Elton-penned plot links some of the flamboyant 70s and 80s rock band's greatest hits into a spectacular stage show.

Behind the scenes

London is, and has always been since the days before Shakespeare, a theatrical city, and there are plenty of opportunities to sample the smell of the greasepaint and the roar of the crowd. The following theatres offer backstage tours where you can explore dressing rooms, wardrobes and costume departments and find out about the elaborate machinery used to get the scenery on and off the stage.

London Palladium

Argyll Street, W1
t (020) 7494 5091
⊖ Oxford Circus
Bus 3, 6, 7, 8, 10, 12, 13, 15, 23, 25, 53, 55, 73, 88, 94, 98, 139, 159, 176, X53
Tour Mon, Tues, Fri at 5.30, Wed, Sat at 12.30pm
Adm £4 per person, regardless of age

Royal National Theatre

South Bank, SE1
t (020) 7452 3400
www.nationaltheatre.org.uk
⊖ /≥ Waterloo
Bus 1, 4, 26, 68, 76, 168, 171, 176, 188, 341, 501, 505, 521, X68
Tour Mon–Sat 10.15, 12.45, 5.30
Adm Backstage tours: £5 per person, concs £4.25

Theatre Royal

Drury Lane, WC2
t 0870 899 3338
www.rutheatres.com
⊖ Covent Garden
Bus 1, 68, 91, 168, 171, 188, 501, 505, 521, X68
Tour Daily, call in advance
Adm Adult £8, child £6

Children's theatre

Going to see a big West End production is all very well, but it's liable to get kids hankering for a life on the stage. Thankfully, London is home to several theatre companies which not only put on their own child-friendly performances, but also offer training and advice (often for free) to aspiring young thespians. Here are some of the best.

Battersea Arts Centre

Old Town Hall, Lavender Hill, SW11
t (020) 7223 2223
www.bac.org.uk
⇌ Clapham Junction
Bus 77, 77A, 345
Open Mon 10–6, Tues–Sun 10–9
Adm drama workshops £4.50; children's theatre: adult £5.75, child £4.50; membership: child £10.75, family £16.50

Organizes activity and theatre workshops for 3–16 year-olds, stages a performance of children's drama every Saturday at 2.30pm.

Half Moon Young People's Theatre

43 White Horse Road, E1
t (020) 7709 8900
www.halfmoon.org.uk
⊖ Stepney Green
⇌ Limehouse
Bus 5, 15, 15b, 25, 40, 106, 253
Open 10–6 (performance times vary)
Adm Performance: adult £3.50, child £3.50

This very serious-minded theatre group runs Saturday workshops on themes from street dance to mask-making. It stages a programme of kids' theatre on Saturdays at 11.30am and 2pm.

Little Angel Theatre

14 Dagmar Passage, Cross Street, N1
t (020) 7226 1787
www.littleangeltheatre.com
⊖ Angel, Highbury & Islington
Bus 4, 19, 30, 38, 43, 56, 73, 341
Open Performances Sat at 11am and 3pm
Adm Adult £7.50, child £5

A wonderful puppet theatre which holds regular weekend performances and also runs a puppet club on Saturday mornings when kids can make and learn how to use puppets. Children must be aged 3 or over.

London Bubble

t (020) 7237 4434
www.londonbubble.org.uk
Times and prices vary, call in advance

This popular roving theatre company moves its mobile show tents around the parks of London during the summer, staying on average one week in each. The plays are aimed squarely at 11 year-olds and under. It also holds workshops for ages 3–6.

Polka Theatre

240 The Broadway, SW19
t (020) 8543 4888
www.polkatheatre.com
⊖ /⇌ Wimbledon, ⊖ South Wimbledon
Bus 57, 93, 155
Open Tues–Fri 9.30–4.30, Sat 11–5.30
Adm Tickets for performances range from £5–£10; a one-day workshop is £25

The capital's only purpose-built children's theatre. Four shows a day are put on during the school holidays, two during term-time. It also runs drama workshops and after-school clubs for all ages. The shows are usually of a very high standard and are a mixture of classics and new work.

Puppet Theatre Barge

Bloomfield Road, Little Venice, W9
t (020) 7249 6876
www.puppetbarge.com
Bus 6, 18, 46
Open Vary, phone ahead
Adm Adult £7, child £6.50

Moored on Regent's Canal, Little Venice, this old working barge is a delightful place to introduce your children to puppetry. The Moving Stage Marionettes Company, which operates the barge, puts on high-quality puppet shows for children and adults throughout the year. It's easy to find: look out for the bright red and yellow awnings. The barge is moored in winter, but in summer sails up and down the Thames, putting on shows.

Regent's Park Open Air Theatre

Regent's Park, NW1
t (020) 7486 2431
www.openairtheatre.org
Adm Tickets for daytime performances start at £9.50 (up to £26) while evening tickets cost a flat rate £6; tickets for family shows are a flat rate £9
⊖ Baker Street
Bus 2, 13, 18, 27, 30, 74, 82, 113, 139, 189, 205, 274

Wheelchair accessible, with adapted toilets, hearing loop and signed performances

This respected theatre company usually puts on some sort of child-friendly show during the summer holidays, as well as Shakespeare and a quality musical (for more details, *see* p.46).

Shakespeare's Globe

Bear Gardens, Bankside, New Globe Wall, Southwark, SE1
t (020) 7902 1400
www.shakespeares-globe.org
⊖ London Bridge
Bus 11, 15, 17, 23, 26, 45, 63, 76, 100, 344, 381, RV1
Open 10–5, daily, for performance times call in advance
Adm Museum: adult £8, child £5.50, concs £6.50, family ticket (2+3) £24, (under-5s **free**)
Saturday 'Child's Play' Workshops **adm** £10
Limited wheelchair access, call disabled access information on **t** *(020) 7902 1409*

On certain select Saturdays, children aged 8–11 can take part in Saturday afternoon 'Child's Play' drama sessions at the Globe's education centre (for more details, *see* p.119).

Tricycle Theatre

269 Kilburn High Road, NW6
t (020) 7328 1000
⊖ Kilburn
Bus 16, 31, 32, 98, 189, 206, 316, 328
Open Performances Sat at 11.30am and 2pm
Adm Performances: adult £4, child £3.50 or £3 in advance; workshops are £20 for a 10-week term

The theatre holds about 300 workshops a year for all ages. It teaches acting, singing, dancing, music, mime, puppetry and circus skills. Its own family theatre performances are both highly innovative and hugely popular, and take place every Saturday of the academic year (Sep–June) at 11.30am and 2pm. The theatre also shows Saturday matinée films for all the family; call for details.

Unicorn Theatre

t (020) 7700 0702
www.unicorntheatre.com

The Unicorn is currently homeless while awaiting work on its new Southwark home to be completed (tentatively scheduled for late 2004). In the meanwhile it will continue to put on performances at a variety of venues including Regent's Park Open Air Theatre.

Pantomime season

The original interactive entertainment. Come December and a collection of ex-sportsmen, soap stars and TV magicians will join a host of professional vaudevillians to produce this most British of institutions. Throughout London you'll find versions of *Aladdin*, *Cinderella* and *Jack and the Beanstalk* in production. Even if you're not a fan, you should still consider taking along the kids, who will love all the singalongs and 'Behind you!' stuff. For details of performances in your area, check out the listings in the *Evening Standard* and *Time Out*.

TV & radio

Being a member of a studio audience for a TV or radio show can be quite a giggle for children. Most shows are free, but, please take note that tickets for the most popular ones are snapped up well in advance and many shows operate age restrictions.

BBC TV and Radio

t (020) 8576 1227
www.bbc.co.uk/whatson/tickets

The BBC also offers backstage tours of its White City studios when you can visit the news and weather centre and see how programmes are made (available to ages 10 and over only). They cost adult £7.95, child £5.95, family £21.95, call **t** 0870 603 0304.

ITV

t (020) 7843 8000, www.itv.co.uk
www.carlton.com

Channel 4

t (020) 7396 4444
www.channel4.com/tickets

Channel 5

t (020) 7550 5555, www.channel5.co.uk
Tickets for ITV, Channel 4 and Channel 5 shows can also be obtained through the following companies:
Carlton, **t** (0115) 964 5234; **Clappers**, **t** (020) 8532 2770; **Fullhouse**, **t** (01299) 829 299; **LWT**, **t** (020) 7261 3261; **Powerhouse**, **t** (020) 7287 0045; **Standing Room Only**, **t** (020) 8870 0111

Kids out

13

Plants and birds

There is plenty of outdoor fun to be had in London. The city is dotted with parks – from great swathes of manicured greenery such as Hyde Park and Green Park to tiny patches of unspoilt wilderness – and there are several urban farms where kids can get close to animals and take part in a variety of art activities. At Kew Gardens and the purpose-built Wetlands Centre in Barnes, it's quite possible to while away a whole day contemplating the wonders of the natural world.

Kew Gardens

Kew, Richmond, Surrey, TW9
t (020) 8332 5622
Infoline t (020) 8940 1171
www.kew.org.uk
≈ Kew Bridge, Kew Gardens
⊖ Kew Gardens
Bus 65, 391, 267, R68 (Sun only)
Open 9.30–dusk
Adm Adult £7.50, under-16s **free**, concs £5.50, blind, partially sighted and wheelchair users **free**
Baby-changing facilities, 2 gift shops, 2 self-service restaurants, coffee bar, bakery, snack shop
Wheelchair accessible, with adapted toilets
Suitable for all ages

When the rain pours down and there's a chill in the air, it's best to head indoors and hide under a blanket. Alternatively, you could pay a visit to the one part of London where tropical weather is guaranteed 365 days a year. And, after 10 minutes spent in the sweltering heat of the Palm House, a huge Victorian conservatory where the conditions are designed to mimic those of a rainforest, you'll never complain about the British weather again.

The Royal Botanic Gardens, to give Kew its proper name, is spread over a 300-acre site on the south bank of the Thames. It has grown, over the course of a 200-year history, into the largest and most comprehensive collection of living plants in the world, with more than one in eight of all flowering plants. There are three enormous conservatories: the above-mentioned Palm House, full of tropical exotica; the late Victorian Temperate House; and the Princess of Wales Conservatory, built in the 1980s and home to both the giant Amazonian water-lilly and Titan Arum, the largest, and possibly the smelliest, flower in the world. There is also a 10-

storey, 50-m high, 18th-century pagoda and a very good restaurant. In summer, however, there's no finer place for a picnic.

WWT Wetlands Centre

Queen Elizabeth Walk, SW13
t (020) 8409 4400
www.wwt.org.uk
≈ Barnes
Bus Train, then 33, 72, 209, 283
⊖ Hammersmith then bus 283
Bus 283
Open 9.30–dusk, feeding times at 12 noon and 3.30pm daily
Adm Adult £6.75, child (4–16) £4, concs £5.50, family ticket £17.50, under-4s **free**
Wheelchair accessible. Baby-changing facilities, shop, self-service restaurant. Suitable for all ages

This innovative site is split into 14 simulated habitats, including arctic tundra and tropical swamp, each inhabited by wildfowl. Picture boards help you to identity what's what and give you a few quiz questions. Though this is obviously a trip best undertaken in good weather when you can follow the keepers as they undertake their daily feeding rounds at 12 noon and 3pm, the centre does boast numerous huts and hides where you can shelter from any showers and still see the wildlife. There's also a visitors' centre where you can pick up children's trails and hire binoculars (£5). It also has a good, spacious ground floor café (with a special children's menu and outside seating) and, upstairs, in the observatory, an interactive area where kids can rediscover life through the eyes of a duck, drangonfly or bird. They can follow migratory patterns across the globe, make some bird sounds, build puzzles or just gaze out over the grounds to see which birds are on the move. There's a small film theatre where visitors can learn more about the centre and the work of the World Wildlife Trust. Seasonal wildlife-themed activities are organized on weekends and, during the school holidays, kids can take part in bat walks, dragonfly hunts and the very popular pond safaris when, armed with nets, they go hunting by the water's edge for tiny creatures to investigate.

Open spaces

Alexandra Palace Park

Muswell Hill, N22
t (020) 8444 7696
www.alexandrapalace.com
⊖ Wood Green
⇌ Alexandra Palace
Bus 184, W3
Open 24hrs a day
Free

'Ally Pally', as it is affectionately known, has had a rather illustrious history. Built in 1862 for the second Great Exhibition, in 1936 it was the site of Britain's first television broadcast. Today, the park is one of the best equipped for sports in the capital. Among its many attractions are a dry-ski slope, several football and cricket pitches, a pitch and putt golf course, an ice rink and a boating lake. There are also a couple of children's playgrounds, complete with sandpits and swings. Both adults and children will enjoy the spectacular views that the park affords over London (for 20p you can take an even closer look through a set of fixed binoculars). Regular funfairs take place during the school holidays and on bank holidays with rides, side shows, children's rides and refreshments. The house also hosts a variety of craft and leisure activity shows, concerts and displays. Redevelopment is currently underway to try and spruce up the park's shabbier corners.

Battersea Park

Prince of Wales Drive, SW11
t (020) 8871 7530
⊖ Sloane Square
⇌ Battersea Park, Queenstown Road
Bus 19, 44, 137, 319, 344, 345
Open Dawn till dusk
Free

Due for redevelopment over the next couple of years, Battersea is nonetheless one of London's best parks for children. There's a small zoo, home to deer, peacocks and wallabies (although its future may still be threatened by the redevelopment), a breezy boating lake, a Victorian Pump House and, best of all, London's largest adventure playground – ropes, gangways, climbing frames, nets etc. – if it can be clambered over, you'll find it here. In summer there are kids' theatre shows and pony rides. For sports fans, there are over 20 tennis courts at the new Millennium arena and also a branch of the London Recumbents, **t** (020) 7498 6543, where you can hire bikes. The park organizes lots of summer events for children, including a teddy bears' picnic. In November there's usually an impressive firework display and bonfire. The Zoo, **t** (020) 8871 7540, is open April–Sept 10–5, daily; Oct–Mar Sat–Sun only 11–3. It costs adult £1.20, child/concs 60p (see p.176 for more details).

Brockwell Park

Herne Hill, SE24
t (020) 7926 0105
⇌ Herne Hill
Bus 2, 3, 37, 196
Open Dawn till dusk daily

Though its main draw is its famous lido (see Evian Lido p.187), especially in summer, the park has much to offer year-round. There are tennis courts, duck ponds, a bowling green, a basketball court, a football pitch and a BMX track, as well as lots of open space to run around in. The First Come First Served Café, at the top of the hill, cooks up all-day breakfast and Sunday lunches, as well as sandwiches and snacks. The park is also home to the Whippersnappers' Workshop Room, which holds daily drop-in music workshops and a free disco on Saturdays. Call **t** (020) 7738 6633 for details.

Crystal Palace Park

Anerley Road, Crystal Palace, SE20
t (020) 8778 9496
⇌ Crystal Palace, Penge West
Bus 2, 3, 63, 122, 137a, 194, 202, 227, 249, 306, 322, 358
Open 7.30am till dusk daily
Dinosaur area open from 9.30am till 1hr before park closes

The park is currently undergoing a major facelift to restore and relandscape the area. Park areas may be closed, so call first, **t** (020) 8778 9496.

Undoubtedly the highlight of the park is the newly restored dinosaur park, a magnificent tableau of dinosaur models which, following a £4 million restoration programme, has been restored to its former glory. Originally conceived by Joseph Paxton 150 years ago, the park was designed to entertain and educate the new urban population during their new-found leisure time.

The site of the Crystal Palace itself, a huge iron and glass structure built for the Great Exhibition of 1851 and which burned down in the 1930s, is now occupied by an enormous TV transmitter that looks a bit like a mini-version of the Eiffel Tower (if you squint).

At present, the Children's Farm and the Boating Lake are closed due to restoration work. The Farm is scheduled to reopen in summer 2004.

There is a one o'clock club for under-5s open year-round, Mon–Fri 9.30–12.30 and 1–4, **t** (020) 8659 6554. There are also special children's events organized in the holidays for 6–12 year-olds, **t** (020) 8778 9496. The café is open daily and available for children's parties.

Dulwich Park

College Road, SE21
t (020) 8693 5737
⇌ North Dulwich
Bus P4, 12, 40, 176, 185, 321
Open Summer 8am–9pm daily, winter 8–4.30 daily
Free

A great place to come after spending the morning gawping at paintings in Dulwich Picture Gallery (see p.161), this beautiful park has a well-equipped children's playground, a boating lake (boats £5.25 for 30mins), tennis courts, horse-riding tracks and a pleasant café (open 9–6, daily, children's menu available). The London Recumbents, **t** (020) 8299 6636, have their base here, where you can hire or buy bikes, trikes and tandem cycles. They also run cycle safety courses on a one-to-one basis, while the resident rangers organize a range of activities from seed hunts to bat walks.

Epping Forest

Epping Forest Field Centre, High Beech Road, Loughton, Essex
t (020) 8508 0028
www.eppingforest.co.uk
⊖ Loughton
Bus 20, 167, 210, 214, 215, 219, 220, 240, 250, 301, 531, 532, 549
Open Field Centre: Mon–Sat 10–5, Sun 11–5
Free

A piece of ancient Britain on the outskirts of modern London. Once part of a huge woodland that stretched from the River Lea to the sea, Epping Forest came into existence 8,000 years ago, just after the last Ice Age. Six thousand years later, Queen Boudicca supposedly fought her last battle here against the Roman Army. Today, this 10-mile crescent is a wonderful mixture of thick dense woodland, grassland, heathland and ponds inhab-

ited by a wide range of wildlife including deer, woodpeckers, foxes and badgers. Close to the station is the excellent field centre which provides maps of the forest and organizes various children's activities, including mini-safaris, nature trails and pond dippings; it also supplies details of walks. The forest also encompasses two listed buildings – Queen Elizabeth's Hunting Lodge (**open** Wed–Sun 1–4 **free**, **t** (020) 8529 6681, and the temple, as well as the remains of two Iron Age earthworks.

Green Park

Piccadilly, W1, and The Mall, SW1
t (020) 7930 1793
See p.92.

Greenwich Park

Charlton Way, SE3
t (020) 8858 2608
See p.152.

Hampstead Heath

Hampstead, NW3
t (020) 7485 4491
⊖ Belsize Park, Hampstead
⇌ Hampstead Heath, Gospel Oak
Bus 24m 46m 168m 214m C2m C11
Open 24hrs a day
Free

After the royal parks, this is London's most famous open space. It's also Central London's most countrified area, one of the few places in the city that actually feels a little bit wild. Once the stamping ground of the poets Keats and Shelley, and of the highwayman Dick Turpin, these 800 acres provide a wonderful setting for a family walk. Kids will enjoy the well-equipped playground by Gospel Oak Station, complete with swings, slides and climbing frame, as well as the funfairs which are regularly set up in summer. Its wide open spaces are ideal for kite-flying, and there is a café nearby on the Parliament Hill side where you can recover. There are some wonderful views of the city, particularly from Parliament Hill (site of the famous lido, see p.187), and the park is also home to Kenwood House where, in summer, concerts are held with firework finales (see p.165). The heath's information centre organizes family activities such as music workshops, bat walks and fishing lessons.

Highgate Wood

Muswell Hill Road, N6
t (020) 8444 6129

⊖ Highgate
Bus 144, W7
Open 7.30am till dusk daily
Free

There's a playground (with an aerial rope slide and a separate, supervised play area for under-5s), a sports ground, an excellent vegetarian restaurant (*see* p.233) and a small patch of ancient woodland that is inhabited by a staggering array of flora and fauna. The wood is home to over 70 species of birds, 12 species of butterfly, 180 species of bats, 80 species of spiders, plus foxes, squirrels and all manner of undergrowth-hugging beetles, slugs and worms. Pick up a nature trail from the woodland centre and head off into the trees.

Holland Park

Kensington High Street, W8
t (020) 8602 2226
⊖ Holland Park, High Street Kensington
Bus 9, 10, 27, 28, 49
Open Dawn till dusk daily
Free

Just off Kensington High Street, this is a lovely manicured park with an orangery, a Japanese Water Garden and free-roaming peacocks and pheasants. Your kids, of course, will ignore all of them, as they head to the park's groovy, multi-level adventure playground. Sticky Fingers restaurant (which on weekends is very child-friendly) is just around the corner (*see* p.232). The ecology centre, **t** (020) 7471 9806, can provide maps and walks.

Hyde Park/Kensington Gardens

t (020) 7298 2100
See p.142.

Regent's Park

t (020) 7486 7905
See p.46.

Richmond Park

Richmond, Surrey
t (020) 8948 3209
www.royalparks.gov.uk/richmond.htm
⊖/≍ Richmond
Bus 72, 74, 85, 371
Open Dawn till dusk daily
Free

This great swathe of west London parkland has long been closely associated with the monarchy. In the 15th century Henry VII had a viewing mound created in the park, allowing him to look out over his kingdom – the mound still stands today and the views remain magnificent, stretching from Windsor Castle in the west to St Paul's Cathedral in the east. Two centuries later, both Charles I and Charles II used the park as a hunting ground. Today, although the hunting has stopped, the park is still home to the Queen's own herds of red and fallow deer which roam the park pretty much as the fancy takes them. A huge variety of other species of wildlife, among them foxes, weasels and badgers, have also made the park their home. There are two public golf courses, some great walking trails and you can hire bikes to explore the park's miles of roads (be aware that the park's roads are open to traffic) from Richmond Park Cycle Hire, **t** (07050) 209 249. There's also a very good park café, the Pembroke Lodge Cafeteria, perched high on Richmond Hill (children's menu available), **t** (020) 8948 7371.

St James's Park

The Mall, SW1
t (020) 7930 1793
See p.93.

Syon Park

London Road, Brentford, Middlesex, TW3
t (020) 8560 0883
www.syonpark.co.uk
⊖ Gunnersbury, then bus ≍ Kew Bridge, then bus
Bus 237, 267
Open Garden: 10.30–5.30 (or dusk if earlier) daily; Butterfly House: Summer 10–5, winter 10–3; Syon House April–Nov Wed–Thurs, Sun and Bank Hol Mon 11–5; Aquatic Experience 10–5.30, daily
Adm House: adult £3.50, child £2.50; house & garden: adult £6.95, child £5.95; Butterfly House: adult £4.95, child £3.95, family £15; Aquatic Experience: adult £4, child £3.50, family (2+3) £12.50, under-3s **free**

Syon Park is a great place to come and get up-close-and-personal with animals. Head for the Butterfly House, where you'll find free-flying butterflies that will settle on your head and arms as you walk around. Afterwards, pop along to the Aquatic House in the great conservatory and say hello to the resident piranhas, crocodiles and turtles before taking a stroll in the park's gorgeous rose garden. On a different plane altogether, Syon Park also has a great indoor adventure playground, Snakes and Ladders (*see* p.157), a model railway and a go-kart track.

Victoria Park

Old Ford Road, E3
t (020) 8533 2057
⊖ Mile End
⇌ Cambridge Heath, Hackney Wick
Bus 8, 26, 30, 55, 253, 277, S2
Open 6am till dusk, daily

Once upon a time, this 218-acre East End park's primary source of entertainment was provided by burning heretics at the stake. Thankfully, today's leisure facilities are a good deal less grisly and include the ornamental gardens, an animal enclosure with goats and fallow deer, tennis courts, a bowling green, an adventure playground, plenty of green open spaces and two lakes, one housing a model boat club, the other a thriving fishing trade.

City farms & zoos

If children won't come to the countryside, then the countryside must come to the children, or so they thought in the early 1970s. At that time, there were growing concerns about the development of London's youngsters. It was felt that they were becoming 'nature deprived'; that they had little concept of what the countryside was like. So the idea of the city farm was born – the aim being to bring a little bit of country life back into the inner city. Here's a selection of some of the best.

Battersea Park Children's Zoo

Albert Bridge Road, SW11
t (020) 8871 7540
⊖ Sloane Square
⇌ Battersea Park, Queenstown Road
Bus 19, 44, 49, 137, 319, 344, 345
Open April–Sept 10–5, Oct–Mar Sat–Sun only 11–3
Adm Adult £2.50, child £1.50, family £8.50

If the rumours are to be believed, then London may soon lose one of its best small zoos. At the time of going to press, it was still uncertain whether the proposed redevelopment of Battersea Park would find a home for the zoo or not, so you'd best get down there while you've still got the chance. You'll find a small Reptile House as well as meerkats, flamingos, emus and wallabies. Children can, if they like, stroke and pet the long-suffering goats and sheep to their heart's content in a special contact area.

Coram's Fields

93 Guilford Street, WC1
t (020) 7837 6138
⊖ Russell Square
Bus 17, 45, 46, 168
Open Summer 9–8 daily, winter 9–dusk
Free

This lovely little park has had a long association with children. It was here that the eponymous Thomas Coram established a foundling hospital in 1747 which, following the building's demolition in 1920, was turned into a children's park. Today, adults can only visit Coram's Fields in the company of a child. In addition to all the lawns, sandpits, paddling pool, basketball court, helter skelter and supervised playground, you'll find the park's highlight, a small farm home to goats, sheep, pigs, chickens, geese, rabbits and guinea pigs.

Deen City Farm & Riding School

39 Windsor Avenue, Merton Abbey, SW19
t (020) 8543 5300
www.deencityfarm.co.uk
⇌ Mitcham
Bus 200
Open Tues–Sun 10–5
Adm Farm: **free**; riding school: £15 for 30mins, £22 for 45mins

A real hands-on experience where children can help with the mucking out of goats, pigs, rabbits and ponies, meet chickens, guinea fowl and geese (as well as a few more exotic wild beasts, such as snakes, ferrets, chinchillas and terrapins) and go for pony and horse rides under the auspices of its riding school. In summer, the farm holds special 'Farmer Days' with tractor rides and barn-dances.

Freightliners City Farm

Paradise Park, Sheringham Road, off Liverpool Road, N7
t (020) 7609 0467
www.freightlinersfarm.org.uk
⊖ Holloway, Highbury & islington
Bus 43, 153, 271, 279
Open Tues–Sun 10–5, 10–4 in winter
Free

Summer playschemes allow visiting kids to get to know the farm's various breeds of sheep, pigs, goats, cattle and poultry. Children are made to feel very welcome and you can purchase free range eggs and bulk meats.

Hackney City Farm

1a Goldsmiths Row, E2
t (020) 7729 6381
www.hackneycityfarm.co.uk
⊖ Bethnal Green
⇌ Cambridge Heath
Bus 26, 48, 55
Open Tues–Sun 10–4.30
Free

In the east end of London, this converted brewery houses a collection of farm animals and runs some popular craft workshops and activity days. Here, kids can have a go at pottery and weaving and find out the proper way to feed animals and shear sheep. There's also an organic café and shop selling eggs, wool, animal hair, meat and pet rabbits.

Kentish Town City Farm

1 Cressfield Close, NW5
t 020 7916 5421
⊖ Kentish Town, Chalk Farm
Bus 24, 27, 31, 46, 134, 168, 214, C1, C2, C11
Open Tues–Sun 9–5
Free

Established in 1973, this was one of the first genuine city (as opposed to working) farms. Children can interact with cows, pigs and goats, and there's a children's garden. Pony rides are available for £1 on weekends (the horse riding club is, unfortunately, only available to Camden residents).

Mudchute Park & Farm

Pier Street, Isle of Dogs, E14
t (020) 7515 0749
DLR Mudchute, Crossharbour Station
Bus D1, D6, D7
Open 9–4, daily
Free

London's largest inner city farm was founded as a working farm at the end of the 19th century on the site of a rubbish dump. It is home to cows, pigs, sheep and even a llama (called Larry). The site also has riding stables (with pony-riding available for under-7s), a wildlife area, a café and swathes of wood and parkland. Kids can join the 'Young Farmer's Club' which organizes workshops with the aim of teaching kids the basics of farming.

Surrey Docks Farm

Rotherhithe Street, SE16
t (020) 7231 1010
DLR Surrey Quays, Canada Water
Bus 225
Open 9–1 and 2–5, daily, closed Mon and Fri during school hols
Free

A tiny farm overlooking the River Thames where you'll find goats, sheep and ducks, as well as a working forge. In summer the farm hosts various craft demonstrations, including metalwork and felt-making, and runs play schemes for youngsters.

Vauxhall City Farm

Tyers Street, SE11
t (020) 7582 4204
⊖ Vauxhall
Bus 2, 36, 77a, 88, 185
Open Tues–Thurs and Sat–Sun 10–5
Free

Next to the MI6 building, Vauxhall City Farm is home to all the usual suspects including pigs, rabbits, sheep, ducks and hens, as well as donkeys and ponies which give rides in summer.

Curious caves

Chislehurst Caves

Old Hill, Chislehurst
t (020) 8467 3264
www.chislehurstcaves.co.uk
Getting there It's off the A222 on the B264 near Chislehurst railway station
Open Daily during school hols, otherwise Wed–Sun, tours hourly 10–4
Adm Adult £4, child £2
Café, gift shop, on-site parking. 1hr from London

This 2,000 year-old tunnel network cut into the side of the Old Hill, Chislehurst is some way outside central London, but is worth a visit. It's a fascinating place that, though resembling natural caves, is actually entirely man-made. The first excavations were made by Druids fleeing the invading Romans, in the 1st century AD. In more recent times, it was used an an ammunition dump in the First World War and, in World War II, became Britain's largest bomb shelter. Today you can take tours in the company of experienced guides right into the caverns' subterranean depths. Though stretching for over 22 miles, the caves are well lit and more spooky than scary. The caves are also available for private parties.

Sports and activities

14

Whether you want to take part or just watch, you'll find London a hive of sporting activity with everything from athletics to windsurfing catered for. The capital's major clubs and sports centres are listed below, along with details of any specific children's schemes or courses that they run. Remember, you can find facilities for tennis, football, basketball and softball in many of London's parks. *See p.173 for details.*

Athletics

Crystal Palace
National Sports Centre, Ledrington Road, Crystal Palace, SE19
t (020) 8778 0131
www.crystalpalace.co.uk
≋ Crystal Palace
Bus 2, 3, 63, 122, 137a, 157, 202, 227, 249, 342, 358, 361, 450

Crystal Palace is the spiritual home of British athletics. Every year it hosts at least one star-studded athletics Grand Prix. Would-be athletes can apply to attend one of their yearly summer sports camps. Alternatively, contact Amateur Athletics Association on t (0161) 231 4494, www.british-athletics.co.uk.

Badminton & squash

Both of these sports are great for promoting dexterity and hand-eye co-ordination. For details of child-friendly clubs contact the **Badminton Association of England**, t (01908) 268400, www.baofe.co.uk or England Squash on t (0161) 231 4494, www.englandsquash.co.uk.

Baseball & softball

Due to an increase in popularity, these two American sports have clubbed together to form the **BaseballSoftballUK** agency. Little Leaguers in search of some action should call t (020) 7453 7000, www.baseballsoftballuk.com.

Basketball

The **English Basketball Association** can help you find anything from a local court to have a knock-about in to a junior level club to join. Call t 0870 774 4225 for details, or visit www.basketballeng-land.co.uk. Wembly Arena hosts basketball matches, t (020) 8902 8833 for details.

Cricket

England's most popular summer game. London's two premier grounds for watching this most tactical of sports are Lord's and the Oval. The county championship season runs from April to September, with four-day matches usually taking place between Thursday and Monday, often with a one-day match sandwiched in between on the Sunday. Both grounds also hold a one-day international match and a five-day international Test Match between England and one of the other eight cricket-playing nations each year – the other nations being Australia, New Zealand, India, Pakistan, Sri Lanka, South Africa, Zimbabwe and the West Indies. Tickets are in the region of £7–£25 – slightly more expensive for international matches. Both Lord's and the Oval run cricket courses for children aged 8 and over, and are enthusiastic supporters of 'Kwik Cricket', an easier, quicker version of the game for younger children.

Marylebone Cricket Club (MCC) and Middlesex County Cricket Club
Lord's Cricket Ground, St John's Wood Road, NW8
t (020) 7266 3825
www.lords.org
⊖ St John's Wood
Bus 3, 82, 113, 139, 189

Surrey County Cricket Club
The Oval, Kennington, SW8
t (020) 7582 6660
www.surreycricket.com
⊖ Oval, Vauxhall
Bus 36, 185

Useful contacts
The following bodies can provide information on sport and venues in and around London.
Sportsline
t (020) 7222 8000
www.sportsonline.co.uk
English Federation of Disability Sport
t (0161) 247 5294
www.efds.net
Sport England
t (020) 7273 1500
www.sportengland.com

Fishing

A bit of string and a bent nail may be all your kids need to get the angling habit. Alternatively, you could decide to invest in some fancy equipment from one of the capital's many tackle shops (try The Reel Thing, 17 Opera Arcade, SW1, t (020) 7976 1830, www.reelthing.co.uk). Either way you will need a licence. Contact the **Environment Agency** (formerly the National Rivers Authority) on t 01734 535 000, www.environment-agency.gov.uk/fish (licences can be bought online). They will also provide a list of fishing sites including some spots along the Thames (home to over 100 types of fish). Coarse and trout fishing licences cost: full £22, 8-day adult £7, child £5, 1-day £2.75.

London Anglers Association
Izaak Walton Road, 2a Hervey Park Road, E17
t (020) 8520 7477
www.londonanglers.net

Football

It has always been the nation's favourite sport, but over the past decade football has reached unprecedented levels of popularity. It now pervades all aspects of popular culture – millions of books, magazines, videos and even records are sold on the back of the game. The most successful players have become pop star-marrying superstars commanding seven-figure salaries, while the top clubs are now stock market listed businesses with massive annual turnovers. Nonetheless, for all this growth, the game itself has remained as simple as ever. It requires the minimum amount of equipment (a ball, basically; goalposts can be fashioned with whatever comes to hand) and can be played practically anywhere. No wonder more British children play football than any other sport.

London is home to over a dozen professional football clubs, the biggest of which – Arsenal, Charlton, Chelsea, Fulham and Tottenham – play in the Premier League, the nation's most prestigious competition. League matches are played at weekends (usually kicking off at 3pm on Saturday), while cup and European matches are played midweek with the big clubs regularly attracting crowds of over 30,000. The games can be passionately exciting and the removal of the hooligan element in the late 1980s has led to more families coming to matches. Most grounds have family enclosures and the facilities, especially at Premier League grounds, are usually excellent. Tickets should be booked as far in advance as possible. A seat at a Premiership match can cost between £25 and £60 per adult, with children half-price. League matches are cheaper at between £15 and £30, with child reductions. England's international matches will be played at a variety of venues around the country until the renovation of the national stadium at Wembley is complete (due to be ready in 2006).

One note of warning, however; if you've never been to a football match before, your children will hear some pretty fruity language. Chanting, singing (often obscene songs about the opposition) and swearing are all an essential part of the experience.

At their best, football clubs can be a focal, unifying point for the local community. Most London clubs now belong to the **Football in the Community** scheme whereby trained coaches organize holiday schools and after-school training for local children (both boys and girls) of all abilities.

Arsenal Football Club
Arsenal Stadium, Avenell Road, Highbury, N5
t (020) 7704 4040
www.arsenal.com
⊖ Arsenal
Bus 4, 19, 29, 43, 153, 236, 253, 271
Tickets £26–£50
102 spaces for wheelchair users

There is a six-year waiting list to become one of the club's 21,000 season ticket holders, although things should improve once their new increased-capacity stadium is completed in a few years' time.

Charlton Athletic
The Valley, Floyd Road, Charlton, SE7
t (020) 8333 4010
www.cafc.co.uk
≈ Charlton
Tickets £15–£35. Wheelchair users call **t** (020) 8333 4000 ext 248

Chelsea Football Club
Stamford Bridge, Fulham Road, SW10
t (020) 7386 7799
www.chelseafc.co.uk
Θ Fulham Broadway
Bus 14, 211
Tickets £29–£49. Wheelchair users call **t** (020) 7385 5545
Club shop, match day crèche for up to 20 children aged 1–5, from 2hrs before kick-off

Crystal Palace
Selhurst Park, White Horse Lane, SE25
t (020) 8771 8841
www.cpfc.co.uk
≈ Selhurst, Thornton Heath
Bus 50, 68, 198
Tickets £18–£25. Wheelchair users call **t** (020) 8768 6080

Tottenham Hotspur Football Club
White Hart Lane, Bill Nicholson Way, 748 High Road, Tottenham, N17
t 0870 420 5000
www.spurs.co.uk
Θ Tottenham Hale, Seven Sisters
Bus 149, 259, 279, W3
Tickets £25–£50. Wheelchair users call **t** (020) 8365 5161
Club shop

West Ham United
Boleyn Ground, Green Street, Upton Park, E13
t (020) 73548 2700
www.whufc.co.uk
Θ Upton Park
Bus 14, 74, 220
Tickets £27–£45

Go-karting

Kids love to pull on their overalls, gloves and helmets, put their foot to the floor and race around a tyre-lined circuit. Apart from the raw thrill of speed (the karts reach a top speed of 30mph), they enjoy the idea of doing something 'grown-up', like driving, in a decidedly 'non-grown-up, go-as-fast-as-you-can' sort of way. London's indoor circuits offer training and racing for mini racing drivers aged 8–16. Everything is done with total care and attention to safety. The centres provide helmets and overalls and rigorous safety advice. Children should go along wearing long sleeves and trousers.

Expect to pay about £30 for an hour-long session.

Docklands F1 City
Gate 119, Connaught Bridge, Royal Victoria Dock, E16
t (020) 7476 5678
www.f1city.co.uk
DLR Royal Albert

Streatham Playscape Kart Raceway
390 Streatham High Road, SW16
t (020) 8677 8677
www.playscape.co.uk
≈ Streatham
Bus 57, 109, 118, 133, 201, 250, 255

Ice-skating

London has half a dozen ice-skating rinks, many of which have popular disco nights. Most will not let children aged under three on the ice. Boots can usually be hired at the door. The average price, including skate hire, is adul: £5–£7, child £3–£5.

Alexandra Palace Ice Rink
Alexandra Palace Way, N22
t (020) 8365 4386
www.alexandrapalace.com/ice.htm
≈ Alexandra Palace
Bus 184, W3

Broadgate Ice Rink
Eldon Street, EC2
t (020) 7505 4068
Θ /≈ Liverpool Street
Bus 133, 141, 172, 214, 271

One of London's few outdoor rinks. It's flooded and frozen between November and March.

Lee Valley Ice Centre

Lee Bridge Road, E10

t (020) 8533 3154

⊖ Walthamstow Central

Bus 158

Don't let the distance put you off, as this large, well-equipped rink has disco sessions from 8.30pm–11pm and is open for general skating from 12 noon–4, daily.

Leisurebox

Queensway, W2

t (020) 7229 0172

⊖ Bayswater, Queensway

Bus 70

London's most famous rink. Come early and watch the pros in action.

Sobell Ice Rink

Hornsey Road, Holloway, N7

t (020) 7609 2166

www.aquaterra.org.uk

⊖ Finsbury Park, Holloway Road

Bus 91

Streatham Ice Arena

386 Streatham High Road

t (020) 8769 7771

www.streathamicearena.co.uk

≥ Streatham Common

Bus 57, 109, 118, 133, 201, 250, 255

Somerset House

The Strand, WC2

t (020) 7845 4600

www.somerset-house.org.uk

⊖ Temple, Charing Cross, Embankment, Covent Garden

Bus 6, 9, 11, 13, 15, 23, 77a, 91, 176

A New York-style open-air ice rink is set up in this grand mansion's courtyard for a few weeks during Christmas and New Year.

Play gyms & gymnastics

Play gyms are a great way to get kids moving and develop co-ordination and motor skills. Gymnastics is also fun for kids both to watch and/or participate in. Contact the **British Amateur Gymnastics Association** on t (01952) 820330, www.baga.co.uk.

Crèchendo

Various locations across London

t (020) 8675 6611

www.crechendo.com

Using toys and soft climbing equipment, younger kids are encouraged to fling themselves around in the name of social development. There are four age groupings from 4 months to 5 years. Kids must be accompanied by a parent or carer. There are 17 Crèchendo centres in London.

Tumbletots, Gymbabes & Gymbobs

Various venues across London

t (0121) 585 7003

www.tumbletots.com

Kids from crawling to pre-school can climb, jump and hang on specially designed equipment, thereby improving their balance, coordination and general physical ability. Older children aged 5–7 can explore equipment designed for adults in a super-vised and safe environment.

Riding

There are dozens of stables and horseriding schools in London, some offering lessons to children as young as two and a half (who presumably have only just got the hang of walking).

Barnfield Riding School

Parkfields Road (off Park Road), Kingston-upon-Thames

t (020) 8546 3616

www.barnfieldriding.co.uk

≥ Kingston

Bus 65, 371

Adm £20 for 1hr lesson

183

ICE-SKATING | PLAY GYMS & GYMNASTICS | RIDING | RUGBY | SKATEBOARDING | SKIING & SNOWBOARDING | SPORTS CENTRES | SWIMMING

The age limit is discretionary. On the Tiny Tots course children as young as two are even allowed to ride.

Dulwich Riding School
Dulwich Common, SE21
t (020) 8693 2944
⇌ West Dulwich
Bus 63, P4, P13
Adm Groups £15 per hour; private lesson £25 per hour
Age limit 10 and over

Ealing Riding School
Gunnersby Avenue, W5
t (020) 8992 3808
⊖ Ealing Common
Bus 207, 607
Adm per 30mins, adult £24, child £17
Age limit Five and over

Hyde Park Riding Stables
63 Bathurst Mews, W2
t (020) 7723 2813
www.hydeparkstables.com
⊖ Lancaster Gate
Bus 7, 15, 23, 27, 36
Adm £49 per lesson
Age limit 5 and over

London Equestrian Centre
Lullingworth Garth, Finchley, N12
t (020) 8349 1345
⊖ Mill Hill East
Bus 13, 82, 112, 143, 260
Adm from £18 per lesson
Age limit 4 and over

Ross Nye's Riding Stables
8 Bathurst Mews, W2
t (020) 7262 3791

Sporting bodies
All England Netball Association
t 01462 442 344
www.england-netball.co.uk
Amateur Athletics Association
t 0121 440 5000
www.british-athletics.co.uk
Amateur Rowing Association
t (020) 8237 6700
www.ara-rowing.org
Amateur Swimming Association
t 0150 926 4357
www.british-swimming.org
Badminton Association
t 01908 568 822
www.baofe.co.uk
British Baseball Federation
t (020) 7453 7000
www.baseballsoftballuk.com
British Canoe Union
t 0115 982 1100
www.bcu.org.uk
British Snowboarding Association
t 0131 445 2428
www.thebsa.org
British Sub-Aqua Club
t 0151 350 6200
www.bsac.com
Croquet Association
t 01242 242 318
www.croquet.org.uk
English Basketball Association
t 0870 774 4225
www.basketballengland.co.uk
English Ice Hockey Association
t 01202 303 946
www.eiha.co.uk
English Ski Council
t 0121 501 2314
www.englishski.org
English Volleyball Association
t 0115 981 6324
www.volleyballengland.org
Golf Foundation
t 01920 876 200
www.golf-foundation.org
Lawn Tennis Association
t (020) 7381 7111
www.lta.org.uk
London Anglers Association
t (020) 8520 7477
www.londonanglers.net
London Gymnastics Federation
t (020) 8529 1142
www.longym.freeserve.co.uk
UK National Cyclists' Organisation
t 01483 417 217
www.ctc.org.uk

www.ridingstable.co.uk
⊖ Paddington
Bus 7, 15, 23, 27, 36
Adm £35 per hour
Age limit 7 and over

Trent Park Equestrian Centre

Bramley Road, Oakwood, N14
t (020) 8363 9005
⊖ Oakwood
Adm per 30mins, adult £22, under-12s £18, under-6s £14
Age limit discretionary

Wimbledon Village Stables

24a High Street, Wimbledon, SW19
t (020) 8946 8579
www.wvstables.com
⊖ /⇌ Wimbledon
Bus 93, 200
Adm from £30 per hr
Age limit 3 and over

Rugby

London has several professional rugby union clubs, many of which offer coaching for children (both boys and girls) and run mini-teams. Club matches are usually played on Saturday afternoons, contact the **Rugby Football Union** on **t** (020) 8892 2000 for more information.

Harlequins

Stoop Memorial Ground, Langhorn Drive, Twickenham, Middlesex
t (020) 8410 6000
www.quins.co.uk
⇌ Twickenham
Bus 281
Tickets £12–£20, wheelchair users **free**
Specific entrance for wheelchair users, adapted toilets

London Wasps

Twyford Avenue Sports Ground, Twyford Avenue, Acton, W3
t (020) 8993 8298
www.wasps.co.uk
⊖ Ealing Common
Tickets adult £23, under-16s £10

Saracens RFC

Vicarage Road Stadium, Watford
t 01923 475 222
www.saracens.com
⇌ Watford High Street
Bus 298, 299, 307
Tickets £10–£30, under-16s £5
Has an entrance for wheelchair users and a reserved section for disabled spectators.

London Irish RFC

Madejski Stadium, Junction 11, M4, Reading, RG2
t (01932) 783 034
www.london-irish.com
⇌ Reading
Tickets adult £10–£25, child £5
Wheelchair access, adapted toilets
Welcomes kids; girls can play up to the age of 12.

London Welsh

Old Deer Park, Kew Road, Richmond, Surrey TW9
t (020) 8940 2368
www.london-welsh.co.uk
⊖ Richmond
Bus 65
Tickets £4–£11, under-16s **free**
Limited facilities for the disabled
Holiday and half-term courses; boys' and girls' teams from under-7s to under-12s.

Skateboarding

Of course, for most kids, the whole point of skateboarding is not to do it in an organized way at special clubs or centres, but rather as you please out on the streets (or at shopping centres and South Bank arts complexes). For many a teenager it's become the ultimate urban activity, practised with an almost religious-like intensity. Those skaters really wanting to test their skills might like to sample the half-pipes, bowls, tombstones, hips, fun boxes and grind boxes (your kids will know what they are) at the following skate parks.

Ally Pally Skatepark

Alexandra Palace, Muswell Hill, N22
⊖ Wood Green
⇌ Alexandra Palace
Bus 184, W3
Open 24hrs daily

Free

The skatepark is between the ice-rink and the children's playground.

Harrow Skatepark

behind Harrow Leisure Centre, Christchurch Avenue, Wealdstone, Harrow, HA3

≥/⊖ Harrow and Wealdstone

Bus H10

Open 9am till dusk daily

Free

There is an outdoor skate park next door to Harrow Leisure Centre.

Meanwhile

Meanwhile Gardens, Great Western Road, W9

⊖ Westbourne Park

Open dawn till dusk daily

Free

London's first skate park built back in 1976.

PlayStation Skate Park

Bay 65, Acklam Road, W10

t (020) 8969 4669

www.pssp.co.uk

⊖ Ladbroke Grove

Bus 7, 23, 52

Open Mon–Fri 11–4 and 5–9, Sat–Sun 10–9

Adm Non-members: £4 for 2 hrs, £7 for 4 hrs; members: £2.50 for 2 hrs, £5 for 4 hrs; membership costs £10 per year

Stockwell Bowl Skatepark

behind Brixton Academy

Stockwell Road, SW9

⊖ Brixton

Open 24hrs daily

Free

South London's most popular skate park, tucked behind the Brixton Academy, is of the old generation of good, concrete outdoor facilities that were designed in the 70s. It's recently been resurfaced with smooth pink concrete and includes a range of bumps and bowls.

Skiing & snowboarding

You don't expect to come to London and go skiing, but you can if you want to. There are a surprising number of dry ski slopes in London. All have nursery slopes for beginners. Prices work out at somewhere in the region of £10–£12 for adults (for a two-hour session) and £5–£6 for children. For more facilities contact the **Ski Club of Great Britain** on **t** (020) 8410 2000, www.ski-club.co.uk

Bromley Ski Centre

Sandy Lane, St Paul's Cray, Orpington, Kent

t (01689) 876 812

www.c-v-s.co.uk/bromleyski

≥ St Mary Kray

Bus 61, 208, R7

Open Mon–Thu 12 noon–10pm, Fri 10am–10pm, Sat 9am–6pm, Sun 9am–8pm, closed Mon in winter

Crystal Palace Ski Slope

Ledrington Road, Norwood, SE19

t (020) 8778 0131

www.crystalpalace.co.uk

≥ Crystal Palace

Bus 2, 3, 63, 122, 137a, 157, 202, 227, 249, 342, 358, 361, 450

Open Mon–Sat 9am–10pm, Sun 9–6

Sandown Sports Club

More Lane, Esher, Surrey

t (01372) 467132

www.sandownsports.co.uk

≥ Esher

Open Mon-Fri & Sun 10-10, Sat 1-8

Sports centres

There are nigh on 200 sports centres in London, offering a huge range of activities from badminton to martial arts. Many have swimming pools and most have special facilities for young children. Some of the best are listed below.

Britannia Leisure Centre

40 Hyde Road, Islington, N1

t (020) 7729 4485

www.britannia.lc.thehealthhub.co.uk

⊖ Old Street

Bus 67, 76, 141, 149, 242, 243, 243A, 271

Recently refurbished, it offers football, tennis, a well-equipped gym, basketball, swimming (including lessons), snorkelling and water polo.

Brixton Recreation Centre

27 Brixton Station Road, SW9
t (020) 7926 9779
⊖ Brixton
Bus 118, 196, 250, P4

Activities catered for include badminton, basketball, gymnastics, swimming, tennis, trampolining. It also organizes holiday play schemes for 5–15 year-olds involving sports sessions in football, gymnastics and basketball, as well as arts and crafts workshops.

Crystal Palace

National Sports Centre, Ledrington Road, Upper Norwood, SE19
t (020) 8778 0131
www.crystalpalace.co.uk
⇌ Crystal Palace
Bus 2, 3, 63, 122, 137a, 157, 202, 227, 249, 342, 358, 361, 450

The home of British athletics, this internationally renowned sports centre boasts an athletics stadium, an Olympic-sized pool and high diving board as well as excellent facilities for badminton, basketball, gymnastics, hockey and martial arts. It stages numerous international sporting competitions and offers teaching and coaching to a high standard. Would-be-athletes can apply to attend one of the centre's annual summer camps.

Michael Sobell Leisure Centre

Hornsey Road, Holloway, N7
t (020) 7609 2166
⇌ Finsbury Park, Holloway Road
Bus 91

A multi-purpose centre offering badminton, basketball, cricket, football, martial arts, squash, table tennis, trampolining and ice-skating.

Oasis Sports Centre

32 Endell Street, WC2
t (020) 7831 1804
⊖ Holborn, Covent Garden
Bus 1, 14, 19, 24, 29, 38, 176

Offering facilities for badminton, football, martial arts, swimming, table tennis and trampolining, Oasis also boasts London's only heated outdoor pool as well as a paddling pool for toddlers.

Queen Mother's Sports Centre

223 Vauxhall Bridge Road, SW1
t (020) 7630 5522
⊖ /⇌ Victoria, ⊖ Pimlico

Bus 2, 36, 185
Badminton, football, martial arts, netball, rounders, swimming.

Swimming

Children just love messing about in water. Whether it's in tropically heated under-5s pools or all-weather lidos, there's something deeply appealing about a good old splish-splash. Most indoor pools run mother and toddler sessions. Expect to pay around £3.50 for an adult, £2 for a child.

Indoor pools

The Arches

Trafalgar Road, SE10
t (020) 8317 5000
⇌ Greenwich
Bus 177, 180, 188, 286, 386
Open 10.30–7 daily
Various water chutes and slides.

Britannia Leisure Centre

40 Hyde Road, N1
t (020) 7729 4485
www.britannia.lc.thehealthhub.co.uk
⊖ Old Street
Bus 67, 76, 141, 149, 242, 243, 243A, 271
Open Mon–Fri 9–9, Sat & Sun 9–6
Water slides, wave machine, pool inflatables and lessons for kids.

Crystal Palace Pool

National Sports Centre, Ledrington Road, Norwood, SE19
t (020) 8778 0131
www.crystalpalace.co.uk
⇌ Crystal Palace
Bus 2, 3, 63, 122, 137a, 157, 202, 227, 249, 342, 358, 361, 450
Open Mon–Fri 9am–9pm, Sat–Sun 9–6
Huge pool complex with an Olympic-size (50m) pool, a 25m training pool, a 20m diving pool (with high diving boards) and an 18m teaching pool.

Fulham Pools

Normand Park, Lillie Road, SW6
t 0870 870 7018
⊖ West Brompton

Bus 74, 190
Open Mon–Fri 9am–9pm, Sat–Sun 9–6
  Water slide, water toys, wave machine and a swimming club for kids.

Latchmere Leisure Centre
Burns Road, SW11
t (020) 7207 8004
www.kinetika.org
⊖ Clapham Junction, Battersea Park
Bus 44, 49, 319, 344, 345
Open Mon–Thurs 7am–9.30pm, Fri and Sat 7am–7pm, Sun 7–6
  Child-friendly indoor pool which includes a seashore slope, wave machine and toddler's pool.

Outdoor pools

  On bright summer days, and even late into the evenings, London's outdoor pools can be delightful. Parents can escape the bustle, lazing by the poolside as their children go berserk in the water while the sun beats down overhead. Prices are roughly the same as for indoor pools.

Evian Lido
Brockwell Park, Dulwich Road, SE24
t (020) 7274 3088
www.thelido.co.uk
⊖ Brixton
⇌ Herne Hill
Bus 3, 37, 196
Open May–Sept Mon–Fri 7am–7pm, Sat–Sun 12 noon–6

Finchley Lido
Great North Leisure Park, High Road, N12
t (020) 8343 9830
⊖ Finchley Central
Bus 263
Open May–Sep 10–7 daily

Oasis Sports Centre
Endell Street, WC2
t (020) 7931 1804
⊖ Covent Garden
Bus 1, 14, 19, 24, 29, 38, 176
Open Mon–Fri 7.30am–8pm, Sat–Sun 9.30–5
  Heated outdoor pool in the heart of London. Also has a toddlers' paddling pool.

Parliament Hill Lido
Parliament Hill, Hampstead Heath (off Gordon House Road), NW5
t (020) 7485 3873

⇌ Gospel Oak
Bus 214, C2, C11
Open May–Sept 7–6, Oct–Feb 7–10.30

Tooting Bec Lido
Tooting Bec Road, SW16
t (020) 8871 7198
⊖ Tooting Bec
Bus 249, 319
Open May–Sept 10–8, daily

Tennis

  If you and your children don't fancy overcoming the obstacles inherent to the Wimbledon experience (see box, p.188), but just want to see some grass court tennis and spot a few famous players (so long as they're male), you might like to visit the Queen's Club's 'Stella Artois' Tournament which takes place a couple of weeks beforehand. The atmosphere here is much more relaxed and tickets are easier to come by (and much cheaper, £10–£15). If your family fancies a game, many public parks have a couple of concrete courts and there are a few tennis clubs in London offering training for children aged 7 and over. Expect to pay about £5–£6 an hour for an outdoor court, £12–£15 inside.

Wimbledon (All England Lawn Tennis and Croquet Club)
Church Road, Wimbledon, SW19
t (020) 8946 2244
www.wimbledon.org
⊖ Southfields, Wimbledon
⇌ Wimbledon
Bus 39, 93 or shuttle bus from any of the above stations

Queen's Club
Palliser Road, W14
t (020) 7385 3421
www.queensclub.co.uk
⊖ Barons Court
Bus 28, 74, 190, 211, 220, 295, 391

Islington Indoor Tennis Centre
Market Road, N7
t (020) 7700 1370
www.aquaterra.org/tennis
⊖Caledonian Road
Bus 73, 274

New balls please

Despite playing host to Wimbledon, the game's premier tournament, Britain's attitude towards tennis is, in truth, rather ambivalent. It has significantly fewer public courts than most other countries and, as a result, significantly fewer top-class players. The last home-grown winner of Wimbledon was Fred Perry (he of the sports shirts) in the late 1930s. Only recently, has Britain managed to find itself a couple of players capable of challenging for top honours and one of those, Greg Rusedski, had to be pinched from Canada. For most of the year, the British public couldn't care less about tennis. During the last two weeks of June, however, it suddenly becomes everyone's favourite sport. Demand for Wimbledon tickets is huge, to put it mildly. In order to buy Centre Court or No.1 Court tickets, where all the big-name matches take place, you have to enter a ballot the previous September, and even then your chances of success are pretty remote. Alternatively, you could try turning up on a matchday and queueing. The queue usually starts several days prior to the championship and can stretch for over a mile. Getting tickets for Wimbledon is not impossible, but it is very difficult – and even if you do get lucky, they're not cheap. Centre Court tickets start at £28 for the first Monday rising to £72 for the final Sunday. Outside court tickets are much better value, starting at £14 for the first Monday (£8 after 5pm) and dropping to £10 for the final weekend (£6 after 5pm), when fewer matches are scheduled. They also give you the chance to buy resale tickets for the show courts which go on sale daily at 2pm.

Regent's Park Tennis Centre

York Bridge Road, NW1
t (020) 7486 4216
www.rptc.co.uk
⊖ Regent's Park
Bus 274

Westway Indoor Tennis Centre

1 Crowthorne Road, W10
t (020) 8969 0992
⊖ Latimer Road
Bus 295

Watersports

Most of the centres listed run courses in sailing, windsurfing, canoeing and rowing – children must be able to swim, usually 50 metres, and there are generally age restrictions. For sailing activities on the Thames try the **Sailing Barge Trust** on **t** (020) 7642 8795, **www**.bargeclub.org; the **Thames Sailing Club** on **t** (01932) 228689, **www**.thamessailing-club.org.uk; or the **Amateur Rowing Association**, **t** (020) 8748 3632, www.ara-rowing.org

Docklands Sailing and Watersports Centre

Millwall Dock, West Ferry Road, E14
t (020) 7537 2626
www.dswc.org
⊖ Mile End
DLR Cross Harbour
Bus D1, D5, D8, P14

Canoeing, windsurfing and sailing sessions are available for ages 8 and over. Kids can also try dragon boat racing and imagine being Vikings.

Islington Boat Club

16–34 Graham Street, N1
t (020) 7253 0778
⊖ Angel
Bus 43, 214
Children must be 9 or over

London Corinthian Sailing Club

Linden House, Upper Mall, W6
t (020) 8748 3280
www.lcsc.org.uk
⊖ Hammersmith
Bus 9, 10, 27

Royal Victoria Dock Watersports Centre

Gate 5, Tidal Basin Road, off Silvertown Way, E16
t (020) 7511 2326
DLR Royal Victoria

Surrey Docks Watersports Centre

Greenland Dock, Rope Street, SE16
t (020) 7237 4009
⊖ Surrey Quays

Westminster Boating Base

Dinorvic Wharf, 136 Grosvenor Road, SW1
t (020) 7821 7389
⊖ Pimlico
Bus 24, C10

Days out

15

Brighton

Getting there By road: The A23 links Brighton directly with London. Alternatively, take the M23 part of the way, rejoin the A23, then follow the signs. The journey should take a little over an hour. By rail: A regular train service runs from London Victoria (30 departures a day), the journey takes around 50mins. Trains also run from London Bridge, Clapham Junction and King's Cross. National Express coaches and Southdown bus services arrive at Pool Valley bus station on Old Steine, not very far from the seafront.
If your kids are aged 5 or over, it's a good idea to travel to Brighton by train. The seafront is an easy 10-minute downhill walk from the station, giving your kids plenty of time to get excited about seeing the sea.
Tourist office 10 Bartholomew Square, **t** 0906 7112255; **t** 0906 1401 506 for children's events and activities. For a free accommodation brochure and guide to Brighton and Hove, **t** 08457 573512 or email: tourism@brighton.co.uk
www.brighton.co.uk/tourist

Britain's seaside resorts tend to have largely similar characteristics. They are cheery and cosy and somewhat old-fashioned. Brighton, however, is different. It's brash and loud and determinedly modern, and remains so all year round. It manages to be both fashionable, with its clubs and designer stores, and yet extremely family-orientated, with lots of child-friendly attractions. There's the pier, of course, with its funfair, arcades and endless supply of giant teddy bears; the Marina, with its arcades and bowling alleys; and, last but not least, the beach itself. Brighton boasts a mighty eight miles of seafront, made up of pebbles rather than sand, so bring your sturdiest pair of sandals. There are good play facilities along the beachfront, which are accessed via decking walkways, including an invitingly sandy volleyball pitch, a basketball court and, further up near the ruined West Pier, an excellent children's play area, complete with children's toilets and baby-changing facilities. Here you'll find a large play pool, brightly coloured lookout posts with turrets and binoculars, a sand and water table and lots of space for picnicking families.

Brighton Museum

Royal Pavilion Gardens, **t** 01273 290 900

www.virtualmuseum.info
Open Tues 10–7, Wed–Sat 10–5, Sun 2–5, Mon open on bank holidays only
Free
Gift shop, café, wheelchair accessible, monthly events for toddlers, families and ages 8 and over

The museum reopened in May 2002 following a £10 million redevelopment This has relocated the entrance to the Pavilion Gardens and made the building much more accessible to visitors. The interior is spacious and light, with a small gift shop and a café. The new archaeology galleries and the local studies centre complement the displays of art, photography and interior design. Families will mostly enjoy the masks and the costume galleries, where children can gawp at the PVC-clad Goths, gasp at the vast girth of George IV's pants or try an Edwardian costume on for size. Downstairs there's an artroom where kids can experience different colours in the spectrum through reading, drawing, colouring and making structures, as well as writing their impressions of the artworks they have seen.

Booth Museum of Natural History

194 Dyke Road, **t** 01273 292 777
Open Mon–Wed and Fri–Sat 10–5, Sun 2–5
Free
Gift shop, mother and baby room, guided tours, wheelchair accessible

Based on the collection of the Victorian naturalist and Brighton resident, Edward Thomas Booth, this holds a fascinating display of insects, butterflies, fossils and animal skeletons. Kids can get up close to all manner of specimens in the new hands-on Discovery Lab and special events are organized during the school holidays.

Brighton Palace Pier

Off Madeira Drive, **t** 01273 609 361
www.brightonpier.co.uk
Open Summer 9am–2am, winter 10am–12 midnight
Adm Free, rides are individually charged
Three bars, various fast food outlets, wheelchair accessible, with adapted toilets

After the beach, this should probably be your first port of call. Reminiscent of an ocean liner on stilts, this beautiful snow-white pier stretches 1,722ft out to sea and is lined with snack bars, stalls and child-friendly attractions. Halfway down you'll find an amusement arcade full of all the latest video games, a few fairground-style stalls and some rather neglected one-arm bandits. Next door is a 250-seat fish and chip restaurant, while beyond this, right at the end of the pier, is a funfair with several gentle carousel-type rides, a small go-kart track, a helter-skelter, a log flume and a rollercoaster. There's free family entertainment in summer ranging from comedy and magicians to live shows featuring favourite kids' TV characters and a host of tribute bands.

Royal Pavilion

North Street, **t** 01273 290 900,
www.royalpavilion.org.uk
Open Oct–Mar 10–5.15; Apr–Sept 9.30–5.45
Adm Adult £5.80, child (under 16) £3.40, family £15 (2+4), £9.20 (1+4)
Queen Adelaide Tearoom, gift shop, children's quiz sheets, mother and baby room, guided tours at 11.30am and 2.30pm, many facilities for the disabled

The Pavilion is, without a doubt, Britain's most over-the-top Royal Palace. Designed by John Nash in the 1810s for the Prince Regent, it's a mishmash of Indian-style exterior and Chinese-style interior. Kids usually respond favourably to its fairytale-like exuberance. Forget notions of taste and style, just come and enjoy the excess.

Brighton Marina

Brighton, **t** 01273 818 504
www.brighton-marina.co.uk
Open 10–6, daily

Quite a way east of the town centre, the Marina is still well worth a visit. It's a nice place to eat, shop and even stay at the stylish Alias Hotel Seattle, **t** 01273 679799, **www.**aliashotels.com. There's also a leisure centre and a large entertainment complex with a cinema, an arcade, ten-pin bowling and pool. Boat cruises around the harbour, to the pier and out to sea are also offered. You can reach the Marina on the Volk's Railway, Britain's oldest electric railway, built in 1883.

Where to Eat

Alfresco

The Milkmaid Pavilion, King's Road Arches
t 01273 206 523
Open 12 noon–10.30, daily

Pleasant, friendly Italian restaurant overlooking the seafront and the kids' playground with an outdoor seating area. Although it doesn't have a children's menu, it is popular with families, especially in summer when it can get very full. High chairs available.

Devil's Dyke

Poynings, **t** 01273 857 256
Open 11.30–10, daily

Family pub overlooking the hugely popular beauty spot of the same name. It offers a children's menu, high chairs, a mother and baby room and outdoor seating on sunny days.

English's

29–31 East Street, **t** 01273 327 980
Open Mon–Sat 12 noon–10.30, Sun 12.30–9.30

Seafood restaurant and oyster bar offering lots of choice for kids with adventurous culinary tastes, something other than cod and chips. There are six separate dining rooms and outdoor seating is available in summer overlooking the busy square frequented by shoppers, buskers and itinerant hair-braiders.

Harry Ramsden's

1–4 Marine Parade, **t** 01275 690 691
Open Mon–Thurs 12 noon–9.30, Fri–Sat, 12 noon–10, Sun 12 noon–9

This branch of the famous northern fish and chip chain is situated opposite the entrance to the pier and Sea Life Centre and can seat over a hundred people. There are two special children's menus, both of which come with a drink and dessert: under-8s can choose from the Harry Chipper's menu for £2.99 and 9–12 year-olds can have the Chart Toppers menu for £3.99. High chairs available. Eat in or takeaway.

The Regency Restaurant

131 King's Road, **t** 01273 325 014
Open 8am–11pm, daily

Traditional seafront fish restaurant with tables on the pavement shaded by coloured umbrellas and a range of locally caught fresh fish and seafood dishes on the menu, plus some tempting puds. Children's menu and high chairs available.

Cambridge

Getting there By air: Stansted airport is about 30 miles south of Cambridge and is linked to the city by a regular bus service (and the M11). By road: Cambridge is 55 miles north of London and can be

reached by the M11 from the south and A14 from the north. Driving into Cambridge city centre, which is largely pedestrianized, isn't really an option unless you take advantage of the city's excellent 'park and ride' scheme. There are five such car parks on the outskirts of Cambridge: Cowley Road/A1309 to the north, Newmarket Road/A1303 to the east, Madingley Road/A1303 to the west, and both Babraham Road/A1307 and Trumpington Road/A1134 to the south of the city. Parking is free, buses leave for the centre every 10 minutes (7am–8pm). An Adult Day Return is £1.50, with up to 3 children under 16 travelling free per paying adult. For details contact Stagecoach Cambus, t 01223 423554. By train: there are frequent services to London King's Cross (50mins) and London Liverpool Street (1hr 10mins). Cambridge station is a mile and a half south of the centre, but served by a regular bus service. By coach: there is an hourly National Express coach service from London Victoria coach station.
Tourist office The Old Library, Wheeler Street.
t 0906 5862526 (premium rate 60 pence per minute) or there is extensive tourist information, including accommodation and other bookings available at **www**.tourismcambridge.com.
The centre has a souvenir shop and has details of guided walking tours led from here by Blue Badge Guides throughout the year (dramatic tours with costumed characters take place in summer)

Cambridge, like its great rival Oxford, is principally famous for its university, one of the oldest and most respected in the world. Like Oxford, it's a very beautiful city with some of the country's most impressive architecture, several delightful parks and the River Cam, which flows to the north and west of the city.

Being smaller and more concentrated than Oxford, it's a great place for pottering, be it on foot, by bike or on the river. The centre of town, where you'll find most of the colleges and university buildings, is largely pedestrianized. The two main thoroughfares, Bridge Street (which turns into Sidney Street, St Andrew's Street and Regent Street) and St John's Street (which becomes Trinity Street, King's Parade and Trumpington Street) are lined with shops, tearooms and bookstores – look out for Galloway and Porter booksellers, 30 Sidney Street, **t** 01223 367876. They also hold a monthly warehouse book sale, with a wide range of quality children's titles at bargain prices.

Cambridge and County Folk Museum
2–3 Castle Street, **t** (01223) 355159
Open Tues–Sat 10.30–5, Sun 2–5; also open Mon from April–Sept 10.30–5
(Please note that the museum will be closed for major improvements to access and toilet facilities from 1 October 2003–September 2004)
Adm Adults £2.50, child 75p, under-5s **free**
Gift shop, guided tours

Housed in a 16th-century, half-timbered farmhouse, this looks at the non-academic side of life in Cambridge, with displays on the people who have lived and worked in this area for the last 400 years. Activity days for children aged 6–10 are organized on some Saturday afternoons, and workshops for 7–11 year-olds are held during the school holidays.

Cambridge Museum of Technology
The Old Pumping Station, Cheddars Lane
t 01223 368650, **www**.cam.net.uk/home/steam
Open Easter–Oct Sun 2–5; Nov–Easter first Sun of every month 2–5
Adm Steaming Days £4, other times £2
Shop, wheelchair accessible, call the museum for dates of 'Steaming Days' and other special events

Housed in a preserved Victorian pumping station, this is filled with the noisy contraptions of the industrial age: boilers, engines and several 'hands-on' pumps, a printing room (where you can print your own souvenirs), a collection of early Cambridge wireless instruments and other local artefacts.

Fitzwilliam Museum
Trumpington Street, **t** 01223 332906
www.fitzmuseum.cam.ac.uk
Open Tues–Sat 10–5, Sun 2.15–5
Please note that the museum is subject to restricted opening due to a major new Courtyard Development. The entire museum will be closed from Jan–June 2004 and the Antiquities Galleries will be closed in Sept 2004 to allow for improved access to the building, including a lift to all floor levels. A new and enlarged café and shop, plus a new gallery space, will also be added.
Free
Café, gift shop, guided tours, mother and baby facilities, limited wheelchair access (but see above)
Not suitable for pushchairs, although baby slings/harnesses available

The city's most respected museum will interest, although you may want to skip cases of European porcelain, Chinese vases and Korean ceramics and head straight to the mummies and painted coffins in the Antiquities Gallery, or the armour and weapons in the Applied Arts section. Family activity sheets are available.

Museum of Archaeology and Anthropology
Downing Street
t 01223 333516, **www**.cumaa.archanth.cam.ac.uk
Open Tues–Sat 2–4.30; phone to check extended summer hours June–Sept
Free

The ground floor 'Rise of Civilization' Gallery, full of ancient pots and bits of flint, is only worth a cursory inspection. Instead, make a beeline for the ethnographic collection on the first floor, a wonderful array of treasures brought back by 18th- and 19th-century explorers: native American feathered headresses, Eskimo canoes and parkas (made from dried walrus hide), scary African tribal masks and suits of Japanese ceremonial armour, all arranged around a 50-ft high totem pole.

Sedgwick Museum of Earth Sciences
Downing Street
t 01223 333456, **www**.sedgwickmuseum.org
Open Mon–Fri 9–1 and 2–5, Sat 10–1
Free (Discretionary donation encouraged)
Shop, some wheelchair access/assistance available

Houses the oldest geological collection in the world (although, in geological terms, this is a pretty slight claim) with various multi-million-year-old rocks and minerals displayed in antique walnut cases. It also has a large collection of fossil dinosaurs. Following a period of redevelopment, (due for completion in spring 2004), the museum will have even more space dedicated to the weird and wonderful world of nature. Planned displays include exhibits on giant dragonflies, how volcanoes work, and investigations into life on other planets.

University Botanic Garden
Cory Lodge, Bateman Street
t 01223 336265, **www**.botanic.cam.ac.uk
Open Jan, Nov, Dec 10–4; Feb and Oct 10–5; March–Sept 10–6
Adm (March–Oct, weekends and Bank hols) Adult £2.50, child (5–17) £2, under-5s **free**

Café–restaurant (summer only), picnic areas, gift shop, mother and baby facilities, guided tours by arrangement, disabled access

The 40-acre University Botanic Garden, just south of the Cambridge's centre, founded in 1762, is the city's most beautiful open space. If you're after a spot where kids can enjoy more uninhibited play, try Jesus Green, to the north of the city centre near the river, a large, open grassy space with a children's play area and an open air swimming pool in summer. Otherwise, just to the west, you'll find Midsummer Common, a huge riverside meadow that plays host to fairs and circuses in summer and a large firework display on 5 November.

Scott Polar Research Institute Museum
Lensfield Road
t 01223 336548
Open Tues–Sat 2.30–4 (except public hols)
Free
Shop, selling relevant children's books on exploration and polar wildlife

This museum of polar life and exploration features original artefacts from Scott's expedition. Sir Ranulph Fiennes' literary defence of Scott's achievements, published October 2003 and entitled simply *Captain Scott*, makes a visit here all the more pertinent.

Punting
The archetypal Cambridge pursuit can be enjoyed every day between Easter and October. Punts can be hired from Magdalene Bridge, Mill Lane, Garret Hostel Lane, the Granta Pub on Newnham Road and the Rat and Parrot pub near Magdalene Bridge. A deposit of around £25 is usually required, while the punts themselves will cost something in the region of £6–£8 per hour. Chauffeured punt trips are also available.

You'll be shown how to use the pole before you set off, but do be aware that it can be a pretty wet and soggy experience, especially during the learning process. However, the Backs do provide an idyllic space in which to dry off and have a picnic while you refine your technique, just remember to stick to the left.

Where to Eat
Cambridge Blue
85-87 Gwydir Street, **t** 01223 361382
Open Mon–Fri 12 noon–2.30 and 5.30–11, Sat 12 noon–3 and 5.30–11, Sun 12 noon–3 and 6–10.30

Family-friendly and refreshingly non-smoking pub, which serves evening and lunchtime meals. Children are allowed in the conservatory and in the large garden, which has a Wendy house and rabbits. Children's menu available.

Cambridge Tea Room

1 Wheeler Street, **t** 01223 357503
Open 10–6, daily

Opposite the tourist information centre, this tearoom serves good cream teas and sandwiches.

Copper Kettle

King's Parade, **t** 01223 365068
Open Mon–Sat 8.30–5.30, Sun 9–5.30

A Cambridge institution overlooking the glorious vista of King's College, where generations of under-graduates have come to discuss the meaning of life over coffee and a Chelsea bun.No credit cards.

Don Pasquale

12 Market Hill, **t** 01223 367063
Open Mon–Thurs 8–6, Fri–Sat 8am–9.30pm, Sun 9–6

With seating on the market square and a plentiful supply of high chairs, this is a fun place to eat pizza and watch the world go by.

Orchard Tea Garden and Restaurant

Mill Way, Grantchester, **t** 01223 845788
Getting there By road or by punt on the River Cam

Lounge in deckchairs under the trees and enjoy a delicious cream tea. You may even spot someone famous; in the 100 years since Rupert Brooke stayed at the orchard, some of the greatest poets, writers, philosophers and scientists have sipped tea here. Visit **www**.orchard-grantchester.com for a 'who's who'.

Oxford

Getting there By road: Oxford is about 48 miles from London and can be reached via the M40. Oxford's efficient 'park and ride' scheme operates daily, (Mon–Sat 5.30am–11.30pm, restricted service on Suns and from Water Eaton) from five sites: Pear Tree and Water Eaton to the north, A44/A40/M40/M6/M1 and A4260; Thornhill to the east, M40/M25; Seacourt to the west/A420 and Redbridge to the south/A34. Journey times are between 8 and 20mins. By train: Services arrive frequently from London Paddington. By bus/coach:

There are regular National Express coach services to Oxford from London Victoria. The Airline, (**t** 01865 785400, **www**.theairline.info) operates coach services between Heathrow (every 30mins) and Gatwick (hourly) to Oxford, day and night.
Tourist information The Old School, Gloucester Green, **t** 01865 726871, **www**.oxfordcity.co.uk

Oxford, of course, is more than just a pretty town for tourists; it's a world famous centre of culture and learning. Home to one of the country's two most prestigious universities, Oxford has, ever since its foundation in the 13th century, been preparing the great and the good for roles in public life. Tony Blair, Bill Clinton, Margaret Thatcher and even Henry VIII all studied at the university, although the term 'university' is slightly misleading – Oxford actually contains several independently operated colleges which together form the university and define the shape of the city. Most of the colleges are open to the public although, to preserve the academic ambience, many operate restricted opening times and charge hefty admission fees. Best for family visits is Christ Church college with its grand dining hall, where Charles I held his parliament, Lewis Carroll ate 8,000 meals and Harry Potter sat beneath the sorting hat awaiting his fate.

With so much accumulated learning and history, you might expect Oxford to be rather dull for children and, approached in the wrong way, it probably would be. But, plan your itinerary carefully and you'll find lots to occupy your days. Oxford actually boasts a good many child-friendly attractions including parks, interactive museums, punts and lots of good spots providing panoramic views of the 'dreaming spires' and surrounding countryside.

Christ Church

St Aldgates
t 01865 276150, **www**.chch.ox.ac.uk
Open Mon–Sat 9–5.30, Sun 1–5.30, closed 25 Dec
Adm Adult £4, child £3
The visitor entrance is at Meadow Gate

A great place for Harry Potter fans; tell the kids that the steps up into the dining hall were where Maggie Smith greeted the new pupils in *Harry Potter and the Philospher's Stone*. The dining hall is also Hogwarts Hall, though somewhat modified by the CGI wizards at Warner Bros in order to seat all four of the school's houses.

Curioxity Science Gallery

The Old Fire Station, 40 George Street
t 01865 247004
Open Sat, Sun and school hols 10–4
Adm Adult £2.50, child £2.20, family £8.80
Hands-on science museum for children full of interactive games and experiments.

Museum of the History of Science

Old Ashmolean Building, Broad Street
t 01865 277280, **www**.mhs.ox.ac.uk
Open Tues–Sat 12 noon–4, Sun 2–5
Free
The museum contains displays of scientific instruments, such as sundials, quadrants, microscopes, telescopes and cameras, dating back to the 16th century (look out for Einstein's blackboard). There's an education room and library.

Pitt Rivers Museum

Parks Road
t 01865 270927, **www**.prm.ox.ac.uk
Open Mon–Sat 12 noon–4.30, Sun 2–4.30
Free
Please note that some sections of the ground floor will be closed until March 2004 for the Court Project. Visitors will be able to see staff working on important conservation work during this time. If you wish to see a particular section of the Court, call in advance to ensure that it will be open.

This elegant Victorian building houses a large ethnographic collection featuring numerous artefacts brought back by Captain Cook from his 18th century journeys of discovery – a witch in a bottle, a puffer-fish lantern, shrunken heads, samurai swords and totem poles are just some of the gruesome horrors bound to attract the children.

Kids can take part in informal Family Friendly Fun sessions every Sunday from 2–4, using backpacks, sorting boxes, quizzes and activity trolleys. Pitt Stops are activity sessions that take place on the first Saturday of every month from 1–4. Sessions begin with a short talk and previous topics include body decoration, puppetry and weapons and armour. Kids can also follow family trails in search of dragons, hats, masks, witches and more.

University Museum of Natural History

Parks Road
t 01865 272950, **www**.oum.ox.ac.uk
Open 12 noon–5, daily (not Easter and Christmas)
Free

Picnic area, some disabled access, children's page on website
Check out the dinosaur galleries, gemstones, extinct species, including the Dodo, and the working beehive (summer only).

The Botanic Gardens

Rose Lane
t 01865 286690, **www**.botanic-garden.ox.ac.uk
Open (April–Sept) Garden: 9–5, daily; glasshouses: 10–4.30; (Oct–Mar) garden: 9–4.30, daily; glasshouses: 10–4
Adm Adult £2, under-12s **free** (**free** to all in winter)
Created in 1621, this is the oldest botanic garden in Britain. You can wander through nine small glasshouses, filled with tropical and sub-tropical plants. From the gardens you can follow the course of the river, though the turnstiles at either end may prove challenging with a pushchair. About half-way along the route and to the left, there's a wooden bridge that leads to the college boathouses. Each boathouse has its own distinctive style and team; if you're lucky you might encounter a training session or even a race.

Port Meadow

Access via Walton Well Road and Thames Towpath
Open Any reasonable time, it is common land
Free
This huge water meadow is the largest green space in Oxford. You can see horses, cows and geese roaming freely.

University Parks

South Parks Road
Open 8am–dusk, daily
Free
Seventy acres of parkland on the west bank of the River Cherwell with gardens, trees, riverside walks and a duck pond.

River trips

Punting, the practice of pushing yourself along the river in a flat-bottomed boat using a long wooden pole, is particularly associated with England's two great university towns. The image of young men in flannels and straw hats mucking about in boats on hot summer days is, for some, as typically English as tea shops and cricket on the village green. It's great fun, if more than a little tricky (young children probably won't be able to handle the heavy pole), but, once mastered, provides a good way of seeing the local countryside. Punts and (for the less adventurous) rowing boats for trips on the River Cherwell down past the Botanic Garden and Christchurch Meadow are available for hire from Magdalen Bridge, Folly Bridge and the Cherwell Boathouse. Sightseeing trips to Iffley, Sandford Lock and Abingdon are also offered from Folly Bridge by Salter Brothers, **t** 01865 243421, www.salterbros.co.uk.

Where to Eat

Bangkok House
42a Hythe Bridge Street
t 01865 200705
Open 12–3, 6–11, daily, booking advised
   The best prawn soup in town and the most beautiful tables to eat it at. Kids will love gazing at the intricate wooden carvings and trying out milder dishes while their parents feast on delicious Thai food. Close to the station; high chairs available.

Donnington Doorstep Family Centre
Townsend Square
t (01865) 727721
Open Mon–Fri 10–4
   Good for a snack or a simple lunch, this drop-in centre has nappy-changing facilities, high chairs and acitivities and toys for children.

Gee's Restaurant
61a Banbury Road
t (01865) 553540
Open 12–2.30 (3.30 Sun), 6–10.30, daily
   This bright Victorian conservatory offers plenty of space for families to spread out over lunch. Kids can choose from simple dishes such as spaghetti or chicken and chips. High chairs available.

The Isis Tavern
On the towpath between Donnington Bridge and Iffley Lock
t (01865) 247006
Open 11–11 (children till 7), daily
   Good pub food and a garden with swings.

Windsor

Getting there By road: Windsor is 20 miles west of London, off the M4 exit 6 and 50 miles northeast of Southampton, off the M3 exit 3. A 'park and ride' service runs between Windsor town centre and Legoland operating at least every 30mins daily from 10.15–6.45 (8.30 during peak season) Additional 'park and ride' is available from Home Park car park on the Datchet Road (B470) to Windsor town centre Mon–Fri 7am–7pm.
By bus/coach: Services leave the Greenline coach stop on Buckingham Palace Road at regular intervals throughout the day, **t** 0870 608 7261
Tourist office Royal Windsor Information Centre, 24 High Street, **t** 01753 743900, www.windsor.gov.uk Above the centre itself is a small exhibition on the history of the town.
   Dominated by the glorious 900-year-old castle, Windsor is a picturesque town with narrow cobbled streets, souvenir shops, ice-cream parlours and tearooms. Visit on a fine summer weekend and it can be overwhelming, but on a midweek morning things are less frenetic. Windsor is really a three-site town: the castle (it's the official residence of the Queen); Eton, the famous public school (where princes William and Harry went to school); and finally (and no doubt your kids will remind you, the *real* reason you came) Legoland (*see* p. 202), one of the country's best theme parks, full of rides, games, models, activity centres, rollercoasters and, no matter when you visit, hordes of fun-seeking kids.
   Eton is open to visitors all year round. Here you can tour the grounds and see the oldest classroom in the world, its ancient desks scored with generations of schoolboy graffiti. If you come in term-time you can see the boys in their distinctive top hats and tailcoats. Nearby are lots of grassy meadows for picnicking and watching the boats on the river.

Windsor Castle
Windsor
t (020) 7766 7304
www.royal.gov.uk
Open Mar–Oct 9.45–5.15 (last adm 4); Nov–Feb 9.45–4.15 (last adm 3)
Adm Adult £11.50, child £6, family £29, under-5s free
Souvenir shop, wheelchair accessible for most areas of castle; car parking in town
   This splendid concoction of towers, ramparts and pinnacles is, today, the official residence of the Queen and the largest inhabited castle in the world – and it is *big*, almost the size of a small town. Although the State Apartments were

ravaged by fire in 1992, you would be hard pressed to tell, following £37 million worth of restoration work. They are today as opulent as they ever were, decorated with hundreds of priceless paintings from the royal collection, including Van Eycks and Rembrandts, as well as porcelain, armour and fine furniture. Children may find them a little dry, however, in which case you should make a beeline for the Queen Mary dolls' house which never fails to illicit a gasp of envy (particularly from the girls). The tombs of knights and kings in St George's Chapel are also worth a look and kids might like to try and guess where the Queen and Prince Charles sit when attending a service (they sit on either side at the back of the choir in two curtained booths). If you've got the energy, climb to the top of the 12th-century Round Tower where, on a clear day, you can see no fewer than 12 counties. The Changing of the Guard takes place outside the Palace on alternate days Mon–Sat at 11am, *see* website for dates.

Windsor Great Park

For something a little more sedate, head to Windsor Great Park, a vast 4,800-acre tree-filled green space stretching out to the south of the town. It contains a 35-acre formal botanic garden, the Swiss Garden, and a huge lake, Virginia Water, with a 100-ft totem pole standing on its banks. The paths are well marked, so it is pushchair-friendly.

According to legend, the ghost of Herne the Hunter is supposed to haunt the park on moonlit evenings. The fearsome figure, dressed in his stag antler headdress and riding a black stallion, appears at the head of a pack of black hounds, which he leads in a midnight chase across the park.

Where to Eat

Crooked House Tea Rooms

51 High Street
t (01753) 857534
Open 9–6, daily

Tearoom housed in the oldest free-standing building in Windsor. The cream teas are a must.

Don Beni

28 Thames Street
t (01753) 622042
www.donbeni.co.uk
Open 12 noon–11, daily

Bright and clean Italian restaurant serving up pizzas and pasta, plus mouth-watering seafood,

meat and fish dishes. Children are welcome and high chairs are available. Takeaway service.

Haagen Dazs Ice-cream Emporium

22 Thames Street
t (01753) 832973
Open Daily 10am–10pm

Wide variety of delicious ice-cream, for a treat.

Puccino's

31 Windsor Royal Station
t 01753 859380

Part of a relatively new chain, with quirky slogans on the sugar sachets to keep the kids amused. Pop in for a quick coffee or pizza and pasta lunch; children's menu and high chairs available. There are other coffee bars in the station, but the friendly service here is a definite bonus.

Royal Oak

Datchet Road (*opposite Windsor and Eton Riverside Station*)
t 01753 865179
Open 11am–11pm, daily

This attractive pub is festooned with flowers in summer and has a patio area, children's menu and high chairs.

Bricks & mortar

Hampton Court

East Molesey, Surrey
t 0870 752 7777
Getting there Hampton Court is just southwest of London near Kingston-upon-Thames, off the A3 and A309 (J12 from the M25). Trains run regularly from London (Waterloo) to Hampton Court Station, or you can take a cruise up the Thames with the Westminster Passenger Service from Westminster Pier.
Open Oct–Mar Mon 10.15–4.30, Tues–Sun 9.30–4.30; Mar–Oct Mon 10.15–6, Tues–Sun 9.30–6
Adm Adult £11.50, child £7.50, concs £8.50, family £34 (2+3), under-5s **free**
Café, restaurant, souvenir shops (look out for the Tudor Kitchen shop which sells a range of Tudor cooking implements and medieval herbs), guided tours, wheelchair access, on-site parking
Suitable for all ages

Hampton Court provides a fabulous day out for children. This grand old building is full of treasures including Henry VIII's state apartments, a series of Georgian rooms and a real tennis court. Children will love the huge Tudor kitchens where every day a Tudor banquet, complete with spit roast, is prepared by cooks in full period dress. It's like stepping into a time-warp where you can see, hear, smell and even taste the days gone by. The guided tours will enchant your children with tales of marriage and murder – this was where Henry VIII lived, remember. Pick up a copy of the daily events programme on arrival and collect your invitation cards to ensure your place on one of the tours.

Henry spent a staggering £62,000 on Hampton court (that's around £18 million in today's money), turning it into the most modern, sophisticated palace in England. Only part of the structure we see today, however, dates from this time. Sir Christopher Wren undertook further rebuilding work in the late 17th century, the most important element of which was the planting of new landscaped gardens. These beautiful gardens have always been as big a draw as the palace itself. The main attraction, of course, is the maze, the most famous in the world. It was planted in 1690 for William III and lures in around 300,000 people a year. There are family trails and audio guides, plus seasonal events including an ice rink at Christmas and carol singing. Very young children can make use of the soft play area in the family room.

Bodiam Castle

Bodiam, Robertsbridge
t 01580 830436
Getting there Bodiam is 10 miles north of Hastings off the B2244. The Kent and East Sussex Steam Railway also makes trips from Bodiam to the nearby town of Tenterden
Open Mid-Feb–Oct 10–6, daily; Nov–mid-Feb Sat–Sun 10–4
Adm Adult £4, child £2, family £10
Café–restaurant with children's menus, gift shop, picnic areas, mother and baby facilities, wheelchair accessible, on-site parking, children's trail, guide and activity backpacks

Bodiam is a proper fairytale castle with round turrets on each corner, crinkly battlements, arrow-slit windows and a portcullis; it is even surrounded by a deep moat. The inside of the castle, most of which is covered in grass, makes a perfect spot for a picnic and there are family events throughout the year, including treasure hunts, arts and crafts acitivities and theatre performances.

Hever Castle

Hever, near Edenbridge
t (01732) 865224, **www.hevercastle.co.uk**
Getting there Hever is about 8 miles west of Tonbridge off the B2027; J6 off the M25
Open Mar–Nov 11–6, daily
Adm Adult £8.40, child £4.60, family £21.40, under-5s **free**
Café with children's meals, gift shop, guided tours, mother and baby facilities, wheelchair accessible, on-site parking, adventure playground

Hever is very much the antithesis of Bodiam, with its antiques, fine tapestries and suits of armour, as well as costumed waxworks of Henry VIII and his six wives (this was where Anne Boleyn, his second wife, lived as a child), and a display of dolls' houses. The castle's picnic-perfect grounds contain a yew maze, a lake and an Italian garden with a lakeside theatre. Here a renowned season of plays, musicals and opera performances takes place each summer. There's also a water maze (from April to October), lined with water jets that spray visitors every time they take a wrong turning.

Leeds Castle

Maidstone
t 01622 765400
www.leeds-castle.com
Getting there Leeds Castle is 40 miles southeast of London near Maidstone off the M20 and B2163. There are direct services from London Victoria to Bearsted, the nearest train station, from where there's a regular shuttle bus to the castle. Eurostar services from London Waterloo stop at Ashford International, 20mins away
Open 1 Apr–Oct 10–5; Nov–Mar 10–3, daily
Adm Adult £9.50, child £6, family £29, under-5s **free**
Gift shops, restaurant, guided tours, some wheelchair access

Leeds Castle looks like a castle should look; dramatic, romantic and mysterious. Set on two islands in the middle of a lake in 500 acres of beautifully sculpted Kent countryside, this was the famously hard-to-please Henry VIII's favourite castle. The interior is stuffed full of precious paintings and furniture, but the 'don't touch' atmosphere means that kids can't really interact with the space. It's a different story, however, in the castle grounds, where a maze, an underground grotto, an aviary and lots of wide grassy spaces to run around on enable kids to let off steam. What's more, family entertainments are put on in the grounds throughout the year. These include treasure trails, craft workshops, animal encounters and a famous Balloon Festival in September.

Hatfield House

Hatfield
t 01707 262823
Getting there Hatfield is 21 miles north of London, 7 miles from the M25 (J23), 2 miles from the A1 (J4) and is signposted from the A414 and A1000. Hatfield train station is immediately opposite. There are regular services from King's Cross, which take approximately 25mins
Open House: Easter Sat–late Sept 12noon–4pm, daily, guided tours only on weekdays; Park and West Gardens 11–5.30, daily (access to gardens only when house is open)
Adm House, park and gardens: adult £7.50, child £4, group (20+) £6.50; Park and gardens: adult £4.50, child £3.50; Park: adult £2, child £1
Restaurant, picnic areas, shop, mother and baby room, guided tours, wheelchair accessible, on-site parking, children's play area, nature trails

Come to Hatfield to see how a real princess lived. This grand, red-brick Jacobean mansion was built in the early 17th century on the site of the Tudor palace where Queen Elizabeth I spent her childhood days. The vast 4,000-acre grounds will probably be of most interest to children, with their formal gardens full of hedges, paths, ponds and fountains and wilderness areas to explore. On your travels, see if you can spot the oak tree under which the young Princess Elizabeth supposedly learned of her succession following the death of her sister Mary in 1558.

The house itself is very grand inside, with its imposing rows of paintings (look for the portrait of Elizabeth) and vast oak staircase (appropriately named the Grand Staircase) decorated with carved figures. Kids will like the National Collection of Model Soldiers, which has over 3,000 miniature figures arranged in battle positions. Craft fairs and theatre productions in the park are among the programmed events that families can enjoy throughout the year.

Knebworth House

Knebworth
t 01438 812661
www.knebworthhouse.com
Getting there Knebworth House is 2 miles from Stevenage; the entrance is directly off J7 of the A1
Open 3–18 April, 29 May–6 June, 3 July–31 Aug, daily; weekends and Bank Hols only: 27–28 Mar, 24 April–23 May, 12–27 June, 4–26 Sept; Park, gardens, playground and railway: 11–5.30, House 12 noon–5
Adm House and grounds: adult £7.50, child £7, family £19 (2+2), under-4s **free**; Grounds only: adult and child £5.50, family £25
On-site parking, café–restaurant, garden terrace tearoom, picnic areas, gift shop, guided tours

Built in the 16th century, Knebworth was originally a simple Tudor mansion, but was covered in Gothic adornments in the 1800s. The interior will be of limited interest with its collections of paintings and armour (quiz sheets available), but it's the grounds that are the real draw. As you head south away from the house you'll encounter a sunken garden surrounded by trees, followed by an exquisite rose garden (just to the right is a pet cemetery), a wildflower meadow and a small maze. Beyond this is a wilderness area and a huge 250-acre park where herds of red deer roam freely.

The biggest attraction for children, however, will inevitably be the Fort Knebworth adventure playground, one of the biggest and best around with lots of derring-do climbing equipment and a great selection of slides, including a suspension slide (you travel down clutching on to a rope), the four-lane Astroglide, where you travel on a helter-skelter-type rush mat down a bumpy plastic chute, a twisting corkscrew slide and a vertical-drop slide. There is also a bouncy castle and a miniature railway, which provides looping 15-minute tours of the grounds. The website gives details of Tudor and Victorian trails for school groups, and has printable pictures of costumed figures and shields for children to add their own designs to and colour in.

Buckets & spades

Eastbourne

Getting there Eastbourne is on the south coast, 21 miles east of Brighton and 18 miles west of

Hastings on the A259, just south of the A27. There are regular train services from London (Victoria) and Brighton.

Tourist information 3 Cornfield Road, Eastbourne, **t** 01323 411400, **www**.eastbourne.org

Eastbourne has a dignified air to it, with elegant Victorian homes and a distinct lack of souvenir shops or candyfloss sellers. Perhaps unsurprisingly, this haven of south coast tranquillity has become a popular retirement home. However, despite its polished veneer, Eastbourne has a good deal to offer in terms of family entertainment. There's the pier, one of the best and most visited in the country; indoor and outdoor adventure play-grounds; The Sovereign Centre leisure complex with four pools and kids' activities; the Museum of Shops; facilities for go-karting, bowling, boating and mini-golf and, of course, the beach – a long stretch of sand and shingle with numerous rock-pools (lifeguards patrol in summer). The seafront is framed by two old towers: the Redoubt Fortress, where classical concerts and firework displays are held in summer, and the Wish Tower, which holds a collection of puppets and props.

Southend-on-Sea

Getting there Southend lies at the southernmost tip of East Anglia, at the mouth of the Thames estuary, 40 miles east of London (reached by the A127). Trains depart from London Fenchurch Street to Southend Central station regularly (1hr) and Liverpool Street to Southend Victoria (45mins). National Express run a frequent service from London Victoria (2.5hrs)

Tourist office 19 High Street, **t** 01702 215120 **www**.southend.gov.uk

Situated on the north bank of the River Thames estuary, Southend offers families Kids Kingdom, a mesmerising inflatable cavern flanked by ball pools, with a soft play haven for under-5s and Sealife Adventure for some fishy tales in the rock-pool demostration area. Visit www.sealifeadventure.co.uk.

There's a sandy beach with facilities for sailing, water-skiing and windsurfing. The Adventure Island fun park on Marine Parade boasts over 40 attractions, some specifically designed for toddlers, while jutting out from the front is the town's most famous feature, Southend Pier, which at over 1.3 miles is the longest pier in the world. The rewards for walking to the end of the pier are some stun-ning coastal scenes.

Nature lovers

Ashdown Forest

Getting there It's just to the southeast of East Grinstead off the A22

Tourist information East Grinstead Tourism Initiative, West Street, East Grinstead, **t** 01342 410121

This great swathe of West Sussex forest and heathland provided the inspiration for A.A. Milne's tales of the famous bear, Winne-the-Pooh. The village of Hartfield is the centre of Pooh country, from where you can visit the 'Hundred-Acre' Wood where most of the Pooh stories were set. Other places which have became familiar through A.A. Milne's stories, such as the Enchanted Place, North Pole and Roo's Sandypit, are all within easy reach of Gill's Lap car park, which can be found just off the B2026. The Ashdown Forest Information Centre, **t** 01342 823583, lies one mile east of Wych Cross on the Hartfield road. Here children can learn more about local flora and fauna in its Exhibition Barn, and there are guidebooks and leaflets detailing walks in the area. There's also a garden with picnic tables and the only public toilets for miles around. Much of the rest of Ashdown is serious walkers' territory, with lots of nature trails and sandy tracks.

Whipsnade Wild Animal Park

Whipsnade, Dunstable
t 01582 872171
www.whipsnade.co.uk

Getting there It's signposted from the M25 (J21) and the M1 (J9 and J12). Green Line buses run from London Victoria, **t** 020 8668 7261. The nearest train stations are Luton (served by King's Cross Thameslink) and Hemel Hempstead (served by Euston)

Open Autumn 10–5, winter 10–4, summer 10–6, Bank Hols 10–7, daily (except 25 Dec)

Adm Adult £12.50, child £9.50, family £39.50 (2+2 or 1+3), under-3s **free**, car entry £9

Café, picnic areas, shop, wheelchair accessible, mother and baby room, on-site parking £3 fee

Please note that the chimpanzee enclosure will be shut for refurbishment until spring 2004

It's always more rewarding looking at animals living in large enclosures that closely resemble their natural environments. Whipsnade, at the last count, boasted no less than 6,000 acres of paddocks for its 2,500 animals to roam around in.

There are four ways to tour Whipsnade: on foot, where you will get to wander among free-roaming wallabies, peacocks and deer; in the safety of your car, for which you have to pay extra; aboard the Whipsnade narrow-gauge steam railway, which takes you on a tour through herds of elephants and rhinos; or, perhaps the best option, aboard the free open-top sightseeing bus, which not only offers elevated views of the animals, but can also deposit you at all the best walking spots.

There's a vast range of animals to see, including Asian elephants, who get to enjoy Europe's largest elephant paddock; white rhinos, who also have plenty of space to run about in; hippos, permanently submerged in muddy water; tigers (come at feeding time when you can see these magnificent beasts on the prowl); giraffes, iguanas, flamingoes, penguins, wolves and many species of birds – including two delightful newcomers, the hornbills named Horatio and Zazu.

The World of Wings flying displays and the Sealion Splash Zone guarantee some up close and personal encounters. Remember to pack a raincoat!

Wildwood Wildlife Centre

t 01227 712111
www.wildwoodtrust.org
Getting there Wildwood is on the A291 between Canterbury and Herne Bay
Open 10–5 (last entry 4, winter 3), daily
Adm Adult £7–£5, child £5.50–£4, family £16–£22

Over 30 acres of ancient woodland are the setting for this wildlife discovery park, which provides children with the opportunity to see a variety of rare and endangered native species from owls and otters to wild boars to beavers. Behind the scenes, Wildwood carries out serious conservation work, although this is not allowed to intrude on the fun to be had from getting close to the animals. Night tours, demostrations and seasonal craft activities are among the exciting events on offer throughout the year.

Theme parks

Chessington World of Adventure

Chessington **t** 0870 444 7777
www.chessington.co.uk
Getting there Chessington is a couple of miles north of Epsom, just off the A243, 2 miles from the A3 and M25 (J9 from the north, J10 from the south). There are regular train services to Chessington South station from London (Clapham Junction)
Open 10–5, daily 10–7 on peak days, now open on selected dates in Dec and Jan
Adm Adult £18–£24, child £14.50–£18 (4–11), family £52–£65 (2+2), under-4s **free**
Fast food outlets, baby-changing, on-site parking, some wheelchair access (safety restrictions apply on some rides – call for detailed leaflet – a limited number of wheelchairs available on request)
Note Height restriction: varies, but is usually 1.2m–1.4m

Chessington has rides for all ages, from top-of-the-range rollercoasters to gentle carousels and roundabouts. The park's most intense rides are the 'Samurai', which spins people round on an enormous rotor blade, 'Ramases' Revenge', which flips its passengers over several times before squirting them in the face with jets of water and the recently souped-up 'Vampire', which swoops and loops over the park's rooftops. Thrill-seekers can visit in summer to sample these rides in the dark or enjoy Hocus Pocus Hall, a 3D adventure full of spooky spells and bubbling potions.

Younger children can enjoy Toytown, the Dragon River log flume, Professor Burp's Bubble Works, the 'Action Man' assault course and Beanoland, with its range of rides themed on Beano characters.

It's easy to forget that, in amongst all the hi-tech gadgetry, there is also a zoo. You can take a quick, theme-park style look at the resident Sumatran tigers, Persian and Clouded leopards and Asian lions, gorillas and meerkats aboard the Safari Skyrail. There are also daily displays by sealions, penguins and hawks; at the 'Creepy Cave' you and the kids can go 'urgh!' at the collection of spiders, insects and other crawling horrors, or soar with the birds in the walk-through aviary.

Legoland

Winkfield Road, Windsor
t 08705 040404
www.legoland.co.uk
Getting there Legoland is 2 miles from Windsor on
the Windsor to Ascot Road, signposted from J6 of
the M4. The bus service from Windsor town centre
to Legoland departs from Thames Street every
15mins during opening times
Open 10–6, daily, park closes later in summer
Adm Adult £18.95–£22.95, child £15.95–£19.95;
2-day ticket adult £32.95, child £29.95
*Seven restaurants/cafés and 11 catering stalls, picnic
areas, mother and baby facilities, wheelchair accessible, wheelchair hire available, adapted toilets,
on-site parking, first aid and lost parent facilities*

A cross between a theme park and an activity
centre, Legoland is now firmly established as one
of the country's top family attractions. As such, it is
a busy place and visitors should expect long
queues, but if you time your trip to arrive early or
stay late (the park stays open until at least 7pm in
summer), you'll manage to make the most of it.

It has some good rides, including two dragon-
themed rollercoasters and a log flume, Pirate Falls.

The most popular attractions are the interactive
zones such as Lego Traffic, where children can
operate electrically powered Lego cars, boats and
balloons. In the Imagination Centre kids are
encouraged to make their own futuristic designs.
Older children can create robotic models or take on
the Extreme Team Challenge water slide, whilst
younger ones can splash around in Explore Land's
Waterworks fountains, dash about in the play
zones and enjoy gentle boat rides.

After all this activity you can head for Miniland
and marvel at the model buildings, complete with
mini Tube train and pleasure boats, or stop off for
a picnic and watch the Wave Surfers in action. In
summer there are shows in the Lego Imagination
Theatre, where you can take a thrilling 4D ride with
the Lego racers – sit near the front if you dare. Very
young kids might prefer a puppet show in the
Explore Theatre, while all the family can marvel at
the acrobatic thrills and spills in the Jack Stone
Stunt Show.

Thorpe Park

Staines Road, Chertsey
t 0870 444 4466
www.thorpepark.com
Getting there Thorpe Park is on the A320 between
Chertsey and Staines (J11 or 13 from the M25).
There's a regular train service from Reading,
Guildford and London (Waterloo) to Staines, from
where you can catch a bus
Open Apr–Nov, times vary, but it usually opens at
10 and closes between 5 and 7.30
Adm Adult £19–£25, child £15.50–£18.50 (4–11 inclu-
sive), family ticket £54–£67, under 1m **free**
*Fast-food outlets, gift shop, baby changing facilities,
first aid centre, some wheelchair access, adapted
toilets, on-site parking. Annual pass available*

Thorpe's impressive range of water rides and
slides make it the perfect option for a hot day, but
do pack waterproofs, swimwear and a spare T-shirt
for good measure. The most fun to be had is on
Tidal Wave, where you plunge 85ft into a wall of
water. Daredevil kids like to wait on the bridge
after their ride to get another soaking as the next
boatload of bold adventurers hit the briney.

Serious white knucklers can also enjoy Nemesis
Inferno's volcanic rumblings as you whizz along
750 metres of suspended track, or head in all direc-
tions at once on Quantuum. Then there's the might
of Collosus to sample, the world's first 10 looping
roller coaster, and 'X:/No Way Out', which, although
not the first rollercoaster to operate in pitch dark-
ness, is certainly the first to force its cargo to travel
at speeds of around 65mph...backwards.

Most of the attractions at Thorpe Park have
clearly been designed to cater for families. Children
are particularly well provided for, with various
themed areas such as Mrs Hippo's Jungle Safari as
well as Model World, which features miniature
versions of the Eiffel Tower, the Pyramids and
Stonehenge. They can also take a boat ride to
Thorpe Farm to bond with the resident goats,
sheep and rabbits.

NEED TO KNOW

SURVIVAL

Being away from home can have its frustrations. Principal among them is you don't necessarily know where everything is, like where to go in an emergency or who to call for advice. London is a big city, it's true, but the following list of essentials should help to put parents' minds at rest and make families feel much more at home.

24-hour chemist
Zafash Chemist
233–235 Old Brompton Road, SW5
t (020) 7373 3506

24-hour dentist
Dental Emergency Care Service
t (020) 7955 2186
www.bda-findadentist.org.uk

Accident and Emergency
University College, London, Hospital
Gower Street, WC1
t (020) 7387 9300
www.uclh.org

Babysitting
Childminders Babysitting Service
t (020) 7935 2049

Emergency
Police, Fire Brigade, Ambulance
t 999 or 112

Getting around
Transport for London
t (020) 7222 1234
www.tfl.gov.uk

Lost property
London Transport Lost Property Office (including Black Cab Lost Property Office)
t (020) 7486 2496

Taxi
Dial-A-Black-Cab
t (020) 7253 5000

Useful websites
NHS Direct
www.nhsdirect.nhs.uk

Either log on or call 0845 4647 to obtain advice from trained hospital staff. This is a vital and reliable service that helps to cut down on unnecessary doctors' appointments and hospital visits, not to mention dragging unwell children out of their beds in the dead of night. Please use it.

A new, and welcome, innovation, particularly useful for visitors, are the NHS walk-in centres. There are nine in the capital (see p.211) and are open to anyone on a drop-in basis. They provide minor treatments, information and advice. The centres are open daily from 7am to 10pm.

Boots The Chemists
www.boots.com

Boots' own website offers an online delivery service for toiletries, baby food, nappies etc., plus advice and details of local Boots' stores and other practitioners.

Maps
www.upmystreet.com

If you're staying in one area for a while you can key in your postcode and find out about all kinds of local services, from dry cleaners to estate agents.

www.multimap.com

Map service that allows you to home in on a particular area and find out about local restaurants, hotels and services.

Practicalities A–Z

Climate

If you've never been to Britain before, you're probably expecting to be consumed in clouds of fog and drizzle the moment you step off the plane. Britain has a reputation for dismal weather – it's the home of the legendary 'pea-souper', after all (long since gone, following strict pollution laws) – and the state of the skies has long been the nation's favourite topic of conversation. The summers are rarely too hot, the winters seldom too cold. However, you may get a brief heatwave in July/August or the occasional week of snow cover in January (plus a small hurricane every 70 years or so) and this does tend to throw the transport system into confusion, so beware.

In London, the average temperature is 22°C (75°F) in July and August, dropping to 7°C (44°F) in December and January. Rainfall is generally at its heaviest in November. The best time to visit is probably late spring or early autumn, when you can look forward to mild temperatures, not too much rain, the odd sunny day and slightly shorter queues at the capital's major tourist attractions.

Electricity

Britain's electrical supply is 240 volts AC. When bringing an electrical appliance from abroad fitted with a two-prong plug, you'll need to purchase an adaptor and probably a transformer as well. British appliances use a type of three-prong, square pin plug that will be unfamiliar to visitors from Europe and North America. All UK plugs have fuses of three, five or 13 amps.

Embassies & consulates

US Embassy
24 Grosvenor Square, W1
t (020) 7499 9000
www.usembassy.org.uk
Open Mon–Fri 8.30–5.30

Australian High Commission
Australia House, The Strand, WC2
t (020) 7379 4334
www.australia.org.uk
Open Mon–Fri 9–5

Canadian High Commission
38 Grosvenor St, W1
t (020) 7258 6600
www.canada.org.uk
Open Mon–Fri 8am–11am

Dutch Embassy
38 Hyde Park Gate, SW7
t (020) 7590 3200
www.netherlands-embassy.org.uk
Open Mon–Fri 9–5.30

High Commission of India
India House, Aldwych, WC2
t (020) 7836 8484
www.hcilondon.org
Open Mon–Fri 9.30–5.30

Irish Embassy
17 Grosvenor Place, SW1
t 0870 162 0844
http://ireland.embassyhomepage.com
Open Mon–Fri 9.30–5

New Zealand High Commission
New Zealand House, 80 The Haymarket, SW1
t (020) 7930 8422
http://nzembassy.com
Open Mon–Fri 10–12 noon and 2–4

South African Embassy
South Africa House, Trafalgar Square, WC2
t (020) 7451 7299
www.southafricahouse.com
Open Mon–Fri 9.30–5

Families with special needs

Wheelchair access to London's public places – its theatres, cinemas, sports grounds etc. – is relatively good. The London Tourist Board's website provides access details for all London's principal attractions, t (020) 7932 2000, www.visitlondon.com/planning_your_visit/information_disabled_people.php.

It also provides a list of wheelchair accessible accommodation, as well as hotels which accept guide dogs. Country-wide information is available from the English Tourism Council, which has produced an 'Accessible Britain' guide in conjunction with the Holiday Care Service, available for £5.99, **t** 0870 606 7204.

Unfortunately, public transport is something of a nightmare for disabled travellers, with access to London's Tubes, trains and buses still rather limited, although Transport for London has introduced 'low-floor' accessible buses on 35 routes. Transport for London's own guide, 'Access to the Underground', has information on what little lift access there is to the city's Tube stations. It's available free from any Tube station or by post from Transport for London Access and Mobility Unit, Windsor House, 42–50 Victoria Street, SW1, **t** (020) 7222 1234. Leaflets detailing 'low-floor' routes and mobility buses, as well as large print, braille maps and audio tapes, are also available.

All black taxis are wheelchair accessible and many have additional aids for disabled travellers including ramps, swivel seats and induction loops. More comprehensive transport information can be found in the 'Access in London' guide, produced by the Access Project, 39 Bradley Gardens, London W13 8HE (a donation of £7.50 towards printing costs is requested). Wheelchair users and blind and partially sighted people are entitled to a 30–50 per cent discount on rail fares and can apply for a Disabled Person's Railcard (£14 a year) at major rail stations, **www**.disabledpersons-railcard.co.uk. A booklet, in PDF format, providing advice on rail travel for disabled passengers can be downloaded from **www**.nationalrail.co.uk/info/disabled. There are currently no discounts on London's buses.

Britain has a growing number of specialist tour operators which specifically cater for the needs of physically disabled travellers, such as Can Be Done, **t** (020) 8907 2400, **www**.canbedone.co.uk. The Association of Independent Tour Operators, **t** (020) 8607 9080, **www**.aito.co.uk, can provide a list, as can RADAR (the Royal Association for Disability and Rehabilitation, *see* below) which also publishes its own guides to holidays and travel. The following organizations will provide information and advice.

Artsline
54 Charlton Street, NW1
t (020) 7388 2227
www.artsline.org.uk

Free information on access to arts venues around the capital. It also publishes a guide 'London: an Access Guide for Disabled People' (£3) and runs a website for disabled theatre-goers, **www**.theatreaccess.co.uk.

Council for Disabled Children
t (020) 7843 1900
www.ncb.org.uk/cdc
Part of the National Children's Bureau, this is a good source of information on travel health and further resources.

Disability Now
6 Markets Road, N7
t (020) 7619 7323
www.disabilitynow.org.uk
Produces a monthly newspaper with holiday ideas written by people with disabilities.

Greater London Association for Disabled People
336 Brixton Road, SW9
t (020) 7346 5800
www.glad.org.uk
Publishes a free London Disability Guide.

Holiday Care Service
2nd Floor, Imperial Buildings, Victoria Road, Horley, Surrey RH6 9HW
t (0845) 124 9971
www.holidaycare.org.uk
Provides information sheets for families on sites that have been assessed by reps according to 'Tourism for All' TFA standards, and also runs an accessible accommodation research service.

Magic Deaf
t (020) 7323 88551
c/o The British Museum, Education Department, WC1
http://magicdeaf.org.uk
Provides details for the hearing impaired about museums and galleries in the capital.

RADAR (Royal Association for Disability and Rehabilitation)
250 City Road, London EC1
t (020) 7250 3222
www.radar.org.uk
Produces guide books and information packs for disabled travellers, including its annual 'Holidays in Britain and Ireland for Disabled People' (£8).

Royal National Institute for the Blind

224 Great Portland Street, London W1
t 08457 669 999 (UK helpline)
t (020) 7388 1266 (for callers from outside the UK)
www.rnib.org.uk
   Advises blind people on travel matters and publishes a hotel guide book for £4.99.

Smooth Groove Guide

www.smoothridegrooveguide.info
   Interactive travel site written by (and for) young disabled people.

Tripscope

t 08457 585 641
www.tripscope.org.uk
   Telephone helpline for disabled people touring in London.

In the US

American Foundation for the Blind

11 Penn Plaza, Suite 300, New York, NY 10011
t 212 502 7600; toll free **t** 800 232 5463
www.afb.org

Mobility International

PO Box 10767, Eugene, Oregon 97440
t 541 343 1284
www.miusa.org

SATH (Society for the Advancement of Travel for the Handicapped)

347 Fifth Avenue, Suite 610, New York 10016
t 212 447 7284
www.sath.org

In Australia

ACROD (Australian Council for the Rehabilitation of the Disabled)

PO Box 60, Curtin Act 2605
t 02 6283 3200
www.acrod.org.au

Infant matters

Babysitters

Finding a reliable and trustworthy childminder in a strange city can be a worrying task. Large hotels usually offer a babysitting service. Small ones may be able to arrange something on request. London also has several reputable agencies offering a network of qualified babysitters, nurses and infant teachers.

Childminders

6 Nottingham St, W1
t (020) 7935 2049/3000
www.babysitter.co.uk

Hopes and Dreams

339–341 City Road, EC1
t (020) 833 9388
www.hopesanddreams.co.uk
   Babysitting from 3 months–5 years. Hotel for over-2s to 11 years old.

Pippa Pop-Ins

430 Fulham Rd, SW6
t (020) 7385 2458
   Award-winning hotel for 2–12 year olds; provides a crèche, nursery school and babysitting services.

Universal Aunts

t (020) 7738 8937
   Provides babysitters, entertainers, people to meet children off trains, and even guides to take children round London.

Breastfeeding

Public breastfeeding is not exactly taboo in London, but you are best off enquiring at individual restaurants as to where you might sit and feed in relative comfort. London's principal airports and train stations, and some of its department stores have mother-and-baby rooms. If in doubt, head for the nearest branch of Boots, though be aware that you may well have to feed your baby while other people change theirs. The main branch of Gap on Oxford Street, close to Bond Street station, has a dedicated nursing mothers' room.

Nappies

You can pick up bumper packs of disposable nappies, such as Pampers or Huggies or an own-name brand, at any London supermarket or major chemist. Some supermarket chains stock Nature Boy & Girl nappies from Sweden, which are 70% biodegradable. If you are worried about the cost (which can be formidable) or damage to the environment, London has plenty of sources of traditional re-usable nappies. Remember that there are nappy laundry services available (*see* below).

Green Baby

345 Upper Street, N1
t (020) 7359 7037
www.greenbabyco.com

Washable nappies and disposables, plus toiletries, buggies and organic clothing available in-store or by mail order, **t** 0870 240 6894.

The National Association of Nappy Services (NANS)

t 0121 693 4949
www.changeanappy.co.uk

Visit the website to find a service in your area. It couldn't be easier.

The Real Nappy Association

PO Box 3704, London, SE26 4RX
t (020) 8299 4519
www.realnappy.com

Send a stamped addressed envelope with two stamps for information and a listing of environment-friendly baby product suppliers.

Sam-I-Am

t 01522 778 926
www.nappies.net

Mail-order cotton nappies.

Snuggle Naps

t 0115 910 7220
www.snugglenaps.co.uk

Mail-order washable, designer nappies.

Insurance

It's vital that you take out travel insurance before your trip. This should cover, at a bare minimum, cancellation due to illness, travel delays, accidents, lost luggage, lost passports, lost or stolen belongings, personal liability, legal expenses, emergency flights and medical cover. The majority of insurance companies offer free insurance to children under the age of two as part of the parent's policy. Also bear in mind annual insurance policies, which can be especially cost effective for families with two or more older children. Always keep the company's 24-hour emergency number close to hand – if you have a mobile, store it in the memory.

The most important aspect of any travel insurance policy is its medical cover. You should look for cover of around £5 million. If you're a resident of the European Union, Iceland, Liechtenstein or Norway, you are entitled to free or reduced-cost medical treatment as long as you carry with you the appropriate validated form. In the EU this is the E111 form, which covers families with dependent children up to the age of 16 (or 19, if in full-time education). Even so, you may have to pay for your medical treatment and then claim your expenses back at a later date, so hang on to your receipts.

In the US and Canada, you may find that your existing insurance policies give sufficient medical cover and you should always check them thoroughly before taking out a new one. Canadians, in particular, are usually covered by their provincial health plans. Few American or Canadian insurance companies will issue on-the-spot payments following a reported theft or loss. You will usually have to wait several weeks and engage in a hefty amount of correspondence before any money is forthcoming. Here is a list of useful insurance contacts.

In the UK

Association of British Insurers

t (020) 7600 3333
www.abi.org.uk

The Financial Ombudsman Service

t 0845 080 1800
www.financial-ombudsman.org.uk

The government-appointed regulator of the insurance industry.

ABC Holiday Extras Travel Insurance

t 0870 844 4020
www.holidayextras.co.uk

Columbus Travel Insurance

t (020) 7375 0011
www.columbusdirect.net

Endsleigh Insurance

t 0800 028 3571
www.endsleigh.co.uk

Medicover

t 0870 735 3600
www.medi-cover.co.uk

World Cover Direct

t 0800 365 121
www.worldcover.co.uk

In the US

Access America
t US/Canada 866 807 3982
www.accessamerica.com

Carefree Travel Insurance
t US/Canada 800 727 4874
www.carefreetravel.com

Travel Assistance International
t US/Canada 800 821 2828
www.travelassistance.com

MEDEX Assistance Corporation
t US 410 453 6300
www.medexassist.com

Lost property

If you lose anything while out and about in London, the chances are it's gone for good. However, you never can tell, and it is always worth checking to see whether some honest citizen has handed your valuable lost item in. If you lose something while on the plane, go to the nearest information desk in the airport and fill out the relevant form as soon as possible.

London Transport Lost Property Office (incorporating the Black Cab Lost Property Office)
200 Baker Street, NW1
t (020) 7486 2496
Open Weekday mornings

Maps

There's little rhyme or reason to the layout of London's streets. Minimal urban planning is a great British tradition – to a Londoner's eyes, nicely arranged grids and blocks are foreign affectations to be resisted at all costs. Your first purchase upon arriving in London should therefore be a good street map – you can pick one up in most newsagents. Stanfords, London's premier map shop has, as you might expect, a wide selection.

If you (or more likely your kids) are computer literate, you can visit **www**.streetmap.co.uk and print out the map of the area you need. If you're hoping to stick around for some time, or have plans to visit attractions on the outskirts of town, you should consider getting hold of a copy of the London A–Z Street Atlas, a must for all disorientated Londoners – almost every household in the capital owns one. It contains street maps of every area in Greater London and is available in a range of formats from a huge, glossy, colour, hardback version to a black and white pocket edition (£19.99 and £2.75 respectively). You will find them stocked at bookstores, newsagents and petrol stations across London.

If you are brave enought to drive in London, you might like to pick up a 'London Parking Map', published by the Clever Map Company or, for out of London, one of the Ordinance Survey's excellent series of annually updated road atlases.

Train, Tube and bus maps are available from main underground and train stations. The most useful is the hybrid Journey Planner which shows both Tube and rail links. You'll find all your cartographic requirements catered for at:

Stanfords
12–14 Long Acre, WC2
t (020) 7836 1321
www.stanfords.co.uk
London's largest map shop.

The Travel Bookshop
13 Blenheim Crescent, W11
t (020) 7229 5260
www.thetravelbookshop.co.uk

Medical matters

Visitors from the EU, Iceland, Liechtenstein and Norway can claim free or reduced cost medical treatment under Britain's National Health Service, so long as they carry with them the appropriate form. In the EU, this is the E111, which covers families with dependent children up to the age of 16 (or 19, if in full-time education). The only things you will be expected to pay for are medical prescriptions (currently £6.10) and visits to the optician or dentist (these are free to children and senior citizens). Visitors from other countries should take out medical insurance.

In an emergency

If you require urgent medical treatment, you should call an ambulance by calling **t** 999 or 112, or drive to the nearest hospital with an Accident and Emergency Department.

Chelsea & Westminster Hospital

369 Fulham Road, SW10
t (020) 8746 8000
⊖ Fulham Broadway

Central Middlesex Hospital

Acton Lane, Park Royal, NW10
t (020) 8453 2257
⊖/ ⇌ Harlesden

Ealing Hospital

Uxbridge Road, Middlesex, UB1
t (020) 8967 5613
www.ealinghopsital.org.uk
⊖ Ealing Broadway

Guy's Hospital

St Thomas Street, SE1
t (020) 7955 5000
www.guysandstthomas.nhs.uk
⊖ London Bridge
Dedicated A&E department for children

Royal London Hospital

Whitechapel Road, E1
t (020) 7377 7000

The London Tube Map

The London Tube map (*see* inside back cover) has become an icon of the city as familiar as Big Ben or a double-decker bus. The first Tube maps, which were drawn up over 100 years ago, were done to scale with spaghetti-like intertwining lines and were practically unreadable. In the 1930s, a young draughtsman called Harry Beck came up with the idea of a new map based on an electrical circuit diagram. On this new map the distances between the stations in central London were extended while those between outer London stations were shortened. The result is one of the clearest and most copied diagrams in the world.

www.bartsandthelondon.org
⊖ Whitechapel
Dedicated A&E department for children

St Mary's Hospital

Praed Street, W2
t (020) 7886 6666
www.st-marys.org.uk
⊖ Paddington

University College London Hospital

Gower Street, WC1
t (020) 7387 9300
www.uclh.org
⊖ Euston Square, Warren Street, Goodge Street

Whittington Hospital

Highgate Hill, N19
t (020) 7272 3070
www.whittington.nhs.uk
⊖ Archway

Minor ailments

In 2000 the NHS set up walk-in centres to cater for people with minor ailments. Use them to avoid hours of waiting at a hospital A&E department. There are nine centres in the capital (*see* below). They are open to anyone on a drop-in basis. The centres are open from 7am to 10pm. There are also some private walk-in centres dotted about, so check first about charges.

Soho Centre for Health and Care

29–30 Soho Square, W1
t (020) 7534 6500
⊖ Tottenham Court Road, Leicester Square

Charing Cross Hospital

Fulham Palace Road, W6
t (020) 8846 7490
⊖ Hammersmith

There are also centres in Parsons Green, SW6; Tooting, SW1;, Tottenham, N18; Edgware HA8; Whitechapel, E1; Newham E13; and Croydon, CRO1.

For more information, contact NHS Direct, **t** 0845 4647 or www.nhs.co.uk.

Chemists/Pharmacies

In Britain, only a limited range of drugs can be dispensed without a doctor's prescription. Chemists will also often stock a selection of basic medical and cosmetic products such as cough mixture, plasters (band-aids), bandages, nappies, vitamins and hairspray. Your local police station can provide a list of late-opening chemists. Otherwise, try the following:

Bliss Chemist

5 Marble Arch, W1
t (020) 7723 6116
Open Until 12 midnight daily

Zafash Chemist

233–235 Old Brompton Road, SW5
t (020) 7373 2798
Open 24hrs a day, 365 days a year

Superstores often have chemists which are open late and on Sundays. **Boots**, **www**.boots.com, is the UK's largest chemist chain. Its branches also usually contain a photographic service. There are branches at 198 Baker Street, W1, **t** (020) 7935 1441; 173–5 Camden High Street, NW1, **t** (020) 7485 5216; Counter Street, Hay's Galleria, SE1, **t** (020) 7407 4276; 4 James Street, Covent Garden, WC2, **t** (020) 7379 8442; 127a Kensington High Street, W8, **t** (020) 7937 9533; 439–441 Oxford St, W1, **t** (020) 7409 2857.

Other useful contacts

Action for Sick Children

c/o National Children's Bureau, 8 Wakley Street, EC1
t (020) 7843 6444
www.actionforsickchildren.org
Provides advice to help parents get the best possible health care for their children.

Action Against Allergies

PO Box 278, Twickenham, TW1
t (020) 8892 2711
Write for a free booklet.

Dental Emergency Care Service

t (020) 7955 2186
www.bda-findadentist.org.uk

Eye Care Information Bureau

t (020) 7357 7730

Medical Advisory Service for Travellers Abroad

t 0113 238 7575
www.masta.org

NHS Direct

t (0845) 4647
www.nhsdirect.nhs.uk

Nurse-led, 24hr helpline offering confidential health advice. You can also get information and advice online.

St John's Ambulance Supplies

t (020) 7278 7888
www.stjohnsupplies.co.uk

Money and banks

The currency in Britain is the pound sterling (written £) which is divided into 100 pence (written p). There are eight coin denominations: 1p, 2p, 5p, 10p, 20p, 50p, £1 and £2 (all issued by the Royal Mint) and four note denominations: £5, £10, £20 and £50 – the last is the most often forged and you'll find that a number of shops and restaurants refuse to accept £50 notes in any circumstances. All notes are printed by the Bank of England (apart from the forgeries, that is).

Most shops and restaurants accept the big name credit and debit cards: Visa, Delta, Mastercard, American Express, Barclaycard, Diners Club, Switch.

The biggest high street banks in London are Barclays, NatWest, HSBC and Lloyds TSB. Most have automatic cash dispensers (or 'holes in the wall') which can be used 24-hours a day and will often dispense money on foreign bank cards. Your bank's international banking department should advise you on this. All banks are open 9.30-3.30, although many are open later (till around 5pm). Some also open on Saturday mornings. The easiest and safest way to carry large sums of money is by using travellers' cheques. These can be changed, for a small commission, at any bank or bureau de change. Try:

American Express

www.americanexpress.com
Terminal 3, Landside Departures, Heathrow Airport, TW6, **t** (020) 8759 6845; 78 Brompton Road, SW3, **t** (020) 7761 7901; 30–31 Haymarket, SW1 **t** (020) 7484 9610; 84 Kensington High Street, W8, **t** (020) 7795 6703; 77 Wilton Road SW1, **t** (020) 7630 6365

Thomas Cook

www.thomascook.com
Victoria Place, SW1, **t** (020) 7302 8660; 1 Marble Arch, W1, **t** (020) 7530 7100; 30 St James's Street, SW1, **t** (020) 7853 6400; 11 Victoria Street, SW1, **t** (020) 7302 8600

Carrying money around

Use a money belt fastened around your waist under a tucked-in shirt or T-shirt. Pickpocketing is rife in certain parts of London, especially busy shopping areas such as Oxford Street. The most recent scams to watch out for are people copying your pin number at cashpoints and then stealing your credit card, and gangs of youths jostling you or swiping something from out of your back pocket. In short, do not put your purse or any other valuables in a back pocket or the rear zipper pocket of your backpack if you wish to see them again. Always keep wallets in your front trouser pockets and hold purses and bags tightly.

National holidays

Britain's national holidays are always arranged to fall on a Monday – Christmas, New Year's Day and Good Friday excepted. This not only allows people to enjoy a 'long weekend', but stops the nation from being cheated out of a holiday that would otherwise fall on a Saturday or Sunday. Shops and services tend to operate according to their Sunday hours and banks are always closed – which is why Britain's national holidays are sometimes also known as bank holidays.

School holidays

State schools
Half-term Autumn, end of October
Christmas two weeks
Half-term mid-February
Easter two weeks
Half-term Spring Bank Holiday, late May/June
Summer six weeks July/August

Private schools
Same half-terms
Christmas 3–4 weeks
Easter 3–4 weeks
Summer 8–9 weeks

Useful numbers
Emergency (Police, Fire Brigade, Ambulance)
t 999 or 112
Operator **t** 100
Directory Enquiries **t** 118500 or 118800 or 118118
International Operator **t** 155
International Directory Enquiries **t** 153

Necessities

Wherever you're travelling with kids, it is always worth taking a packet of wet wipes, a full change of clothing, toys to fiddle with, drinks and snacks, plus some empty, disposable bags for unforeseen eventualities. Other items you might like to consider which could be picked up in London include:
► a torch/flashlight
► matches/lighter
► a night light
► safety pins
► an extension cord
► needle and thread
► a roll of sticky tape
► a net shopping bag
► moisturizing cream
► travel socket converters
► mild soap and baby shampoo
► playing cards, paper & crayons
► a forehead thermometer

One-parent families

There are various organizations in London offering advice and support for single parents travelling with children.

One Parent Families
255 Kentish Town Road, NW5
t (020) 7428 5400
www.oneparentfamilies.org.uk
Runs a lone parent helpline, **t** 0800 018 5026

Gingerbread
16–17 Clerkenwell Close, EC1
t 0800 018 4318 or (020) 7336 8183
www.gingerbread.org.uk

One-Parent Family Holidays
t 01465 821 288
www.opfh.org

Opening hours

The traditional opening times for shops and offices in London are 9am until 5.30pm, although many shops are now open from 10am until 7pm. Most shops have one nominated day, usually Wednesday or Thursday, on which they stay open late, until 8 or 9pm. Sunday opening, most commonly between 12 noon and 5pm, has become the norm in recent years. Some of the capital's corner shops and supermarkets stay open 24-hours a day. Pubs and restaurants, however, observe very strict licensing laws – no alcohol can be served outside the period 11am–11pm – although there are increasing calls for Britain to adopt more open-ended, Euro-style opening hours.

Post offices

You can buy stamps, post parcels and pay bills in London's post offices Mon–Fri 9–5.50 and Sat 9–12 noon, although if you want to send a postcard, most of the capital's newsagents sell stamps. The cost of sending a letter (under 60g) first class to anywhere in the UK or second class to anywhere in Europe is 28p, while a postcard costs 38p to Europe and 42p to anywhere else. Post boxes, painted the same distinctive red as the capital's buses and older phone boxes, are common. You'll find post offices at 24–28 William IV Street, Trafalgar Square, WC2, **t** (020) 7930 9580; 105 Abbey Street, SE1, **t** (020) 7237 8629; 43–44 Albemarle Street, W1, **t** (020) 7493 5620; 81–89 Farringdon Road, EC1, **t** (020) 7242 7262; 54–56 Great Portland Street, W1, **t** (020) 7636 2205; 24–27.

For more about Royal Mail services, visit **www.**royalmail.com. For complaints, call **t** 0345 740 740.

The golden rules
▶ Don't leave valuables in your hotel room.
▶ Keep most of your money in travellers' cheques.
▶ Keep all your valuables in a money belt fastened around your waist under a tucked shirt or t-shirt.
▶ Only keep small amounts of money in your wallet or purse. Keep your wallet in your trouser pocket and hold purses and bags close to your body with the flap facing inwards and the strap over your shoulder.
▶ Steer clear of unfamiliar areas of the city late at night.
▶ Try to avoid travelling alone on the Underground late at night.
▶ Do not leave bags hanging over chairs.
▶ Take care on busy shopping streets.

Safety

London is still a relatively law-abiding place, but in an emergency you can call the police, fire brigade or ambulance services on **t** 999 or 112. As a tourist, the crimes you are most likely to fall victim to are pickpocketry and petty thieving. London's busiest shopping districts – Oxford Street, Covent Garden, King's Road, Kensington High Street – are often targeted by organized gangs of pickpockets, but as long as you remain vigilant and take sensible precautions with your valuables, you should be able to enjoy a trouble-free holiday.

Of course, when travelling with children, you need to be extra vigilant. When on the streets or in a crowded place, make sure you never let them out of your sight. Always keep your children in front of you and continually take a head count. Under-2s can be kept safe on a wrist-rein. In the event that you do get separated, encourage your children to remain in one place and wait for you to find them. It is a good idea to supply youngsters with a whistle to blow in case they lose sight of you in busy areas. A bright cap or jacket makes them much easier to spot. If you have more than one child, colour match their clothes so that you only have one thing to watch out for. Older children may be trusted enough to explore by themselves within bounds. Even so, always establish a central, easy-to-find meeting place. Ensure your children carry identification at all times and make sure you have an up-to-date photograph of them, too.

Telephones

There are still some red phone boxes left in London, although not nearly as many as the postcard industry would have you believe. British Telecom began removing these cast iron monoliths in the early 90s, with the intention of replacing them with lighter, cheaper, plastic booths. The public raised such a fuss, however, that BT was forced to leave a significant number standing. They are still quite common in parts of the West End, but have almost completely disappeared from the suburbs, apart from in sleepy hamlets and villages.

Although British Telecom lost its monopoly for supplying the nation with telephones when it was privatized in 1984, it's still by far Britain's most popular phone company. The majority of the capital's public phone booths are BT-owned, although there are now several other companies, including Mercury and AT&T, operating payphones. In fact, there are now very few streets in central London that don't have at least one public phone. In particular, look out for the orange, European-looking Interphones. For some reason, these have proved to be London's least popular public phone booths and, as such, are the kind you are most likely to find unoccupied. All London's main Tube and train stations have ranks of public phones.

You can buy excellent prepaid phone cards, such as Gnanam or Tele2, which can be used from any phone using a pin number on the back of the cards. Ask at local newsagents.

Most modern pay phones accept coins (any denomination from 10p up, the minimum call charge is 20p) and phone cards (available in denominations of £1, £2, £5, £10 and £20 from newsagents or post offices), although some only accept one or the other. Some booths let you pay by swiping a credit card. If possible, avoid using the phone in your hotel room as it is quite normal for the hotel to treble or even quadruple the call rate.

Britain's domestic phones employ an unusual wide type of phone jack, and if you need to plug in a phone brought from abroad or a modem, you may have to buy an adaptor.

International calls are cheapest in the evening after 6pm and on weekends. The international dialling code is 00 followed by the country code:

United States and Canada 1
Ireland **353**
France **33**
Italy **39**
Germany **49**
Australia **61**
New Zealand **64**

The telephone code for London itself is 020 (which you needn't dial for calls made within the city) followed by either a 7 (for central London) or an 8 (for outer London). If dialling from outside the UK, remember to omit the initial 0.

The phone numbers of businesses and shops are listed in the Yellow Pages, available for £5 from BT. Also, check out their website at **www**.yell.co.uk.

Time

London is the official home of time. The prime meridian, the line of 0° longitude, runs through the quiet, southeast London borough of Greenwich and, since 1884, Greenwich Mean Time (GMT) has been the standard against which all other times are set. GMT is generally one hour ahead of western Europe. In summer, however, Britain switches to British Summer Time (BST) which is one hour ahead of GMT. Britain is five hours ahead of New York, eight hours ahead of San Francisco and 10 hours behind Tokyo and Sydney. In everyday conversation, the majority of Londoners will use the 12-hour clock – 9am, 3pm etc. – but timetables are more often given using the 24-hour clock.

Tipping

Ten to 15 per cent is the usual rate in restaurants, taxis, hairdressers etc. You are not obliged to tip, however, especially if the service was unsatisfactory. You would not normally tip a bartender in a pub. Restaurants sometimes add a service charge of 10–15 per cent, which should be shown on the menu. Tipping staff such as chambermaids and porters is discretionary, but much appreciated.

Useful parenting websites
www.allkids.co.uk
www.babycentre.co.uk
www.babydirectory.com
www.babyworld.com
www.familiesonline.co.uk
www.familycorner.com
www.forparentsbyparents.co.uk
www.kidsinmind.co.uk
www.kinderstart.com
www.mumsnet.com
www.naturalparentinguk.com
www.parents-news.co.uk
www.parentscafe.co.uk
www.practicalparent.org.uk
www.storknet.com
www.ukchildrensdirectory.com
www.ukparents.co.uk

Toilets

The whereabouts of the nearest toilet is perhaps the single most important piece of information a parent can have. Most mainline stations have public toilets (20p per visit!) as do London's principal department stores and some fast food outlets (notably McDonald's and Burger King). Pubs and restaurants, however, will sometimes only let you use their facilities (even in an emergency) if you're going to buy something. Public toilets on the streets of London are few and far between. The old-fashioned underground toilets have largely been phased out (there is still one in Leicester Square), but have yet to be replaced with an adequate number of street-level loos. You will come across the odd, free-standing automatic toilet known as a 'super loo' but, be warned, your 20p entitles you to a maximum 15 minutes' use of the facilities, after which the door will swoosh open revealing you (in whatever stage of undress) to the street. If in Covent Garden, check out the loos in St Paul's Churchyard, which have won awards for cleanliness and 'ambience'.

Tourist information

www.visitlondon.com
t (020) 7932 2000
t 090 6866 3344, recorded information (charged at the not inconsiderable sum of £1 per minute).

London Tourist Offices

Heathrow Terminals 1,2,3 Underground concourse

Waterloo International Terminal
Open 8.30am–10.30pm

Accommodation booking service
t (020) 7932 2020

British Visitor Centre
1 Regent Street, Piccadilly Circus, SW1
Open Mon–Fri 9–6.30, Sat–Sun 10–4

Greenwich Tourist Information Centre
Pepys House, 2 Cutty Sark Gardens, SE10
t 0870 608 2000
Open 10–5, daily

Liverpool Street Station
Liverpool Street Underground station, EC2

Victoria Station
Station Forecourt, SW1

Further Information

The most up-to-date information on the city's attractions and cultural life is provided by the nation's main daily newspapers – the *Daily Telegraph*, *The Times*, the *Daily Mail*, the *Independent* et al – and, in particular, by the London daily *Evening Standard*, which produces a listings magazine *Metro Life* every Thursday (with a special Kids' Section), and the *Guardian*, whose own listings magazine *The Guide* accompanies its Saturday edition. You should also check out *Time Out*, the capital's best selling weekly listings magazine, available in all major newsagents.

Sleep

The perfect family-friendly hotel should have all the facilities parents expect (large, well-equipped bedrooms; comfortable public rooms where they can relax in peace and quiet, sometimes away from the children; a babysitting/baby listening or crêche service and a decent restaurant, with a menu that extends beyond pizza and chips) as well as all the things kids need (cots, high chairs, reasonable meal times, a supervised activity area, a swimming pool or garden). However, it should above all display a welcoming attitude to all members of the family, whatever their age or status.

The London Tourist Board runs an accommodation booking service dealing with everything from five-star luxury hotels to long stay apartments and hostels, **t** (020) 7932 2020, **www.**visitlondon.com/planning_your_visit/accommodation.php, office@london.nethotel.com.

Hotels

If money is no object, you could, of course, go the five-star route: The Ritz, the Savoy, Claridges, the Dorcheser, these are some of the most famous names. They're all centrally located with family suites and excellent facilities and all offer a guaranteed supply of petting and pampering – and all will charge £400 plus a night for a family of four; and even then there's no guarantee that your boisterous kids will be welcome in the restaurants and public rooms. At the other end of the scale are the budget hotels. A good one in the centre of town should set you back around £100 a night, for which you should get a TV, shower or bath, phone and breakfast. It can be even cheaper if you're willing to share a bathroom with other guests.

The big chains

The well-known international hotel chains are virtually guaranteed to be a safe bet. True, this type of hotel can be rather impersonal – their principal clients are, after all, businessmen, not families – but you can, at least, be sure that the rooms will be clean and well-equipped and the service reliable. Furthermore, many hotels offer a range of competitive packages and deals for families, as well as activity programmes and children's menus in their restaurants, and some provide babysitting, baby-listening, cots and high chairs as standard. **Novotel**,

the French-owned chain, offer Summer Fun Breaks which include family entry to a nearby attraction, while the Forte Group (who own the **Travelodge** chain among others) have, in the past, offered discounts of up to 50 per cent on some of their London hotels, a deal which includes reduced entry for kids to a West End show.

Best Western
t 0800 393 130
www.bestwesternhotels.com
Doubles from £75 (prices do vary enormously, depending on the size and facilities of the hotel; this is by no means the minimum in all Best Western hotels)

Choice Hotels
t 0800 444444
www.choicehotelseurope.com
Doubles from around £100

The Choice Hotels group, which also includes Comfort Inns, Quality Inns and Sleep Inns, offers a range of family deals (for instance, at the time of going to press, a four-night family break for two adults, two children could be had for as little as £255). All rooms have playstations and DVD players and the restaurants offer an 'Adventure Kids' menu. Some hotels also have a pool.

Holiday Inn
t 0870 400 8161
www.holiday-inn.co.uk
Doubles from £60

Family-friendly chain where children under 17 stay for free and under-12s eat for free. They also offer a range of family deals.

Novotel
t (020) 8283 4500
www.novotel.com
Doubles from £115

Novotel, who operate hotels across the capital, are one of the most child-friendly chains around. Kids stay for free in their parents room (and also get breakfast for free), are given games when they arrive and also have special indoor play area. Most hotels also have an outdoor play area and some have a pool. All Novotel restaurants offer a children's menu and have a special 'children's corner' where kids can go after they've finished eating to allow their parents to enjoy their meal in peace.

Queens Moat Houses

t 0646 213 214
www.moathousehotels.com
Doubles from £120

Thistle

t 0870 3339 292
www.thistlehotels.com
Doubles from £120

Travel Inn

t 0870 238 3383
www.travelinn.co.uk
All rooms £44.95

Travel Inn also operate 'London Family Leisure Deals' offering a room and breakfast for up to two adults and two children, plus free entry to selected attractions (including the Tower of London, Madam Tussaud's and the London Dungeon) for £95.

Travelodge

t (0800) 850 950
www.travellodge.co.uk
All rooms from £44.95

Recommended hotels

The following are hotels which go out of their way to welcome and provide facilities for families.

22 Jermyn Street

22 Jermyn Street, SW1
t (020) 7734 2353
www.22jermyn.com
⊖ Piccadilly Circus
Doubles from £210, **suites** from £335

Small luxury hotel behind Piccadilly Circus which welcomes children with their own newsletter, 'Kids' Talk', and a supply of games, children's videos, a list of local child-friendly restaurants and even teddy bear dressing-gowns. 24-hour room service; extra beds and cots available.

Ashley Hotel

15–17 Norfolk Square, W2
t (020) 7723 3375
www.ashleyhotels.com
⊖/≥ Paddington
Doubles from £75, **family rooms** from £89

Cheap and cheerful family-run hotel (50 rooms) in three warren-like houses on a quiet square near Paddington Station. The family rooms are quite cramped (with tiny ensuite shower rooms), but from £89 per night, they are still relatively good value. There are special rates for children sharing with parents and no charge for babies.

The Athenaem

116 Piccadilly, W1
t (020) 7499 3466
www.athenaeumhotel.com
⊖ Green Park
Doubles from £285, **apartments** from £520

The Athenaeum is an upmarket hotel-apartment complex set in a row of elegant Piccadilly townhouses that prides itself on its family-friendliness. All the hotel rooms are sumptuously appointed – if a bit chintzy – and each apartment comes complete with sofas, TV, video, hi-fi, washing machine and kitchen, allowing you to live a totally self-contained existence (but with the hotel's facilities on call 24-hours a day). Guests are entitled to free use of the Athenaeum spa, gym and CD and video library.

Blooms Hotel

7 Montague Street, WC1
t (020) 7323 1717
www.bloomshotel.co.uk
⊖ Russell Square
Doubles from £205

Lovely small hotel set in an 18th-century townhouse near the British Museum. There are no specific children's facilities, but it's happy to welcome families and the staff are friendly and helpful. There's a pretty, paved, walled garden, 24-hour room service and extra cots are available. Under-10s stay for free in their parent's room.

Concorde Hotel

50 Great Cumberland Place, W1
t (020) 7402 6169
www.concorde-hotel.com
⊖ Marble Arch
Doubles from £90, **triples** from £99

With the same owners as the equally family-friendly Bryanston Court next door, this is a small, friendly hotel with a large, comfortable lounge and well-appointed bedrooms. Triple rooms can cost as little as £99 and there are cots, high chairs and a babysitting service available. They also have furnished apartments (complete with kitchens) in an adjacent building that are very popular with families.

County Hall Travel Inn Capital

Belvedere Road, SE1

t 0870 2383 300
www.travelinn.co.uk
⊖/⇌ Waterloo
All rooms Mon–Fri £82.95 per room, Fri–Sun £79.95

Centrally located, excellent value hotel above the London Aquarium, next to the new London Eye and just across the Thames from the Houses of Parliament. Part of the Travel Inn chain, this hotel provides reliable, no-frills accommodation with extra cots and children's menu available.

Crescent

49–50 Cartwright Gardens, WC1
t (020) 7387 1515
www.crescenthoteloflondon.com
⊖/⇌ Euston
Doubles from £90

One of several hotels on this Bloomsbury Crescent just north of the British Museum, this is

perhaps the pick of the bunch. The rooms are fairly basically equipped, but cheap for the location. Ground-floor rooms available (but no lift to upper floors). No charge for children under-2s; cots and high chairs available and babysitting by arrangement.

Durrants Hotel

George Street, W1
t (020) 7935 8131
www.durrantshotel.co.uk
⊖ Bond Street
Doubles from £140, family from £180

Smart, very traditional family-run hotel (90 rooms), housed in an 18th-century building behind the Wallace Collection and within easy reach of Bond Street. It has a comfortable lounge – lots of pine and mahogany panelling – a good restaurant (dinner from 6pm) and can arrange a babysitting service. Extra cots and high chairs available.

Dolphin Square Hotel

Dolphin Square, Chichester Street, SW1
t (020) 7834 3800
www.dolphinsquarehotel.co.uk
⊖ Westminster
Suites from £100, although prices do rise considerably in the high season

One of the few all-suite hotels in London, the Dolphin Square combines the benifits of an apartment complex with the facilities of a top-notch hotel. Right in the heart of London on the north side of Parliament Square, next to the river and set in its own gardens, it boasts a grand selection of one, two and three-bedroom suites, an 18-m pool, tennis courts, a shopping mall and a spa.

Edward Lear

28–30 Seymour Street, W1
t (020) 7402 5401
www.edlear.com
⊖ Marble Arch
Doubles from £74, family from £99 (prices go down the longer you stay)

Extremely friendly hotel, just 50 yards from Oxford Street, housed in two 18th-century townhouses that were once the home of the famous nonsense verse writer (and composer of *The Owl and the Pussycat*) Edward Lear. His illustrated limericks adorn the public rooms. The bedrooms are quite spacious but not necessarily ensuite, and there's no charge for under-2s or for children under

---

Family-friendly hotel checklist

Here is a list of things to look out for when hotel-hunting.
▶ special family packages or discounts. Do remember that British hotels tend to charge per person rather than a room rate, so cramming everyone into the same room doesn't always make sound economic sense. However, many hotels do allow children sharing their parents' room to stay free of charge.
▶ a choice of family rooms with three or more beds
▶ rooms with interconnecting doors
▶ a constantly monitored baby-listening service
▶ access to whatever leisure facilities there might be. Nothing is guaranteed to put a damper on a child's spirits more than being told they can't use the swimming-pool
▶ cots and high chairs
▶ children's meals. Are they healthy, served at a conveniently early time, in a family-friendly location, and if not, are children welcome in the restaurant?
▶ designated play areas for children. If there's an outdoor play area, is it safe and supervised?
▶ supplies of toys, books and, even better, computer games
▶ a babysitting service
▶ a crêche
▶ organized activities for children
▶ qualified child-care staff

13 sharing their parents' room at weekends. Extra cots available.

Goring

Beeston Place, Grosvenor Gardens, SW1
t (020) 7396 9000
www.goringhotel.co.uk
⊖/⇄ Victoria
Doubles from £195, family from £375

Right in the heart of Royal London, a stone's throw from Buckingham Palace and the great parks, this is a very grand, upright, traditionally British sort of establishment that nonetheless does its best to accommodate the needs of families. The public rooms are furnished in country house-style with open fires in winter, the bedrooms are sumptuous with all mod cons and there's a large private garden. Guests are entitled to free use of the local health club and there's a babysitting service available.

Hart House Hotel

51 Gloucester Place, W1
t (020) 7935 2288
www.harthouse.co.uk
⊖ Baker Street, ⊖/⇄ Marylebone
Doubles from £105

Very smart B&B housed in a West End Georgian mansion. The rooms vary in size – those near the top tend to be the largest and brightest – and are decorated in a variety of styles ranging from antique to modern. Toys are provided for the kids, there are extra cots and a babysitting service is available.

Hilton Metropole

225 Edgware Road, W2
t (020) 7402 4141
www.hilton.com
⊖ Marble Arch
Doubles from £120, although prices do rise considerably in the high season

Recently refurbished and extended, the Hilton is a superb family choice. Kids stay for free in their parents' room and there's a swimming pool, a children's menu available in the restaurant and a babysitting service (not to mention great views out over London from the 23rd floor). High chairs and video games also available.

Parkwood

4 Stanhope Place, W2
t (020) 7402 2241

⊖ Marble Arch
Doubles from £74, family from £99 (prices go down the longer you stay)

Owned by the same people as the Edward Lear, this small hotel is just a few yards from Hyde Park. It boasts several large, bright family rooms as well as a gallery of pictures by children who have visited the hotel. Extra beds, cots and high chairs available plus babysitting by arrangement.

Pippa Pop Ins

430 Fulham Road, SW6
t (020) 7385 5706
⊖ Fulham Broadway

This friendly establishment is a hotel just for children. Up to 12 kids can stay here for between a night and a week. Activities are organized on weekends and during the school holidays. Childred aged 2–5 can attend the day nursery, and there's an after-school service where children can be picked up from school and given tea and homework supervision until they are collected by their parents. There's a second hotel 'Pippa Pop-Ins on the Green' at 165 New King's Road, SW6.

Hotel La Place

17 Nottingham Place, W1
t (020) 7486 2323
www.hotellaplace.com
⊖ Baker Street
Doubles from £120, family from £150

Small, family-owned hotel on a quiet street near Madame Tussaud's, with a good restaurant (supper served 6–8.30, high chairs available), pleasantly furnished rooms and a welcoming atmosphere. Babysitting can be arranged.

Apart'hotels

A relatively new concept for the UK, these self-catering apartments have all the facilities you'd expect at home, plus hotel services on call 24-hours a day. There are two room sizes: a studio (sleeps four) or apartment (sleeps six) and prices start at £107 a night, though some are cheaper if you stay for over a month. The French company **Citadines, t** (0800) 376 3898, **www**.citadines.com has complexes in Covent Garden, South Kensington, Trafalgar Square and the Barbican.

Bed & breakfast

A British institution, these are small guest houses or private houses (usually located in residential areas outside the city centre) which hire out rooms at a reasonable price. Although you may have to share a bathroom, it is possible to get accommodation for as little as £10–20 per person per night. To find out how welcoming a potential B&B is to families, try asking the following questions.

▶ Are there cots and high chairs available?
▶ Is it possible to have separate children's meals at a time that suits them?
▶ Are the children expected to eat with the adults or at separate tables?
▶ Is there running-around space for children?
▶ Is there a comfortable lounge for the adults to relax in once the children have gone to bed?

The following agencies all have extensive lists of B&Bs throughout London.

Host and Guest Service
103 Dawes Road, SW6
t (020) 7385 9922
www.hostandguest.co.uk
Throughout London. From £20 per person per night. You can download a brochure from the website.

London Bed and Breakfast Agency
71 Fellows Road, NW3
t (020) 7586 2768
www.londonbb.com
Throughout London. Double rooms from £22 per person per night, though they also offer much more expensive accommodation.

Uptown Reservations
50 Christchurch Street, SW3
t (020) 7351 3445
www.uptownres.co.uk
Upmarket self-catering apartments in Kensington, Knightsbridge and Chelsea. Family rooms from £125; double rooms from £95.

Renting a flat

For a stay of several weeks, or even months, it is probably worth thinking about renting a flat. Not only does this make sound economic sense, it will also give you the chance to become familiar with the local community – meeting the neighbours, shopping in the local grocery stores, etc. Self-catering also allows you to do what you like when you like. You can get up when it suits you, nurse your colicky newborn at 3am and scramble eggs whenever your toddler gets peckish. Again, there are some important questions that are worth asking.

▶ How far is your accommodation from the nearest shops, supermarket, launderette, restaurants, transport and park?
▶ How many bedrooms does the flat have? The phrase 'sleeps 6' does not necessarily mean that there will be three bedrooms; often a sofa in the living room converts into a bed, and you may even need to rearrange the room in order to create enough sleeping space.
▶ Are cots supplied and, if so, is there an additional charge for them?
▶ Are the children's rooms fitted with bunk beds and, if so, do these have safety rails?
▶ Is the garden or pool fenced off and are there any nearby ponds, streams or other potential hazards?
▶ Is it safe for children to play unsupervised in the garden?
▶ Can babysitting be arranged locally?

Holiday Serviced Apartments
273 Old Brompton Road, SW5
t (0845) 060 4477
www.holidayapartments.co.uk
Can supply serviced and unserviced apartments all over London; two-bed flats from £900 per week.

AAE Shortlets
1 Princess Mews, Belsize Crescent, NW3
t (020) 7794 1186
www.aaeshortlets.co.uk
Apartments in northwest London; two-bed flats from £700 per week.

Euracom
Stanmore Towers, 8–14 Church Street, Stanmore, HA7

t (020) 8420 7666
www.euracom.co.uk
Two-bed flats from £550 per week plus booking fee. You can download a PDF brochure from the website.

Globe Apartments
36 James Street, W1
t (020) 7935 9512
www.globeapt.com
Two-bed flats from £600 per week.

Home exchange

The principle could not be easier: you hand your home over to another family, while they take on yours. You need to supply details of your home and family to an agency which lists you in their directory. References may be checked and a holiday agreement exchanged for added security.

The advantages of home exchange are obvious. You automatically have someone to care for your home, and even your pets, while you are away. Most importantly, exchanging homes with a family with children the same age as yours means their home is certain to be child-proofed and stocked with all the baby equipment you need to make your holiday fun and hassle-free. The savings can also be huge. Your only real expenses are signing up with an agency, transport to your destination and the usual holiday expenses.

Before you take the plunge, be specific about what you require from a visiting family and the sort of daily or weekly upkeep you expect, such as feeding pets, watering plants, tidying the house and taking telephone messages.

To organize a home exchange contact one of the following:

In the UK
NCT House-Swap Register
t 01626 360 689
www.nctpregnancyandbabycare.com
Membership fee £25.85
Run by the National Childbirth Trust, its register only lists families with at least one child under 12.

Intervac Home Exchange
t 01225 892 208
www.intervac.com

Homelink International
t 01344 842 642
www.homelink.org.uk
Membership fee £95

Home Base Holidays
t (020) 8886 8752
www.homebase-hols.com

In the US
Homelink USA
t 800 638 3841
www.homelink.org

Trading Homes International
t 310 798 3864
www.trading-homes.com

International Home Exchange
t (0800) 877 8723
www.homeexchange.com

Youth Hostels

Forget the dowdy image of cheesecloth, mung beans and compulsory acoustic guitar sessions; youth hostels have smartened up their act and offer family rooms with no chore rotas attached. Apart from being cheap and easy-going, youth hostels can also more easily accommodate larger family groups.Most hostels allow under-3s to stay for free and can provide cots and high chairs. The hostels at Hampstead and Rotherhithe also offer a children's menu. The best YHA hostels in London are listed below, for reservations call **t** (020) 7373 3400, **www.**yha.org.uk

City of London Youth Hostel
36 Carter Lane, EC4, **t** (020) 7236 4965
⊖ St Paul's
Beds in dormitory from £20 (5–17 year olds), £24 (18 and over); 4-bed rooms from £96.50 incl breakfast

Hampstead Heath Youth Hostel
4 Wellgarth Road, NW11, **t** (020) 8458 9054
⊖ Golders Green
Double room from £47

Rotherhithe Youth Hostel
Salter Road, SE16, **t** (020) 7232 2114
⊖ Rotherhithe, Canada Water
Double room from £47

Eat

Happily, the number of restaurants prepared to cater for the often fickle fancy of children is growing all the time. Sunday lunchtime, in particular, is often designated 'family time' in many eateries, with some even laying on entertainment in the form of magic shows and face-painting.

Cheap Eats

Café in the Crypt
St Martin-in-the-Fields, WC2, t (020) 7839 4342
🚇 Charing Cross
Open Mon–Sat 10–8, Sun 12 noon–8 (hot food 12 noon–3.15 and 5–7.30)

Atmospheric subterranean café whose semi-dungeonesque appearance should appeal to youngsters. With a wide selection of hot dishes, snacks and vegetarian choices available, this is a good place to come after a hard morning's sightseeing. Half portions are (rather logically) half price. High chairs available.

Chelsea Kitchen
98 King's Road, SW3, t (020) 7589 1330
🚇 Sloane Square
Open Mon–Sat 8am–11.30pm, Sun 9am–11.30pm
Sells a wide range of (very cheap) sandwiches, salads and pasta dishes.

Ed's Easy Diner
362 King's Road, SW3, t (020) 7352 1956
🚇 Sloane Square
12 Moor Street W1, t (020) 7439 1955
🚇 Tottenham Court Road
O2 Centre, 255 Finchley Road, NW3
t (020) 7431 1958, 🚇 Finchley Road
Branches open Sun–Thurs 11.30am–12 midnight, Fri–Sat 11.30am–1am
It's a bit noisy, but the burgers and chips in this mock 1950s 'rock 'n' roll' diner (complete with jukebox) are good and they have a very reasonably priced kids' menu (£4.45). High chairs available.

Giraffe
6–8 Blandford Street, W1, t (020) 7935 2333
🚇 Baker Street
46 Rosslyn Hill, NW3, t (020) 7435 0343
🚇 Hampstead
29–31 Essex Road, N1, t (020 7359 599
🚇 Old Street, 🚆 Essex Road
For details of other branches, visit **www.giraffe.net**
Branches open 8am–11.30pm daily

How much?
Unless otherwise indicated you should be able to get a meal for one adult and one child, at whatever time, for less than £25–£30
When?
London restaurants tend to serve lunch between 12.30 and 3pm and dinner between 7 and 10pm.

With its bright, colourful decor and piped world music, Giraffe has a rather groovy, youthful ambience. Both adults and children are well catered for – adults with a selection of inventive breakfast, lunch and dinner menus; children with a Kids' Pack filled with games and puzzles and a children's menu (just £4.95) of simple dishes (veggie noodles, sausages, burgers etc.) and large fruity shakes served with a giraffe-shaped stirrer. Non-smoking throughout. High chairs available.

Goddard's Pie House
45 Greenwich Church Street, SE10
t (020) 8293 9313, **www.pieshop.co.uk**
🚆 Greenwich, **DLR** Greenwich, Cutty Sark
Open Mon–Fri 10–6.30, Sat–Sun 10–7.30
Traditional London food served up by the restaurant's fifth generation of Goddard's – minced beef, steak and kidney, eel or cheese and onion pie, accompanied by a large potion of mash and topped with a bright green parsley sauce known as liquor. And if you've still got room after that, the restaurant does an excellent blackberry and apple pie, served with a generous helping of ice cream.

Manze's
87 Tower Bridge Road, SE1, t (020) 2407 2985
www.manze.co.uk, 🚇 London Bridge, Tower Hill
Open Mon 11–2, Tues–Thurs 10.30–2, Fri 10–2.15, Sat 10–2.45
Manze's is the oldest pie and mash shop in London (it first opened in 1862) and, despite the many competing eateries, still one of the most popular with queues that regularly stretch right down the street at lunchtime (when it's open). The food is traditional and determinedly unglamorous – minced beef pies, jellied eels and big dollops of mash all topped with liquor (parsley sauce) – not to mention very cheap. Where else can you feed a family of 4 for under £15?

Pollo
20 Old Compton Street, W1, t (020) 7734 5917

⊖ Leicester Square, Tottenham Court Road
Open 12 noon–12 midnight daily

Long-established budget diner selling a range of reasonable pasta dishes. A little dingy with its ancient formica tables, but plenty of atmosphere.

African

Calabash

Africa Centre, 8 King Street, WC2, **t** (020) 7836 1936
⊖ Covent Garden
Open Mon–Fri 12.30–3 and 6–11

Situated in the Africa Centre's basement, this provides a welcome alternative to the seemingly ubiquitous American-style menu. It specializes, as you might expect, in African dishes such as cous-cous, groundnut stew and Yassa (grilled chicken cooked in a lemon sauce). If your kids are at all adventurous (and some, so I'm told, are) they'll love this. You can get reduced price children's portions.

American

Big Easy

332–4 King's Road, SW3, **t** (020) 7352 4071
⊖ Sloane Square
Open Mon–Sat 12 noon–11.30, Sun 12 noon–11

If your kids like seafood, then you've come to the right place. This excellent, Louisiana-style diner specializes in huge plates of prawns, crabs and lobster (they also do burgers and ribs). Children get their own menu (£4.95), along with paper and crayons. The best pictures are displayed in the 'Big Easy Little Urchins Under Sea Club Gallery'. High chairs available.

Bodeans

17 Poland Street, W1, **t** (020) 7287 7575
⊖ Oxford Circus
Open Mon–Fri 12 noon–11, Sat–Sun 12 noon–10.30

This American-style smokehouse has counter service upstairs and a restaurant downstairs, with TV screens showing American sports for adults and a chic, black pad for the kids to lounge in, with TV showing the latest cartoons and films. Kids eat free at weekends.

The High Chaparral

35 Greenwich Church Street, SE10, **t** (020) 8293 9143
⇌ Greenwich, **DLR** Greenwich, Cutty Sark
Open Mon–Sat 12 noon–11, Sun 12 noon–10

Fun little Tex Mex diner where you can load up on fajitas, enchiladas and nachos.

Maxwell's

8/9 James Street, WC2, **t** (020) 7836 0303
⊖ Covent Garden, Embankment, Leicester Square
76 Heath Street, Hampstead, NW3
t (020) 7794 5450, ⊖ Hampstead
Branches open 11am–12 midnight daily

The children's menu (£7.25) at this diner-style eaterie is full of games and puzzles; there are join-the-dots, pictures to colour in and word searches. It features lots of kids' favourites, including chicken nuggets fish 'stix', burgers and hot dogs, as well as a few tasty surprises of its own – Mega Chocolate Madness Cake and deep-fried ice cream. The pavement seating outside provides good views of the musicians and 'robot' men who busk this patch. Do be aware that the restaurant is rather less family-friendly during the evening, when it fills up with groups of young revellers.

Texas Embassy Cantina

1 Cockspur Street, SW1, **t** (020) 7925 0077
www.texasembassy.com, ⊖ Charing Cross
Open Mon–Thurs 12 noon–11, Fri–Sat 12 noon–12 midnight, Sun 12 noon–10.30

Popular Tex-Mex diner just a stone's throw from Trafalgar Square, housed in the former headquarters of the White Star Shipping Line (which owned the ill-fated Titanic). Its name is a reference to the brief period between 1836–45 when Texas was an independent country and opened an embassy in London near this spot. Children are catered for with a dedicated menu (which entitles them to unlimited drinks refills) of Tex-Mex-lite cuisine plus games, puzzles and balloons. Outside tables and high chairs available.

British

Rock and Sole Plaice

47 Endell Street, WC2, **t** (020) 7836 3785
⊖ Covent Garden
Open 11.30–10.30, daily

The oldest fish and chip shop in the capital (it opened in 1871) and still one of the best, serving large portions of battered fish and big fat chunky chips. Outside seating and high chairs available.

Seashell

49–51 Lisson Grove, NW1, **t** (020) 7224 9000
⊖ Marylebone
Open Mon–Fri 12 noon–2.30 and 5–10.30, Sat 12 noon–10.30

Two floors serving crisp fish and crunchy chips; a long-time favourite of Londoners.

Stanley's

6 Little Portland Street, W1, **t** (020) 7462 0099
www.rkstanleys.co.uk, ⊖ Oxford Circus
Open Mon–Sat 12 noon–11

With its old-style 1950s décor and sausage-heavy menu, this is a good, fun choice. Children's portions, baby-changing facilities and high chairs available.

Greek

Daphne

83 Bayham Street, NW1, **t** (020) 7267 7322
⊖ Camden Town
Open Mon–Sat 12 noon–2.30 and 6–11.30

Warm, welcoming and very popular Greek restaurant with a lovely sunny roof terrace. Children's portions and high chairs available.

Hot & Spicy

Blue Elephant

3–6 Fulham Broadway, SW6, **t** (020) 7385 6595
www.blueelephant.com, ⊖ Fulham Broadway
Bus 11, 14. 28, 211, 295, C4
Open Mon–Fri 12 noon–3 and 7–12 midnight, Sat 7–11, Sun 12 noon–3.30

Famous Thai restaurant offering great value, super-spicy Sunday lunchtime meals for £22 per head, with entertainment laid on for children. Kids will love the restaurant's jungle-like décor.

Chutney Mary

535 King's Road, SW10, **t** (020) 7351 3113
www.realindianfood.com, ⊖ Fulham Broadway
Open Mon–Sat 12 noon–2.30 and 5.30–11.30, Sun 12.30–3

The twin sister of Veerswamy (see below), this pleasant, modern Indian restaurant is very popular with familes, particularly on Sundays when they offer a children's menu for £7 consisting of a mixture of mild curry dishes and reliable standbys for fussy eaters – fish fingers, burgers etc. There is a very pleasant conservatory. High chairs available.

Masala Zone

9 Marshall Street, W1, **t** (020) 7287 9966
www.realindianfood.com, ⊖ Oxford Circus
Open Mon–Sat 12 noon–2.30 and 5.30–11.30, Sun 12.30–3

This brightly-coloured, subtly-lit diner is the latest venture by the excellent Chutney Mary Group and offers a menu mainly comprised of inexpensive street food dishes, which are piquant and sweet rather than overly spicy. There's also a Children's Thali (£3) available on request. The chicken burger comes highly recommended. Weekday lunchtimes are pretty busy and there's no booking, but the no smoking policy throughout and roomy upstairs level are plus points for those with pushchairs in tow.

Veeraswamy

99–101 Regent Street, W1, **t** (020) 7734 1401
www.veeraswamy.com, ⊖ Piccadilly Circus
Open Mon–Sat 12 noon–2.30 and 5.30–11.30, Sun 12.30–3

Owned by the same people who run Chutney Mary and Masala Zone, this is a great child-friendly Indian restaurant (it claims to be the UK's oldest) where you can sit and watch the world go by while your kids demolish mountains of popadoms. Sunday is the restaurant's designated family day when they offer a special children's menu for £7 (made up of lightly spiced Indian dishes), and there are crayons, colouring books and goodie bags for the kids to enjoy while they wait for their food. High chairs available.

Italian

Cantina del Ponte

Butler's Wharf Building, Shad Thames, SE1
t (020) 7403 3403, **www.**conran-restaurants.co.uk
⊖ London Bridge, Tower Hill
Open Mon–Sat 12 noon–3 and 6–11, Sun 12 noon–3 and 6–10

Terribly swish with its riverside setting, canopied terrace and terracotta mural of an Italian market-place, Cantina del Ponte is a real gourmet's delight. As with most Conran restaurants, it's also very family orientated, offering a children's menu full of kiddy-friendly favourites – pastas, pizzas, soups – that are a cut above the norm.

Carluccio's

Fenwick, New Bond Street, W1, **t** (020) 7629 0699
⊖ Bond Street
2 Nash Court, Canary Wharf, E14, **t** (020) 7719 1749
⊖ Canary Wharf
12 West Smithfield, EC1, **t** (020) 7329 5904

⊖ Farringdon
www.carluccios.com
Branches open Mon–Fri 8am–11pm, Sat
10am–11pm, Sun 10am–10pm

Though the branches of this small chain of restaurant-delicatessens can get crowded in the evenings, they make an excellent spot for lunch when families are treated to a real Mediterranean welcome. There are plenty of simple ravioli and spaghetti dishes for children and (if they're good) ice cream bombes for pudding. And once you've finished eating, you can always browse the delicatessan for supplies. High chairs available.

La Lanterna
6–8 Mill Street, SE1, **t** (020) 7252 2420
⊖ Tower Hill
Open 12 noon–11

Small, homely, traditional Italian restaurant serving good reasonably priced fare. Half portions and high chairs available. It can get quite crowded, especially in the evenings when live music is staged at the next door café.

Monza
6 Yeoman's Row, SW3, **t** (020) 7591 0210
⊖ South Kensington, Knightsbridge
Open Tues–Sun 12 noon–2.30 and 7–11.30, Mon
7–11.30 only

A small, quaint Italian restaurant offering a range of pizza, pasta and risotto dishes to suit all tastes. Family-orientated with excellent service, its walls are decorated with motor-racing memorabilia (Monza hosts the Italian Formula 1 Grand Prix).

Oriental

Benihana
37–43 Sackville Street, W1, **t** (020) 7494 2525
⊖ Piccadilly Circus, Green Park
77 King's Road, SW3, **t** (020) 7376 7799
⊖ Sloane Square
100 Avenue Road, NW3, **t** (020) 7586 9508
⊖ Swiss Cottage
www.benihana.co.uk
Branches open Mon–Tues 6pm–11pm, Wed–Fri 12
noon–3 and 6–11, Sat–Sun 12 noon–11

Fun Japanese noodle chain for families looking to experiment. Several dishes are specifically designed for children's tastes and kids, for their part, enjoy watching the skilful chefs preparing the food at their tables – Ninja style. Children's enter-

tainment is laid on on Sunday afternoons at the Swiss Cottage branch. High chairs available.

China, China
3 Gerrard Street, W1, **t** (020) 7439 7502
⊖ Leicester Square

A good place to grab a quick bowl of noodles in between bouts of sightseeing.

Chuen Cheng Ku
17 Wardour Street, W1, **t** (020) 7437 1398
⊖ Leicester Square

Has the longest menu in Chinatown, which can prove a little daunting – just ask for the day's specials, you're unlikely to be disappointed. If you're hoping to impress the waiters with your grasp of Cantonese, try asking for the following: Tsun Guen (mini spring rolls), Pai Gwat (steamed tiny spare ribs) or Har Gau (rice dumplings stuffed with shrimps). It's extremely child-friendly, with booster seats, high chairs and baskets of goodies for good little kiddies.

New World
1 Gerrard Place, W1, **t** (020) 7734 0396
⊖ Leicester Square

One of the best places to introduce your children to the joys of Chinese food. On Sundays it's packed with families tucking into bowls of dim sum – (Chinese dumplings, the restaurant's speciality). Try the special child-size mini dim sum.

Royal China
40 Baker Street, W1, **t** (020) 7487 4688
⊖ Baker Street
Open Mon–Sat 12 noon–11, Sun 11–10

One of the capital's best Chinese restaurants outside of Chinatown itself. Children are warmly welcomed and the dim sum is superb. Children's menu and high chairs available.

Royal Dragon
30 Gerrard Street, W1, **t** (020) 7734 1388
⊖ Leicester Square

Excellent dim sum and a family-friendly atmosphere, particularly on Sundays.

Tiger Lil's
75 Bishop's Bridge Road, W2, **t** (020) 7221 2622
⊖/⇌ Bayswater, Royal Oak
15a Clapham Common, SW4, **t** (020) 7720 5433
⊖ Clapham Common
270 Upper Street, N1, **t** (020) 7226 1118
⊖ Highbury & Islington

www.tigerlils.com
Branches open Mon–Fri 6pm–11.30pm, Sun 12 noon–11

Tiger Lil's offers a unique interactive dining experience which children of all ages will happily enjoy. Rather than order items from a menu, you are invited to collect together a plateful of fresh ingredients (from a selection of pre-prepared meat, fish and vegetable slivers) – which you then take to one of three chefs who will cook it while you wait – this in itself is very impressive with flames leaping spectacularly from super-heated woks. It's certainly not the place to go for a quiet meal, but it is lots of fun. Children's portions, high chairs and crayons are available.

Pizzas

Gourmet Pizza Company
Gabriel's Wharf, 56 Upper Ground, SE1
t (020) 7928 3188, ⊖ Waterloo
7–9 Swallow Street, W1, **t** (020) 7734 5182
⊖ Piccadilly Circus
Branches open 12 noon–10.30

Small, rather upmarket chain serving reliably excellent pizzas including a few rather unusual combinations – sauteed leak and pecorino cheese, salami and artichoke etc. Thankfully, the kids menu is a little more conservative. High chairs available.

Pizza on the Park
11 Knightsbridge, SW3, **t** (020) 7255 5273
www.pizzaonthepark.com
⊖ Hyde Park Corner, Knightsbridge
Open Mon–Fri 8.15am–12 midnight, Sat–Sun 9.30am–12 midnight

This bright, cheery pizza restaurant is the perfect place to fill up after a morning spent in the park or nearby museums. Colouring books, crayons and balloons are handed out at weekends when you may also be able to hear live jazz being played. Chidren's portions and high chairs available.

Pizza Piazza
39 Charing Cross Road, WC2, **t** (020) 7437 1686
⊖ Leicester Square
www.pizzapiazza.co.uk
Branches open 11.30am–12 midnight daily
This is a firm favourite with the kids. The menu doubles as a board game and children are given an activity pack when they arrive, full of animal cards, badges and colouring books. The kids' menu,

featuring mini pizza and simple pasta dishes, is imaginative and fun.

Pizza Pomodoro
51 Beauchamp Place, SW3, **t** (020) 7589 1278
www.pomodoro.co.uk
⊖ Knightsbridge
Open 12 noon–1am daily

Overlooking the very swanky Beauchamp Place, this is only really family friendly at lunchtimes (the evenings often being given over to live music) when it's fun to sit at a window table watching the great and the good of Knightsbridge parading up and down in their high fashions. The interior is decorated with pictures of the owner standing with famous patrons, such as Clint Eastwood and Sylvester Stallone. In case you're interested, '*Pomodoro*' is the Italian for tomato.

Pizza Organic
20 Old Brompton Road, SW7
t (020) 7589 9613, ⊖ South Kensington
75 Gloucester Road, SW7, **t** (020) 7370 6575
⊖ Gloucester Road
www.pizzapiazza.co.uk
Open 11.30am–12 midnight daily

An avowedly environmentally-conscious restaurant, Pizza Organic, which is run by the same people as Pizza Piazza, offers stone-baked pizzas and a children's menu featuring the 'O-People'; six cartoon characters designed to teach children all about the exciting world of organic produce (good) and GM foods (bad). The restaurant's organic menu was designed by Jamie Oliver.

Posh Nosh

Bluebird
350 King's Road, SW3
t (020) 77559 1000
www.conran-restaurants.co.uk
⊖ Sloane Square
Open Mon–Fri 12.30–3 and 6–11.30, Sat 12 noon–4 and 6–11.30, Sun 12 noon–4 and 6–11

More than just a restaurant, Terence Conran's flagship 'gastrodome' comprises a foodshop, a flower market, a bar, a café and a club, in addition to a huge restaurant illuminated by a giant skylight. Despite its grand appearance, it encourages family trade, particularly at Sunday lunchtimes with dishes from the children's menu (fish and chips, sausage and mash, linguine and tomato sauce) costing £6.25. Otherwise the set menu is £12.50 during the week (2 course) and £15 at weekends (three courses). Outdoor tables and high chairs available.

Brown's

82–84 St Martin's Lane, WC2, **t** (020) 7497 5050, ⊖ Leicester Square

47 Maddox Street, W1, **t** (020) 7491 4565 ⊖ Oxford Circus, Bond Street

114 Draycott Avenue, SW3, **t** (020) 7584 5359 ⊖ South Kensington

Branches open 12 noon–12 midnight

Well-to-do but ever family-friendly brasserie chain. Children get their own menu (£3.95) and crayons can be requested. The restaurants occasionaly run deals whereby under-12s get to eat for free if accompanied by an adult. Be warned, it can be a bit pricey.

Oxo Tower Restaurant

Oxo Tower, Barge House Street, South Bank, SE1 **t** (020) 7803 3888, **www**.oxotower.co.uk ⊖ Waterloo, Blackfriars

Open Mon–Sat 12 noon–3 and 6–11.30, Sun 12 noon–3.30 and 6.30–10.30

Serves great food and can offer some of the most stunning river views to be found anywhere in the capital (it's particularly magical at night). They offer a special brasserie kids' menu at weekends.

The People's Palace

Royal Festival Hall, South Bank Centre, SE1 **t** (020) 7928 9999, **www**.peoplespalace.co.uk ⊖/≥ Waterloo

Open Mon–Sat 12 noon–3 and 5.30–11, Sun 12 noon–3 and 5.30–8

A very grand eaterie offering superb river views and a refined contemporary European menu. Best suited for older, better behaved children. The two course children's menu (sausage and mash, pasta, chicken and chips etc.) is a not inconsiderable £10.

Searcy's

Level I, Barbican Centre, EC2 **t** (020) 7588 3008, ⊖ Barbican

Open Mon–Fri 12 noon–2.30 and 6–10.30, Sat–Sun 12 noon–3 and 5–6.30

This bright, airy modern-looking diner overlooks the Barbican's central courtyard and fountains. It's a bit hi-falutin' (not to say a touch pricey), but does its best to accommodate families.

Pubs

Anchor Inn

34 Park Street, Bankside, Southwark, SE1 **t** (020) 7902 1400, ⊖/≥ London Bridge

Open Mon–Sat 11am–11pm, Sun 12 noon–10.30

One of the grand inns of old London town, this 18th-century pub was built on the site of a 15th-century predecessor and can count Dr Johnson among its former patrons (he supposedly wrote part of his dictionary here). It serves decent pub fare and has an outdoor terrace where you can sit watching life on the river. Inside is a small collection of Elizabethan artefacts found nearby. It's just a few dozen yards from Shakespeare's Globe.

Cadogan Arms

298 King's Road, **t** (020) 7352 1645 ⊖ Sloane Square

Bus 11,19, 22

Open Mon–Sat 11am–11pm , Sun 12 noon–10.30 *Kids welcome to 8pm*

How could we fail to recommend this namesake establishment? Sadly we can claim no link with this traditional King's Road local, complete with roaring fires and cosy nooks, but we can at least vouch for its child-friendly atmosphere and affordable child-sized portions of burgers, chicken or sausage and chips.

Cutty Sark

Ballast Quay, off Lassell Street, SE10 **t** (020) 8858 3146

≥ Greenwich, **DLR** Greenwich, Cutty Sark

Open Mon–Sat 11am–11pm, Sun 12 noon–10.30

A little further downriver from the Trafalgar Tavern, the Cutty Sark is another lovely riverside park with great views of the Millennium Dome and Canary Wharf. Decorated in a nautical style with bits of old ships adorning the walls, it offers a children's menu made up of the usual fare – sausages, chicken nuggets etc. – for a reasonable £2.75.

Dickens Inn

St Katherine's Way, **t** (020 7488 2208) **www**.dickensinn.co.uk, ⊖ Tower Hill, Tower Gateway, **DLR** London Bridge

The best of both worlds, this Tower stalwart (one of the oldest buildings on this stretch of the river) houses a pizzeria (upstairs) to keep the kids happy and a pub (downstairs) where adults can enjoy a pint (or two). In summer, it's a great spot for dining alfresco with its balconies overlooking the dock. It stands next to the 'Grand Turk' a full-size replica of an 18th-century 'Man of War'. Children's portions, high chairs and baby-changing available.

The Engineer

65 Gloucester Avenue, NW1, **t** (020) 7722 0950
⊖ Camden Town, Chalk Farm
Open Mon–Fri 12 noon–3 and 7–11, Sat–Sun 12.30–3.30 and 7–11 (kids' menu 12 noon–3, daily)

Gastropubs are all the rage with the parenting set, mainly because of their more relaxed café-bar atmosphere, where it's okay to linger over a coke and a newspaper as well as enjoy the quality of the food. Often they stock a more discerning array of drinks, including decent wines, teas and coffee. The Primrose Hill area is very popular with families, so several of its pubs are family-friendly, but this one throws a special childrens' menu (available daily from 12 noon–3pm) and some crayons into the mix. Bar snacks, dining room upstairs, yard at the back.

The Trafalgar Tavern

Park Row, SE10, **t** (020) 8858 2437
⇌ Greenwich, **DLR** Greenwich, Cutty Sark
Open Mon–Sat 11.30am–11pm, Sun 12 noon–10.30

Just east of the Royal Naval College, this friendly pub has been welcoming visitors since 1837. In the mid-19th century, Liberal cabinet ministers used to gather here on the Sunday after Whitsun to feast on whitebait caught from the Thames. Unfortunately, the pollution of the river put an end to their revelries in 1868. Today, the refurbished pub provides an elegant setting for a riverside meal and and whitebait is even back on the menu, although it's no longer caught in the Thames. Children's menu available.

Tea-Time Treats

Fortnum & Mason Fountain Room

181 Piccadilly, W1, **t** (020) 7734 8040
www.fortnumandmason.co.uk, ⊖ Piccadilly Circus
Open Mon–Sat 7.30am–11pm

A wonderfully elegant tea room set in the basement of the Queen's grocers. They offer a children's menu, but the highlight here is definitely their wide and delicious range of specially made ice creams, sorbets, sundaes and sodas. It's a haven of old-fashioned style and charm, suitable for older children. Once you've finished your ice cream, pop outside to watch the workings of the famous Fortnum & Mason clock.

Gloriette Patisserie

128 Brompton Road, SW3, **t** (020) 7589 4750
⊖ Knightsbridge
Open Mon–Sat 7am–7pm, Sun 9–6

This is a great place for anyone with a sweet tooth. Boasting a fantastic selection of tempting cakes, from creamy chocolate gateaux to glazed fruit tarts, it also sells a wide variety of snacks, ranging from salads to assorted tasty sandwiches.

Patisserie Valerie

215 Brompton Road, Knightsbridge, SW3
t (020) 7823 9971, ⊖ Knightsbridge
Open Mon–Fri 7.30–7, Sat 8–7, Sun 9–6
105 Marylebone High Street, W1
t (020) 7935 6240, ⊖ Baker Street, Bond Street
Open Mon–Fri 7.30am–8.30pm, Sat 8am–8.30pm, Sun 9–6.30
43 Old Compton Street, W1, **t** (020) 7935 6240
⊖ Leicester Square
Open Mon–Fri 7.30–7, Sat 8–7, Sun 9–6
8 Russell Street, Covent Garden, WC2
t (020) 7240 0064
⊖ Covent Garden, Leicester Square
Open Mon–Sat 7.30am–8.30pm, Sun 8–7
27 Kensington Church Street, W8
t (020) 793 79574, ⊖ High Street Kensington
Open Mon–Fri 7.30–7pm, Sat–Sun 8–7
www.patisserie-valerie.co.uk

First established in the 1920s by Belgian-born baker Madame Valerie, each branch of this patisserie-cum-café chain has a pleasant continental ambience and stocks a wonderful array of sticky treats as well as savoury snacks and salads.

Ritz Hotel

150 Piccadilly, W1, **t** (020) 7493 8181
www.theritzhotel.co.uk, ⊖ Green Park
Tea 1.30pm, 3.30pm and 5.30pm daily

Afternoon tea at the Ritz is rather steep at £29 a head, but the setting and the sight of the cakes, sandwiches and scones piled high on silver platters make it an experience few children are likely to forget. Book well in advance (at least three months for a weekend) and dress smartly (no jeans).

Treat Eats

Hard Rock Café

150 Old Park Lane, W1, **t** (020) 7629 0382
www.hardrock.com, ⊖ Hyde Park Corner

Open Mon–Thurs 11.30am–12 midnight, Fri–Sat 11.30am–1am, Sun 11.30am–11.30pm

Younger kids can enjoy the colour-in menu (£4.25, featuring macaroni cheese or fried chicken, as well as the staple burger and chips) and the collection of toys. Their older siblings will love the videos and spotting the jackets of surprisingly diminutive rock stars. Cross the road to the shop afterwards and be sure to go downstairs to the **Vault** for a tour of the curious bits and bobs left behind on the road to eternal stardom. Bo Diddley's home-made guitar, John Lennon's military jacket and Buddy Holly's trademark specs are among the highlights.

Planet Harrods

Fourth Floor, Harrods, 87–135 Brompton Road, SW1 **t** (020) 7730 1234, ⊖ Knightsbridge
Open Mon–Sat 10–7, Sun 12 noon–6

An American-style restaurant where cartoons play constantly on big screens.

Planet Hollywood

13 Coventry Street, W1, **t** (020) 7734 6220
www.planethollywood.com
⊖ Leicester Square, Piccadilly Circus
Open Sun–Thurs 12 noon–11, Fri–Sat 12 noon–12 midnight

Somewhat beleaguered, this once mighty chain is still hanging in there. Always filled with tourists and noisy beyond measure, it's nonetheless worth a look if you're in the area. Kids like the garish posters and cabinets full of movie memorabilia. The food is expensive (the kid's menu is £7.95) but perfectly reasonable (burgers, ribs etc.) and there is a 75-seat preview theatre.

Rainforest Café

20 Shaftesbury Avenue, W1, **t** (020) 7434 3111
www.therainforestcafe.co.uk
⊖ Leicester Square, Piccadilly Circus
Bus 3, 12, 14, 19, 22, 38
Open Sun–Thurs 12 noon–11, Fri–Sat 12 noon–12 midnight
Suitable for all ages

A wonderful theme restaurant, particularly popular with young children. As the name suggests, the tables and chairs have been placed in among the trees and foliage of an artificial rainforest. Inhabiting the dense undergrowth are various mechanical animals, including chimps, monkeys, alligators, birds and snakes, who come alive every 15 minutes to whoop and chatter

following a rather loud artificial thunderstorm. Games and face-painting are laid on at weekends. The grill-style menu is tasty, albeit rather expensive. The 'Wild Bunch' children's menu is a rather hefty £9.95. There's also a great shop upstairs.

Smollensky's

105 The Strand, WC2, **t** (020) 7497 2101
⊖ Embankment, Charing Cross
Open Mon–Wed 12 noon–12 midnight, Thurs–Sat 12 noon–12.30am, Sun 12 noon–5.30 and 6.30–11
Bradmore House, Queen Caroline Street, Hammersmith, W6, **t** (020) 8741 8124
⊖ Hammersmith
Open Mon–Sat 12 noon–2.30 and 5.30–11
62 Carter Lane, EC4, **t** (020) 7248 4220
⊖ St Paul's, Blackfriars
Open Mon–Fri 11.30am–11pm
For details of other branches, visit www.smollenskys.co.uk

This is the restaurant that started the whole craze for putting on children's entertainment at weekends – kids can have their faces painted, watch a Punch and Judy show, take part in magic tricks and eat something from the American-style kids' menu (£4.95). Parents will appreciate the tinkling piano music and succulent grill steaks and fish specials. Children's entertainment on Saturday and Sunday afternoons, book in advance.

Sticky Fingers

1a Phillimore Gardens, W8, **t** (020) 7938 5338
www.stickyfingers.co.uk
⊖ High Street Kensington, Holland Park
Bus 9, 10, 27, 28, 31, 49, 94
Open 12 noon–12 midnight daily

The owner, Bill Wyman, used to play bass guitar for the Rolling Stones and the restaurant is filled with rock and roll memorabilia – all of which will probably be lost on the restaurant's younger visitors. Nonetheless, they will enjoy the burgers and fries (children's menu £7.25) and the magic shows, activities and face painting that are laid on on Sunday afternoons. High chairs available.

TGI Friday's

6 Bedford Street, WC2, **t** (020) 7379 0585
⊖ Covent Garden, Leicester Square
Open Mon–Sat 12 noon–11.30, Sun 12 noon–11
29 Coventry Street, W1, **t** (020) 7379 6262
⊖ Piccadilly Circus

Open Mon–Thurs 12 noon–11.30, Fri 12 noon–12 midnight, Sat 11am–12 midnight, Sun 12 noon–11 www.tgifridays.co.uk

An ever-popular choice, this lively Tex-Mex diner offers three separate children's menus: a 'baby organic' menu for infants aged 4–15 months (free when their parents dine); a 'Kinder Suprise' menu for under-6s which features fish fingers, chicken nuggets, hot dogs etc. and comes with a Kinder Surprise egg; and the 'Clubhouse Menu' for 6–11 year-olds made up of slightly more grown-up fare – burgers, ribs, fajitas etc. High chairs, booster seats and colouring books available.

Vegetarian
Food For Thought
31 Neal Street, WC2, **t** (020) 7836 0239
⊖ Covent Garden
Open Mon–Sat 12 noon–8.30, Sun 12 noon–5

Cheap and friendly serving quiches, salads, soups etc. It can get a little crowded, so turn up for an early lunch to be sure of a seat.

Manna
4 Erskine Road, NW1, **t** (020) 7722 8028
www.manna-veg.com, ⊖ Chalk Farm
Open Mon–Sat 6pm–11pm, Sun 12.30–3 and 6–11
Spacious, popular and highly regarded veggie restaurant.

Oshobasho
Highgate Wood, Muswell Hill, N10
t (020) 8444 1505, ⊖ Highgate
Open 8.30–7.30 daily, the park gates close at 8.30pm

Extremely popular vegetarian restaurant in the idyllic setting of Highgate Wood. Familes flock to its large outdoor seating area at the weekends. There's also a children's play area. If you're feeling adventurous after your meal, pick up a nature trail from the next door woodland centre and head off into the trees. *See p.175.*

Food Chains
Ask Pizza
197 Baker Street, NW1, **t** (020) 7486 6027
⊖ Baker Street
48 Grafton Way, W1, **t** (020) 7388 8108
⊖ Warren Street
121 Park Street, W1, **t** (020) 7945 7760
⊖ Marble Arch
103 St John Street, EC1, **t** (020) 7253 0323

⊖ Farringdon
56 Wigmore Street, W1, **t** (020) 7224 3484
⊖ Bond Street
www.askcentral.co.uk
Branches open 11.30am–11.30pm

Pizza Express' main rival for the title of 'best pizza chain', Ask also specializes in thin-crust, Italian-style pizzas and has a similar continental ambience. There's no special children's menu, but families are made to feel very welcome with children's portions and high chairs readily available.

Belgo
Belgo Centraal, 50 Earlham Street, WC2, **t** (020) 7813 2233, ⊖ Covent Garden
Open Mon–Thurs 12 noon–11.30, Fri–Sat 12 noon–12 midnight, Sun 12 noon–10.30
Belgo Noord, 72 Chalk Farm Road, NW1, **t** (020) 7267 0718, ⊖ Chalk Farm
Open Mon–Fri 12 noon–3 and 6–11, Sat 12 noon–11.30, Sun 12 noon–10.30
Also *see* branches of **Bierodrome,** their gastropub counterparts, **open**: 12 noon–12 midnight daily
173-4 Upper Street, N1, **t** (020) 7226 5835, ⊖ Angel
44-48 Clapham High Street, SW4, **t** (020) 7720 1118, ⊖ Clapham Junction
67 Kingsway, Holborn, WC2, **t** (020) 7242 7469
⊖ Holborn
www.belgo-restaurants.com

Belgo Nord and Belgo Centraal make up the two branches of this very fashionable restaurant. All welcome children with open arms and free food (under-12s eat free, 1 adult per 2 kids). While adults try some Belgian specialities such as Moules Marinières (mussels with celery and onion) or chilled asparagus with Ardennes ham, children can tuck into the restaurant's more child-friendly (albeit still Belgian-centric) fare – wild boar sausages and mash, followed by waffles with fruits and white chocolate sauce – from the colour-in 'Mini-Belgo' menu (£4.95). Be warned, the restaurant is very trendy and, as a result can get pretty busy, especially at weekends.

Café Rouge
29–31 Basil Street, SW3, **t** (020) 7584 2345, ⊖ Knightsbridge, **Open** Mon–Sun 12 noon–3
Victoria Place, 115 Buckingham Palace Road, SW1
t (020) 7931 9300, ⊖ Victoria
Open Mon–Sun 8.30am–11pm
46 James Street, W1, **t** (020) 77487 4847
⊖ Bond Street

Open Mon–Sat 10am–11pm, Sun 10am–10.30pm
15 Frith Street, W1, **t** (020) 7437 4307
⊖ Leicester Square, Tottenham Court Road
Open Mon–Sat 10am–11pm, Sun 10.30am–11pm
34 Wellington Street, WC2, **t** (020) 7836 0998
⊖ Covent Garden, **Open** Mon–Sun 10am–11pm
Hay's Galleria, SE1, **t** (020) 7378 0097, ⊖ London Bridge
Open Mon–Fri 9am–10.30pm, Sat–Sun 12 noon–6
Hillgate House, Limeburner Lane, EC4, **t** (020) 7329 1234, ⊖ Blackfriars, **Open** Mon–Fri 8am–10.30pm
Ibis Hotel, Stockwell Street, SE3, **t** (020) 8293 6660
DLR Greenwich, Cutty Sark
Open Mon–Sun 10.30–11pm
For details of other branches, visit **www.cafer-ouge.co.uk**

Extremely child-conscious French café chain. There are two children's menus – one aimed at toddlers, offering gloopy favourites like mashed potato and omelette, while the other features mini-portions from the adult menu. The chain also produces a very grand activity pack with stickers, puzzles, crayons and Kinder-style construction toys.

Café Pasta

2–4 Garrick Street, WC2, **t** (020)7497 2779
⊖ Leicester Square
15 Greek Street, W1, **t** (020) 7734 7430
⊖ Tottenham Court Road
182–184 Shaftesbury Avenue, WC2, **t** (020) 7379 0198, ⊖ Leicester Square
www.pizzaexpress.co.uk/cpasta.htm
Branches open 11.30am–12 midnight, daily

Pizza Express' pasta-mad sibling, this displays many of the same qualities: attractive decor, good food and a genuinely family-friendly atmosphere achieved without recourse to games or gimmicks. High chairs available.

Caffè Uno

5 Argyll Street, W1, **t** (020) 7437 2503, ⊖ Oxford Circus
100 Baker Street, W1, **t** (020) 7486 8606, ⊖ Baker Street
28 Binney Street, W1, **t** (020) 7499 9312, ⊖ Charing Cross, Leicester Square
24 Charing Cross Road, WC2, **t** (020) 7240 2524, ⊖ Charing Cross, Leicester Square
9 Kensington High Street, W8, **t** (020) 7937 8961, ⊖ High Street Kensington
40–42 Parkway, NW1, **t** (020) 7428 9124, ⊖ Camden Town

37 St Martin's Lane, WC2, **t** (020) 7836 5837, ⊖ Leicester Square
64 Tottenham Court Road, W1, **t** (020) 7636 3587, ⊖ Goodge Street
www.caffeuno.co.uk
Branches open 11am–11pm daily

Good for a quick pizza or bowl of pasta, Caffè Uno is a very reasonably priced Italian chain. The children's menu features the kids' cartoon favourite 'Arthur' and and offers a choice of simple pizza and pasta dishes (spaghetti bolognese etc.) plus the odd Anglicized addition (fish and chips), two scoops of ice cream and a free drink – all for £3.95. High chairs available.

Fish!

Cathedral Street, SE1, **t** (020) 7407 3803
⊖ London Bridge, Borough
Open 11.30–11, daily
County Hall, 3b Belvedere Road, SE1, **t** (020) 7901 6734, ⊖ Waterloo
Open 11.30–3 and 5–11, daily
www.fishdiner.co.uk
Branches open Mon–Sat 11.30am–11pm, Sun 12 noon–10.30

Fish! is about as far from the traditional British chippy as it's possible to get. Its greatest strength is the quality and choice it offers. Not only are there about 12 different varieties on offer every day, but you can also choose the way in which it is cooked. Although children may baulk at some of the choices, they're bound to find something they like on the children's menu – which entitles them to two courses (they can choose chicken and chips if fish doesn't take their fancy), a drink and dessert for £6.95. They are also given a Kids' Pack of games and puzzles. High chairs available.

Pizza Express

125 Alban Gate, London Wall, EC2, **t** (020) 7600 8880, ⊖ Barbican, St Paul's
Open Mon–Fri 11.30–11, Sat 12 noon–10, Sun 12 noon–8
133 Baker Street, W1 **t** (020) 7486 0888, ⊖ Baker Street, **Open** 11.30am–12 midnight, daily
21–22 Barret Street, W1, **t** (020) 7629 1001, ⊖ Bond Street, **Open** 11.30am–12 midnight, daily
9–12 Bow Street, WC2, **t** (020) 7240 3443, ⊖ Covent Garden, **Open** 11.30am–12 midnight, daily
7 Beauchamp Place, Knightsbridge, SW3, **t** (020) 7589 2355, ⊖ Knightsbridge;
Open Mon–Sat 11.30am–12 midnight

Cardamom Building, Shad Thames, SE1,
t (020) 7403 8484, ⊖ Tower Hill, London Bridge
Open 11.30am–12 midnight daily
7 Charlotte Street, W1, **t** (020) 7580 1110
⊖ Goodge Street
Open Mon–Sat 11.30am–11.30pm, Sun 11.30–11
4 Church Street, Greenwich, SE10, **t** (020) 8853
2770, DLR Greenwich
Open 11.30am–12 midnight daily
30 Coptic Street, Bloomsbury, WC1 **t** (020) 4636
3232, ⊖ Holborn, Tottenham Court Road
Open 11.30am–12 midnight daily
26 Cowcross Street, EC1, **t** (020) 7490 8025,
⊖ Farringdon, Open 11.30–11, daily
49 Curtain Road, EC2, **t** (020) 7613 5426,
⊖ Liverpool Street, Old Street
Open 11.30am–12 midnight daily
10 Dean Street, W1 **t** (020) 7439 8722, ⊖ Tottenham
Court Road, **Open** 11.30am–12 midnight, daily
20 Greek Street, W1, **t** (020) 7734 7430, ⊖Leicester
Square, **Open** 11.30am–12 midnight daily
152 King's Road, SW3, **t** (020) 7351 5031; ⊖ Sloane
Square, **Open** 11.30am–12 midnight daily
2 Salisbury House, London Wall, EC2, **t** (020) 7588
7262, ⊖ Barbican, St Paul's, Bank, Liverpool Street
Open Mon–Fri 11.30–10.30
80–81 St Martins Lane, WC2, **t** (020) 7836 8001,
⊖ Covent Garden, **Open** 11.30am–12 midnight daily
13–14 Thayer Street, London, W1 **t** (020) 7935 2167
⊖ Oxford Circus, **Open** 11.30am–12 midnight, daily
The White House, 9c Belvedere Road, SE1, W1
t (020) 7928 4091; ⊖ Waterloo
Open 11.30am–12 midnight daily
85 Parkway, NW1, **t** (020) 7267 2600,⊖ Camden
Open 11.30am–12 midnight, daily
www.pizzaexpress.co.uk
  Serving tasty, thin-crust Italian style pizzas (plus
a few pasta dishes such as lasagne and canneloni),
this is by far the best pizza chain in London.
Whichever one you choose, you won't go far
wrong. Some of the more popular branches offer
crayons and colouring books.

Tootsies

35 James Street, **t** (020) 7486 1611, ⊖ Bond Street
107 Old Brompton Road, SW7, **t** (020) 7581 8942
⊖ South Kensington
120 Holland Park Avenue, **t** (020) 7229 8567
⊖ Holland Park
198 Haverstock Hill, NW3, **t** (020) 7431 7609
⊖ Belsize Park

For details of other branches visit **www**.tootsies-
restaurants.co.uk
Branches open 11.30am–12 midnight
  Upmarket, rather trendy burger chain serving
American-style food in generous portions. Children
are given colouring books and crayons. Main
courses from the childrens' menu (burger and
chips, sausage and mash, chicken sandwich etc.)
are around £3.50, with desserts £2.25 and milk-
shakes £1.50. High chairs available.

Wagamama

11 Jamestown Road, NW1, **t** (020) 7487 4688
⊖ Camden Town
Open Mon–Sat 12 noon–11, Sun 12.30–10
26 Kensington High Street, W8, **t** (020) 7376 1717
⊖ High Street Kensington
10a Lexington Street, W1, **t** (020) 7292 0990
⊖ Bond Street
4a Streatham Street, WC1, **t** (020) 7323 9223,
⊖ Tottenham Court Road
101 Wigmore Street, W1, **t** (020) 7409 0111,
⊖ Oxford Circus
www.wagamama.com
Branches open Mon–Sat 12 noon–11, Sun 12.30–10
  Though rather canteen-like with its long refec-
tory tables, this fast-growing noodle house chain
is surprisingly family-friendly, although the
(inevitable) hustle and bustle may appeal more to
older children. High chairs available.

Yo! Sushi

52 Poland Street, **t** (020) 7287 0443
⊖ Oxford Circus, Tottenham Court Road
County Hall, Belvedere Road, SE1, **t** (020) 7928 8871;
⊖ Waterloo
95 Farringdon Road, Clerkenwell, EC1, **t** (020) 7841
0785
⊖ Farringdon
www.yosushi.co.uk
Branches open 12 noon–12 midnight daily
  A dining experience unlike any other – you pick
sushi dishes from an enormous conveyor belt
whilst your drinks are prepared by a special drinks-
mixing robot. Children get a games bag and their
own menu, which offers such authentic Japanese
delicacies as fish fingers and chicken nuggets and
comes with a pair of special child-friendly chopsticks. During the week under-12s eat for free. High
chairs and clip-on baby seats available.

Shop

As far as families are concerned, there are two types of shop: those that children visit under duress – clothes shops are a good example – and those that parents visit under duress – Hamleys, for instance. Inevitably, after a shopping trip, one half of the family will be left feeling pretty grumpy and upset, either because they've been made to try on a particularly nasty sweater, or because they've been dragged through a seething mass of teddy bears. We've done our best to cover both types from the most granny-friendly knitwear shops to the most overwhelming toy stores.

Arts, crafts & hobbies

The Bead Shop
21a Tower Street, WC2
t (020) 7240 0931
www.beadworks.co.uk
⊖ Covent Garden
Bus 6, 9, 11, 13, 15, 23, 77A, 91, 176
Open Mon 1–6, Tues–Fri 10.30–6.30, Sat 11.30–5
   Getting kids to make their own jewellery is a great way of filling a spare afternoon. The Bead Shop, tucked away behind Cambridge Circus, near Covent Garden, provides thousands of coloured baubles, beads and fasteners needed to complete your creations.

The Candle Shop
30 The Market, Covent Garden, WC2
t (020) 7439 4220
www.candlesontheweb.co.uk
Bus 6, 9, 11, 13, 15, 23, 77A, 91, 176   ⊖ Covent Garden
Open Mon–Fri, Sun 10–7, Sat 10–8
   If anyone in your family is interested in candle-making, this is the place to come. It stocks a variety of colourful kits and holds regular candle-making demonstrations.

Comet Miniatures
44–48 Lavender Hill, SW11
t (020) 7228 3702
www.comet-miniatures.co.uk
≋ Clapham Junction   Bus 77, 77A, 345
Open Mon–Sat 9.30–5.30
   A haven of hobbydom, Comet sells all manner of collectibles – rare Japanese toys, film figures etc. – as well as thousands of plastic aircraft assembly kits.

> ### Go fly your kite
> ▶ the maximum height for kite flying in the UK is 60m.
> ▶ never fly near overhead power cables.
> ▶ don't fly near buildings or trees.
> ▶ don't fly over or near other people.
> ▶ always wear sunglasses, whatever the weather, to protect your eyes against harmful UV light.

Kite Store
48 Neal Street, WC2
t (020) 7836 1666
⊖ Covent Garden
Bus 6, 9, 11, 13, 15, 23, 77A, 91, 176
Open Mon–Wed, Fri– Sat 10–6, Thurs 10–7
   The Kite Store sells just about every size, shape and colour of kite imaginable. It also stocks a range of aerobatic toys including boomerangs, yo-yos and water-powered rockets. Pride of place, however, goes to the cutting-edge 'flexifoil' kites, which are capable of lifting a grown man clear of the ground.

London Dolls House Company
29 The Market, Covent Garden, WC2
t (020) 7240 8681
www.london-dolls-house.sagenet.co.uk
⊖ Covent Garden
Bus 6, 9, 11, 13, 15, 23, 77A, 91, 176
Open Mon–Sat 10–7, Sun 12 noon–5
   On Covent Garden's lower level, this shop houses a wonderful collection of miniature homes, each of which is a perfect recreation of period style – from Georgian and Victorian to Art Deco and the ultra-modern – each with appropriate stacks of beautifully crafted furniture and accessories for the serious enthusiast.

Stanley Gibbons
399 The Strand, WC2
t (020) 7836 8444
www.stanleygibbons.com
⊖ Charing Cross
Bus 6, 9, 11, 13, 15, 23, 77A, 91, 17
Open Mon–Fri 9–5.30, Sat 9.30–5.30
   The biggest name in the world of stamps, the Stanley Gibbons stamp emporium on the Strand has become a Mecca for collectors from all over the world. As well as a vast collection, it also has a museum, a show room and even an auction house. It's very grand and attracts some seriously wealthy

enthusiasts but, nonetheless, is still a great place for kids to come and start a collection by picking up a £1 bag of assorted stamps.

Baby & nursery

Dragons of Walton Street
23 Walton Street, SW3
t (020) 7589 3795
www.dragonswaltonstreet.com
⊖ South Kensington
Open Mon–Fri 9.30–5.30, Sat 10–5

This is where society mothers come to furnish their nurseries in the latest designer fittings. The hand-made, hand-painted furniture is undeniably beautiful, but also exorbitantly expensive.

Nursery Window
83 Walton Street, SW3
t (020) 7581 3358
www.nurserywindow.co.uk
⊖ South Kensington
Open Mon–Sat 10–6

Not nearly as grand as the nearby Dragons, Nursery Window is still rather well to do. It sells a cheery range of fabrics, toys and accessories.

Green Baby
345 Upper Street, N1
t (020) 7359 7037
www.greenbaby.com
⊖ Angel
Bus 4, 19, 30, 38, 43, X43, 56, 73, 171a, 214
Open Mon–Sat 10–5

Baby goods for the environmentally-conscious, such as washable nappies and organic toiletries. Also stocks pushchairs and Baby Trekkers.

Mothercare
www.mothercare.com
Branches open Mon–Wed, Sat 10–7, Thurs–Fri 10–8, Sun 12 noon–6
107–115 Long Acre, WC2, **t** (020) 7240 9549,
⊖ Covent Garden
173 Oxford Street, W1, **t** (020) 7437 7722,
⊖ Oxford Circus
461 Oxford Street, W1, **t** (020) 7629 6621,
⊖ Bond Street
85 King's Road, SW3, **t** (020) 7376 5634
⊖ Sloane Square

This is perhaps the country's most famous and reliable children's chainstore. It's been around for years and is still selling, toys, nursery equipment, well-made, reliable clothes and maternity wear at reasonable prices. Also has a nappy delivery room and a mother and baby room.

Books & comics

London's book scene is dominated by three giant multinationals: Waterstone's, Books Etc and Borders. All operate a chain of huge bookstores throughout the capital (Waterstone's, Piccadilly is the largest bookshop in Europe) with good, well-stocked children's sections and comfortable interiors. For something a little different, try Foyle's in Charing Cross Road. Its famously sprawling layout make tracking a book down a real adventure, and the children's section is fantastic.

Harrods, Selfridges and the dedicated kids' department store, Daisy and Tom, have also all got great children's book departments (*see* pp.243–4).

A network of smaller, specialist bookstores including several dedicated children's bookstores are mostly located on the outskirts of town. These include the Golden Treasury (Southfields and Fulham), the Children's Bookshop (Muswell Hill), The Bookworm (Finchley) and Word Play (Crouch End). The Children's Book Centre is the only children's bookshop in central London which is full of Enid Blyton, Roald Dahl and J.K. Rowling favourites as well as colouring books, pop-up books and, for the modern up-to-date child, CD-Roms.

In a more teenage vein, if your kids are big Spider Man comic fans, try Gosh! on Great Russell Street where you can pick up *Marvel* and *DC* back copies (as well as compilations of newspaper strip cartoons such as Peanuts and The Far Side), or Comic Showcase at 63 Charing Cross Road. For science fiction, head for Forbidden Planet on New

Oxford Street, which has a huge collection of SF comics, books and models.

Chains & large bookshops

Books Etc
www.booksetc.co.uk
Branches open 9.30–8, Sunday 12 noon–6
30 Broadgate Circle, EC2, **t** (020) 7628 8944,
⊖ Liverpool Street; 70 Cheapside, EC2, **t** (020) 7236 0398, ⊖ St Paul's; 9–13 Cowcross Street, EC1, **t** (020) 7608 2426, ⊖ Farringdon; 176 Fleet Street, EC4, **t** (020) 7353 5939, ⊖ St Paul's; 263 High Holborn, WC1, **t** (020) 404 0261, ⊖ Holborn; 54 London Wall, EC2, **t** (020) 7628 9708, ⊖ Moorgate; 23 Piccadilly, W1, **t** (020) 7437 7399, ⊖ Piccadilly Circus

Borders
www.bordersstores.amazon.com
Branches open Mon–Sat 8–11, Sun 12 noon–6
120 Charing Cross Road, WC2, **t** (020) 7379 8877,
⊖ Tottenham Court Road; 203–207 Oxford Street, W1, **t** (020) 7292 1600, ⊖ Oxford Circus

Foyle's
113–19 Charing Cross Road, WC2
t (020) 7437 5660
www.foyles.co.uk
⊖ Tottenham Court Road
Bus 14, 19, 24, 29, 38, 176
Open Mon–Sat 9–6, 9–7

Waterstone's
www.waterstones.com
Branches open Mon–Sat 9.30–8, Sun 12 noon–6
203–206 Piccadilly, W1, **t** (020) 7851 2400, ⊖ Piccadilly Circus; 82 Gower Street, WC1, **t** (020) 7636 1577, ⊖ Goodge Street; 99–101 Old Brompton Road, SW7, **t** (020) 7581 8522, ⊖ South Kensington; 128 Camden High Street, NW1, **t** (020) 7284 4948, ⊖ Camden Town; 9/13 Garrick Street, WC2, **t** (020) 7836 6757, ⊖ Leicester Square; 11 Islington Green, N1, **t** (020) 7704 2280, ⊖ Angel; 193 Kensington High Street, W8, **t** (020) 7937 8432, ⊖ High Street Kensington; 150 King's Road, SW3, **t** (020) 7351 2023, ⊖ Sloane Square; 28 Margaret Street, W1, **t** (020) 7580 2812, ⊖ Oxford Circus; 39–41 Notting Hill Gate, W11, **t** (020) 7229 9444, ⊖ Notting Hill Gate; 19–23 Oxford Street, W1, **t** (020) 7434 9759, ⊖ Tottenham Court Road; The Grand Building, Trafalgar Square, WC2, **t** (020) 7839 4411, ⊖ Charing Cross

Children's & specialist bookshops

The Bookworm
1177 Finchley Road
t (020) 8201 9811
⊖ Golders Green
Bus 7
Open Mon–Sat 9.30–6

Children's Book Centre
237 Kensington High Street, W8
t (020) 7937 7497
www.childrensbookcentre.co.uk
⊖ High Street Kensington
Bus 9, 10, 27, 28
Open Mon, Wed, Fri–Sat 9.30–6.30, Tues 9.30–6, Thurs 9.30–7, Sun 12 noon–6

Children's Bookshop
29 Fortis Green Road, NW10
t (020) 8444 5500
⊖ East Finchley
Bus 7
Open Mon–Sat 10–6

Comic Showcase
63 Charing Cross Road, WC2
t (020) 7434 4349
⊖ Covent Garden
Bus 6, 9, 11, 13, 15, 23, 77A, 91, 176
Open Mon–Wed 10–6, Thurs–Sat 10–7

Forbidden Planet
71 New Oxford Street, WC1
t (020) 7836 4179
⊖ Tottenham Court Road
Bus 8, 25
Open Mon–Sat 10–6; Thurs–Fri 10–7

The Golden Treasury
www.thegoldentreasury.co.uk
Branches open Mon–Fri 10–6, Sat 9.30–5.30
29 Replingham Road, SW18, **t** (020) 8333 0167, ⊖ Southfields; 95–97 Wandsworth Bridge Road, SW6, **t** (020) 7384 1821, ⇌ Clapham Junction

Gosh! Comics
39 Great Russell Street, WC1
t (020) 7636 1011
⊖ Tottenham Court Road
Bus 7
Open 10–6, Thurs–Fri 10–7

The Lion and the Unicorn
19 King Street, Richmond, TW9
t (020) 8940 0483
⊖/⇌ Richmond
Bus 72, 74, 85, 371
Open Mon–Sat 10–6

Word Play
1 Broadway Parade, Crouch End, N8
t (020) 8347 6700
⊖ Archway, Highgate
⇌ Crouch Hill
Bus 43, 271
Open Mon–Sat 9–5.30, Sun 11–5

Clothes & shoes

Anthea Moore Ede
16 Victoria Grove, W8
t (020) 7584 8826
⊖ Gloucester Road
Bus 49
Open Mon–Sat 9.30–5
Made-to-measure classic party dresses for parents who like their little girls to look just so. There's also a baby clothes section. *Expensive.*

Barney's
6 Church Road, Wimbledon, SW19
t (020) 8944 2915
⊖ Wimbledon
⇌ Wimbledon
Bus 93
Open Mon–Sat 10–6, Sun 12 noon–5
Just up the hill from the All England Tennis Club, this is the perfect place to pick up an outfit on your way to Centre Court. It stocks all the big names in children's design – Catimini, Roobarb & Custard, Paul Smith and Elle. *Expensive.*

Brora
www.brora.co.uk
Branches open Mon–Sat 10–6
344 Kings Road, SW3, **t** (020) 7352 3697,
⊖ Sloane Square
66 Ledbury Road, SW3, **t** (020) 7229 1515,
⊖ Notting Hill Gate
Cashmere galore, all the way from a mill in Scotland. Makes for the most luxurious babygros and booties around. *Expensive.*

Buckle My Shoe
18–19 St Christopher's Place, W1
t (020) 7935 5589
www.bucklemyshoe.co.uk
⊖ Bond Street
Bus 6, 7, 10, 12, 13, 15, 23, 73, 94, 98, 113, 135, 137, 139, 159, 189
Open Mon–Sat 10–6, Thurs 10–7
Snazzy, modern footwear for snazzy modern kids with the emphasis on soft leather and classic Italian designs. It also stocks a small clothing range. *Mid-Range– Expensive.*

Catimini
52a South Molton Street, W1
t (020) 7629 8099
www.catimini.com
Open Mon–Sat 10–6, Thurs 10–7
Funky printed romper suits, dresses and coordinating accessories. Catimini is one of the top names in contemporary children's wear. Mail order available. *Expensive.*

The Clark's Shop
www.clarks.co.uk
Branches open Mon–Sat 10–6.30, Thurs 10–8, Sun 12 noon–6
260 Oxford Street, W1, **t** (020) 7499 0305, ⊖ Oxford Circus; 476 Oxford Street, W1, **t** (020) 7629 9609, ⊖ Bond Street; 203 Regent Street, W1, **t** (020) 7734 1339, ⊖ Oxford Circus; 98 Kensington High Street, W8, **t** (020) 7937 4135, ⊖ High Street Kensington; 99 Cheapside, EC2, **t** (020) 7606 6754, ⊖ Bank, St Paul's
Having your feet measured here is one of the rituals of British childhood. The shoes and the designs are classic, affordable, comfortable and utterly dependable. *Inexpensive–Mid-Range.*

Clementine
73 Ledbury Road, W11
t (020) 7243 6331
⊖ Notting Hill Gate
Bus 7, 23, 27, 28, 31, 52, 70, 302
Open Mon–Sat 10–6.30
Adorn your kids and their bedrooms with the clothes and furniture range from this charming shop. Simplicity is the key, from light, cotton clothing to attractive bed linen. *Expensive.*

The Cross
141 Portland Road, W11
t (020) 7727 6760

⊖ Notting Hill Gate
Bus 7, 23, 27, 28, 31, 52, 70, 302
Open Mon–Sat 10.30–6

Super cool shop filled with trendy labels such as Little Punk for budding style divas as well as the more practical OshKosh range. *Mid-Range–Expensive.*

Gap Kids
www.gapkids.com
Branches open Mon–Sat 10–8, Sun 12 noon–6
145 Brompton Road, SW3, **t** (020) 7225 1112, ⊖ Knightsbridge; 208 Regent Street, W1, **t** (020) 7287 5095, ⊖ Oxford Circus; 121–123 Long Acre, WC2, **t** (020) 7836 0646, ⊖ Covent Garden; 122 King's Road, SW3, **t** (020) 7823 7272, ⊖ Sloane Square; 223–225 Oxford Circus, W1, **t** (020) 7734 3312 376–384 Oxford Street, W1, **t** (020) 7408 4500, ⊖ Oxford Circus; 473–475 Oxford Street, W1, **t** (020) 7409 7517, ⊖ Bond Street

Sweatshirts, T-shirts, denims etc. which are renowned for their durability. Some branches also contain a subsidiary, Baby Gap, which sells a colourful range of practical babywear and toddler clothes. *Mid-Range.*

Gotham Angels
23 Islington Green, N1
t (020) 7359 8090
⊖ Angel
Bus 4, 19, 30, 38, 43, X43, 56, 73, 171a, 214
Open Mon–Wed, Fri 10.30–7, Thurs 10.30–8, Sat 10–6, Sun 12 noon–6

Fab coordinated outfits for designer mothers and daughters, plus trendy torso hugging T-shirts and baby vests for wannabe überbabies. *Expensive.*

Gymboree
198 Regent Street, W1
t (020) 7494 1110
www.gymboree.com
⊖ Oxford Circus
Bus 3, 6, 12, 13, 15, 23, 53, 88, 94, 139, 159, X53
Open Mon–Sat 10–7, Thurs 10–8pm, Sun 11.30–5.30

Large store selling everything from swimsuits to winter woollen coats. *Mid-Range.*

H&M Hennes
www.hm.com
Branches open Mon–Sat 10–6.30, Thurs 10–8, Sun 12 noon–6pm
174–6 Oxford Street, W1, **t** (020) 7612 1820, ⊖ Oxford Circus; 123 Kensington High Street, W8, **t** (020) 7937 3329, ⊖ High Street Kensington; 261 Regent Street, W1, **t** (020) 7493 4004, ⊖ Oxford Circus

Inexpensive children's clothes made from natural fibres in trendy but tasteful colours and designs. Some branches have computer terminals where kids can play games on the Hennes website. *Inexpensive–Mid-Range.*

Humla Children's Shop
Branches open Mon–Sat 10.30–6.30
23 St Christopher's Place, W1, **t** (020) 7224 1773
13 Flask Walk, NW3, **t** (020) 7794 7877

One of the best children's chains around, the Scandinavian-based Humla sells some wonderfully earthy original design clothes (knitwear is a particular speciality) as well as traditional wooden toys, mobiles and bunkbeds. *Mid-Range–Expensive.*

Instep
45 St John's Wood High Street, NW8
t (020) 7722 7634
⊖ St John's Wood
Bus 6, 13, 16, 82, 98, 113
Open Mon–Sat 9.30–5.30

A sort of halfway house between Clark's and Buckle My Shoe, this is an excellent place to pick up everything from school shoes and sandals to ballet pumps. Also stocks some continental designs. *Mid-Range.*

Jigsaw Junior
www.jigsaw-junior.com
Branches open Mon–Sat 10.30–6
126–127 New Bond Street, W1, **t** (020) 7491 4484, ⊖ Bond Street; 65 Kensington High Street, W8, **t** (020) 7937 3572, ⊖ High Street Kensington; 124 King's Road, SW3, **t** (020) 7589 5083, ⊖ Sloane Square; 57 Regent Street, W1, **t** (020) 7734 7604, ⊖ Oxford Circus

Stocks a good range of colourful children's clothes plus miniature versions of adult clothes for fashion-conscious teenagers. Prices are fairly reasonable. *Inexpensive–Mid Range.*

Joanna's Tent
289b King's Road, SW3
t (020) 7352 1151
⊖ Sloane Square
Bus 11, 19, 22, 211, 319
Open Mon–Sat 10–6, Sun 1–5

Top-of-the range designer kids' clothes – Junior Armani, Paul Smith for Kids etc. – all at designer prices. *Expensive.*

Marks & Spencer

www.marksandspencer.co.uk
Branches open Mon–Sat 10–6.30, Thurs 10–8, Sun 12 noon–6
458 Oxford Street, W1, **t** (020) 7935 7954, ⊖ Marble Arch; 173 Oxford Street, W1, **t** (020) 7437 7722, ⊖ Oxford Circus; 143 Camden High Street, NW1, **t** (020) 7267 6055, ⊖ Camden Town; 113 Kensington High Street, W8, **t** (020) 7938 3711, ⊖ High Street Kensington

The high temple of British underwear, Marks sells an excellent range of sturdy, classic children's designs. Best of all, if you have second thoughts, you can take your purchases back for a full refund, no questions asked. *Inexpensive–Mid-Range.*

Miki House

107 Walton Street, SW3
t (020) 7838 0006
www.mikihouse.co.uk
⊖ Knightsbridge
Bus 10, 19, 52, 74, 137
Open Mon–Sat 10–6

Nice, bright cheerful clothes; lots of red and yellow T-shirts and shirts, corduroy dresses etc. – all bearing the smiling Miki bear motif. *Mid-Range.*

Mothercare

See p.238
Inexpensive–Mid-Range.

Next

www.next.co.uk
Branches open Mon–Fri 10–6.30, Thurs 10–8, Sun 12 noon–6
54/60 Kensington High St, W8, **t** (020) 7938 4211, ⊖ High Street Kensington; 15–17 Long Acre, WC2, **t** (020) 7420 828, ⊖ Covent Garden; 203 Oxford Street, W1, **t** (020) 7434 0477, ⊖ Oxford Circus; 327–399 Oxford Street, W1, **t** (020) 7409 2746, ⊖ Oxford Circus; 160 Regent Street, W1, **t** (020) 7434 2515, ⊖ Piccadilly Circus; 11 Strand, WC2, **t** (020) 7930 0416, ⊖ Charing Cross

High street staple selling good kidswear. *Inexpensive–Mid-Range.*

O'Neill

www.oneilleurope.com

Branches open Mon–Sat 10–7, Thurs 10–8, Sun 12 noon–6
7 Carnaby Street, W1, **t** (020) 7734 3778, ⊖ Oxford Circus; 9–15 Neal Street, WC2, **t** (020) 7836 7686, ⊖ Covent Garden

For the cool street surfer look that older kids and teens are after. *Mid-Range.*

Paul Smith for Children

40–44 Floral Street, WC2
t (020) 7379 7133
www.paulsmith.co.uk
⊖ Covent Garden
Bus 6, 9, 11, 13, 15, 23, 77A, 91, 176
Open Mon–Wed, Fri 10.30–6.30, Thurs 10.30–7, Sat 10–6.30, Sun 1–5

Innovative designer clothes for parents who really want to go to town. Swimsuits and separates for eye-catching occasions. *Expensive.*

Please Mum

www.pleasemumlondon.com
Branches open Mon–Sat 10–6.30, Thurs 10–7.30
69 New Bond Street, W1, **t** (020) 7493 5880; 85 Knightsbridge, SW1, **t** (020) 7486 1380

Lovely bright, colourful clothes and special occasion outfits for children aged between 0 and 15 and parents with healthy bank balances. *Expensive.*

Semmalina

225 Ebury Street, SW1
t (020) 7730 9333
⊖ Sloane Square
Bus 19, 22, 137, C1
Open Mon–Sat 9.30–5.30

A real fairytale shop with dolls' houses, jewels and a drawbridge play area. It sells a good range of funky labels as well as its own clothing line. A good place to off-load some pocket money. *Expensive.*

Slam City Skates

16 Neal's Yard, WC2
t (020) 7240 0928
www.slamcity.com
⊖ Covent Garden
Bus 6, 9, 11, 13, 15, 23, 77A, 91, 176
Open Mon–Sat 10–6.30, Sun 1–5

All you need for the baggy, laid-back skater look. Decks and accessories are also available if you want to do more than just look the part. *Mid-Range.*

Tartine et Chocolat

66 South Molton Street, W1

t (020) 7629 7233
⊖ Bond Street
Bus 7, 23, 27, 28, 31, 52, 70, 302
Open Mon–Sat 10–6
Adorable babywear from Paris. *Expensive.*

Trotters
www.trotters.co.uk
Branches open Mon–Sat 9–6.30, Wed 9–7, Sun 10–6
127 Kensington High Street, W8, **t** (020) 7937 9373,
⊖ High Street Kensington; 34 King's Road, SW3,
t (020) 7259 9620, ⊖ Sloane Square
The clothes are good but designery – Paul Smith and Ralph Lauren are prominent labels – and there's a wide selection of toys and books to keep the kids amused while parents browse and make their purchases. *Mid-Range–Expensive.*

What Katy Did
49 Kensington Church Street, W8
t (020) 7937 6499
⊖ Notting Hill Gate
Bus 7, 23, 27, 28, 31, 52, 70, 302
Open Mon–Fri 10.30–6, Sat 10–6.30
Cute little boutique full of unusual labels. *Expensive.*

Young England
47 Elizabeth Street, SW1
t (020) 7259 9003
www.youngengland.com
⊖ Sloane Square, Victoria
Bus C1
Open Mon–Fri 9.30–5.30
A rather patriotic establishment. All the clothes are made in England using home-grown materials and are based on traditional designs.

Department stores

London is home to some of the shopping world's most famous department stores. There's Harrods, of course (*see* below and p.145), and Harvey Nichols in Knightsbridge; Barkers on Kensington High Street, and Selfridges and John Lewis on Oxford Street. All have good children's clothes and/or toy departments. There's one department store in London, however, devoted solely to children. Daisy & Tom is a Harrods for the under-15s. Founded by

bookshop mogul Tim Waterstone (and named after two of his children), it provides pretty much everything a child could want – books, toys, games, a play area, a carousel, an automated puppet show – as well as catering to the more mundane concerns of parents with its extensive range of clothes, baby equipment and pushchairs. It's even got a hairdressing salon where kids can pick up a First Haircut certificate.

Barkers
63 Kensington High Street, W8
t 0870 160 7247
www.houseoffraser.co.uk
⊖ High Street Kensington
Open Mon–Wed, Fri 10–7, Thurs 10–8, Sat 9.30–7, Sun 12 noon –6
Wheelchair and pushchair accessible, with adapted toilets, parent and baby room, children's wear department, café

Daisy & Tom
181–3 King's Road
t (020) 7352 5000
www.daisyandtom.com
⊖ Sloane Square
Bus 11, 19, 22, 211, 319
Open Mon–Wed, Fri 9.30–6, Thurs–Sat 9.30–7, Sun 11–5
Wheelchair and pushchair accessible, with adapted toilets, parent and baby room, children's wear department, toy department, children's book department, play area, café

Dickins & Jones
224–244 Regent Street, W1
t 0870 160 7262
www.houseoffraser.co.uk
⊖ Oxford Circus, Piccadilly Circus
Open Mon–Wed, Fri–Sat 10–7, Thurs 10–8, Sun 12–6
Wheelchair and pushchair accessible, with adapted toilets, parent and baby room, children's wear department, café

Harrods
87–135 Brompton Road, SW1
t (020) 7730 1234, **f** (020) 7581 0470
www.harrods.com
⊖ Knightsbridge
Bus 10, 19, 52, 74, 137
Open Mon–Sat 10–7, Sun 12 noon–6
Wheelchair and pushchair accessible, with adapted toilets, parent and baby room, children's wear

department, toy department, food department, café, car park
For further details *see* p.145.

Harvey Nichols

109–125 Knightsbridge, SW1
t (020) 7235 5000
www.harveynichols.com
⊖ Knightsbridge
Bus 10, 19, 52, 74, 137
Open Mon–Fri 10–8, Sat 10–7, Sun 12 noon–6
Wheelchair and buggy access, adapted toilets, parent and baby room, car park, children's wear department, food market, café

House of Fraser

318 Oxford Street, W1
t 0870 160 7258
www.houseoffraser.co.uk
⊖ Oxford Circus
Bus 6, 7, 10, 12, 13, 15, 23, 73 94, 98, 113, 135, 137, 139, 159, 189
Open Mon–Wed, Fri–Sat 10–8, Thurs 10–9 Sun 12 noon–6
Wheelchair and buggy access, adapted toilets, parent and baby room, children's wear department, café

John Lewis

278–306 Oxford Street, W1
t (020) 7629 7711
www.johnlewis.co.uk
⊖ Oxford Circus
Bus 6, 7, 10, 12, 13, 15, 23, 73 94, 98, 113, 135, 137, 139, 159, 189
Open Mon– Wed, Fri–Sat 9.30–7, Thurs 9.30–8
Wheelchair and pushchair accessible, with adapted toilets, parent and baby room, children's wear department, play area, café

Selfridges

400 Oxford Street
t (020) 7629 1234
www.selfridges.co.uk
⊖ Oxford Circus
Bus 6, 7, 10, 12, 13, 15, 23, 73 94, 98, 113, 135, 137, 139, 159, 189
Open Mon–Sat 10–8, Sun 12 noon–6
Wheelchair and pushchair accessible, with adapted toilets, parent and baby room, car park, children's wear department, toy department, café

Markets

For antique toys, head towards Notting Hill for Portobello, (the world's largest antiques market) or Camden Passage in Islington. For bric-à-brac and the odd discovery, Brick Lane on Sunday mornings is well worth a visit – be sure to turn up early if you want to get the best bargains. Going to Brick Lane market also gives you a chance to see a fascinating but less well-known part of London. For trendy clothes, music and what-nots, Camden is worth a look, while Greenwich on Saturdays and Sundays has a good range of market fodder, from CDs and clothes to antique furniture, bric-a-brac and toys.

Brick Lane

Brick Lane, E1 and surrounds
⊖ Aldgate East, Shoreditch, Bethnal Green, Liverpool Street
⇌ Liverpool Street
Open Sun 6am–1pm

Camden Lock

Camden Lock Place, off Chalk Farm Road, NW1
t (020) 7284 2084
www.camdenlock.net
⊖ Camden Town, Chalk Farm
⇌ Camden Road
Bus 24, 27, 29, 31, 134, 135, 168, 214, 253, 274, C2
Open Sat, Sun 10–6; some stalls stay open throughout the week

Camden Passage

Camden Passage, off Islington High Street, N1
⊖ Angel
Bus 4, 19, 30, 38, 43, X43, 56, 73, 171a, 214
Open Wed 7–2, Sat 8–4

Greenwich

Stockwell Street, SE10 and surrounds
⇌ Greenwich
Bus 53, X53, 177, 180, 188, 199, 286, 386
Open Sat–Sun 9–5

Portobello

Portobello Road. W11 and surrounds
⊖ Notting Hill Gate, Ladbroke Grove, Westbourne Park
Bus 7, 23, 27, 28, 31, 52, 70, 302
Open Sat–Sun 5.30am–3pm

Music & computer games

London is home to several vast record emporia, each with floors filled with copious amounts of CDs, tapes, videos, DVDs and computer games.

Computer Exchange (LEX)
32 Rathbone Place, W1
t (020) 7636 2666
⊖ Tottenham Court Road
Open Mon–Sat 10–7

Game
www.game.uk.com
100 Oxford Street, W1, **t** (020) 7637 7911, ⊖ Oxford Circus, Tottenham Court Road
10 Victoria Place, Buckingham Palace Road, SW1, **t** (020) 7828 9913, ⊖ Victoria
124 Camden High Street, NW1, **t** (020) 7428 5961, ⊖ Camden

HMV
150 Oxford Street, W1
t (020) 7631 3423
www.hmv.co.uk
⊖ Oxford Circus
Bus 6, 7, 10, 12, 13, 15, 23, 73 94, 98, 113, 135, 137, 139, 159, 189
Open Mon–Sat 9.30–8, Sun 12 noon–6

Tower Records
1 Piccadilly Circus
t (020) 7439 2500
www.towerrecords.co.uk
⊖ Piccadilly Circus, W1
Bus 3, 6, 9, 12, 13, 14, 15, 19, 22, 23, 38, 53, 88, 94, 139, 159
Open Mon–Sat 9am–12midnight, Sun 12 noon–6
Bus 3, 6, 9, 12, 13, 14, 15, 19, 22, 23, 38, 53, 88, 94, 139, 159

Virgin Megastore
225–229 Piccadilly W1
t (020) 76930 4208
www.virginmega.co.uk
⊖ Piccadilly Circus
Bus 9, 14, 19, 22, 38
Open Mon–Sat 9–6, Sun 10.30–4.30

Shopping centres

Lacking the charm or character of some of the central London shopping areas, shopping centres do at least offer the convenience of having shops, restaurants and leisure facilities under one roof. They also have crêches, thereby allowing you a couple of hours relaxing retail therapy.

Bluewater
Greenhithe, Kent
t 0845 602 1021
www.bluewater.co.uk
⇌ Greenhithe
Open Mon–Fri 10–9, Sat 9–8, Sun 11am–5pm
Still the big daddy of shopping centres, the massive Bluewater not only offers some 320 shops (including branches of Marks & Spencer, House of Fraser and Daisy&Tom), dozens of fast-food outlets and chain restaurants, a multiplex cinema and the Kids Village Crêche (which takes children between the ages of two and four on weekdays and two and eight on weekends and bank holidays), but also has facilities for a range of activities (including a fishing lake, a Wintergarden, an outdoor play area, a boating lake and cycle paths) for when you begin to wither under the constant glare of the fluorescent shop lighting. Of particular note to health-conscious parents, however, the centre has a unique fresh-air, air-conditioning system and is non-smoking throughout.

Brent Cross Shopping Centre
Brent Cross, NW4
t (020) 8202 8095
www.brentcross-london.com
⊖ Brent Cross, Hendon Central
Open Mon–Fri 10–8, Sat 9–7, Sun 11–5
Around 90 shops (including branches of Boots, Marks & Spencer, Next and John Lewis), plenty of places for food and a children's play centre called the Nipperboat.

Lakeside Thurrock
West Thurrock, Essex
t 01708 869933
www.peoplelovelakeside.co.uk
⇌ Lakeside
Open Mon–Fri 10am–10pm, Sat 9–7.30, Sun 11–5
Over 300 shops (including branches of the Disney Store, House of Fraser, the Early Learning

Centre, the Games Workshop and Marks & Spencer) and food outlets, market stalls, cinema and a Stay 'n' Play Crêche for 2–7 year-olds.

Xscape
602 Marlborough Gate, Milton Keynes
t 01908 200020
www.xscape.co.uk
≈ Milton Keynes
Open From 9am, closing times vary

Retail and leisure centre with shops, a cinema, a bowling alley, indoor climbing walls and a fitness club. The real treat here is the Snozone, the country's largest 'real' snow slope. You'll find none of that funny dry netting stuff here; Snozone uses snow-cannons and keeps the temperature at a constantly chilly -2°C, making it suitable for proper skiing and snowboarding. Lessons are offered.

Consumer associations
Baby Products Association
The Coach House, Erlegh Manor
Vicarage Road, Leighton Buzzard, LU7 9EY
t (01296) 662 2789
Can provide a leaflet on purchasing baby equipment, both new and second-hand, and produces a yearbook listing suppliers of baby products throughout the country (£15).
British Toy and Hobby Manufacturer's Association
80 Camberwell Road, SE5 0EG
t (020) 7701 7271
www.btha.co.uk
Operates a toy information service, including plenty of advice on how to choose toys for disabled children.
Citizen's Advice Bureau
www.nacab.org.uk
Offers advice on, among other things, what to do if you cannot get a refund on faulty goods. Branches are all over London. Check the website or directory enquiries for details of your nearest branch.
Office of Fair Trading
Fleetbank House, 2–6 Salisbury Square, EC4 8JX
t 0845 722 4499
www.oft.gov.uk
Can give detailed advice about your rights as a consumer.

Specialist shops

Not all of London's shops are classifiable into neat categories and some shops even revel in their acute specialization on a single theme. Here are a couple of the best.

Anything Left Handed
57 Brewer Street, W1
t (020) 7437 3910
wwwanythingleft-handed.co.uk
↝ Piccadilly Circus
Open Mon–Fri 10–6, Sat 10–5
Bus 3, 6, 12, 13, 14, 15, 23, 38, 53, 88, 94, 139

Shop for left-handers selling everything from corkscrews to boomerangs. There's a kid's club on the website.

The Back Shop
14 New Cavendish Street, W1
t (020) 7371 5232
www.thebackshop.co.uk
↝ Bond Street
Bus 135, C2
Open Mon–Fri 10–5.45, Sat 10–2

If your children suffer from bad posture, this is the place to come for chairs a nd desks designed to help them sit up straight.

Sports shops

Niketown
236 Oxford Street, W1
t (020) 7612 0800
www.nike.com
↝ Oxford Circus
Bus 6, 7, 8, 10, 12, 13, 15, 23, 25, 55, 73, 94, 98, 113, 135, 137, 139, 159, 176, 189
Open Mon–Wed 10–7, Thurs–Sat 10–8, Sun 12 noon–6

The Nike swoosh is one of the world's most recognizable logos. Lately, it's been trying to pull off a similar trick with the sports shop opening vast 'temples' of sportswear in the major cities of Europe and America. See p.60 for more details.

Lillywhites
24–36 Regent's Street, W1
t 0870 333 9600

↔ Piccadilly Circus
Bus 3, 6, 12, 13, 15, 23, 53, 88, 94, 139, 159, X53
Open Mon–Sat 10–7, Thurs 10–8, Sun 12–6

This is a well-established sports equipment store catering for everyone from footballers and cricketers to abseilers, skateboarders and canoeists.

JD Sport

www.jdsports.co.uk
Branches open Mon, Tues, Sat 9–8, Wed–Fri 9am–9pm
145 Kensington High Street, W8, **t** (020) 7937 0523, ↔ High Street Kensington; 104 King's Road, SW3, **t** (020) 7823 8182, ↔ Sloane Square; 267 Oxford Street, W1, **t** (020) 7491 7677, ↔ Oxford Circus

Well-stocked sportswear chain, particularly in the trainer department.

JJB Sports

120 Oxford Street, W1
t (020) 7636 0696
www.jjb.co.uk
Bus 3, 6, 12, 13, 15, 23, 53, 88, 94, 139, 159, X53
↔ Oxford Circus
Bus 6, 7, 10, 12, 13, 15, 23, 73 94, 98, 113, 135, 137, 139, 159, 189
Open Mon–Sat 10–7, Thurs 10–8, Sun 12 noon–6

Very busy and chaotic sportswear shop with good range of reduced-price clothing and footwear.

Soccerscene

56–7 Carnaby Street, W1
t (020) 7439 0778
www.soccerscene.co.uk
↔ Oxford Circus
Bus 6, 7, 10, 12, 13, 15, 23, 73 94, 98, 113, 135, 137, 139, 159, 189
Open Mon–Sat 9.30–7

Easily the best football shop in London. You can pick up the kit of almost any team in the world here, as well as any amount of balls, boots and shin pads, not to mention books, magazines and videos galore.

Toys & games

Cheeky Monkeys

202 Kensington Park Road, W11
t (020) 7792 9022

www.cheekymonkeys.com
↔ Notting Hill Gate
Bus 7, 23, 27, 28, 31, 52, 70, 302
Open Mon–Fri 9.30–5.30, Sat 10–5.30

Nice selection of wooden toys and imaginative fancy dress outfits. There are four other branches across town.

The Disney Store

www.disneystore.co.uk
Branches open Mon–Sat 10–8, Sun 12 noon–6
360–66 Oxford Street, W1, **t** (020) 7491 9136
↔ Oxford Circus
9 The Piazza, Covent Garden, WC2,
t (020) 7836 5037
↔ Covent Garden

The store is full of lovable characters as familiar as friends, as well as a vast array of cartoon-related merchandise: videos, play figures, mugs and costumes, clothes and games. The video screen belting out classics never fails to attract children.

Early Learning Centre

36 King's Road, SW3
t (020) 7581 5764
www.elc.co.uk
↔ Sloane Square
Bus 11, 19, 22, 211, 319
Open Mon–Sat 9–6, Wed 9–7, Sun 11–5
The Early Learning Centre is concerned about the impact toys can have on a child's development. Uncontroversial, wholesome fun is the name of the game, and the toys, aimed mainly at the pre-school age group, are uniformly excellent. The shop has several special play areas where kids can try out the toys.

Hamleys

188–196 Regent Street, W1
t (020) 7734 3161
www.hamleys.com
↔ Oxford Circus
Bus 3, 6, 12, 13, 15, 23, 53, 88, 94, 139, 159, X53
Open Mon–Fri 10–8, Sat 9.30–8, Sun 12 noon–6

London's premier toy store, Hamleys has six floors of the latest must-have playthings. *See* p.59 for more details. There's a much smaller branch of Hamleys at Covent Garden, 3 The Market, The Piazza, Covent Garden, WC2; **t** (020) 7240 4646, open Mon–Wed Fri–Sat 10–7, Thurs 10–8, Sun 12 noon–6.

Harrods

87–135 Brompton Road, SW1
t (020) 7730 1234
www.harrods.com
⊖ Knightsbridge
Bus 10, 19, 52, 74, 137
Open Mon–Sat 10–7

Harrods has the best toy department of any department store. The Toy Kingdom on the fourth floor even rivals Hamleys for the sheer range of toys on offer. You can find everything, from limited edition Steiff Teddies and third-size Ferraris with full leather interior to the latest video games. There's also a well-stocked children's bookshop and, next door, Planet Harrods, an American-style restaurant where cartoons play constantly on big screens. Throughout the year the toy department organizes various events and activities for children, including such delights as Teddy Bear Days and Easter Egg hunts.

Just Games

71 Brewer Street, W1
t (020) 7437 0761
⊖ Piccadilly Circus
Bus 6, 12, 13, 14, 15, 19, 23, 38, 53, 88, 94, 139, 159, X53
Open Mon–Sat 10–6, Thurs 10–7

Just Games stocks all the family favourites, including such long-lived classics as Monopoly, Jenga, Snakes & Ladders, Cluedo and Mouse Trap alongside any number of chess sets, backgammon boards and domino sets.

Traditional toys

Parents who despair of modern trends in toy design will be pleased to know that there are several shops in London specializing in more traditional toys. These range from miniature theatre sets and handpainted wooden puppets to carved wooden animals, kaleidoscopes and paper aeroplanes. Look out for the Hill Toy Company, Benjamin Pollock's Toy Shop (where miniature theatre sets are a particular speciality; *see* p.81), mail order specialists Tridias and the self-explanatory Traditional Toys, which stocks old-fashioned toys from all round the world.

Hill Toy Company

71 Abingdon Road, W8
t (020) 7937 8797
www.hilltoy.co.uk
⊖ High Street Kensington
Bus 9, 10, 27, 28, 31, 49
Open Mon–Fri 9.30–5.30, Sat 10–5

Benjamin Pollock's Toy Shop

44 Covent Garden Market, WC2
t (020) 7379 7880
www.pollocks-coventgarden.co.uk
⊖ Covent Garden, Leicester Square
Bus 6, 9, 11, 13, 15, 23, 77A, 91, 176
Open Mon–Sat 10.30–6, Sun 12 noon–5pm

Peter Rabbit & Friends

42 The Market, Covent Garden, WC2
t (020) 7497 1777
www.peterrabbit.com
⊖ Covent Garden
Bus 6, 9, 11, 13, 15, 23, 77A, 91, 176
Open Mon–Sat 10–8, Sun 10–6

Rainbow

253 Archway Road, N6
t (020) 8340 8003
⊖ Highgate
Bus 43, 134, 263
Open Mon–Sat 10.30–5.30

Tridias

25 Bute Street, SW7
t (020) 7584 2330
www.tridias.co.uk
⊖ South Kensington
Bus 49, C1
Open Mon–Fri 9.30–6. Sat 10–6

Traditional Toys

53 Godfrey Street, SW3
t (020) 7352 1718
⊖ South Kensington
Bus 11, 19, 22, 49, 211, 319, 345
Open Mon–Fri 10–5.30, Sat 10–6, Sun 11–4.30

Quiz answers

1

The Underground, or more commonly, the Tube, is the correct name for the English subterranean rail system.

2

Mercury, Venus, Earth, Mars, Jupiter, Saturn, Uranus, Neptune, Pluto.

3

The Ashes are the burnt remains of the stumps, which were presented to the English team by the ladies of Melbourne following an English tour of Australia. It's also the name given to the Test Match series that takes place between the two countries every two years. The winner receives a replica urn – the original can be seen in the museum at Lord's Cricket Ground.

4

West Ham.

5

1,656.

6

They make up the yellow set on the board of the London version of Monopoly.

7

The answer is c), a whopping 17,000, or roughly one for every 350 people living in the capital.

8

Decency Boards were wooden panels that ran along the top deck of old horse-drawn buses. They were designed to prevent unscrupulous gentlemen from getting a crafty look at ladies' ankles.

9

It is named after an aviary that James I had installed near this avenue.

10

Sir Henry Tate, of Tate & Lyle sugar fame, invented the sugar lump and so made his fortune.

11

They both have blue blood running through their veins. Of course, the Royal Family actually has red blood, like everyone else. 'Blue blood' is an expression used to denote that someone has aristocratic ancestry. Lobsters, on the other hand, do actually have blue blood.

12

A groundling was the name given in Elizabethan times to a member of the audience who watched a play standing in front of the stage.

13

Richard III. His evil scheme, if he was responsible, didn't do him much good, however. Within a couple of years he too was dead, slain at the Battle of Bosworth Field by the future Henry VII.

14

Parading through the streets of London as part of the Lord Mayor's Show (*see* London's Year for November, p.37).

15

The Royal Mint. The Bank of England is Britain's central bank and the only bank in England and Wales that can issue paper money. It's also the bank of all the High Street banks such as Natwest, Barclays and Lloyds TSB. Many, many billions of pounds are stored in its vaults.

16

a) Triceratops means 'three-horned face'.
b) Deinocheirus means 'terrible hand'.

c) Baronyx means 'big claw'.

17

It took 10 years to build the Victoria & Albert Museum's current home. On its completion in 1899 it was given its royal name, having previously been nicknamed the 'Brompton Boilers'.

18

It took Sir Francis Chichester nine months and one day to sail around the world.

PICK YOUR BRAINS about ...

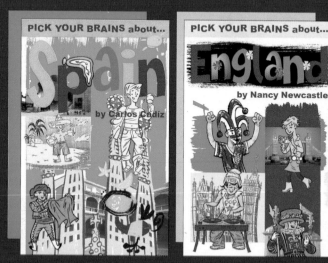

At last enquiring young minds can discover Europe in an entertaining and inventive new series.

CADOGANguides